Can the World Be Governed?

Studies in International Governance is a research and policy analysis series from the Centre for International Governance Innovation (CIGI) and WLU Press. Titles in the series provide timely consideration of emerging trends and current challenges in the broad field of international governance. Representing diverse perspectives on important global issues, the series will be of interest to students and academics while serving also as a reference tool for policy-makers and experts engaged in policy discussion. To reach the greatest possible audience and ultimately shape the policy dialogue, each volume will be made available both in print through WLU Press and, twelve months after publication, accessible for free online through the IGLOO Network under the Creative Commons License.

Can the World Be Governed?

Possibilities for
Effective Multilateralism

*   *   *

Alan S. Alexandroff, editor

Wilfrid Laurier University Press

[WLU]

Wilfrid Laurier University Press acknowledges the financial support of the Government of Canada through its Book Publishing Industry Development Program for its publishing activities. Wilfrid Laurier University Press acknowledges the financial support of the Centre for International Governance Innovation. The Centre for International Governance Innovation gratefully acknowledges support for its work program from the Government of Canada and the Government of Ontario.

Library and Archives Canada Cataloguing in Publication

Can the world be governed? : possibilities for effective multilateralism / Alan S. Alexandroff, editor.

(Studies in international governance series)
Co-published by: Centre for International Governance Innovation.
Includes bibliographical references and index.
ISBN 978-1-55458-041-5

1. International organization. 2. International cooperation. 3. International relations. 4. International economic relations. 5. Security, International. I. Alexandroff, Alan S. II. Centre for International Governance Innovation III. Series.

JZ1318.C36 2008   341.2   C2007-907600-9

Co-published with the Centre for International Governance Innovation.

Cover image by Stefan Hermans. Cover design by Blakeley. Text design by Barry A. Norris.

© 2008 The Centre for International Governance Innovation (CIGI) and Wilfrid Laurier University Press

∞

This book is printed on Ancient Forest Friendly paper (100% post-consumer recycled).

Printed in Canada

Contents

*   *   *

Introduction

Alan S. Alexandroff

* * *

In the foreword to a May 2007 publication of the Centre for International Governance Innovation (CIGI), John English, the think tank's executive director, summarizes CIGI's mandate as follows:

> CIGI strives to find and develop ideas for global change by studying, advising and networking with scholars, practitioners and governments on the character and desired reforms of multilateral governance. (Dayaratna-Banda and Whalley 2007)

With evident editor's prejudice, I believe this volume on global governance reform fits well within that mandate; I also believe it achieves a degree of success.

The evolution of the volume and its chapters on global governance reform require some elaboration. Assembling the authors and their various perspectives on global governance reform took considerable effort, as I describe more fully at the end of this Introduction. One task, however, engendered some notable discussion among the authors and CIGI officials: identifying an appropriate title for this collection of global governance issues. At CIGI's 2006 annual meeting, at which a number of the authors presented their papers, several had time between panels to ponder an appropriate "cap" or "umbrella" for the volume. Out of those discussions and several subsequent editorial ones, and not without some controversy, the volume carries the main title, *Can the World Be Governed?*

One concern raised in the discussions about the title was whether readers might imagine this volume to concern itself with world government or perhaps some form of global federalism. Ferry de Kerckhove raises this perspective directly, noting that it is expressed by idealists who urge "a transformation from a multilateral system at the service of national interests to a true system of world governance" (236). This is not, however, what the authors focus on in this book—indeed, given their theoretical, policy, and practical interests, such a focus would be unlikely. As contemporary "students" of global politics, and with many international relations specialists among them, they recognize the continuing critical importance of sovereignty and national interest in international relations. Thus, the principal attention throughout the book is on multilateralism—what Arthur Stein describes in the following broad foundational terms:

> Although unilateralism remains an ever-present possibility and although international organizations reflect the power and interests of their members, the growing number of such organizations, as well as international laws and agreements, over the past century makes multilateralism an existential reality. (49–50)

Stein also suggests that the contemporary global structure of states is a form of "weak confederalism."

Multilateralism, then, is the key to global governance and its reform. Yet multilateralism is not restricted to a common or simple definition. As broadly understood in these pages, multilateralism includes multistate international organizations but, more broadly and additionally, principles, rules, and norms that apply to these states.

Looking at multilateralism in the context of global governance, as we do throughout this volume, is designed to assess the adequacy of a number of key international organizations of global governance, generally in a formal, but increasingly also an informal, institutional form. But whereas international lawyers—one strong audience examining international organizations—have been drawn principally to the institutionalization, if not the legalization, of international organizations in the post–World War II era, political scientists, including many of the authors in this volume, have approached international institutions much more broadly.[1] Where the lawyers focus on the names, addresses, and secretariats—in other words, the more formal international institutional aspects—political scientists broaden the multilateralism focus. As Stein describes elsewhere (forthcoming), political scientists expanded their examination to include first regimes and then institutions, or the "rules of the game," where, among other things, both formal and informal organizations reside. Indeed, Richard Rosecrance divides international institutions into not just formal and informal ones but "hard" and "soft" and even "medium" institutions before concluding that a Great Power coalition—again, an informal organization— "when it can be achieved, is the most effective international regulator" (86). For Rosecrance, the coalition is the operative institution.

Thus, not only do the chapters in this volume include analysis with formal/informal dimensions but also analysis in which organizations, principles, norms, and rules are relevant to looking at multilateralism and the adequacy of global governance and reform proposals. Equally, in the circumstances in which these organizations and behaviors—the "rules of the game"—seem wanting, a number of the authors suggest what kinds of reforms might improve global governance—that is, global economic development, security, or prosperity—in the wider terms international relations scholars have identified.

In analyzing and recommending reforms of current multilateral institutions, the authors naturally engage the significant global governance reform literature. Stein tackles analytically the reform wave; indeed, many of the chapters are grounded in the reform proposals in this literature or made by policy makers. With authors examining so many dimensions of multilateralism, including international economic as well as security institutions, it is, of course, difficult to expect a common view of reform in global governance. Yet common themes do emerge that go some way in uniting the chapters. In particular, there is some commonality in the questions the

---

1. For a thorough review of the international lawyers' perspective on international organizations, see Alvarez (2006). For a strong political science contrast, see Stein (forthcoming).

authors seem to be asking about global governance and its possible reform. And, I believe, some common outcomes emerge.

Multilateralism and
Global Governance Reform

The typology shown in Table 1 reveals, I hope, how the authors capture what Stein calls the "what and why" of global reform. The authors have a broad purchase on the questions of global governance and global reform: each attempts to address why reform is being urged for the organization or sector or functional area. In addition, they address generally the prospects for reform and the ways they foresee reform occurring.

Robert Wolfe, Eric Helleiner and Bessma Momani, Ferry de Kerckhove, and James Fearon examine in some depth proposed reforms for a number of critical formal international organizations—namely, the World Trade Organization (WTO), the International Monetary Fund (IMF) and the United Nations Security Council. All these authors look at reforms that would craft some rebalancing of membership and leadership on the basis of "legitimacy," not just power; their focus is on possible reconfigurations that would provide greater support for global governance and its institutions, though often balanced against efficacy—the organization's ability to achieve certain outcomes.

These organizations offer a wide range of leadership formulas, from the presumed inclusion of all states to the WTO's consensus principle to the Permanent Five (P5) states that have veto authority in the Security Council for binding resolutions. In his detailed chapter on the WTO, Wolfe suggests that the global trading system seems to work well on a day-to-day basis. Nevertheless, analysts have raised questions about the difficult, and possibly failed, Doha Round of trade negotiations. In particular, they have speculated that the Doha Round's failure might challenge the continued global governance of world trade. Yet Wolfe's response is far from conventional: while admitting that the WTO is not necessarily efficient, he sees it as providing a vital "learning" setting, especially for the organization's many developing member states. The Doha Round permits the articulation of a wide set of interests in the multilateral setting and affords

Table 1: *Multilateralism and Global Governance Reform*

	Determinants of Structure and Outcome	
	Legitimacy/Efficacy	Largely Driven by the Distribution of Power
Institutions International organizations — formal	Wolfe Helleiner & Momani de Kerckhove Fearon	Ikenberry Drezner
International organizations plus norms, rules, and principles — informal	Collier Stein	Goff Rosecrance

its members the opportunity to learn the rules and norms of the global trading system. Thus, Wolfe believes, reform of the WTO's consensus rule and the Single Undertaking would undermine critical aspects of global governance in the international trade.

Helleiner and Momani raise the key issue of the declining power of the IMF and the crisis that this challenge to a critical postwar financial institution poses for global governance. In the IMF, there is a relatively narrow leadership in the form of a limited set of influential states. Reform proposals range across a wide set of issues and cover the adequacy and legitimacy of current leadership as well as the organization's performance. Helleiner and Momani suggest, however, that these proposals are unlikely to be transformative but palliative or corrective, and would not set a new direction for the IMF's governance. Some of the reforms might revitalize the organization, but they would be manifestly difficult to achieve. As is true with many other cases of reform, the challenge of governance reform appears larger and more difficult especially where reforms seek outcomes along the legitimacy/efficacy continuum. Meanwhile, as Helleiner and Momani point out, the IMF's functions might have been altered permanently by its recent shift away from a key goal or outcome—lending. Moreover, serious objections have been raised over reform proposals designed to focus on the Fund's surveillance role. The authors suggest that the crisis of IMF power, and now function, might not be easy to resolve.

Fearon and de Kerckhove, the two remaining authors in this group, examine in different ways but in some depth the challenge of reform of the UN, especially the Security Council and the continued leadership of the P5.

Fearon takes an analytic approach to global institutional reform, examining contemporary threats to peace and security, including internal war, state breakdown, and WMD terrorist threats. He then focuses on how to adapt and reform international organizations to best promote future peace and security. He looks at and discards unilateral action before examining how contemporary threats to peace and security could be tackled through reform of current multilateral organizations. With security challenges firmly in his sights, he also looks at the creation of a new security organization from scratch, and determines that such an organization would need to combine legitimacy and effectiveness, perhaps through some form of weighted voting or nonpermanent membership. Furthermore, he argues, "[v]otes should be weighted by criteria that are dynamic in the sense of being able to reflect changes in the international distribution of population and influence" (182). Among the criteria he would use to weight votes are a state's population, economic size, and its contributions to the organization and to peacekeeping. He also questions whether the organization's general membership, or a Security Council-like body within it, should include only democracies.

Like Wolfe and Helleiner and Momani, de Kerckhove takes a close look at formal institutional reform, but extends his analysis to reform of a variety of UN institutions. In this sense, his chapter forms a more detailed narrative to accompany Fearon's analytic look at Security Council reform. It reminds us how difficult the path to reform might be. Here, the reform agenda set out by Kofi Annan when he was UN secretary-general falls victim, apparently, to promising too much. Indeed, de Kerckhove describes the reform failure as "a beautiful vision for the World's Federalists," and notes that the agenda appears increasingly to be about security issues that have "turned off" many member states from the developing world. In addition, he suggests, the focus of Security Council reform on the legitimacy of the P5's leadership has crippled, or at least harmed, a more wide-ranging debate about the reform agenda. Nevertheless, de Kerckhove presses forward, attempting to look at a more fully global perspective for reform, even though it appears to be at odds with the outcome of the UN's 2005 Summit.

With our next two authors the perspective shifts, as both John Ikenberry and Daniel Drezner examine global governance reform with a focus more directly on power and the structural distribution of power among states in the global system.

Ikenberry has become a well-known proponent of liberal institutionalism in international relations, and in his chapter he examines US ambivalence about multilateralism. Although the United States is acknowledged as the chief architect and champion of international organizations and rules since World War II and although it remains the most powerful and influential state in the international system, it has acted unilaterally in a variety of well-known instances. Ikenberry chronicles a number of contemporary shifts in the international system and how they have altered the incentives for the United States to act unilaterally rather than multilaterally. Yet, notwithstanding two dramatic shifts in the system—the rise of unipolarity and the weakening of Westphalian sovereignty in the global system—Ikenberry sketches a possible US leadership agenda that would entail that country's recommitting to multilateral governance. Although he describes a full agenda of multilateral recommitment, he also acknowledges that future global governance likely will be more informal, bilateral and domestically centered.

Drezner, meanwhile, challenges some fundamental thinking of liberal institutionalists, noting—as do Wolfe, Helleiner and Momani, and Fearon —that there is a growing mismatch between the distribution of power within and without international organizations. This is true, according to Drezner, especially for US-dominated organizations, as many of them are. Drezner points out, however, that not only is it particularly difficult to rewrite the rules and leadership of current international organizations, but such efforts lead to stalemate and reform failure. Yet, in the face of such failure and sclerosis, Drezner points out—as do Ikenberry and Stein—that there seems to be a proliferation of new international organizations; indeed, he describes the current situation as "a world thick with institutions." This proliferation, however, creates another sort of problem for global governance: bluntly, the problem of choice. Drezner asserts that powerful states use this increase in the number of international organizations and rules for their own benefit. Far from states generally benefiting from the thickening array of such organizations, the structure permits the powerful to forum shop, which enables them to receive the greatest advantage from the current structure. This forum shopping by the powerful undermines more rules-based and rules-neutral international governance. Thus, the current system maintains international organizations that remain power incongruent—where a mismatch remains in the distribution of power between the organization and the external international system, and where the thickening of international institutions might well undermine rules-based multilateralism.

In the lower right quadrant of Table 1 are Richard Rosecrance and Patricia Goff, who, while maintaining a focus on power and power distribution, look beyond reform of formal institutions and explore the reform of rules and norms as well.

Rosecrance examines a continuum of structures from the formal to the informal, including international institutions—empires, alliances, and others—that he calls "softer institutional linkages." He suggests that, in the end, Great Power coalitions remain the most effective international regulators. He further suggests that a Great Power concert could arise in the current context through the participation of powerful states within the extant variety of institutions—whether soft, medium, or hard—that could form the basis of future global governance. Rosecrance also reminds us that cooperation represents a far more important instrument of international politics than is frequently recognized in the analysis of global politics. The motivation for cooperation in the contemporary setting is a consequence of both common goals and common opponents. Thus, in the current global governance realm, collective action by the Great Powers could crystallize into active opposition to Islamic extremism and nuclear proliferation. In addition, Great Powers could derive further unity from the collective search for economic prosperity. As Rosecrance suggests, "[i]t is their participation in a variety of decisionmaking organizations that brings Great Powers together and that legitimizes and represents their common interests in a variety of international contexts" "(106).

Goff, too, looks beyond the distribution of power to the formation and redefinition of norms and principles in the international system. Such a focus, according to Goff, will get us to what John Ruggie, one of multilateralism's chief analysts, suggests are the "ideas" underpinning the system. Goff begins with the changing distribution of power among the Great Powers. She warns against global governance analysis, in which the United States occupies too pivotal a role, and notes the redistribution of power in the international system to the so-called BRIC countries (Brazil, Russia, India, and China). What influence these states will have on future global governance remains an open question but a more balanced examination is warranted, according to Goff. In addition, Europe and nonstate actors need to be factored into any examination of contemporary global governance. Beyond the distribution of power, however, are ideas—the organizing principles and rules of the international system. As Goff argues, "[t]hese organizing principles, intended to operate regardless of the power capabilities of individual participants, represent an aspect of multilateralism that is often lost in contemporary debates" (395). She argues for the need "to shift our focus to outcomes and to the ideas, goals, and aspirations underpinning multilateral action" (398).

Finally, we come to the bottom left quadrant of the typology in Table 1, where Paul Collier and Arthur Stein are situated. The analysis of both authors seems to be less determined by the distribution of power among states—or, at least, they explore elements of the wider legitimacy of global governance leadership. Both authors also examine ideas and outcomes and the so-called rules of the game.

Collier tackles the challenging question of development—specifically, the failure of African development. Global development policy is rife with ideological clashes among analysts, activists, and donor countries. Collier enters the fray without apology. He argues that African development failure is a product not of poverty but of divergence. He suggests that one can identify what he calls the "bottom billion"—the poor of the developing world—by the divergence of per capita income, a phenomenon particularly acute in Africa. From Collier's perspective, the solution is clear and simple: growth. As he writes, "[d]ivergence is inescapably about growth: it simply means that growth rates differ, and it can be rectified only by raising growth rates in the societies at the bottom" (243).

Having identified the goal as growth, Collier suggests that the developed countries—specifically the members of the Organisation for Economic Co-operation and Development (OECD)—need to develop instruments other than just aid to promote African development, including trade, military intervention, and governance standards (both corporate and governmental) to tackle development failure in Africa. He argues, however, that the policies of the OECD countries are uncoordinated and represent each country's particular interests. "[W]hat is needed," he says, "is the cooperation of a group of countries that are sufficiently allied and sufficiently large to be effective" (281). Not all states need to do everything—some might specialize in particular development policy instruments. For example, he suggests that the Group of 8 major industrial countries might focus on aid, trade, and governance standards while the P5 focuses on security. He also anticipates the likely need to include China and India in development policies, and suggests that a larger international organization—say, a G20—would be more appropriate to tackle global development.

Stein provides the widest analytic scope of inquiry of multilateralism of any of the authors in the volume. Indeed, in some ways, his wide-ranging inquiry might place him in a number of the boxes in the typology in Table 1. Stein begins his inquiry with an examination of the reform motivation in contemporary international relations. He notes the general disappointment about the state of global governance and the many reform proposals. But he is careful to differentiate among the many reform proposals. As he suggests, reform proposals come in a number of different forms and for different reasons. Such reform proposals can be simply palliative, to deal with discontent over a particular institution without solving the underlying problems; they can be corrective, to deal with existing international institutions; and they can be transformative, to change the way institutions behave or even to create new institutions and expand the scope of global governance. As Stein declares, "[u]nderstanding the prospects for reform requires a sense not only of the nature of the reform but also of the nature of the complaints expressed about current practices. As in other areas of politics, there is much shadow play and posturing in the politics of institutional reform" (42).

Two elements define Stein's analysis of global governance. The first is the logic of the system, which demands that global governance be incentive compatible, meaning that states choose to act in their national interest and can do so either in conjunction with others—multilateralism—or unilaterally. Stein's first element, the question of multilateralism versus unipolarity or hegemony, is a theme that weaves through a number of chapters of this book. Stein argues that, although all states—not just the hegemon—are able to choose between one approach and the other, the consequences of the choices made by more powerful states are more consequential for global governance. Further, the choice of each state, whether powerful or not, is determined by its assessment of the costs and benefits of the available opportunities and ongoing constraints. Stein concludes, however, that states generally see multilateralism as preferable as long as they perceive that course as capable of achieving their national interest. This apparent preference is critical in an understanding of global governance.

The second element in Stein's analysis is the existential reality of multilateralism and the reality of what he describes as a weak confederal structure of the international system. The contemporary system of states, and their interests, according to Stein, generates multilateralism." But the foundation of multilateralism—and here he parts company with a number of authors who focus more directly on power distribution—is not defined purely by the distribution of power in the system. There is something beyond just a strict power distribution, which Stein has left in his chapter as "history." What is clear, however, is that the many organizations, laws, and agreements of contemporary global governance make multilateralism an existential reality in contemporary international relations. Stein concludes: "We live in a world of weak confederalism precisely because states find independent decision making inadequate to their governance needs; they thus prefer forms of joint decision making and governance, yet they are unprepared to relinquish core elements of their autonomy and independence" (75).

This tension between sovereignty and global governance persists in all global governance institutions. Thus, in the surge of reform proposals and the proliferation of international institutions, it is important to gauge the motivation behind institutional creation and the call for reform. Perhaps the motivation stems from heightened expectations of "more" global governance or from the failure of organizations, principles, and rules—in other words, as Stein makes clear, as a result of both success and failure. Calls for reform might also grow out of a wish to alter an organization's mandate or to devise a new one, perhaps to correct its limitations or failings. In still other instances, reform proposals might stem from politicians' need to assuage certain domestic interests, with little or no intention that such reforms be successfuly implemented. Clearly, however, not all reform proposals are alike, and a picture of a rising tide of reform proposals might say little about the need for, or the prospects of, genuine reform of contemporary global governance institutions.

Almost all the chapters start with an examination of the distribution of power among states, and there is a general presumption that the distribution of power shapes and reshapes multilateralism. Goff raises the effect of the BRICS on the reform of institutions, as do Wolfe (on WTO reform) and Helleiner and Momani (on IMF reform). At the same time, both Goff and Drezner warn of overemphasizing the dominance of the United States. What appears evident, however, from the empirical chapters is how difficult it might be to reconfigure organizations—in terms of either leadership or principles and rules—to reflect any new distribution of power.

Whether they focus on specific organizations or more generally on international institutions, all the authors seek to determine the character of future organizations and international institutions. Ikenberry suggests that, in future, we are likely to see less multilateralism and more informal, bilateral, and domestic-centered governance arrangements. Fearon raises the prospect of a competing security organization to the current "universal" UN, one that might require each member country to be democratic. Rosecrance suggests that global governance might need to rely on formal, or more possibly informal, new "grand coalitions" built not necessarily on common values or polities (such as democracy) but on common interests. The organizational and institutional forms might vary—in some instances, the goal might be to further a rules-based, principles-driven system; in others, international cooperation of the powerful might be the principal goal. The result, however, is that "effective" organizations are likely to be less multilateral, less permanent, and less easy to see.

Global governance and the reform of global governance are at the heart of this volume. I hope—and I daresay the authors do, too—that readers come away with a better understanding of the possibilities and the challenges of both in contemporary global politics.

The Evolution of a Book

In 2005, I proposed to Daniel Schwanen, CIGI's chief operating officer and director of research, that we convene a Global Institutional Reform (GIR) Workshop. I suggested that the workshop focus on global governance —in particular, on the effectiveness of current international organizations and institutions and on an assessment of global governance reform proposals. Subsequently, a preliminary meeting was held at the Woerner House near Waterloo in September 2005, at which it was decided to call for a series of papers on global governance reform to be presented at CIGI's annual meeting in fall 2006. Always a predilection of mine, I urged that, in convening the workshop, we examine the full spectrum of global governance institutions, from security through economic and humanitarian.

Soon after the decision to proceed with the workshop and the research papers, Daniel and I determined that there was much to be gained in partnering with Princeton University's Woodrow Wilson School of Public and International Affairs.[2] With the active cooperation of my colleague at Woodrow Wilson, G. John Ikenberry, we arranged commitments from and retainers for a number of scholars. In addition, John and I agreed to hold a "dry run" for the draft papers commissioned for the GIR Workshop in the summer preceding CIGI's 2006 annual meeting.

In mid-August 2006, the authors gathered to discuss their presentations at Woodrow Wilson's House on the Princeton campus. In addition to the presenting authors, a number of colleagues were kind enough to take a bit of summer time and join us for what turned out to be a most enjoyable day-and-a-half of heated, but friendly discussion, great meals, and some excellent wine chosen by our host, John Ikenberry. I must thank invited guests Miles Kahler, Rohr Professor of Pacific International Relations, University of California, San Diego; Ferry de Kerckhove, Department of Foreign Affairs and International Trade, Ottawa; Steven E. Miller, editor-in-chief of *International Security* and Director, International Security Program, Belfer Center for Science and International Affairs, John F. Kennedy School of Government, Harvard University; Andrew Cooper, Distinguished

---

2. CIGI already had a connection with the Woodrow Wilson School, since Anne-Marie Slaughter, its dean, sits on CIGI's International Advisory Board of Governors.

Fellow and Associate Director, CIGI; and Steven F. Bernstein, Associate Professor of Political Science and then acting director of the Centre for International Studies, Munk Centre for International Studies, University of Toronto.

This lively group joined with the paper presenters and we found ourselves well entertained by their drafts and defenses of various aspects of global institutional reform: Paul Collier on development; Eric Helleiner and Bessma Momani on the IMF; John Ikenberry on US foreign policy; Richard Rosecrance on Great Power alliances; David Smith, a member of the CIGI International Advisory Board of Governors and Executive Director of the Centre for Global Studies, University of Victoria, on Canadian foreign policy; Arthur Stein on multilateralism; and Robert Wolfe on the WTO.

In addition to organizing the draft papers and advancing the workshop discussions, we invited workshop members to join a virtual GIR community at a Web site called IGLOO.[3] At the site, we made available to community members, among other things, many of the reports containing reform proposals issued by or on behalf of various international organizations.

Many of the authors who had presented drafts at Princeton then made rather more polished presentations in panels at the 2006 annual CIGI meeting, held at CIGI's base in Waterloo, Ontario; they then began to revise their papers for this volume. Meanwhile, as the shape of the volume began to emerge, some of the authors suggested possible additions. Ferry de Kerckhove, for example, suggested that a paper on the 2005 UN Leaders' Summit might be a useful addition to the draft papers already under way, since it was evident from the significant number of reform proposals on various aspects of the UN that there would be a real benefit in directly addressing the UN reform process.[4]

---

3. IGLOO stands for International Governance Leader and Organizations Online. The technology is the product of several innovators who have sought to leverage local technology and talent to facilitate international governance research over the Web. IGLOO now houses many online organizations concerned with aspects of global governance.
4. It also tied at least one chapter to an earlier CIGI publication, Heinbecker and Goff (2005), about which I will have some thoughts in the Conclusion.

Meanwhile, I had proposed that we divide the book into two sections, one focusing on the theory and analysis of global governance reform and the other an empirical section focusing more on the challenge of reforming particular international organizations. Of course, the division is not precise—for example, Collier is clearly concerned with both specific multilateral development initiatives, such as the UN's Millennium Development Goals, and the theory of development initiatives.[5] Then, a number of additional possibilities came to mind, one of which grew out of a presentation Daniel Drezner of Tufts University made at the University of Toronto in which he raised questions about the creation of international organizations by Great Powers. As he described it, the proliferation of international organizations had led to, among other things, forum shopping, nested and overlapping institutions, and regime complexes that had come to play key roles in shaping the pattern of global governance. This position, as you will see, is in contrast to the liberal institutionalist school represented by Ikenberry in his chapter on the United States. It is a pleasure to have Drezner's revised version of his earlier presentation in this book. Finally, Arthur Stein alerted me to a report on reforming international institutions prepared by James Fearon of Stanford University for the International Task Force on Public Goods, in which he examined various reform proposals for the UN Security Council. I am pleased that he agreed to provide a shorter version of that report for this book.

Although the volume then seemed complete, Daniel Schwanen suggested an addition. At a panel during CIGI's 2006 annual meeting, Patricia Goff, a Senior Fellow of CIGI, had provided a perspective on multilateralism in which she raised a number of issues on which other authors in this volume had commented. Here, she develops some of the themes she identified in her panel remarks and offers comments on the theoretical and empirical contributions of the other authors in the volume.

A volume such as this cannot possibly be completed without the avid assistance of many hands. My thanks to the numerous CIGI staff members who helped usher the authors and their chapters along. Thanks also to Brian Henderson and his staff at Wilfrid Laurier University Press for

---

5. Collier expands on many of his arguments in his recent book, *The Bottom Billion* (2007).

pressing forward on publication. My great thanks as well to our diligent copy editor, Barry Norris—the wonders of the Internet made his location in New Brunswick no impediment to timely editing and revision. And, of course, a very special thanks to Daniel Schwanen, without whose constant support this volume would not have reached fruition; I know all the authors are grateful for his consistent support and guidance. Finally, a reminder that the views expressed here are not necessarily those of CIGI or its Board of Directors.

So here it is—a collective enquiry into multilateralism and whether the world can be governed.

References

Alvarez, José E. 2006. "International Organizations: Then and Now." *American Journal of International Law* 100 (2): 324–47.

Collier, Paul. 2007. *The Bottom Billion: Why the Poorest Countries Are Failing and What Can Be Done about It.* Oxford: Oxford University Press.

Dayaratna-Banda, O.G., and John Whalley. 2007. "After the MFA, the CCAs (China Containment Agreements)." Working Paper 24. Waterloo, ON: Centre for International Governance Innovation. May.

Heinbecker, Paul, and Patricia Goff, eds. 2005. *Irrelevant or Indispensable? The United Nations in the 21st Century.* Waterloo, ON: Wilfrid Laurier University Press.

Stein, Arthur. Forthcoming. "Neoliberal Institutionalism." In *Oxford Handbook on International Relations*, edited by Christian Reus-Smit and Duncan Snidal. New York: Oxford University Press.

Incentive Compatibility and Global Governance:
Existential Multilateralism, a Weakly Confederal World, and Hegemony

Arthur A. Stein

*   *   *

The twentieth century was the century of international institutions. Although some international organizations can trace their origins back to the nineteenth century, and international institutions more broadly go back centuries, the number grew tremendously in the past hundred years. In 1909, a clearinghouse for information on international organizations listed 37;[1] by the end of the century, there were more than 6,400.

For some, the set of international organizations already in existence at the beginning of the twentieth century augured world government. In a work entitled *International Government* and published in 1916 in the midst of World War I, Leonard Woolf wrote, "in every department of life, the beginnings, and more than the beginnings, of International Government

My thanks to Alan Alexandroff, Steve Bernstein, Paul Collier, Patti Goff, Eric Helleiner, John Ikenberry, Miles Kahler, Jeff Legro, Steve Miller, Richard Rosecrance, and Bob Wolfe for comments.

1. See the Web site: http://www.uia.org/statistics/organizations/ytb299.php. The clearinghouse began as the Central Office of International Associations and later became the Union of International Associations. It has regularly published data on international organizations since 1910. For a brief history of the organization, see http://www.uia.org/uia.

already exist." In fact, Woolf noted, "the recognition of international interests, and that national interests are international interests, and *vice versa*, was the great social discovery of the last 100 years." This view was seconded by political scientist Mary P. Follett shortly after the United States' entry into World War I, who wrote that nations "have fought for national rights," but these "are as obsolete as the individual rights of the last century." Moreover, Follett argued, the United States held the key to the emergence of internationalism: "the contribution of America to the Great War will be told as America's taking her stand squarely and responsibly on the position that national particularism was in 1917 dead" (quoted in Iriye 2002, 18, 20).

Yet, almost a century later, the growth of international organizations has not brought world government—indeed, there is great disappointment about the state of global governance. The end of the Cold War, although as momentous and consequential as the end of any protracted war between great powers, differed from its predecessors, the two World Wars, in that it brought no great efforts at building international institutions.[2]

The past decade and a half has been an era of great disquiet and uncertainty, one characterized simultaneously by globalization and heightened tribalism, and marked by profound concern about the continued viability and the need for reform of international institutions. Global developments are seen as challenging both the nation-state and international organizations.[3]

---

2. Ikenberry (2003a, 2003b), however, disagrees. He sees the expansion of the North Atlantic Treaty Organization (NATO) and the launching of the North American Free Trade Agreement, Asia-Pacific Economic Cooperation, and the World Trade Organization (WTO) as constituting the pursuit of an institutional agenda comparable to that which followed World Wars I and II. I argue that this more recent agenda is not on a par with the earlier eras and that it constitutes adaptation of existing institutions rather than a major effort of institutional construction. I discuss the effect of extant institutions on the post–Cold War era later in this paper.

3. The implications of globalization for the size of the state system are discussed in Rosecrance and Stein (2006). In this paper, I use the terms organization, institution, and regime largely interchangeably, though they are subtly different. The literature on organizations focuses on concrete entities with buildings, addresses, and employees. Regimes and institutions refer to a broader set of phenomena, although there is continued disagreement on their defining parameters. Here, my focus is primarily on concrete organizations, although

It has also been an era of unparalleled—for some, unchecked—US power. US dominance has meant that some look to the United States to lead (Mandelbaum 2005), while others fear US unilateralism. No one would argue today, as Follett did in 1917, that the United States would press the argument that "national particularism [is] dead."

Ironically, the remarks by Woolf and Follett from nearly a century ago sound prescient today. Intervening events and current trends provide ammunition for those who would agree with their remarks, as well as for those who would find them idealistic and utopian: not only can one contest their views about the trajectory of international relations, but, in the current setting, one can also question the United States' continued commitment to multilateralism, much less internationalism.

A great deal of dissatisfaction with global governance exists today, and many proposals for the reform of international organizations continue to be proffered. In this paper, I develop an argument about the requisites for international governance and the reform of international institutions. First, I distinguish between social engineering and governance at the global level and at the domestic level, and argue that international governance, especially, must be compatible with incentives. I then discuss the implications of incentive compatibility for the continuing import of power and interests and for the choice between going it alone and working with others through international institutions. I argue that the option of unilateralism exists for many states, not just Great Powers—that both unilateralism and multilateralism reflect power, interests, and historical legacy.

Then, I discuss the relationship between incentive compatibility and civil society, and the effect of the growth of democracies on the construction of international institutions. I argue that, increasingly, global institutions have to be compatible with societal preferences as well as with governmental ones. I then address the dissatisfaction with international institutions and demands for reform, arguing that many expressions of dissatisfaction should not be taken seriously and that some reforms are purposely illusory—indeed, arguments about the inadequacy of governance and the need for reform can be exercises in posturing.

---

many of my arguments apply to broader concerns. For a review of this literature, see Stein (forthcoming).

Even the United States continues to show a preference for multilateralism, and I argue that it does so for reasons of both domestic and international legitimacy. I then suggest that multilateralism is an existential reality in a world best characterized as weakly confederal. Following this is a discussion of the requisites of multilateralism, in which I argue that unilateralism is not just about a state's going it alone but about the existence of active disapproval of its actions.

In the final section, I delineate some criteria for constructing institutions, and argue that institutional design and reform should be incentive compatible and commensurate with the problems they are intended to deal with, that international institutions should allow differentiated commitments and encompass member states with shared interests. Throughout, I stress that debates about international governance mirror those about domestic governance, and that similar political dynamics are evident in both domains.

Incentive Compatibility and International Governance

The instruments available for governance and social engineering at the global level differ from those at the domestic level. Within societies, governments have an array of tools with which to coerce changes in individual behavior. Governments can socialize individuals and use the media and information flows to shape the ways in which individuals view the world. They can also induce behavioral change by manipulating the incentives that individuals face. In short, governments function at a supra level of authority in relation to the individuals whose behavior they seek to engineer.[4]

International institutions, in contrast, do not have at their disposal comparable bases of power. In international politics, no higher-level

---

4. Lukes (1974) adds the shaping of individuals' preferences as another way in which governments exercise power. Foucault (1977) explores what he terms the "microphysics of power," emphasizing institutions of repressive social control. Strikingly, even with such instruments, there remains a great deal of illegal and deviant individual behavior within societies. Also striking is the absence of these instruments of control at the international level.

authority has the tools to engineer the behavior of governments in ways that governments can shape the behavior of their citizens.[5] The decisions of international organizations reflect the interests of their constituent governments, and enforcement depends on them as well. We are thus left with the reality that global governance must reflect the interests of states. The optimism of Woolf and Follett about world government depended on state interests. Woolf's argument hinged on "the recognition…that national interests are international interests," whereas, for Follett, national rights were obsolete and "national particularism was…dead."

International organizations thus arise and are fashioned to serve the interests of states. Global governance and the design of institutions depend on incentives and on constructing arrangements that are compatible with such incentives.[6]

Power, Interests, and International Institutions

That international institutions must be incentive compatible implies that the verities of international politics continue to be important. International institutions are the creations of self-interested states that are confronting a variety of problems and that prefer outcomes arrived at through joint, as opposed to individual, decision making (Stein 1982, 1990, chap. 2). A recognition of the importance of international organizations and their role thus does not require one to conclude, as Iriye (2002, 158–59) does, that power

---

5. Persuasion exists internationally, but not in the sense in which it functions domestically. Internationally, persuasion functions through information about options and payoffs, and thus is inherently about the interests of the actors. Coercion exists internationally, but it is more successful in deterring, rather than compelling, the behavior of Great Powers; even when successful, the compulsion of behavior typically works against the weakest, least relevant states. To give but one example, trade liberalization requires agreement among major economic actors, and it would be impossible for the United States to force Japan to open its domestic markets to international forces; such coercion could occur only with respect to small and irrelevant players in the trading world (Stein 1984).

6. This does not mean that there are no agency issues or that international organizations do not develop some degree of independence (Haftel and Thompson 2006).

relations among major states constitute the traditional view "presented in conventional vocabulary and frameworks" and that international organizations are part of "an alternative definition of international relations [that has] been gaining strength and that a new vocabulary might be needed to note that development."

The Option of Unilateralism

The need for incentive compatibility means that states have the choice between acting on their own and acting in conjunction with others, between working through existing international organizations and ignoring them, between following the extant strictures of international law and ignoring them. That remains as true today as it has been for centuries. What is different today, however, is the broad range of possibilities that exist for acting in conjunction with others. The choice between unilateralism and multilateralism exists not only for the United States—the context in which most discussions of this arise—but also for others. Indeed, the choice of going it alone, separate from its efficacy and advisability, is open to all.

Every one of the list of particulars adduced as evidence of US unilateralism is available as an option for other, nonhegemonic powers. For example, the Bush administration has been castigated for choosing not to ratify the Kyoto Protocol but instead introducing its own "Clean Skies" initiative. Yet, in Canada, the Conservative Party's election triumph in January 2006 has had much the same effect on ending Canada's adherence to the protocol. The consequences of joining or not may be different, both for the country making the choice and for all others, but the choice remains.

The point applies as well to the use of force. The United States is not the only country to use force unilaterally and without international approval. Australia, for example, has twice intervened militarily in East Timor, once at the request of the international community and once at the request of the East Timorese government—in the latter case, Australia acted according to its perceived national interests and without seeking the approval of the Security Council. The issues for any power are capability and cost. A state has the choice of acting on its own if it has the ability to do so and is willing to bear the cost. For example, Israel chose to attack the Osirak reactor in Iraq in 1981—it had the ability to do so and it was willing to pay the political costs of going ahead.

Unilateralism is, of course, more consequential the more powerful the state that exercises it. A middle power that pursues a unilateral course can be seen benignly as a free rider or malevolently as a system challenger, but a hegemon that pursues unilateralism is likely to be upsetting the very possibility of a cooperative solution. Moreover, to the extent that multilateral institutions constitute a mechanism by which others are able to constrain a hegemonic power, unilateral policies by such a power pose a larger set of challenges to other states in the system than merely the issue at hand. Thus, the US (and Canadian) response to Kyoto is not about the protocol itself, but a symbol of a larger problem.

Unilateralism, Multilateralism, and State Interests

Unless one is prepared to argue that states do not know, or are willing to act contrary to, their own interests, unilateral action must be seen as being in a state's interest. The choice of multilateralism over unilateralism must perforce also be in a state's interest. That both unilateralism and multilateralism reflect state interests poses an analytic problem, however, especially for those who recommend institutional reform.

Singer, Walsh, and Wilkening (2004), for example, recognize the role of state interests, then trip all over themselves in defining unilateralism and multilateralism. They note that countries cannot be convinced "to act for long in ways that are incompatible with their own interests"; rather, they act in terms of how they see their interests, "not how an outside power thinks they ought to." The authors define multilateralism as "an approach to foreign policy that seeks durable solutions to major international security problems through cooperation based on mutual interests as prescribed by dialogue." They contrast this approach with a characterization of unilateralism as "ad hoc cooperation based on coalitions willing to act according to the self-perceived interests of a major power as defined by its own *dictat*" (p. 8).

The authors' caveat that cooperation is "based on mutual interests as prescribed by dialogue" seems at least slightly at odds with the presumption that states perceive their own interests in their own terms and not in terms of what others think they should want. By suggesting that "self-perceived interests of a major power [are] defined by its own *dictat*," the authors merely restate what they say is true of all states—that they see their own interests in their own terms. Thus, the discussion of the cooperation of unilateralism is contradictory. States are said to join coalitions of the willing and to act according to the interests of a major power, which violates the presumption that states do not act "in ways incompatible with their own interests." Alternatively, that cooperative coalitions of the willing exist must mean that coalition members see it in their interest to join. Both multilateralism and unilateralism are seen as entailing cooperation and, in the end, the only coherent difference between the two definitions is that multilateralism seeks durable solutions and unilateralism is about ad hoc cooperation. But there is nothing in the nature of these terms to suggest they are about durability or ad hoc-ery.

Recognizing that foreign policy is rooted in state interests leads to the understanding that the choice between multilateralism and unilateralism is in the service of the same objective, and that the choice reflects an assessment of the costs and benefits of available opportunities and extant constraints. It is fallacious to suggest that multilateralism is in a state's interest but unilateralism is not, because any action, especially a unilateral one, must be in a state's interest. Thus, those who argue in favor of multilateralism must do so on the basis of a calculation of the cost effectiveness or efficiency of such action.[7] They could argue that some policy makers have made the wrong calculation about the relative costs of unilateralism and multilateralism, but such an argument implies that the environment is ambiguous enough that people can draw contradictory assessments of net

---

7. For a discussion of competing bases for assessing self-interest, see Stein (1990).

    Here, normative arguments on behalf of multilateralism face a problem. Ikenberry (2003b, 55) argues that the United States has created and supported only those multilateral institutions it could dominate or in which it found that the gains from "locking other states into enduring policy positions" was worth more than the costs of reduced policy autonomy. But it is hard to square this positive view of multilateralism with normative arguments that encourage US multilateralism and arguments that US policy has been hijacked by various factions of the Bush administration.

benefits and that the matter should be self-correcting as political leaders periodically learn anew the lesson of unilateralism's higher costs.

Alternatively, proponents of multilateralism could argue that, although unilateralism might be in a country's interest, there are negative spillovers, in the form of unintended costs borne in other areas, as well as positive spillovers, benefits that accrue in other areas by forgoing unilateralism in one domain. This would imply that, while unilateralism might indeed be better on some issues, its negative externalities must be paid in other settings.[8] Proponents of multilateralism could also frame their argument around calculations of enlightened self-interest—that longer-term benefits accrue from short-term self-abnegation.

The point I develop below is that, by and large, states do see multilateralism as a preferable way to achieve their objectives if that option can lead to success. But multilateralism must also be in their interest.[9] Moreover, if states perceive international organizations to be in need of reform, their interest in multilateralism must be sufficiently great as to exceed the expected costs of reform; otherwise, unilateralism or ad hoc multilateralism will be the result.

The Balance of Power and International Institutions

Earlier epochs of institutional formation, characterized by a multiplicity of Great Powers, were either multipolar or bipolar. Since 1990, however,

---

8. Ironically, one could make this argument concerning the Iraq War. The United States was able to topple Saddam's regime, and at minimal international cost. The problem arose with the negative spillovers, which first and foremost included the unwillingness of others to take part in postwar reconstruction and governance. The costs of the war have come from the occupation, which might well have been avoided if those who opposed the war had taken part in postwar peacekeeping and stabilization.

9. I thus disagree with Kagan (2002a, 2002b), who argues that the United States is instrumentally multilateralist whereas Europeans are principled multilateralists. He cites French president Jacques Chirac as an example of the European approach, but France has not sought Security Council approval to intervene militarily in its former African colonies. On the other hand, Kagan does recognize that most US officials are at least pragmatic multilateralists and that, even in the United States, there are no true unilateralists to be found.

the global distribution of power has changed fundamentally. The world has become unipolar or hegemonic, which, in turn, has affected the creation and evolution of international institutions.[10]

Multilateralism reflects a basic reality of international politics: the distribution of power. Modern multilateralism, consisting largely of the international institutions that have developed over the course of the past 150 years, has emerged in quite different settings. In the first wave, which emerged during a multipolar age, the ability to fashion arrangements for a multilateral setting was critical. The standard criticism that the League of Nations failed, in part, because the United States did not join is a critique that the institution's design was not compatible with the interests of all the parties needed to make it work. In contrast, the United Nations was designed for a multipolar age, but largely functioned in a bipolar one. Any new multilateralism thus has to deal with the core reality of the changed distribution of power. Whether one regards the world today as unipolar or hegemonic, or the United States as a hyperpower, this changed reality affects all states. It also changes their incentives for, and expectations from, multilateral arrangements. Any new institutions will perforce be built on the foundations of this new reality.

Although the United States is far and away the world's dominant power, domain-specific distributions of power also matter. In economic terms, indeed, the world is arguably multipolar, rather than unipolar, and the United States cannot act as unilaterally on economic and financial issues as it can on military ones. In addition, the continuing existence of a balance of nuclear terror imposes constraints even on the United States' exercise of unilateral military power.

If the nature of global governance merely reflects the distribution of power, then unilateralism reflects unipolarity, multilateralism reflects multipolarity, and bipolarity occupies some middle ground that one imagines is closer to unipolarity. In a world of one Great Power, one would expect that power to act unilaterally if power considerations were all that mattered. In a world of a number of Great Powers, power considerations

---

10. In Stein (1984), I noted the irony of scholars of international political economy who talk of "hegemonic stability theory" in an era that security scholars characterize as bipolar or multipolar.

would imply some degree of multilateralism if the powers were to co-operate on international issues. In a bipolar world, one would expect little multilateralism to the extent that each power did not really need allies, absent a joint condominium between the two Great Powers. The question, then, is: how did we get multilateral institutions in an age of bipolarity? There are two answers.

One answer is that liberalism trumped bipolarity—that the United States as a liberal power created liberal institutions (Ikenberry 2001)—and that liberalism is somehow linked with multilateralism. My own argument (Stein 1984) is that, although the United States took a more active role in pressing liberalization following World War II, it also accepted and fostered illiberal practices. US liberalism was confined to US allies and clients, while adversaries experienced the brunt of US intolerance. The United States was willing to provide access to its markets and to accept an asymmetric bargain that tolerated others' illiberal practices, in part for political reasons. Those on the outside of that system paid the prohibitively high tariffs that remained as a legacy of Smoot-Hawley and, in the case of adversaries, were subject to detailed lists of items prohibited for export. The United States has been similarly illiberal on the movement of people, prepared to deny visas for visiting scholars and authors because of their political views and to deny Americans the freedom to travel to countries it sanctions. Comparable arguments can be made about US treatment of capital movements and its practice of supporting illiberal governments if they were anti-communist and undercutting democratic regimes and free elections out of a fear of communism. In short, any argument about US policy as driven by a general ideology of liberalism is problematic.

An alternative answer is that the bipolar reality of the Cold War meant that there were few global institutions, and they functioned only when the two superpowers agreed—for example, at the UN Security Council. What we think of as successful multilateral institutions were subsystemic, not global, and consisted of the members of one bloc. In effect, the multi-lateral order, especially institutions dealing with security, trade, and finance, was essentially an anti-communist rather than a global order. Ironically, then, many subsystemic organizations only became truly global with the end of the Cold War.

There is today a debate in the United States about the implications of unipolarity. For some, this era represents an opportunity for the United States to play an imperial role, to provide the global benefits of empire (Ferguson 2004; Lal 2004). For others, unipolarity is inherently short lived and will generate countervailing coalitions, which eventually will restore a balance of power.[11] Within the latter group are those arguing that US unipolarity can be extended and balancing avoided and limited through a self-conscious self-abnegation on the part of the United States through an emphasis on multilateralism. In my view, however, US unipolarity is occurring in a setting of existential multipolarity, in which the options of both unilateralism and balancing are few, constrained, and, at the extreme, ultimately self-defeating.

The overwhelming power of the United States has meant that both its disinterestedness and its concerns overwhelm multilateral efforts and that, if necessary, other countries, though unable to challenge the United States militarily, can stymie efforts by the United States to have international institutions rubber-stamp its preferences and actions. The result is both a desire for US leadership in the construction of multilateral governance and a fear of US domination of the resulting constructions.

Multilateralism and the Historical Moment

Changes in the distribution of power do not occur in an institutional vacuum. Typically, a set of enduring international institutions continues to function in their respective regions, functional areas, and domains. In contrast to earlier eras, the international institutional structure changed only somewhat as a direct result of the end of the Cold War.

Then there is the matter of history. The effects of the two World Wars were so profound, and the existing international organizational infrastructure so relatively weak, that, in effect, the design of international organizations had to start from scratch following each war—the League of

---

11. There is already an extensive literature on whether or not others have begun to balance US power; if they have not, why not; and if they have, whether this constitutes a new and different kind of soft balancing. See the discussion in the summer 2005 issue of *International Security*.

Nations, for example, did not survive World War II and a completely different organization was created after the war. That is not the case today.

At the end of the Cold War, there was a deep and rich array of existing international organizations. Thus, we are witnessing, perhaps for the first time in world history, the adaptation of international organizations to new circumstances and the adaptation of Great Powers to international organizations, not their creation anew. The organizational developments of the post–Cold War world consisted largely of adaptations of existing institutions. On the one hand, changing conditions and needs did not lead to the construction of new security institutions; instead, NATO was expanded to include new members and new out-of-area missions. On the other hand, the end of the economic Cold War was met not with the creation of new institutions but with the decision of major powers, such as China, to join an existing organization, the WTO. China had little choice but to accept the rules of the world trading order. The situation, and the negotiated outcome, might have been different had China been there at the time the organization was being designed. If the organization did not exist and were being negotiated now, the rules might well be more accommodating of China's expressed preferences for entry.

The nature of existing organizations affects not only new entrants but also extant members. The United States belongs to many organizations, is party to many agreements, and has many commitments. It must decide whether the change in relative power internationally should be the basis for exercising exit and voice or whether loyalty remains the order of the day. One implication is that the problem of US unilateralism antedates the current administration.[12] The phrase "coalition of the willing," so often used by and attributed to the Bush administration, originated in the Clinton administration. The following quotation from a 1998 op-ed piece makes the point clearly:

> The United States has a penchant these days for joining international negotiations that spin out of control. We went to Kyoto to talk about climate change and discovered we couldn't sign the treaty. We went to Ottawa to talk about landmines and found our military problems ignored

---

12. For a discussion of US ambivalence regarding international organizations, see Luck (1999, 2003), among others.

by other states. We may be the "indispensable country," as Secretary of State Madeleine Albright likes to say. But we often set ourselves up as Alamo holdouts, criticized as the indispensable country with indefensible positions. (Wedgwood 1998)

Table 1 was originally compiled to demonstrate US recalcitrance with respect to international treaties. Reordering the list by date, however, shows that US reluctance to join particular treaties predates the George W. Bush administration.[13] In fact, since 1990, US administrations have had to accommodate themselves simultaneously to the existential reality of a rich environment of multilateral institutions and to the heightened possibility of unilateralism in a unipolar world. The issue of accommodating new power realities is also a problem that middle powers—especially former Great Powers—have to face. In effect, the distribution of marbles has changed, but the players are less willing to allow the one who is accumulating the marbles to have more of a say.

This, then, is what is new about the new multilateralism: historical organizations are dealing with a quite different distribution of power, and any new institutional arrangement will be constructed in the shadow of hegemony.[14] The challenge of today is how to adapt existing organizations so that they remain compatible with the incentives of the United States, and how to fashion new multilateral arrangements in a unipolar age.[15]

---

13. To re-emphasize the point regarding Kyoto, see Ward, Grundig, and Zorick (2001), who note that "analysis of climate change negotiations typically links states' bargaining positions" to various factors that, for the United States, can include "heavy dependence on fossil-fuel use; the influence of its domestic fossil fuel lobby, articulated especially through the possibility of a Senate veto of ratification of the treaty; and concerns about loss of competitiveness if China was to be exempted from obligations under the climate-change regime" (439). Their work antedates the George W. Bush administration, however, and even de-emphasizes the US position in the global balance of power.
14. I use this formulation to make the point that it is not simply the current distribution of power, but also expectations about the future distribution of power, that matters for institutional design today.
15. As Weiss describes it, the real challenge is "to identify those [cases] where Washington's tactical multilateralism kicks in" (2004, 137). See also Boulden and Weiss (2004).

Table 1: *US Contrarianism and International Treaties*

Treaty	US Action	Description
Pre–George W. Bush administration		
International Covenant on Economic, Social, and Cultural Rights	Signed Oct. 5, 1977, never ratified	US maintains that such rights are "aspirational," not inalienable or enforceable. 142 countries have ratified.
Convention on Discrimination against Women	Signed July 17, 1980, never ratified	US remains one of handful of countries, including Iran and Sudan, not to ratify
Convention on the Rights of the Child	Signed Feb. 16, 1995, never ratified	At the UN, only the US and Somalia have not ratified
Comprehensive Test Ban Treaty	Signed Sep. 24, 1996, never ratified	US Senate voted in 1999 to reject ratification. Nuclear Posture Review of 2002 hints of a return to testing.
Chemical Weapons Convention	Signed Jan. 13, 1993, ratified Apr. 25, 1997	US set extensive limitations including which facilities can be tested, and providing for a "national security" basis for refusing inspection.
UN Framework Convention on Climate Control (UNFCCC) and the Kyoto Protocol	Ratified UNFCCC Oct. 15, 1992; signed Kyoto Protocol Nov. 12, 1998, never ratified	Of industrialized states, only the US, Australia, and Israel have not ratified the protocol. The US did ratify the UNFCCC, but has not complied.
Mine Ban Treaty	Opened for signature Dec. 3–4, 1997, entered into force March 1, 1999, US never signed	Turkey only other NATO nonsignatory, Cuba only other Western Hemisphere nonsignatory.
George W. Bush administration		
Biological and Toxin Weapons Convention (BWC) and Draft Proposal	Signed Apr. 10, 1972, ratified Mar. 23, 1975, rejected draft proposal June 2001	US rejected negotiated draft proposals to strengthen enforcement mechanisms thought of as inadequate, and refused to return to negotiations.
Anti-Ballistic Missile Treaty	Signed and ratified summer 1972, US unilateral withdrawal Dec. 13, 2001	US is first major power unilaterally to withdraw from a nuclear arms control treaty. The Bush administration wants to pursue missile defense to deal with "terror threats."
Rome Statute of the International Criminal Court	Signed Dec. 31, 2000, unsigned June 6, 2002	Unprecedented "unsigning." US pressing countries for bilateral agreements to exempt US military and government personnel from court's jurisdiction.

Source: Quenemoen 2003.

Incentive Compatibility, Civil Society, and the New Multilateralism

Increasingly, international institutions have to be incentive compatible with societal as well as governmental interests. The world is experiencing a third wave of democratization. The international system today includes a larger number of states, a larger proportion of which is democratically governed. The mobilization of civil societies and the spread of democratic governance have tremendous implications for the future development of international institutions. Once, international institutions reflected the interests of governments in their interactions with one another. Democratization often brings with it a heightened sense of nationalism (Snyder 2000) and a preference for unilateralism; increasingly, however, reform proposals reflect societal pressures (Keck and Sikkink 1998). The critical issue then becomes that of the alignment of state and society.

There is the prospect of a disconnect between domestic politics and the foreign policy of democratic governments, between the executive and legislatures, between governments and their citizens on the desirability and acceptability of the fetters of multilateralism. One possibility is that citizens might have a greater preference for multilateralism than does their government. More typically, governments recognize the benefits of, and the need for, multilateral institutions but have a difficult time selling them at home. This is one aspect of US unilateralism. In Table 1, for example, half the cases of US contrariness (and five of the seven cases prior to the George W. Bush administration) consist of international agreements and protocols that the US government signed but that the US Senate did not ratify.[16]

Indeed, one can argue that the key constraint to multilateralism on the part of the United States is not the executive branch's pursuit of hegemony in a unipolar world but a legislature and a society unwilling to accept as much multilateral internationalism as successive presidents have desired. Table 2 makes clear that, although both Republican presidents (Reagan and Nixon) and Democrat presidents (Truman and Clinton) pushed through significant numbers of international treaties, only a small proportion of

---

16. Indeed, this problem of the lack of congressional approval has led to an increased use of executive agreements on the part of US administrations (Martin 2000).

Table 2: *Treaty Actions of US Administrations from Grover Cleveland to George W. Bush*

President	Treaty Actions during Presidency	Of Treaties Signed, Number Ratified during Presidency
George W. Bush	6 signed; 10 ratified 1 signature nullified 1 ratification withdrawn	0
Bill Clinton	32 signed; 30 ratified	10
George H.W. Bush	13 signed; 10 ratified	2
Ronald Reagan	14 signed; 19 ratified	5
Jimmy Carter	14 signed; 8 ratified	3
Gerald Ford	2 signed; 10 ratified	1
Richard Nixon	17 signed; 19 ratified	7
Lyndon Johnson	7 signed; 16 ratified	4
John Kennedy	6 signed; 4 ratified	0
Dwight Eisenhower	13 signed; 8 ratified	6
Harry Truman	16 signed; 14 ratified	9
Franklin Roosevelt	0 signed; 6 ratified	0
Herbert Hoover	1 signed; 4 ratified	0
Calvin Coolidge	1 signed; 0 ratified	0
Woodrow Wilson	0 signed; 1 ratified	0
William Taft	1 signed; 1 ratified	0
Grover Cleveland	0 signed; 1 ratified	0

Source: Jurewicz and Dawkins 2005, 21.

Note: No treaties were signed or ratified after Roosevelt's second term in office. Presidents did not all serve the same length of time, and some faced Senates controlled by their opposition.

these agreements were ratified. Indeed, every president since Eisenhower has seen the ratification of more treaties signed by a predecessor than of those he has signed. Moreover, President George W. Bush's record does not seem out of line with that of many modern presidents, especially Republicans (see Table 3).

An analysis of international treaties (Jurewicz and Dawkins 2005) finds that the United States has ratified only 160 (or 29 percent) of 550 active

Table 3: *Treaty Actions per Year in Office, US Administrations from Harry Truman to George W. Bush*

President	Treaties Signed per Year	Treaties Ratified per Year	Signed and Ratified during Presidency per Year
George W. Bush	1.5	2.4	0.0
Bill Clinton	4.0	3.8	1.3
George H.W. Bush	3.3	2.5	0.5
Ronald Reagan	1.8	2.4	0.6
Jimmy Carter	3.5	2.0	0.8
Gerald Ford	0.8	4.0	0.4
Richard Nixon	3.1	3.5	1.3
Lyndon Johnson	1.4	3.1	0.8
John Kennedy	2.1	1.4	0.0
Dwight Eisenhower	1.6	1.0	0.8
Harry Truman	2.0	1.8	1.1

Source: Jurewicz and Dawkins 2005, 21.

Note: At the time the source was published, George W. Bush had served one month of his second term. Ford served two years and six months. Nixon served a full first term and one year and six months of his second term. Johnson served one year and two months of his first term and a full second term. Kennedy served two years and ten months. Truman served three years and eleven months of his first term and a full second term. Some presidents faced Senates controlled by their opposition for some or all of their terms in office.

treaties. Yet this aggregate statistic masks interesting trends by issue and type of agreement: many more treaties that deal with national security or that facilitate trade and resource usage are ratified than treaties on human rights, labor rights, and the environment.

It might be that the United States is less willing than other countries to constrain its sovereignty in some areas. But the issue of a disconnect between governmental and societal preferences is not confined to the United States. Many elected governments discovered that their support of the United States in the war in Iraq ran counter to the preferences of a majority of their citizens. In addition, we often hear of Arab governments that privately support various Western positions but do not do so publicly because of fear of opposition from the "Arab street."[17]

Alternatively, it might be that the United States takes the signing of international agreements more seriously than do other countries, and thus is less likely to sign agreements merely for show without the intention of adopting them. This might especially be the case given the standing of international law in domestic law and the access available to US courts and the remedies they can dispense.[18] In contrast, the multilateralism of autocracies can entail merely illusory commitment, in which public cooperation with other nations is matched by covert defection and internal violations of international commitments.[19] There is no small irony to be found in assessing the correlation between treaty ratification and actual performance for democracies and autocracies. Although castigated for its failure to sign various international treaties, the United States has a better record in some areas than many signatories.

In the past, multilateralism was the product of a smaller set of states, fewer of whom were liberal democracies. Multilateralism in the modern world must be consistent with the levels of domestic political mobilization in prospective members.

Dissatisfaction and the Demand for Reform

That international organizations reflect the interests of states suggests that we should approach reform proposals with some degree of skepticism. There seems to be a continuous level of dissatisfaction with international

---

17. One way to read the disjuncture between state and society in the United States and the Middle East is captured in the following quotation: "In Washington, officials lie in public and tell the truth off the record. In the Mideast, officials say what they really believe in public and tell you what you want to hear in private" (Friedman 2006).

18. This is still an additional reason for the presidential use of executive agreements rather than treaties. Compliance with such agreements remains an executive prerogative and not subject to societal intervention via the judicial process.

19. Striking examples include the lack of compliance with commitments under the Nuclear Non-Proliferation Treaty (NPT), and those regarding human rights and women's rights.

institutions and a perpetual industry that proposes reform.[20] Commissions and reports pour forth recommending one international reform after another, but, like their domestic counterparts, they gather dust. Yet dissatisfaction does not necessarily equal failure that requires reform. Dissatisfaction often accompanies the best that can be done.

Prospective social engineers must assess the realities of international politics before contemplating reform or institutional construction. World politics reflects an equilibrium between power and interests, and might not be amenable to change. If both the absence and existence of international institutions reflect the interests of states, then the workings of international politics at any point in time constitute an equilibrium outcome. Demands for new institutions and for the reform of extant ones might then simply reflect dissatisfaction with an extant equilibrium.

That the world reflects an equilibrium and is unlikely to change explains why reform proposals often come from former officials. In the military context, it is retired generals who recommend reforms to do away with interservice rivalry—proposals they would never have championed when they were on active duty because such reforms do not reflect the interests of active duty officers. Blue ribbon commissions of former government leaders that recommend the strengthening of international institutions are of a similar character. When it is former leaders who are making reform recommendations, it is a good indication that reform is not in the interests of those currently in power.

Political outcomes, in both the domestic and international arenas, often reflect compromise among conflicting interests. The result might be an equilibrium outcome that is no one actor's ideal. Every actor can then complain about the outcome and proffer various alternatives, while remaining fully aware that nothing will change. Even if one actor obtains its ideal, others will surely not. Dissatisfaction by some or all is thus a political reality of governance, domestic or global, and not an indication of any prospect of reform.

---

20. Weiss and Young (2005) note that the sixtieth anniversary of the United Nations was remarkably like the fiftieth in the calls for reform. Winkelmann (1997) traces Security Council reform proposals, while Archibugi (1993) discusses reform proposals floated in the wake of the end of the Cold War.

Intended Institutional Failure

The failure of institutions is often interpreted as a failure for them to work as intended. But there are times when institutions work exactly as intended, leaving many actors frustrated. For example, the US political system is often decried as slow, cumbersome, and imperfectly responsive, yet it functions as intended by the Founding Fathers, who wanted an institution to calm and mediate popular passions—thus, the frustrations experienced with the institution reflect its functioning as intended.[21]

The United Nations has worked exactly as intended and constructed, and this is the reason for the disaffection with it. During the Cold War, the institution did relatively little, as the conflict between the two superpowers precluded the Great Power cooperation necessary for it to do much. Following the end of the Cold War, the UN briefly became a more central actor in international politics, as the Great Powers could agree on some policies and were interested in an institutional rubric for their joint efforts. Much of the recent disaffection with the UN has to do with the heightened expectations generated during the early 1990s.

Feigned Dissatisfaction, Scapegoats, and Political Cover

Some expressed dissatisfaction with international institutions is feigned. State officials often criticize institutions that they prefer to have as scapegoats and providers of political cover. Their criticism is entirely for show, as are their proposals for reform.

Within national governments and international institutions, one sees feigned dissatisfaction repeatedly. Members of the US Congress happily criticize the Federal Reserve Board and use it as a scapegoat for inflation or deflation, but prefer to keep the Fed independent. They prefer to have the Fed pursue policies that it and most members of Congress find appropriate

---

21. Ironically, many of the same people who express frustration with the workings of the US political system are also appalled at any effort to change it. A good example is provided by Democrats' reactions to President Franklin Roosevelt's 1938 plan to pack the Supreme Court with appointees more sympathetic to his political agenda.

while retaining the ability to criticize the institution. In this way, they can demonstrate to their constituents that they feel their pain while signaling that they are not at fault.

International institutions play a similar role. National politicians are often happy to castigate international institutions while adopting the policies they recommend, knowing that such policies are best for their countries. The international equivalent of politicians' feigned criticism of central banks, for example, is the criticism of the International Monetary Fund (IMF) by politicians for imposing conditions the politicians themselves want to adopt; in this way, government officials can offload the blame for necessary but unpopular economic reforms onto the IMF (Vreeland 2003).[22] Indeed, blaming the institution is in the tradition of politicians who look to avoid blame (Weaver 1986). Thus, expressed dissatisfaction and proposals for reform are not necessarily consonant with a true preference for reform.

Institutions as Process and the Bicycle Metaphor

Dissatisfaction can also spring from success, rather than failure. This occurs when institutions are perceived as part of an ongoing process and stems from concerns that the process needs to be maintained or failure will result.

Some international objectives—Middle East peace and free trade, for example—are recognized as difficult things that can be achieved only in incremental steps. Middle East peace is seen as a process requiring many steps that cannot be taken without some degree of trust and gradual reconciliation. The metaphor used for the Middle East peace process is that of riding a bicycle: one must continue to pedal or fall off (Ross 2004, 350).

---

22. The argument has even been made that national politicians look to international organizations as a way of gaining autonomy from domestic pressures (Wolf 1999; Koenig-Archibugi 2004). Rather than losing autonomy from joining international organizations, national governments gain autonomy from more overbearing domestic pressures. In this way, international institutions undercut democratic governance. One study finds that political leaders choose legal dispute resolution as a means of obtaining political cover (Allee and Huth 2006).

This leads to an emphasis on maintaining the process and a sense that, if forward movement stops, disaster is at hand. The successes achieved are ignored, and the focus is on maintaining the process.

Something similar exists on the issue of world trade. Achieving liberalization is a long and extended process: complete openness to international markets cannot be achieved in one fell policy swoop; rather, it requires slow adjustment and the development of constituencies interested in continued and sustained openness. Thus, trade liberalization has proceeded in stages, with one trading round following another, and each tackling issues untouched by earlier rounds. Indeed, the very success in dealing with one set of issues brings new issues to the fore (Stein 1993). And at each round, there is concern that failure to proceed spells disaster, as if what has already been accomplished by way of liberalization would be undone.

It is such a progressive vision of process and movement that is at the heart of some of the expressed dissatisfaction with international institutions. But in such cases, it is the very success of the institutions that is in a sense responsible for the pressure to do more. In these matters, the least difficult issues are resolved first and the most difficult ones confronted at later stages. Agreements on easier matters provide no guarantee of continued progress. Dissatisfaction with the pace and with stumbling blocks is a price of the slow process that constitutes success, and not necessarily an indication of failure.

Institutional Failure, Complainants, and Stakeholders

Institutions also generate dissatisfaction by complainants who are not direct stakeholders capable of undertaking reform. This is true whenever the actions of stakeholders generate externalities for those who are not members of the institution. Outsiders who bear the costs complain and want reform of the institution, but it is the inside stakeholders who control the possibility of reform—and unless they are dissatisfied, nothing will happen.

The US Congress provides a simple example. Members of Congress like a system of campaign finance that allows them to outspend their challengers vastly, if it does not dissuade challenge entirely, and in which incumbency is virtually a guarantee of re-election. Voters might not like that outcome, but politicians do. The disaffected reformers are voters, but it is politicians who must approve any reform proposal. When voter disaffection is great enough, politicians have every incentive to undertake reforms that make only a cosmetic difference, not real change.

Does reform of international institutions have the same characteristics? Many activists in civil society find international institutions inadequate, yet that is not the same as when states find them inadequate. Too often, reform recommendations come from the ranks of global civil servants who staff international institutions but have minimal real authority, or from academics, international lawyers, and nongovernmental organizations (NGOs) who want institutions and their member governments to do things they do not want to do. Reform proposals also come from states that are excluded from one form of global governance or another.[23]

Reform results from the interests of stakeholders. Nonstakeholders can effectuate reform when they can affect the incentives of stakeholders —or they can create alternative institutions.

The Kabuki Dance of Demand and Supply

The political dynamics I have described lead to charades of politics, in which reform is demanded but not really desired and in which proffered reform is illusory. States and the politicians who direct them complain at times and argue for reform, but prefer things to remain unchanged. And when the pressures for reform become unstoppable, states and the politicians who direct them supply reform without change, dealing with political pressures in a wholly illusory fashion.

Politicians often face pressure, for example, for protectionism from particularistic interests who have been hurt by increased trade openness. Yet, they are also aware that continued free trade is optimal for the society as a whole. In such a case, politicians need to appear to be responsive to protectionist demands while not actually offering serious protection—a stand that characterizes many US trade policies (Goldstein 1993). Similarly,

---

23. An example of this is the proposed reform for increasing the number of permanent members of the UN Security Council.

politicians face pressures to deal with immigration flows. Domestic residents concerned about national identity as well as their jobs press for tight immigration controls. On the other hand, immigration flows reflect demands for labor. Clever politicians respond by promoting policies that appear responsive to demands for immigration control while simultaneously allowing flows to continue (Rudolph 2006).

In many cases, instead of adopting illusory policies to deal with demands for reform, politicians propose changes in the process that either have no hope of adoption or would not deliver change even if adopted. Rather than propose or pass balanced budgets, for example, politicians argue for a line item veto or a budget committee or a constitutional amendment. Weaker still, they propose commissions to study the problem.

Similarly, politicians around the world are feeling the pressure to democratize, and have every incentive to generate the appearance of democratization that does not threaten their hold on power (Sweet 2001). We thus witness liberal reforms with continued one-party rule.

There is, in short, a stylized dance of institutional reform that has to be separated from the real thing. There are complainants who have no power and powerholders whose complaints constitute scapegoating and blame avoidance. There are reform proposals that are not real reforms. There are demands for reform that do not reflect a true desire for reform, and there are proffered reforms that are intended to be illusory.

Palliative, Corrective, and Transformative Reforms

Reform efforts and recommendations come in different forms and for different reasons. It is possible to distinguish among palliative, corrective, and transformative reform recommendations for international institutions.

Palliative institutions and reforms are intended to deal with the fallout of extant problems without really solving them. Institutions for dealing with refugees, for example, do not address in any fashion the underlying source of the problem; rather, they deal with the pain. Similarly, palliative reforms for extant organizations are intended to deal with the problems generated by international institutions. Recommendations intended to spruce up the image of the UN are palliative.

Corrective reforms are ones intended to fix extant problems—to restore institutions to their past healthy status. Examples of corrective reforms are recommendations for transparency intended to deal with the rise of corruption.

Transformative reforms are intended to chart new institutional territory —to get extant institutions to function differently, to tackle new issues, or to create new international institutions and expand the scope of global governance.

Transformative reforms are the hardest to achieve because they require the states that are the constituents of international institutions to defer some aspect of their sovereignty and expand the extent of governance above the nation-state. Ironically, without careful empirical assessment, I would venture to say that most reform efforts are of this type, and intended to push the agenda of global governance. Such reforms often originate among idealists in civil society and in NGOs, and are about universalizing a set of values and practices that exist in some societies but that are hardly universal; they are also portrayed as progressive.[24] Such reforms move beyond the small but active reform industry when they are intended to deal with widely perceived problems and reflect the interests of major states and their governments.

Understanding the prospects for reform requires a sense not only of the nature of the reform but also of the nature of the complaints expressed about current practices. As in other areas of politics, there is much shadow play and posturing in the politics of institutional reform.

International Institutions as Cargo Cults

Finally, there are those who want international cooperation but who mistake international institutions for international cooperation—they seem to believe that, if one creates institutions, international cooperation will follow. The problem is that institutions are vehicles for achieving

---

24. This has led one scholar to characterize such efforts as "the new cultural imperialism" (Lal 2004). More broadly, Lal argues that there is a fundamental difference between spreading materialist values and spreading Western moral values. The former are accepted, the latter generate a backlash.

cooperation that are designed by states with an interest in joint, rather than individual, decision making.

Absent states that are interested in achieving outcomes other than those that can be achieved through individual decision making, the argument for institutions resembles that of a cargo cult. Nobel physicist Richard Feynman (1985) gives the following example of people who see the form but do not understand the process. He tells the story of South Sea islanders who experienced prosperity when US military aircraft used their islands during World War II. They remembered how it had been when the planes flew and they wanted those days, and the planes, to return. So they cleared the runways, rebuilt the towers, and put men with earphones in the towers. They had the form exactly right, but the planes of the US military did not return. The islanders did not understand the causal process. In a sense, those who design institutions, hoping cooperation will follow, also miss the causal sequence.

Institutions might engender cooperation, but they first require cooperation. This core reality bedevils many liberal arguments. Many see trade as the route to international cooperation, yet trade requires trade agreements and thus itself requires cooperation as a prerequisite.[25]

The Roller Coaster of Heightened and Dashed Expectations

The post–Cold War era has been one of great hope for, and great frustration with, global governance. During the Cold War, the reality of bipolar conflict and competition meant that truly global governance depended on the rare prospect of an alignment of superpower interest or disinterest. Governance efforts, therefore, were more typically less than global. But the end of the Cold War meant the end of the old mechanisms of control and brought new problems to the fore.

At first, there were depictions of a period of a new concert of powers (Rosecrance 1992) and a flurry of UN activity. During the early 1990s,

---

25. This point underlies the problem of selection bias in the empirical assessment of the effect of institutions. Scholars have attempted to demonstrate that institutions are effective in generating state compliance, but the problem is that states join institutions with which they intend to comply.

there was a series of peacekeeping missions and a sense that the Security Council could act truly as an institution of collective security. There were hopes for expanded prospects for global governance and a renewed focus on reforms that would be required to make extant institutions function in a new age.

Such hopes were only somewhat dashed by the slaughter in Rwanda, which generated an outpouring on the need for humanitarian intervention. Now, in the wake of the Iraq War, there is further disillusionment. Ironically, then, much of the concern about international institutions stems not just from the Bush administration's style or policies but also from the elevated expectations generated during the 1990s.

This roller coaster of heightened expectations and the disappointments of reform and expanded governance have masked the reality of the continuing growth in, and demand for, multilateral institutions.

Summary on Reform

Demands for reform provide no necessary indication that reform is either desired or desirable. At the same time, reforms themselves do not necessarily imply that anything will change. Nor do they imply that change will necessarily constitute an improvement. Citizens within societies have discovered that, even when there are market failures, the construction of governmental regulatory regimes to deal with them can generate government failures that are far worse than the market failures they were intended to address. This is precisely the nature of one of the lines of criticism of the major international financial institutions. In such cases, transformative reforms, although pitched as progressive, may turn out to be regressive.

Reforms embody different objectives and have different implications. Some merely deal with fallout, some try to correct problems that have arisen with time, others try to push forward an agenda for global governance.

International reforms, whether serious or illusory, merely palliative or truly progressive, typically depend on more, not less, international cooperation. They are intended to reduce the scope of state autonomy, not to increase it. As such, reforms depend on and serve to increase multilateralism, and unilateralism is seen as their foil.

The Continuing Preference for Multilateralism

Despite changes in the global distribution of power, despite the difficulty of meeting the requisites of incentive compatibility for state and society, and despite the illusory character of many discussions of global governance, there is a continuing demand for international institutions and multilateralism, even on the part of the United States.

A General US Interest in Multilateralism

When people talk of multilateralism or the lack of it, they really have in mind the United States and whether it is going it alone or in concert with others. Since the United States is the lone remaining superpower, other countries have a heightened interest in having it act in concert with them, rather than going it alone. For the United States to act in concert with others, however, it must have an interest in doing so; thus, any call today for multilateralism has perforce to take into account US interests.

At the same time, the United States actually prefers multilateral solutions, for the following reasons. First, it is the lone remaining superpower only in the military, not the financial, sense. As a superpower, it is unique in being a net debtor and in having much of its debt held by another state of some power: China. Although the situation constitutes a balance of financial terror in that China could exercise its weapon only at great cost, it remains the case that the United States is financially constrained.

Second, the United States has repeatedly sought financial support. During the Cold War, it regularly pressed its allies to increase their payments in support of US military installations. Since the end of the Cold War, it has asked or pressed for financial contributions for expensive endeavors.

Third, the United States necessarily restrains itself militarily, as it has throughout the nuclear age, because unbridled use of its military power has enormous political consequences for itself.

In a post-imperial age, in which populations are mobilized and mobilizable, Great Powers need the support of others to demonstrate that their actions are not solely self-interested. The United States has repeatedly justified its actions, not as a matter of self-interest, but in universalistic terms, and such justifications ring hollow if other nations do not support

US objectives or actions. As a result, even during the Cold War, the United States pressed for allied assistance for its extensive military operations in Korea and Vietnam; it has continued to seek such support for its post–Cold War operations.

Peculiarly, the United States is so powerful militarily that it needs the help of others to deal with the challenges it faces. In conventional military engagements, it cannot be challenged, much less defeated. Instead, the United States confronts unconventional warfare in extraterritorial engagements and terrorist attacks both at home and abroad. Dealing with terrorist attacks or with unconventional warfare more broadly necessarily requires the support of other countries, because such conflicts entail political, not solely military, solutions.

In short, the United States has had, and continues to have, an interest in multilateralism.

The US Interest in Multilateralism and the War in Iraq

Although castigated for acting unilaterally, in fact the United States put together a substantial "coalition of the willing"—the Bush administration claimed initially that 49 countries had "publicly committed to the Coalition" (United States 2003)—to wage war in Iraq. The coalition was derided because some of the countries were small and insignificant, yet the list also included the United Kingdom, Japan, Italy, South Korea, Turkey, and Australia—ranked second, fourth, seventh, tenth, fourteenth, and fifteenth in the world in terms of defense spending in 2004 (SIPRI 2005).[26]

The United States has carried the bulk of the military effort in Iraq, and easily could have undertaken the entire operation without any support (setting aside the issue of access provided by neighboring countries). The assistance provided by most of the coalition is so marginal that it is largely symbolic. Nevertheless, in waging the effort, the White House trumpeted the coalition. The press release announcing the list of coalition partners emphasized four features of the coalition. The first two were standard

---

26. These rankings are based on market exchange rates, rather than on purchasing power parity.

measures of power: the combined population and combined gross domestic product of coalition countries. The other two features, however, were unrelated to issues of power: "Every major race, religion, ethnicity in the world is represented" and "The Coalition includes nations from every continent on the globe" (United States 2003). Thus, the coalition was presented, first, as an agglomeration of resources and capabilities and, second, as broadly representative by race, religion, ethnicity, and region. Given how little the other nations provided by way of capability, however, it seems that what the United States sought was their representativeness.

Multilateralism and International Legitimacy

A set of questions arises from a White House emphasis that a coalition was waging the war and the marginal character of that contribution. Why did the United States seek others' support, and why did the others offer it? Since their contributions were not coerced, what was being exchanged?

States that undertake collective efforts need both capability and legitimacy. The United States sought a coalition to wage the Iraq War not for its capability but for the legitimacy it would extend to the US-dominated operation. The coalition was not an old-fashioned alliance of capability aggregation. As even the White House press release noted, "[c]ontributions from Coalition member nations range from: direct military participation, logistical and intelligence support, specialized chemical/biological response teams, over-flight rights, humanitarian and reconstruction aid, to political support" (United States 2003). In short, political support was as important as any military capability.[27]

Similarly, opposition to the US military effort by France, Germany, and Russia was significant not because of any military opposition they might have offered or any capability they might have extended to Iraq, but because their political opposition undercut the legitimacy of US actions.

---

27. On the issue of legitimacy, begin with Franck (1988); Hurd (1999); and Clark (2003). Note that my characterization of legitimacy as the affirmation of non-particularistic interests differs from that of Hurd (1999) and is quite close to Thompson's (2006) argument that international organizations provide strategic information transmission. My point is that the information transmitted about the broad support for a course of action is precisely what legitimacy is about.

When people talk about multilateralism, then, they mean more than a set of states that combine their capabilities to achieve some objective. They also have in mind the legitimacy that comes from states' acting in concert because their objectives are not particularistic national interests but common interests.

Multilateralism and Domestic Legitimacy

Multilateralism is about obtaining not only international legitimacy, but also domestic legitimacy. In a world in which international institutions need to be compatible with societal incentives as well as governmental ones, multilateralism also provides domestic legitimacy to governments that need the support of citizens to sustain their foreign policies.

The relationship between multilateralism and domestic legitimacy can be assessed by asking simple questions. Are political leaders punished or rewarded for flouting the norms of the international community, or even for ignoring the outside world? Do leaders find it important to obtain international support for their foreign policy positions?

Arguments have been made for two diametrically opposed logics characterizing the relationship between the outside world and internal politics. On the one hand, the outside world is a source of legitimacy for both domestic and foreign policy. States want the recognition of others. Individual leaders go to summits with others as a way of establishing their political legitimacy. The acceptance of a government as an interlocutor by the outside world enhances its internal legitimacy. Membership conditionality is an effective instrument in eliciting contested domestic change (Kelley 2004). Unilateral policies risk, or ensure, the hostility of the outside world, and a regime that practices them runs the risk of losing domestic support and legitimacy. Governments thus prefer multilateralism as a way not only to reduce costs but also to bolster the internal acceptability and legitimacy of foreign policy—and even of domestic policy, as Solingen (1998) and Snyder (2000) have argued in different settings.

On the other hand, the argument has also been made that pressure from the outside world can reinforce domestic political legitimacy—that political elites can use outside pressure to heighten domestic support and generate nationalistic fervor in conflicts with the outside world. External pressure can delegitimate internal domestic opposition and make possible the expansion of state power. Indeed, Nincic (2005) argues that this is the major consequence of sanctions—collective sanctions have rarely generated foreign policy shifts, but in many cases have strengthened the sanctioned regime. Pushed to the extreme, this view suggests that unilateral policies can go down well domestically, and also that regimes can purposely instigate conflict with the outside world as a way of bolstering their position at home —an argument that constitutes the heart of diversionary theories of war.

Ironically, one can see both arguments at work in US policy toward Iraq across the two Bush administrations. In 1990, the first Bush administration was readily able to mobilize world support to oppose Iraq's invasion and occupation of Kuwait. It had a more difficult time mobilizing domestic support, however, and indeed required a UN resolution in order to obtain a congressional resolution—and that just barely. In contrast, in 2002 and 2003, in the wake of 9/11, the George W. Bush administration easily garnered domestic support for the war in Iraq even in the face of the opposition of key allies.

This discussion implies—its theoretical incompleteness notwithstanding —that multilateralism can result from either a strong, confident government or a weak one in need of external legitimacy. Conversely, unilateralism can also result from a strong regime unconcerned with external affirmation or a weak one needing external conflict to generate defensive patriotism.

This suggests that an important component of unilateralism is not merely the international strength of the regime in having the capability that unilateralism requires, but also its internal strength or weakness. Unilateralism might also reflect a societal preference, not merely a governmental one. Yet, multilateralism too emerges as a product of multiple forces, sometimes reflecting regime strength, binding and linking its society to others, sometimes reflecting regime weakness and the need for external legitimacy.

Existential Multilateralism in a Weakly Confederal World

Although unilateralism remains an ever-present possibility and although international organizations reflect the power and interests of their members, the growing number of such organizations, as well as international laws and agreements, over the past century makes multilateralism an existential reality. The world consists of overlapping clubs in every region and every functional domain. Indeed, the number of intergovernmental organizations well exceeds the number of states in the system, and there are so many international treaties and agreements that it is impossible to compile a complete list.[28] Thus, although the option of unilateralism is available, the existence of such a large array of international institutions and agreements sustains a multilateralist reality.

A debate is ongoing in the security literature about deterrence and the options confronting states armed with nuclear weapons. There have always been those who have argued that deterrence is a policy choice: states could eschew deterrence and choose to procure nuclear weapons and develop doctrines of war fighting, and with sufficient nuclear superiority could engage in nuclear war. The competing view, however, is that deterrence is an existential reality once nuclear-armed states face each other (Bundy 1984). Relative numbers and military doctrines do not matter. Rather, the reality that both have weapons, that no defense is perfect, that no pre-emptive strike can assure that every weapon is destroyed, and that even one such weapon can cause so much damage as to exceed any potential political benefit imagined in its use, all combine to create deterrence as an existential reality, not a doctrinal choice. However much governments procure weapons and espouse doctrines to the contrary, deterrence is simply a fact of life, one which constrains nuclear states.

The same point can be made about multilateralism: it is an existential reality. Much as governments try to deny the reality, much as they try to go it alone, in the end they are constrained by the reality that they can do little of any consequence without acting in conjunction with important others. One can say that even the Bush administration is aware of this. Blowing things up is something the United States can accomplish on its own—

---

28. One reason it is so difficult to determine the number is that the UN's central database of treaties is incomplete because only some international treaties are deposited with the secretary-general. Others are deposited in specific countries, international organizations that are not part of the UN, and with specialized agencies of the UN (Jurewicz and Dawkins 2005).

although even there, it needs others' approval for the use of overseas bases and for overflight permissions—but it can do little else. In one domain after another, the United States is looking for the support of others and discovering this hard reality of international politics.

Virtually any concern of the US government requires a multilateral response (Nye 2002). Typically, international cooperation is most limited in the area of security, but whether the issue is the war on terror or combating the proliferation of nuclear weapons, the United States cannot achieve its objectives alone. It can take specific steps on its own, but achieving its objectives at an acceptable cost requires the assistance of others, or at least their forbearance and acquiescence. Even Bush Republicans make this point: Richard N. Haass, the initial director of policy planning at the State Department during the Bush presidency, said (2003),

> The United States is the most powerful country in the world by almost any measure of power. That said, however, what is noteworthy about this world is how, for all of our power, we can't meet most of the challenges we face on our own. And we certainly can't meet any of the challenges we face better on our own than [we can by] cooperating with others.

He went on to add that "the most interesting debates are not the debates between unilateralism and multilateralism, but what kind of multilateralism," by which he meant the choice between a universal and a regional forum, between an extant formal one and an ad hoc coalition of the willing, and how to give the latter "a dimension of legitimacy" and acceptability. "Those are the real foreign policy questions," he said, "not whether there is a unilateral option, because, quite honestly, there isn't one."

Indeed, the entire critique of the Bush administration implies that multilateralism is an existential reality. Were that not the case, the United States would not be castigated for acting unilaterally. The benchmark expectation is that states act multilaterally, and it becomes a matter of comment when they choose not to. We would not bother to characterize any state as unilateralist if the benchmark expectation was that states act on their own—in such a case, we would note multilateralism as the unusual behavior. The refrain of the United States as unilateralist makes clear that the benchmark expectations are now multilateral.

Existential multilateralism, however, limits the range of state calculations, including that of the United States. The view of the Clinton administration, whose rhetorical commitments to international institutions vastly exceeded its actual practice, was characterized as "multilateralism if we can, unilateralism if we must."[29] In contrast, the view of the George W. Bush administration, whose verbal contempt for international institutions has vastly exceeded its actual practice, has been characterized as "unilateralism if we can, multilateralism if we must."[30] These two characterizations, in effect, narrow the scope of state decisions and bound them by a realization that there are cases in which there is no choice but to engage in multilateralism and that the ability to fulfill state objectives is such that the recourse to unilateralism is smaller than it once was for states.

A Weakly Confederal World

In fact, one could argue not only that multilateralism is an existential reality but that weak confederalism is the nature of modern reality. There are many intergovernmental organizations and many rules for state conduct. Yet, the confederal system is weak: it lacks fiscal authority and depends on the voluntary contributions of states, it has no standing army and depends on the willingness of member states to provide forces, and it is powerless to resolve conflicts among its constituent members.[31] As with past confederations, the structure of cooperation reflects the power and interests of members, their need for some cooperation, and their desire for autonomy. And as with past confederations, there are frustrations with the limitations of weak confederalism.

---

29. There are slight variations on the phrase. Something like it appears in the national security strategy document of 1995, and another version is attributed to then secretary of state Madeleine Albright. The phrase quoted here is from Senator John Kerry's 2004 presidential campaign (Schwenninger 2004).
30. This point was made by former Republican senator and Clinton defense secretary William Cohen and by Pascal Boniface of the Paris-based Institut de relations internationales et stratégiques (see United States 2005).
31. I deliberately characterize the system as confederal, rather than as a confederation, for it is not just one confederation but a system of confederations.

This confederation differs from others, however, in that efforts to strengthen confederal authority have proceeded along multiple tracks. Some have focused on one central locus of governance, such as the United Nations, but in many cases, states have proceeded to construct a federal world along functional lines. Rather than transfer increasing authority over time from one issue area to another to a central confederal authority, member states have created strong institutions but only in discrete functional domains.[32]

The General Problem of Unintended Institutional Failure

In this weakly confederal system, there is the same spirited debate about the proper role of institutional solutions to problems. The same quandary exists at the international level as at the national level: do governmental responses to market failures always improve the situation? Increasingly, people realize that there is also a problem of government failure, in which government policies generate worse outcomes than the market failures they were intended to alleviate. Within domestic society, this has led to some governmental deregulation and privatization and generated ongoing debates between those recommending market-based solutions and those promoting governmental regulatory ones. At the international level, it consists of a challenge to the presumption that the construction of more international institutions is always a good thing.

In some cases, both a market response to an international problem and a regulatory one entail the creation of an institution. The development of an international emissions trading regime constitutes the application at the global level of a domestic market solution for dealing with pollution. It required a treaty and constitutes an institution. It contrasts with the regulatory alternative that simply mandates reductions by locale and firm,

---

32. This view of a weak confederal world puts me at odds with those who make a number of different arguments. I disagree with the view that "world political institutions cannot be created by the governments of existing states" (Murphy 1999) as well as with those who view second-order representation as constituting a democratic deficit.

but which also would have been an institution—though likely a more bureaucratic one.

In other cases, market solutions allow states to maintain autonomy, and are institutions in only the broadest sense of their being rules of behavior. An example is that of floating exchange rates, where markets, rather than some international agreement and monitoring institution, determine the value of traded currencies.[33]

There are those who argue that the development of international organizations has not always constituted an improvement in world affairs (Gallarotti 1991). Indeed, one development economist, a former research administrator at the World Bank, argues that the major international economic organizations have become "the major purveyors of global illiberalism" (Lal 2005, 503; see also Easterly 2006). Or, as another assessment describes the results of efforts at international economic policy coordination, "it only grafts government failure onto the international system" (Sally 2001, 55). Not surprisingly, in some areas, recommendations for global governance reform run the gamut from expansion to abolition. In the case of international financial institutions, there may be as many academics who recommend the complete abolition of the IMF as recommend an expansion of its activities and reform of its governing rules.

In short, the same hard-nosed questions must be addressed at the global level as at the domestic one. What tasks are appropriate for government? What problems are preferably resolved by market solutions? What issues require intergovernmental organizations and which are better dealt with by NGOs, the international equivalent of domestic philanthropic and civic organizations?[34] And when is the proposed international organization likely to result in an international government failure that is worse than the problem that led to its creation?

---

33. Ironically, the switch in international monetary regimes did not do away with the IMF; rather, it led to a transformation in the nature of the Fund's role (Stein 2001).
34. Governments have begun to outsource many international activities, including humanitarian, developmental, and security assistance. This creates new agency problems and perverse incentives for NGOs (Cooley and Ron 2002).

The Requisites of Multilateralism

The world abounds with international institutions. Regional ones are purposely subsystemic, but even most functional ones are less than universal. That institutions are not universal but constitute coalitions of the willing and the agreeable raises the question of the requisites of multilateralism.

How Many Are Needed?

Even though the United States put together a substantial coalition in support of its war in Iraq, the exercise was not seen as multilateral. Was it because critical countries did not take part? Was it because the participation of most, except for the United Kingdom, was rather minimal? Was it because major countries not in the coalition actively opposed its efforts? Is the difference between Gulf I and Gulf II not in the number of coalition members nor in the extent of their contribution but that no major country opposed Gulf I? Is it simply that Gulf II lacked a UN Security Council resolution—the difference thus being an announced French intention to veto versus a Chinese abstention?[35] Or is it that, in Gulf I, the United States appeared to be more constrained by the needs, concerns, and interests of its coalition partners?

This raises important questions about the requisites of multilateralism: how many countries must take part? what level of participation by others must there be? what level of restraint on particularistic self-interest must exist for a policy to be called multilateral? Conversely, how much opposition and by how many and whom undercuts the legitimacy of multilateral efforts? Moreover, does multilateralism require more than merely a signal of commitment? These questions about multilateralism can be put in

---

35. Criticism of the United States often conflates unilateralism and ad hoc multilateralism. US actions have been characterized at times as unilateral not because the United States acted alone but because it ignored extant international institutions (such as the Security Council) in favor of an ad hoc coalition of the willing. But this raises the question of what institutional imprimatur is required. Is the circumvention of the UN acceptable as long as an alternative is obtained? In the case of Kosovo, the United States and others circumvented the Security Council but obtained NATO agreement.

terms of the United States, specifically: what must it do, or what level of support must it obtain, or in what ways must it allow its freedom of action to be curtailed, for its actions to be seen as multilateral?

The issue of requisite numbers is not merely one of appearance but import. Trade liberalization did not historically require that all countries reduce their barriers but that the largest trading states do so. Controlling missile proliferation requires agreement and adherence among the states capable of building and selling such weapons. Significant reductions in greenhouse gases might not require the adherence of all nations but only that of significant polluters. In such cases, the requisites of multilateralism are determined by the nature of the domain and the distribution of power or activity among countries.

Multilateralism Requires More than Common Values

In discussing an upcoming summit with German chancellor Angela Merkel, President George W. Bush said, "Listen, the first thing that has to happen diplomatically for anything to be effective is that we all agree on the goal. And we've agreed on the goal, and…now that we've got the goal in mind, we're working on the tactics" (2006). In his own inimitable way, the president put his finger on a core issue of multilateralism: the necessity for agreement on both tactics and goals, means and ends. The existence of common interests or values is but the first step toward the kinds of policy alignment that multilateralism need perforce entail.[36]

In a book entitled *Renegade Regimes*, Miroslav Nincic (2005) argues that there are four important currently accepted and widely shared norms, and that their violation—through the pursuit of weapons of mass destruction, the support of or engagement in acts of terrorism, a large-scale assault on human rights, and territorial aggression—makes states into renegades.

---

36. This discussion finesses what I believe to be an important and underappreciated distinction between common values and common interests. For a start, see Frieden's (1999) distinction between changeable policy preferences and abiding values.

Yet, we have recently observed repeatedly that multilateralism breaks down not because of an absence of agreement on objectives, but because of a disagreement on tactics. The disagreements on dealing with Iran provide just one example. No country has publicly stated its support of a nuclear Iran. China and Russia have said "they don't want a nuclear-armed Iran" (Reuters 2006, quoting Under Secretary of State Nicholas Burns) and have even voted with the United States in the UN against the government of Iran. But they have also expressed their opposition to sanctions and military attacks. Does the agreement on the basic objective of a non-nuclear Iran constitute multilateralism or does the disagreement about how to deal with Iran constitute a failure of multilateralism?

Much the same can be said about the war in Iraq as a quintessential case of a failure of multilateralism. The broad support that the United States had in opposing Saddam Hussein's regime became whittled away dramatically when it pressed for military action. The disagreement was over tactics, not overriding objectives or views of the regime.

Moreover, what is seen as a failure of multilateralism occurs only after the failure of attempts to obtain agreement on tactics when there is an agreement on goals. The United States tried to obtain a broad consensus to oppose Saddam Hussein. It obtained a unanimous Security Council resolution, but one that reflected agreement on ends and only the most minimal agreement on means. It was the failure to agree on the use of force and the US decision to go ahead notwithstanding that is seen as the rupturing of multilateralism.

This discussion implies that criticisms of the Bush administration as having failed to provide international leadership are semantically miscast. The Bush administration tried to lead, but found important countries unwilling to follow. One could criticize these other countries for a lack of followership, but the inability to get others to follow becomes characterized as a failure of leadership. Ironically, the unipolarity implicated in making US unilateralism possible did not simultaneously generate a willingness by others to follow US hegemony. The collapse of Soviet power simultaneously increased the United States' freedom of action while reducing US leverage on prospective supporters, including its allies.

The public nature of position taking and its constraints in open societies also implies tremendous difficulty in pursuing coordinated but discordant policies. Take the classic case of good cop/bad cop strategies. The United States is in many ways the bad cop in recent world affairs, always threatening the use of force and not appearing at all pliable on the possibility of negotiated solutions. Many US allies end up playing the role of the good cop, decrying the use of force, pressing for international agreement, and encouraging miscreants about the prospects for accommodation and their reintegration into the community of nations. Although the role of the bad cop may be helpful, as some allies admitted was the case when the United States threatened military action to force Iraq to allow UN inspectors back into the country, it nonetheless complicates the international relationships of democratic governments.

All this implies that multilateralism, if it is to mean joint action in dealing with problematic global issues, must entail agreement not only on core values but also on the means of achieving desired outcomes in world affairs. But does it also imply that the price of multilateralism is the broad acceptance of the least common denominator when there is disagreement among a core group of states (however that core is defined) about tactics? Is the price of multilateralism that it is subject to a unit veto?

I have argued that multilateral action requires agreement on both objectives and tactics. Yet, there are tactical differences among states engaged in concerted action, which raises the question of the differences that are compatible with sustained multilateralism. Is it possible to sustain multilateralism on the basis of agreement on principles, values, and objectives, while still recognizing divergent tactical approaches? Several points can be made.

First, the line between strategic and tactical can be blurry, as can the line between ultimate and instrumental objectives.

Second, there can be a division of labor when both goals and strategies are agreed on. Countries can fight in concert but still provide different forms of military capability. Similarly, countries can provide debt relief in different forms. My point is simply that there must be broad agreement on goals and on the nature of policy.

Third, views of governments are rarely going to be so aligned that there will not be some disagreement among them. Any assessment of national politics clearly demonstrates that there is always the prospect of disagreement. Politicians, even when operating within a narrow spectrum of difference, can always parse in order to distinguish themselves and thus signal disagreement. The ability to play Goldilocks is ever present, if only to argue about too little or too much, too soon or too late.

Fourth, given possibilities for differentiation, what constitute departures from collective action can be contested. Imagine that a group of countries agrees on an objective and a strategy—for example, the agreement to provide collective defense under NATO—but one country chooses to act as a free rider, to shirk on its contribution. This would still constitute concerted action with substantial agreement—the shirking does not vitiate the multilateral character of the enterprise.

On the other hand, there are cases in which a free rider can be seen as destroying the ability to achieve an objective and, thus, as undercutting multilateralism. Take the case of debt relief. Developed countries might agree that the poorest countries need some debt relief, but if a country extends little if any relief, it is, in effect, insisting that the relief provided by others be used to compensate it (by having its loans repaid on terms much closer to those originally extended). In such a case, those that extend real debt relief might well argue that the attempt to be a free rider is essentially destroying the possibility of multilateral debt relief. This is why collective debt relief exercises can be quite complicated to work out and require the agreement of all large lenders. Not extending relief on terms acceptable to the others can indeed be seen as reneging on any agreement to extend relief. In effect, the degree of acceptable differentiation has itself to be agreed on.

Ironically, then, multilateralism can be sustained by acquiescence, not just agreement. An abstention in the UN Security Council on a sanctions resolution constitutes acquiescence that, in effect, sustains a legitimated multilateral response. It constitutes both a willingness to let a joint measure pass and a commitment to abide by it. Indeed, this has been the norm in Great Power cooperation in recent years: multilateralism has been sustained through the venue of the Security Council by a willingness to eschew the veto. Here, the West has rarely obtained China's affirmative agreement; rather, it has more typically obtained China's acquiescence.

All this makes the assessment of multilateralism and an understanding of its requisites somewhat complicated. Some things, however, are clear: when one observes joint operations, one clearly sees multilateralism, and when one observes public disagreement and opposition, one clearly sees the absence of multilateralism.

My point is that the perceived collapse of multilateralism in recent years has occurred at times over disagreements on policy, not overall objectives. No country has stood up for the sovereign right of ethnic cleansing, and all oppose nuclear weapons proliferation except for those that threaten it—and even Iran claims that its actions are justified within the bounds of peaceful use and extant international agreements. The disagreements are over how to achieve those objectives: through diplomacy, engagements, and inducements, or through the threat, and use, of force. This means that even the existence of an international community and a set of agreed-on norms of conduct are insufficient to assure multilateral responses to miscreants.

Multilateralism and the Absence of Disapproval

Multilateralism and unilateralism constitute two attitudes toward the external world. It is interesting to contrast this distinction with a different typology of state behavior. Jeff Legro (2006) distinguishes three types of states: trustees, hermits, and rebels. Rebels are states interested in upending the established order (the revolutionary Soviet Union was one example). Hermits are isolationists interested in separating themselves from the world (Tokugawa Japan, for example). Trustees are states that are neither hermits nor rebels, but are integrated into the international community and upholders of the existing order.

How does Legro's typology fit the multilateralism/unilateralism dichotomy? Hermits are certainly not multilateralists, but isolationism would not qualify as unilateralism if the latter presumes some degree of involvement with the outside world. Rebels have activist foreign policies, and although one can imagine a group of rebel countries acting in tandem, they would constitute a distinct minority of the states in the system and would act in opposition to others; historically, however, rebels have tended to act on their own.

But even if all rebels are unilateralists, not all unilateralists are rebels. Indeed, not all unilateralists are merely pursuing particularistic national interests. One of the striking aspects of US unilateralism has been the assertion by US administrations to be vouchsafing universal interests and values. Indeed, arguments such as hegemonic stability theory portray a unilateralist Great Power as providing collective goods without much support.

Overlaying these alternative typologies of state behavior makes it clear, I believe, that unilateralism captures a wide range of policies, from those intended to upset the international order to those that constitute go-it-alone efforts to sustain the order. To make the point clearer, imagine a community of states bound by most-favored-nation free trade agreements. Then, suppose a group of countries creates, in tandem, a regional customs union that violates their larger obligations and constitutes their defection from the liberal regime. Finally, imagine there is one Great Power that continues to maintain open markets, in keeping with the established order. We would hardly characterize the actions of the power that maintains its commitments, but now being the only one to do so, as unilateralist. I am less certain, but I believe we also would not call the group defection multilateralism.

I am certain that there are those who would argue that the United States' intervention in Iraq was a Great Power's unilateral maintenance of an established order in the face of others' defection from their obligations. Imagine, for example, if the United States were prepared to intervene in, say, Darfur to put a stop to ethnic cleansing and genocide, but was the only one willing to do so—would other countries describe such an intervention as unilateralist?

What I am getting at is that, when we characterize state behavior as unilateral, we mean more than a state's acting on its own; we have in mind a state that acts on its own without the approval or acquiescence of other countries. In the trade case above, the states that defect from liberal commitments still approve of—and actually desire—the Great Power's maintenance of open markets.[37] I would assume the same to be true of the hypothetical Darfur intervention—that it would be approved by others who would be happy to sit on the sidelines.[38]

---

37. Decoupling unilateralism/multilateralism from the substance of policy and its progressive/regressive character is discussed by Robinson (2000), who provides criteria for determining what constitutes progressive unilateralism.

38. An interesting example is provided by the recent agreement on nuclear technology between the United States and India. Critics of the arrangement argue

All this suggests that the multilateral/unilateral disjuncture is more about the approval of others than about how many states act jointly and how much each contributes. More pointedly, multilateralism is about the absence of others' disapproval, while unilateralism is behavior in the face of others' disapproval. Thus, what distinguishes the 1991 Gulf War from the 2003 Iraq War is the absence of disapproval in the former case, not how many countries joined in or how much they contributed. It is also why a Security Council abstention—that is, acquiescence rather than approval—still sustains multilateralism. It is the presence or absence of disapproval that is key. It is also why there can be regimes that have mechanisms for excused cheating, where the fact of being excused keeps departures from being seen as unilateralist and as cheating (Stein 2000, 244–49).

All this raises the question of whose disapproval matters. Clearly, the disapproval of immediate target states does not. Iraqi objections in 1991 and 2003 did not count in this sense; Sudanese objections to intervention in Darfur surely would not matter. The objection must come from states that are not immediate parties.

Constructing Institutions

The foregoing discussion of incentive compatibility, the requisites of multilateralism, and the nature of the world today generates core criteria for institutional design and construction. These criteria are key to successful social engineering. They must reflect the international distribution of power and contain the requisite set of countries for objectives to be accomplished. They must be compatible with the self-interest of states that must comply with their strictures. Institutions must be commensurate with the problems they are intended to solve and the challenges they face.

---

that it fundamentally undercuts the NPT and simply encourages would-be proliferators. Supporters argue, rather, that it deals with a core problem of the treaty and brings into the regime a state that had been kept outside it. Thus, this action on the part of the United States is portrayed as unilateralism in the service of multilateralism. In the short term, the reaction of other major powers will be key to how the action is seen. In the long term, how it is viewed will also depend on how well it works out.

Incentive Compatibility

The most successful social engineers have been economists. Their success derives from their recognition that voluntary behavioral change requires that the self-interested incentives of individual actors be compatible with the behavioral change that policy intends to make. This requirement follows from the requirement that change reflect voluntarism rather than coercion.[39]

Intergovernmental organizations are products of states' choices and, although they are affected by NGOs and civil society, change operates through the decisions of governments and reform efforts have to be compatible with the constellation of governments' interests and concerns and reflect their assessment of the problem, their relative bargaining power, and so on. As with recommendations for campaign finance reform that must run the gauntlet of the very politicians who would be subject to the reforms, so recommendations for international institutional reform must pass muster with the nation-states that would be subject to the strictures of new institutional arrangements.

But international institutions must be incentive compatible not only with national governments but, increasingly, with their domestic societies. That an increasing number of states are run by representative, elected governments means that international agreements have to be compatible with societal incentives. They must not only reflect the national interests, as seen by the governments that negotiate and sign, but also meet the requisites of domestic ratification as well as domestically sanctioned compliance. Global governance increasingly will require not merely a mutuality of state interests but a convergence of societal preferences as well.

The prospects for global governance will be held hostage to a variety of state-society interactions, sometimes in the form of executive-legislative relations. The relative support for multilateralism by elites and publics

---

39. One indication of the idealist roots of modern social constructivists in international relations is their failure to recognize that the social constructions of the twentieth century include Nazi aryanization, Soviet collectivization, the Chinese Cultural Revolution, the Cambodian killing fields, and ethnic cleansing, and whose costs total in the hundreds of millions of human lives, vastly exceeding the war casualties of the century.

and different political parties, as well as the propensity of officials to lead or follow their publics and the rules will determine the prospects for supranational arrangements.[40] Outcomes will vary between unified and divided governments. Governments that face re-election will act differently than lame ducks. Outgoing governments might sign multilateral agreements in the hope of locking in their successors, or of freeing their successors from a politically difficult decision, or in the knowledge that their successors will not ratify the agreements and thus be embarrassed. But durable multilateralism has to survive changes in governing parties and coalitions in democratic signatories.

Finally, it should be noted that incentive compatibility is not the same as normative compatibility. There are international reform efforts that are compatible with the norms held by many but not with their incentives. Perhaps the most poignant example is provided by the effort to enshrine a "responsibility to protect." The very phrase associated with the argument reveals all: there is a sense of a duty, not necessarily a desire or a willingness, to protect. In everyday language, we talk of states and individuals as pursuing their interests, but not their duties—duties are more typically shirked than pursued.

Task Expansion and Mission Creep

Solving or dealing with any problem brings the choice of using old institutions or creating new ones. The existence of a problem suggests that existing institutions allowed it to occur, so they require some reform, if only that of task expansion—or what is derogatorily characterized as "mission creep." Whether to recast or to build also entails the choice of ad hoc-ery or permanence.

---

40. Note that trade liberalization in the United States required major institutional transformations to the rules of the political game. First, rather than have the executive negotiate trade treaties that would then be subject to congressional approval, a system developed of advance authorization for percentage tariff reductions. Second, Congress bound itself through fast-track authority to vote on trade agreements without amendment. Prior to this change, the workings of US politics precluded sustained liberalization despite widespread recognition that it was in the country's interest (Hody 1996).

When a problem arises, the initial reaction is to look for existing institutions whose task can be expanded to include dealing with it. This is especially the case where the institution is seen as already successful in its domain and not as the source of the problem. Thus, following the toppling of its government in 2001, Afghanistan was made a NATO operation—a vibrant, functioning organization whose tasks had already been extended to include out-of-area operations in the Balkans now moved into southern Asia.

Conditions are ripe for a new institution when a problem arises that is not associated with an existing institution whose tasks cannot be expanded or whose members are unwilling to expand its tasks. For example, the perceived weaknesses of the NPT meant the need for a new institution to control the spread of missile technology, while disagreement among its members meant that NATO did not go into Iraq as it had Afghanistan.

One implication of commensurability is that it is easier to create new institutions to deal with new problems or new crises generated by old problems than to propose reforms, simply because of frustration with the workings of extant institutions. This is especially the case when the problem is seen as reflecting an institution's failure. Extant institutions already reflect past negotiations and compromises, and constrain the direction of organizational development. In short, there is a path dependence to global governance.

Forum Shopping

The net result of the past history of institutional construction and reconstruction is that there exist many arrangements with overlapping functional and geographic domains. That leaves states with a choice of the institutions they want to use to deal with the problem. For example, the United States and others opted to take the problem of the Balkans to NATO rather than to the UN. And this leads to the problem of forum shopping.

Within countries, actors can choose between some combination of lobbying, capturing, and litigating in dealing with their interests.[41] They can try to obtain favorable laws from the legislature, favorable regulations

---

41. For a model that deals with two of the three, see Rubin, Curran, and Curran (2001).

from bureaucracies, and favorable rulings and judgments from courts. In federal systems, they can work at different levels of governance. Within the legal system, they can choose between different courts and jurisdictions.[42]

Since the world now has clubs that overlap in both their memberships and functional domains, forum shopping is now an international possibility.[43] Forum shopping expands the possibilities of strategic contestation, and it creates one more way in which the powerful can assure themselves of favorable outcomes.[44] Yet forum shopping has not created domestic chaos, and one might as readily expect international equivalents to domestic mechanisms for dealing with the problems of venue selection and choice of law.

Commensurability

To be successful, a solution must be commensurate with the problem it is intended to solve. If the proposed solution is inadequate, it might make reform more palatable but it ensures that the problem continues—in effect, it becomes an example of illusory reform.[45] Yet, a proposed solution that overreaches is also a recipe for failure.

Despite the need for commensurability, there remain benefits from overreaching. Would-be reformers need to ask whether they should strive for the achievable or for the desirable. To strive for the former is to compromise but to accomplish, to strive for the latter is to trade the benefits

---

42. They can also choose between competing certifiers (Lerner and Tirole 2006).
43. The possibility of ad hoc international coalitions of the willing makes the international context even more complicated.
44. Alter and Meunier (2006) cite an example of the resolution of a trade dispute that might have been complicated by forum shopping. Elsewhere in this volume, Drezner even argues that forum shopping reintroduces the very anarchy that institutions were meant to ameliorate. Note, however, that the strategy of forum shopping, and even "regime shifting" (Helfer 2004), is open not just to the powerful: as economic integration proceeds, private actors as well as governments will exercise forum shopping (Koch 2006).
45. US gun laws are a case in point. Another example is European levels of acceptable pollution that are set so high that there is less demand for pollution credits than there are credits for sale in the market.

of setting an ideal standard but at the cost of failure. Let us call the former *pragmatic reformers*, the latter *utopian idealists*. Pressing for unachievable ideals is to accept the failure to achieve an objective in the hope of setting a marker and a tone for a conversation. In the United States, those who have pressed for an equal rights amendment or gay marriage present clear examples of failed objectives whose success is measured by the extent to which they have changed the conversation and made possible other pragmatic, achievable changes. An international example is provided by the lawyers who achieved only "marginal tangible successes at The Hague" in the late nineteenth century but who "achieved greater accomplishments by advancing discourse on disarmament and arms control" by providing the "terminology" which "allowed more focused debate in the twentieth century" (Keefer 2006, 1).

Clubs, or the Community of States

Many of the items discussed above translate directly into core issues of institutional design. The discussion of the requisites of multilateralism, for example, implicates the criterion of membership. Some institutions are global, whereas others consist of a subset of countries. This choice between inclusivity and exclusivity is central to the design of institutions.

One way to proceed is to involve the community of all nations—to create institutions for the purpose of global governance. Here, nothing short of universality is deemed acceptable: even if not all join, the institutions are nevertheless deemed to apply to all.[46]

The alternative is to take a developmental approach—to construct more limited and focused institutions and allow them to develop. One striking feature of international organizations is that they have grown more intrusive over time, encroaching on sovereignty in ways their founders could scarcely have imagined. The IMF, for example, has over time expanded the scope of its conditionality and oversight. Originally prescribing only a macroeconomic policy mix and an end to subsidies, the Fund now prescribes judicial independence and a host of good governance requirements (Stein 2001).

---

46. This is one way international law is created.

Progressive reformers thus confront a choice. They can include more nations (or draft an agreement that obtains more signatories) and accomplish less initially, but in the hope for growth over time in the constraints on sovereignty. Alternatively, they can create institutions that include fewer nations but that tackle a wider range of issues and/or entail more initial intrusiveness and constraint.

Either choice has a progressive logic associated with it. The former relies on development and accretion to expand the scope of the regime, as has happened, for example, with the NPT, which, in the past decade and a half, has imposed heightened scrutiny because of the discovery of Iraq's clandestine nuclear program. But an expansion of scope is not always assured. The Bush administration, for example, withdrew from negotiations on—and thus brought to a halt efforts to deal with—the perceived inadequacy of enforcement under the Convention on Biological and Toxin Weapons. The agreement remains in force, but the effort to strengthen the regime has faltered.

A different set of developmental possibilities exists in which deeper cooperation among a smaller set of countries constructs an "institution of the willing," but one with agglomerative properties. An institution that offers collective benefits only for members becomes a magnet for new adherents. Trade arrangements that include most-favored-nation clauses or that create common markets or free trade areas have that property. Such "regime creation by accretion" is characteristic of international institutions that are "clubs of agglomeration" (Rosecrance and Stein 2001, 225–26) that change the incentives for future prospective entrants.[47] Moreover, as Downs, Rocke, and Barsoom (1998) show, the sequential admission of members based on a preference for cooperation results in an institution that exhibits more cooperation than could have been achieved by an initial strategy of complete inclusion. Those on the outside might prefer not to have to choose between joining and staying out; they might even have

---

47. In a comparison of European integration in different policy areas, Kölliker (2001) finds that those with excludable network effects are those in which initial differentiation eventually results in long-run convergence. For a discussion of the link between the nature of the good and the inclusiveness of governance arrangements, see Kölliker (2006).

preferred to join initially when they could have had a larger role in writing the rules.[48]

Implied in this debate is the issue of how much to link reforms across domains and how much to depend on historical development. For instance, organizations intended to promote trade liberalization have been pressed to expand their tasks by taking on a set of tangential issues, including environmentalism, workers' rights, and human rights. As another example, the successful reduction of classical barriers to trade shifted the trade liberalization agenda to include nontariff barriers, which are really discordant domestic public policies and practices (Stein 1993). There are also calls for political liberalization to be placed on the agenda as a component of trade liberalization, leading to a debate between those who want to rely on historical development for economic liberalization to generate political reform and those who want to press political liberalization as part of the development of an international community.

Differentiation

Another important feature of institutional design is differentiation, the importance of which both the construction of international institutions and their reform must recognize. More states will bind themselves to multilateral governance arrangements if they have some ability to differentiate between their temporal and issue commitments.

In constructing an integrated Europe, it has long been recognized that deeper integration could be achieved by allowing states to adjust at different rates, by allowing deeper integration in some domains than others, and by allowing some states to integrate at a deeper level than others. In the first dimension, time, states can approach particular objectives at different speeds. In the second dimension, a spatial one, some members can achieve a greater level and depth of integration than others. In the third dimension, one of issues, states have some ability to choose the policy areas in which they want to participate.[49]

---

48. Some realists (for example, Gruber 2000) have sought to portray this as coercion, but it is hardly the coercive vision of classical realism (see Rosecrance 2001).

49. Stubb (1996) provides an extensive list of English, French, and German terms for these three dimensions.

Similar differentiation can be found in other multilateral arrangements. An example is in the contributions by members of the coalition in Iraq: had the United States insisted on each member's making a particular effort, it would obviously have had fewer coalition partners, but by accepting different contributions, the United States increased the number of countries willing to take part.[50]

Differentiated commitment, then, is one way to meet the requirements of commensurability and incentive compatibility, to be both inclusive and exclusive, and to take the most that can be achieved while setting in place the possibility for development and expansion.[51] Organizations with different categories of membership, different timetables for full adherence, and some conditional ability to opt out as needed make it possible to create an expansive multilateralism.

A Typology of Organizational Reform

Any exercise in institutional development begins with the question of whether an existing problem should be dealt with by an existing institution or by the creation of a new one. If the problem derives from the perceived failure of extant organizations, the focus will be on reform. If the problem is something new, typically there will be some debate as to whether to extend the prerogative and scope of an extant organization or construct a new one. As a start, this implies that a range of choices—institutional, constitutional, structural, and systemic—constitutes reform.

Institutional Reform

The simplest reform is merely to tinker with the process or procedure to improve efficiency. We might call this institutional reform. Suggested

---

50. Even then, some states were prepared to encourage and support the United States in private but not in public, a sign that US actions were consonant with their leaders' interests but not with societal preferences.
51. Gilligan (2004) demonstrates that there is no broader-deeper tradeoff once states are allowed to set their policies at different levels. In the language used here, differentiated commitment makes possible more inclusive institutions.

improvements in financial accountability and demands for increased transparency are examples of such process reforms. They can be presented as good in themselves and/or as needed to generate improved outcomes. Transparency, for example, is usually presented as both. Changing the lines of reporting of subunits or adding a secretariat are also examples of process reforms.

Process reforms are the least transformative of extant arrangements. They are the reforms typically suggested by politicians who are looking for illusory responses to constituent pressures. Some of the reports done at the behest of the UN secretary-general are of this type, and are largely public relations exercises intended to generate greater support for the organization.

Another example of an illusory reform is modifying the distribution of voting rights in the IMF in the hope that this would somehow affect the perceived legitimacy of the institution or states' willingness to borrow from it. The IMF is, after all, a bank that needs to be repaid, and it attaches conditions precisely to ensure that it will be repaid. At the same time, states join the IMF because they have little choice, and would borrow from other, less-demanding sources if they were available. Thus, changing the distribution of voting rights on the IMF executive board would hardly change these two fundamental aspects of the workings of the institution.

Constitutional Reform

A higher-order form of change is constitutional reform. Although it is hard to draw a fine line between institutional and constitutional reform, I would argue that, for example, changes in decision rules—the mechanisms for aggregating diverse preferences into a collective choice—are at the heart of constitutions, as are the broad policy domains that are organizational purviews, and that such changes constitute constitutional reform. Examples would include removing the unit veto in the EU or adding members to the UN Security Council.

The difference between institutional reform and constitutional reform can be illustrated by the reforms proposed for the United Nations Human Rights Commission (UNHRC). I would characterize some of these proposals —such as appointing an advisor to monitor the human rights effects of anti-terrorism measures (Nelson 2004)—as institutional reforms. The process change was recommended on the presumption that it would lead to policy changes, and the fight was over the process rather than the actual outcome—a common feature in politics. By contrast, proposals to change how and which countries are selected for the UNHRC—such as those that would disqualify any country under Security Council sanctions from serving on the UNHRC or that would require selected countries to obtain a two-thirds' vote in the General Assembly—are constitutional reforms.

Structural Reform

Another kind of reform is to change the structure of an institution. Examples of such changes, which are on a par with a constitutional change in their prospective consequences, would be to add a dispute resolution mechanism to an international organization or to add a permanent military capability to European institutions. Allowing NATO to undertake out-of-area operations was a structural reform.

Some reforms are hard to categorize and assess, even by the participants debating them. For example, the UN replaced the Human Rights Commission with a Human Rights Council, a reform advertised as structural since the new council would have higher status and greater accountability. But the United States opposed the change, arguing that it was purely cosmetic—in effect, arguing that the change was an illusory one that would leave the acronym the same and outcomes essentially unchanged.

Structural reforms are about changing the operational capability of an institution. They focus directly on what the institution does, not on its administrative procedures. Procedural reforms are often proffered in the hope that they will lead to changes in outcome, not just process.

Systemic Reform

Finally, states can decide that no extant institution can deal with the problem and that a new one is needed. I label this systemic reform, because it reflects a need to change the system of international institutions. An example of systemic reform was the creation of a Missile Technology Control Regime to deal with the proliferation of missiles, rather than expanding the scope of the NPT.

A Final Comment

This mapping of the nature of reform is correlated, but not perfectly, with the characterization of the intent of reform I presented above. Transformative reforms require greater change than palliative ones and thus are less likely to be merely procedural in character. Ironically, reform proposals often focus on bureaucratic and procedural recommendations even though substantive change is desired. Addressing operational capability is ignored or deferred in favor of a focus on the administrative and procedural. Ironically, even as the United States has grown in relative power and emerged as the world's sole superpower, institutional and constitutional reforms of a variety of institutions typically have focused on increasing the number of states that are treated as players and on flattening the distribution of relative voting power.

The Role of Middle Powers

Given its hegemony, the United States' actions are inherently suspect. Other countries have reason to be concerned that the United States is pursuing its particularistic interests, and its pronouncements on behalf of universal values are greeted with suspicion and cynicism. Despite its own good track record on adhering to international agreements, the George W. Bush administration has discovered that its unmasked contempt for international organizations does not help in the pursuit of requisite multilateralism.[52] This leaves key middle powers with the ability to act as interlocutors, intermediaries, and interceders. The Europeans are playing that role with regard to Iran, and regional powers in the western Pacific are playing it with North Korea on the issue of nuclear weapons proliferation.

The ranks of middle powers include sufficient diversity that their agreement on a set of issues cannot simply be derided as Western or European or even wealthy. Their views cannot be cast as those of the poor interested

---

52. This raises the interesting question of how much of George W. Bush's international reputation has to do with style rather than substance. Note that here, too, the Bush administration merely traveled a well-worn path: Canadian diplomat David Malone characterized "the Clinton administration's instinctive penchant for UN-bashing whenever in a tight spot from which blame might be delegated" (2003, 90).

in redistribution or the rich interested in maintaining privilege, nor can they be cast as those of security free riders or of aspiring imperialists. The heterogeneity in their ranks, and even their measure of disinterestedness (in the sense of not having a direct stake), makes possible a set of commitments to transcendent objectives and means. In a unipolar age, their international role is in no way diminished and in many ways heightened, for they provide legitimacy through their affirmation of nonparticularistic interests.

A Community of Democracies

The requisites of incentive compatibility and commensurability suggest that a community of democracies is a categorization without much relevant content for international organizations. The Community of Democracies has met every two and a half years since 2000 and has organized itself as a caucus at the UN. Yet, about all that these democracies have been able to agree on is that they share certain values associated with their form of internal governance. The obvious question then arises: is that enough to translate into shared foreign policy interests?[53]

There are, in fact, deep divisions among the world's democracies even as regards the promotion of democratic governance. The difficulty the EU has had in crafting a common defense and security policy should provide pause to any global effort to organize democracies. The nations of the EU, all democracies, already bound by common governance structures in some domains, and sharing geopolitical concerns, have talked about, but made little progress toward, a common defense and security policy.

In addition to doubt about a common interest for such an international institution, there is the question of whether the set of democracies is commensurate with any international governance problem. On most issues, the set of democracies simply excludes too many important countries that have to be party to viable governance arrangements in most domains. In the end, the Community of Democracies has been able to agree only in a

---

53. In fact, the first problem in creating such an institution is determining which countries are sufficiently "democratic" to join. The Community of Democracies chose to deal with this problem by including democratizing countries, and has been criticized for some of the nations included.

most general way to support the aim of promoting democratic governance and "to collaborate on democracy-related issues in existing international and regional institutions" (Council for a Community of Democracies 2000).

Conclusions

This is an age of contradiction. The world's colossus does not, and cannot, have the imperial ambitions of past hegemons. The nature of modern reality is such that no power completely controls its own fate, and self-sufficiency is more of a mirage than ever. The requisites of daily life, and the solutions to most of the problems states face, require international cooperation. The nature of travel, communication, production, and exchange defines an age of globalization, yet tribal values preclude a political convergence to match economic integration.

We live in a world of weak confederalism precisely because states find independent decision making inadequate to their governance needs; they thus prefer forms of joint decision making and governance, yet they are unprepared to relinquish core elements of their autonomy and independence.

This state of affairs leaves many unhappy, some because they believe that a strong global confederation or federation is long overdue, others because they fear the implications of overbearing centralized political power. Technological change will continue to generate new issues and problems that require new forms of governance. The age-old questions fought out at the local and national levels will be refought at the global level: what aspects of governance can be decentralized, what require greater centralization? what governance functions are best performed by what kinds of institutions operating at what level (local, national, regional, global)? where should the dividing line between public and private reside? what issues require regulation and what should be left to the market and private actors (with governance merely entailing tinkering with property rights)? are organizations required, and should they be formalized and institutionalized?

The questions of governance remain a challenge. In a changing world in which perfection has not been attained, there is always some dissatisfaction with the state of governance and calls for reform. That is as true for domestic politics as it is for international politics.

In this paper, I have tried both to encourage and to challenge would-be architects of global governance. Despite arguments that international institutions are weakening (Ikenberry 2005, 2006), my emphasis has been on the existential reality of multilateralism and the structural reality of weak confederalism in the midst of a unipolar age. Moreover, the demand for global governance will only increase with globalization and technological change. Yet, demands for reform are insufficient and realized reforms are often illusory, and the requisites of political constructions are many and substantial. Those who work in the vineyards of progressive reform (at whatever level of governance) need only recall Maya Angelou's (1993, 89-92) admonition that,

> Of course, there is no absolute assurance that those things I plant will always fall upon arable land and will take root and grow, nor can I know if another cultivator did not leave contrary seeds before I arrived. I do know, however, that if I leave little to chance, if I am careful about the kinds of seeds I plant, about their potency and nature, I can, within reason, trust my expectations.

The existing architecture of international politics is testament both to the possibilities and limitations of global governance.

This paper is part of a recent reversal of roles. Whereas, in the past, as Weiss (2005, 367) notes, academics "made the case for dramatic reforms" only to have the "practical folks…throw cold water and call instead for incremental changes," today "we are witnessing the opposite." Now, it is the diplomats and international civil servants who use "hyperbolic rhetoric" and the academics who provide the sober assessments. This paper is a further plea for realistic global construction.

References

Allee, Todd L., and Paul K. Huth. 2006. "Legitimizing Dispute Settlement: International Legal Rulings as Domestic Political Cover." *American Political Science Review* 100 (2): 219–34.

Alter, K.J., and S. Meunier. 2006. "Nested and Overlapping Regimes in the Transatlantic Banana Trade Dispute." *Journal of European Public Policy* 13 (3): 362–82.

Angelou, Maya. 1993. *Wouldn't Take Nothing for My Journey Now*. New York: Random House.

Archibugi, Daniele. 1993. "The Reform of the UN and Cosmopolitan Democracy: A Critical Review." *Journal of Peace Research* 30 (3): 301–15.

Boulden, Jane, and Thomas Weiss. 2004. "Tactical Multilateralism: Coaxing America Back to the UN." *Survival* 46 (3): 103–14.

Bundy, McGeorge. 1984. "Existential Deterrence and Its Consequences." In *The Security Gamble: Deterrence Dilemmas in the Nuclear Age*, edited by Douglas MacLean. Totowa, NJ: Rowman & Allanheld.

Bush, George W. 2006. "President discusses the economy, participates in press availability." Press release. Washington, DC: White House. April 28. Available at Web site: http://www.whitehouse.gov/news/releases/2006/04/20060428-2.html.

Clark, Ian. 2003. "Legitimacy in a Global Order." In *Governance and Resistance in World Politics*, edited by David Armstrong, Theo Farrell, and Bice Maiguashca. New York: Cambridge University Press.

Cooley, Alexander, and James Ron. 2002. "The NGO Scramble: Organizational Insecurity and the Political Economy of Transnational Action." *International Security* 27 (1): 5–39.

Council for a Community of Democracies. 2000. Final Warsaw Declaration: Toward a Community of Democracies. Warsaw. June 27. Available at Web site: http://www.ccd21.org/articles/warsaw_declaration.htm.

Downs, George W., David M. Rocke, and Peter N. Barsoom. 1998. "Managing the Evolution of Multilateralism." *International Organization* 52 (2): 397–419.

Easterly, William. 2006. *The White Man's Burden: Why the West's Efforts to Aid the Rest Have Done So Much Ill and So Little Good*. New York: Penguin Press.

Ferguson, Niall. 2004. *Colossus: The Price of America's Empire.* New York: Penguin Press.

Feynman, Richard P. 1985. *"Surely You're Joking, Mr. Feynman!": Adventures of a Curious Character.* New York: W.W. Norton.

Foucault, Michel. 1977. *Discipline and Punish: The Birth of the Prison.* New York: Pantheon Books.

Franck, Thomas M. 1988. "Legitimacy in the International System." *American Journal of International Law* 82 (4): 705–59.

Frieden, Jeffrey A. 1999. "Actors and Preferences in International Relations." In *Strategic Choice and International Relations,* edited by David A. Lake and Robert Powell. Princeton, NJ: Princeton University Press.

Friedman, Thomas L. 2006. "Mideast rules to live by." *New York Times,* December 20.

Gallarotti, Giulio M. 1991. "The Limits of International Organization: Systematic Failure in the Management of International Relations." *International Organization* 45 (2): 183–220.

Gilligan, Michael J. 2004. "Is There a Broader-Deeper Trade-off in International Multilateral Agreements?" *International Organization* 58 (3): 459–84.

Goldstein, Judith. 1993. *Ideas, Interests, and American Trade Policy.* Ithaca, NY: Cornell University Press.

Gruber, Lloyd. 2000. *Ruling the World: Power Politics and the Rise of Supranational Institutions.* Princeton, NJ: Princeton University Press.

Haass, Richard N. 2003. "Interview: We Can't Meet Most of the Challenges We Face on Our Own." New York: Council on Foreign Relations. Available at Web site: http://www.cfr.org/publication.html?id=6107.

Haftel, Yoram Z., and Alexander Thompson. 2006. "The Independence of International Organizations: Concept and Applications." *Journal of Conflict Resolution* 50 (2): 253–75.

Helfer, Laurence R. 2004. "Regime Shifting: The TRIPS Agreement and New Dynamics of International Intellectual Property Lawmaking." *Yale Journal of International Law* 29: 1–83.

Hody, Cynthia A. 1996. *The Politics of Trade: American Political Development and Foreign Economic Policy.* Hanover, NH: University Press of New England.

Hurd, Ian. 1999. "Legitimacy and Authority in International Politics." *International Organization* 53 (2): 379–408.

Ikenberry, G. John. 2001. *After Victory: Institutions, Strategic Restraint, and the Rebuilding of Order after Major Wars*. Princeton, NJ: Princeton University Press.

———. 2003a. "Is American Multilateralism in Decline?" *Perspectives on Politics* 1 (3): 533–50.

———. 2003b. "State Power and the Institutional Bargain: America's Ambivalent Economic and Security Multilateralism." In *US Hegemony and International Organizations: The United States and Multilateral Institutions*, edited by Rosemary Foot, S. Neil MacFarlane, and Michael Mastanduno. New York: Oxford University Press.

———. 2005. "A Weaker World." *Prospect* 116 (November): 30–33.

———. 2006. "The Weakening of Global Institutions." *TPM Cafe: America Abroad*. May 4. Available at Web site: http://americaabroad.tpmcafe.com/node/29504.

Iriye, Akira. 2002. *Global Community: The Role of International Organizations in the Making of the Contemporary World*. Berkeley: University of California Press.

Jurewicz, Patricia, and Kristin Dawkins. 2005. *The Treaty Database: U.S. Compliance with Global Treaties*. A Report from the Global Cooperation Project of the Institute for Agriculture and Trade Policy. Minneapolis, MN. Available at Web site: http://www.tradeobservatory.org/library.cfm?refID=60426.

Kagan, Robert. 2002a. "Multilateralism, American style." *Washington Post*, September 13.

———. 2002b. "Power and Weakness." *Policy Review* 113 (June-July): 5–23.

Keck, Margaret E., and Kathryn Sikkink. 1998. *Activists beyond Borders: Advocacy Networks in International Politics*. Ithaca, NY: Cornell University Press.

Keefer, Scott Andrew. 2006. "Building the Palace of Peace: The Hague Conference of 1899 and Arms Control in the Progressive Era." *Journal of the History of International Law* 8 (1): 1–17.

Kelley, Judith. 2004. "International Actors on the Domestic Scene: Membership Conditionality and Socialization by International Institutions." *International Organization* 58 (3): 425–57.

Koch, H. 2006. "International Forum Shopping and Transnational Lawsuits." *Geneva Papers on Risk and Insurance-issues and Practice* 31 (2): 293–303.

Koenig-Archibugi, Mathias. 2004. "International Governance as New *Raison d'État?* The Case of the EU Common Foreign and Security Policy." *European Journal of International Relations* 10 (2): 147–88.

Kölliker, Alkuin. 2001. "Bringing Together or Driving Apart the Union? Towards a Theory of Differentiated Integration." *West European Politics* 24 (4): 125–51.

———. 2006. "Governance Arrangements and Public Goods Theory: Explaining Aspects of Publicness, Inclusivenenss and Delegation." In *New Modes of Governance in the Global System: Exploring Publicness, Delegation and Inclusiveness*, edited by Mathias Koenig-Archibugi and Michael Zürn. New York: Palgrave Macmillan.

Lal, Deepak. 2004. *In Praise of Empires: Globalization and Order*. New York: Palgrave Macmillan.

———. 2005. "The Threat to Economic Liberty from International Organizations." *Cato Journal* 25 (3): 503–20.

Legro, Jeffrey. 2006. "Trustees, Hermits, and Rebels: The Sources of International Identity." Paper presented at the Workshop on Political Economy, National Security, and International Relations, University of California, Los Angeles, May 12.

Lerner, J., and J. Tirole. 2006. "A Model of Forum Shopping." *American Economic Review* 96 (4): 1091–1113.

Luck, Edward C. 1999. *Mixed Messages: American Politics and International Organization, 1919–1999*. Washington, DC: Brookings Institution Press.

———. 2003. "American Exceptionalism and International Organization: Lessons from the 1990s." In *US Hegemony and International Organizations: The United States and Multilateral Institutions*, edited by Rosemary Foot, S. Neil MacFarlane, and Michael Mastanduno. New York: Oxford University Press.

Lukes, Steven. 1974. *Power: A Radical View*. New York: Macmillan.

Malone, David M. 2003. "US-UN Relations in the UN Security Council in the Post-Cold War Era." In *US Hegemony and International Organizations: The United States and Multilateral Institutions*, edited by Rosemary Foot, S. Neil MacFarlane, and Michael Mastanduno. New York: Oxford University Press.

Mandelbaum, Michael. 2005. *The Case for Goliath: How America Acts as the World's Government in the 21st Century*. New York: Public Affairs.

Martin, Lisa L. 2000. *Democratic Commitments: Legislatures and International Cooperation*. Princeton, NJ: Princeton University Press.

Murphy, Cornelius F., Jr. 1999. *Theories of World Governance: A Study in the History of Ideas*. Washington, DC: Catholic University of America Press.

Nelson, Anna. 2004. "NGOs slam UN human rights body for going soft." *Neue Züricher Zeitung*, March 15. Available at Web site: http://www.globalpolicy.org/ngos/ngo-un/rest-un/2004/0315slam.htm.

Nincic, Miroslav. 2005. *Renegade Regimes: Confronting Deviant Behavior in World Politics*. New York: Columbia University Press.

Nye, Joseph S., Jr. 2002. *The Paradox of American Power: Why the World's Only Superpower Can't Go It Alone*. New York: Oxford University Press.

Quenemoen, Marianna. 2003. "US Position on International Treaties." New York: Global Policy Forum. July. Available at Web site: http://www.globalpolicy.org/empire/tables/treaties.htm.

Reuters. 2006. "Russia, China oppose Iran attack." May 3. Available at Web site: http://archive.gulfnews.com/articles/06/05/03/10037245.html.

Robinson, Ian. 2000. "Progressive Unilateralism? U.S. Unilateralism, Progressive Internationalism, and Alternatives to Neoliberalism." Foreign Policy in Focus, Discussion Paper 3. November 15. Available at Web site: http://www.fpif.org/papers/unilateralism.html.

Rosecrance, Richard. 1992. "A New Concert of Powers." *Foreign Affairs* 71 (2): 64–82.

———. 2001. "Has Realism Become Cost-Benefit Analysis?" *International Security* 26 (2): 132–54.

Rosecrance, Richard, and Arthur A. Stein. 2001. "The Theory of Overlapping Clubs." In *The New Great Power Coalition: Toward a World Concert of Nations*, edited by Richard Rosecrance. Lanham, MD: Rowman & Littlefield.

———, eds. 2006. *No More States?: Globalization, National Self-Determination, and Terrorism*. Lanham, MD: Rowman & Littlefield.

Ross, Dennis. 2004. *The Missing Peace: The Inside Story of the Fight for Middle East Peace*. New York: Farrar, Straus and Giroux.

Rubin, P.H., C. Curran, and J.F. Curran. 2001. "Litigation versus Legislation: Forum Shopping by Rent Seekers." *Public Choice* 107 (3-4): 295–310.

Rudolph, Christopher. 2006. *National Security and Immigration: Policy Development in the United States and Western Europe since 1945*. Stanford, CA: Stanford University Press.

Sally, Razeen. 2001. "Looking Askance at Global Governance." In *Guiding Global Order: G8 Governance in the Twenty-First Century*, edited by John J. Kirton, Joseph P. Daniels, and Andreas Freytag. Burlington, VT: Ashgate.

Schwenninger, Sherie R. 2004. "A World Neglected: The Foreign Policy We Should Be Having." *The Nation*, October 18. Available at Web site: http://www.newamerica.net/publications/articles/2004/a_world_neglected.

Singer, Clifford, James Walsh, and Dean Wilkening. 2004. *Reinventing Multilateralism*. Urbana-Champaign, IL: University of Illinois, Urbana-Champaign, Arms Control, Disarmament, and International Security. Available at Web site: http://www.acdis.uiuc.edu/Reinventing/index.shtml.

SIPRI (Stockholm International Peace Research Institute). 2005. "The 15 Major Spenders in 2004." Available at Web site: http://www.sipri.org/contents/milap/milex/mex_major_spenders.pdf.

Snyder, Jack L. 2000. *From Voting to Violence: Democratization and Nationalist Conflict*. New York: W.W. Norton.

Solingen, Etel. 1998. *Regional Orders at Century's Dawn: Global and Domestic Influences on Grand Strategy*. Princeton, NJ: Princeton University Press.

Stein, Arthur A. 1982. "Coordination and Collaboration: Regimes in an Anarchic World." *International Organization* 36 (2): 299–324.

———. 1984. "The Hegemon's Dilemma: Great Britain, the United States, and the International Economic Order." *International Organization* 38 (2): 355–86.

———. 1990. *Why Nations Cooperate: Circumstance and Choice in International Relations*. Ithaca, NY: Cornell University Press.

———. 1993. "Governments, Economic Interdependence, and International Cooperation." In *Behavior, Society, and International Conflict*, vol. 3, edited by Philip E. Tetlock, Jo L. Husbands, Robert Jervis, Paul C. Stern, and Charles Tilly. New York: Oxford University Press for the National Research Council of the National Academy of Sciences.

———. 2000. "The Justifying State: Why Anarchy Doesn't Mean No Excuses." In *Peace, Prosperity, and Politics*, edited by John E. Mueller. Boulder, CO: Westview Press.

———. 2001. "Constrained Sovereignty: The Growth of International Intrusiveness." In *The New Great Power Coalition: Toward a World Concert of Nations*, edited by Richard Rosecrance. Lanham, MD: Rowman & Littlefield.

————. Forthcoming. "Neoliberal Institutionalism." In *Oxford Handbook on International Relations*, edited by Christian Reus-Smit and Duncan Snidal. New York: Oxford University Press.

Stubb, Alexander C-G. 1996. "A Categorization of Differentiated Integration." *Journal of Common Market Studies* 34 (2): 283–95.

Sweet, Catherine Elizabeth. 2001. "Democratization without Democracy: Strategic Politicians and the Emergence of Pseudodemocracy in Morocco." Ph.D. diss., University of California, Los Angeles.

Thompson, Alexander. 2006. "Coercion through IOs: The Security Council and the Logic of Information Transmission." *International Organization* 60 (1): 1–34.

United States. 2003. White House. "Operation Iraqi Freedom: Coalition members." Press release. March 27. Washington, DC. Available at Web site: http://www.whitehouse.gov/news/releases/2003/03/20030327-10.html.

————. 2005. Department of State. Media Reaction Branch. "President Bush's Europe trip: 'Real dialogue' or 'symbolic gesture'?" Washington, DC. Available at Web site: http://www.globalsecurity.org/military/library/news/2005/03/wwwh50302.htm.

Vreeland, James Raymond. 2003. "Why Do Governments and the IMF Enter into Agreements? Statistically Selected Cases." *International Political Science Review* 24 (3): 321–43.

Ward, Hugh, Frank Grundig, and Ethan R. Zorick. 2001. "Marching at the Pace of the Slowest: A Model of International Climate-Change Negotiations." *Political Studies* 49 (3): 438–61.

Weaver, R. Kent. 1986. "The Politics of Blame Avoidance." *Journal of Public Policy* 6 (4): 371–98.

Wedgwood, Ruth. 1998. "The pitfalls of global justice." *New York Times*, June 10, p. A35.

Weiss, Thomas G. 2004. "The Sunset of Humanitarian Intervention? The Responsibility to Protect in a Unipolar Era." *Security Dialogue* 35 (2): 135–53.

————. 2005. "An Unchanged Security Council: The Sky Ain't Falling." *Security Dialogue* 36 (3): 367–69.

Weiss, Thomas G., and Karen E. Young. 2005. "Compromise and Credibility: Security Council Reform?" *Security Dialogue* 36 (2): 131–54.

Winkelmann, Ingo. 1997. "Bringing the Security Council into a New Era: Recent Developments in the Discussion on the Reform of the Security Council." *Max Planck Yearbook of United Nations Law* 1: 35–90.

Wolf, Klaus Dieter. 1999. "The New Raison d'État as a Problem for Democracy in World Society." *European Journal of International Relations* 5 (3): 333–63.

A Grand Coalition and International Governance

Richard Rosecrance

*   *   *

Current proposals to reform the United Nations Security Council by admitting Germany or Japan to permanent member status are unlikely to be accepted. Reform of the International Monetary Fund (IMF) to give Far Eastern nations, particularly China, more voting leverage also will not pass muster if it were to undermine the veto the United States—with its 17 percent share—effectively has over IMF decisions. Indeed, no form of "democratization" of the leadership of international institutions will be effective if it substitutes greater "inclusion" for "representation" of the nations that, in fact, possess the economic and military power to carry out international operations. Reform will be effective, however, if it devolves responsibility on the Great Powers—the United States, China, the European Union, Japan, Russia, and perhaps India. These agglomerations of power provide legitimacy to international reform and convey the capability necessary to carry it out. They represent the crucial elements in any long-term program of reform for the international system, and they are essential to bring governance and peace to the world.

Of course, all effective means of international governance involve strengthening ties among nations, and many links and institutions already join them together. Some of these are "soft" institutional procedures, like those reflected in votes in the UN General Assembly or in the muted and decentralized strictures of international law. Between the hard and soft institutional approaches are "medium" institutions such as the World Trade Organization (WTO) and the IMF: though theoretically universal in scope, they have bite only on particular issues and cover only a few realms of activity. Then there are hard institutional processes, such as votes in the UN Security Council that reflect Great Power consensus.[1]

Empires and alliances also restrict state options and provide a degree of governance within their sphere. Broadly speaking, while empires have occasionally succeeded in the past, they cannot solve the problems of the world today. Alliances sometimes regulate behavior among their number, but it is less certain that they govern the actions of their targets—indeed, they sometimes exacerbate relations through positive feedback. It is by no means clear, for example, that alliance bipolarity reduces conflict—it might enhance it.

In this paper, I review a range of proposed solutions to the problem of international governance—from empire to alliances to the softer institutional linkages—before generally concluding that a concert of Great Powers, when it can be achieved, is the most effective international regulator.

The Prospects of Empire

Empire united much of the civilized world under the aegis of Rome, but it has seldom worked since. It was efficient then because tributary and nearby agglomerations of power were linked to Rome and, for a time, provinces and client states benefited through an extensive network of

---

1. Paul Kennedy (2006, 73–74) is skeptical that the UN Security Council can do much, whether or not it is reformed:

    Since 1950 the vast majority of American military actions were either not sanctioned by the Security Council at all (Vietnam, Central America) or were "contracted out" operations where the Council thought it had no real purview (Korea, the First Gulf War, Mogadishu, Afghanistan) … it was not pleasant for liberal internationalists at the dawn of the first decade of the twenty-first century to consider that the UN's primary organ for security might be becoming merely a rubber stamp for the world's largest and most assertive member.

international trade. Egypt, Spain, Gaul, and Italy traded wine, grain, oil, perfume, glassware, and textiles with one another. When Rome was attacked by barbarians across the Rhine in the fourth century, trade and transport, encumbered by military vehicles, also diminished, making commerce risky and costly. Only luxury trades remained, then autarky began to intrude. The Romans raised taxes to reconstruct roads, but travel on them was frequently interrupted by brigands. The interdependence of Rome and its tributary areas proved the empire's undoing as transport costs rose and food could no longer be imported from remote areas. A much more primitive, land-based economy then emerged, and Rome collapsed from within. Rome never succeeded in developing a stable, cooperative relationship with its provinces and tributary states, and no military danger forced them all to work together. Rome prevailed for a time because of the unmatched power of the Roman legion, but the need to travel greater and greater distances ultimately attenuated its strength. Other challengers not bound into the mutually supporting network of international trade and Roman law eventually emerged on the frontier.

The notion that one state today could establish a Roman-like empire over all the others is ludicrous. No one has the military strength to do this, and shallow strategic reach is not the equivalent of the Roman legion and the extension of Roman roads and legal systems. The United States cannot do it, as Iraq proves. Neither does the United States have the economic strength to achieve imperium elsewhere—it is, in fact, growingly dependent on others.

Still, many call for the United States to be more imperial, even though its ambit would fall far short of arrogating the entire world. In 1897, Britain controlled one-quarter of the world's land area and one-seventh of its population; today, there are many large agglomerations of power and territory. In the face of Russia, China, the EU, and India, US power is inadequate to achieve imperial rule even over an area equal to that of the British Empire. Niall Ferguson, perhaps the most persuasive proponent of an imperial US strategy, recognizes that the door is closing on the opportunity for such an attempt—indeed, it might already be shut. David Abernathy, for example, finds intrinsic contradictions in colonialism that lead to its own demise: "[A]s government tried to slow down political change, growing numbers of colonial residents asked why their protostate should not move more rapidly forward toward state sovereignty. Critics complained in effect, 'The metropole has taken us 80 percent of the way. Why not finish the task? If our rulers won't do it, we will'" (2000, 327). Eric Hobsbawm, in charting imperial decline, emphasizes the catalytic effect of defeat in war: "What fatally damaged the old colonialists was the proof that white men and their states could be defeated, shamefully and dishonourably, and the old colonial powers were patently too weak, even after a victorious war, to restore their old positions" (1996, 216).

In any event, even if the United States believed it could extend its empire militarily, further US military exertions likely would only bid up costs without pacifying the dissenting province. Though militarily strong, the United States is economically weaker than it used to be and cannot carry a larger burden; indeed, it might have to lay down some of what it now seeks to lift.

Alliances

But empire might not be necessary. Some believe that alliances of major players might suffice. In the early days of the Cold War, the North Atlantic Treaty Organization (NATO) brought together western and central Europe, with Japan an important associate in the Far East, in a kind of grand alliance. In this complex of nations, individual countries usually adjusted their behavior to that of the group.[2] Whether the success of NATO internally was also a success externally remains an open question. At the most severe levels of the Cold War, NATO and the Warsaw Pact, by mutually checking each other, at least achieved a nuclear peace—there was no World War III. But bipolarity did not regulate the domestic lives of its participants, and international economic cooperation was limited to one side of the bipolar alignment.

The most successful alliance system in Western history was that of Bismarckian Germany. Bismarck did not produce a universal system,

---

2. This was not always true. France took its forces out of the NATO command after 1958.

because France was always excluded. Nonetheless, by 1887, the German chancellor had developed alignment networks that linked Austria, Russia, and Britain with Berlin. Since France would do nothing without a strong ally, the system was pacific. The arrangement, as historians point out, was "inconsistent" because Germany was allied to two powers, Austria and Russia, that were opposed to each other—rivals over territory in the Balkans. Yet the German link restrained them both. And if Germany could not fully restrain Russia by itself, Britain would be Berlin's accomplice. In fact, Bismarck's alliance system was successful in part because it represented an overbalance of power. Germany was restricted, not by the one remaining outside power, France, but by the internal operations of its own alliances with Russia and Britain. In Paul Schroeder's (1989) analysis, alliances were tools for mutual restraint, ways for allies to manage one another's policies. When "the pilot was dropped" in March 1890, however, the new emperor, Wilhelm II, decided not to renew the "Reinsurance Treaty" with Russia, leaving that country isolated and free to form an alliance with France. When that happened, the alliance bipolarity that led to World War I began to consolidate itself. Instead of acting as a restraint, alliances became a goad to greater power and opposition in the system.

NATO, however, does not appear to be the modern-day equivalent of Bismarck's system. It leaves out key powers—Russia, China, India—while important European members seek to downplay the alliance because of the intrinsically one-sided nature of its internal negotiations, which favor the United States, the strongest military member. Since negotiations between the United States and the EU are more equal outside the NATO military sphere, European countries are likely to opt increasingly for addressing the United States through collective EU forums. Thus, it does not appear that the NATO edifice can be restructured.

Institutions

As Robert Keohane (1984) points out, international institutions have to solve the problems of free riding and the so-called Prisoner's Dilemma: if one member offers cooperation, it is in the interest of others to free ride on the first member's contribution. Keohane suggests the problem can be solved by relying on "satisficing" as the *vade mecum* of cooperation, whereby members will not insist on full rationality in decision making but will cooperate even when it might not be wholly in their interest to do so. Experiments in social psychology show, of course, that, where player-members expect to have an on-going relationship with each other over time and where their number is small, cooperation can still exist despite the dictates of strict "rationality"—people are not, in Amartya Sen's memorable phrase, "rational fools." But even here, the institution they join or support has to be capable of producing results, otherwise few will want to remain members. Also, the Prisoner's Dilemma shows that, if the same players play a game many times over, cooperation tends to develop as long as no one knows when the game will end. If an end is specified, the lack of cooperation on the last play will influence earlier plays, and co-operation will collapse at the beginning. Tom Schelling (1978) shows that a multiparty Prisoner's Dilemma might lead to initial cooperation, but after a K-group (which first establishes cooperation) has been formed, sub-sequent participants will be tempted to take a less cooperative line—indeed, as Raiffa (1982) shows, business school students almost always do so, and countries frequently behave like business school students.

How is it, then, that there is any cooperation at all in international relations? Should not every state be a free rider? In fact, in international relations, there is—in general and with exceptions—more cooperation than one would expect from a free-rider and public-goods point of view, at least partly because countries often gain prestige from cooperating or from joining high-status international clubs. Getting into the fraternity of the "great" or the "exclusive" is attractive to national leaderships. Countries like to win Nobel Prizes, for example, for their international performance and standing. This is why Norway and Canada routinely stand high in international forums: they are the conscience of others, in that they have few axes to grind and still contribute beyond their share. Sometimes, they make the United States feel guilty, no doubt much to their satisfaction!

But we cannot solve the problem of international cooperation today by wishing that all countries were like Canada. Some countries in the Middle East—perhaps Syria and Iran—actually gain local prestige by not contributing and by not joining, but effectively opposing, arrangements most major players in the system desire. Tentative victories won by standing up to the United States and its Israeli ally certainly contribute to prestige among Muslim populations, though few concrete benefits are thereby gained. In fact, one might hazard the guess that had oil not been abundant in the Middle East, cooperation between Muslim regimes and the rest of the world would have been far more marked than it is at the moment. In one sense, cooperation among Middle Eastern players, given their interests, is probably considerably less than one might have predicted from a game theoretic point of view. The failure to cooperate is supported by oil revenues: conflict in the Middle East has become affordable and thus tolerable.

There are different kinds of institutions. Some, as we saw at the outset, are essentially "soft" institutions. They do not contribute much; they do not pay for much; they do not constrain much. Countries in these bodies do not have to ante up, and both Prisoner's Dilemma and free-rider incentives apply significantly. The General Assembly of the United Nations and the UN Human Rights Council are examples: they do little and they achieve little, and few take them seriously except when the Security Council is deadlocked. Paul Kennedy remarks: "What, finally, can one say about the General Assembly? This is, after all, the closest approximation we have of the parliament of man, yet its limpness is apparent to all" (2006, 274). Kennedy pays UN institutions the ultimate compliment, but even he recognizes that they are not yet "the parliament of man" and may never be.

The IMF and the World Bank are "medium" institutions. They are governed by Great Powers, and they might not always intervene to help countries in trouble. Debt forgiveness has been on the world's agenda for several years, yet nothing has been done to achieve it. Countries facing default sometimes ask for a "bailout," but—even if offered—they have to meet such strict conditions to get it that complying with them might doom the regime in power. Although there is a great deal of inequality among nations, the IMF and the World Bank have done little to reduce it. China is a member of the WTO, but its rapid economic development was not due to international financing or special trade concessions. Rather, its arrangements were made with private parties—corporations in whose interest it is to produce in a low-cost, high-quality economic environment. These companies helped to guarantee that Chinese production for Western corporations would be sold in their countries.

Economic Linkages

The functioning of institutions depends on the strength of the economic links among major parties and institutional members in the system. Today, globalization dwarfs even the strongest state. As Jagdish Bhagwati writes, "globalization intensifies interdependence among nation-states and increasingly constrains their ability to provide for the welfare of their citizens" (2005, 13). No state is fully independent economically, except perhaps those that are not engaged in trade, finance, tourism, migration, or other exchanges with their neighbors—a category in which only the most impoverished nations would be found. Those that have embarked upon international trade understand that the costs and prices of imports and exports are critical to sustaining that trade. If nations wish to export in order to get funds to invest at home to sustain their economic development, they need to achieve high quality and low price to succeed in world markets. Their corporations, whether private or state, need to meet international competition, which is now exceedingly keen in most areas. Of course, corporations and sales abroad are sometimes subsidized. Competitive products are kept out of the domestic market through tariffs or other restrictions. But such tactics frequently lead to objections lodged with the WTO, with unpredictable results. It is far better to compete on price by lowering costs.

Production supply chains—outsourcing—make this possible (see Jones 2000). Countries can move their production overseas or contract with a foreign supplier to produce it, at costs lower than those that could be achieved domestically. US and European industry have remained competitive by producing abroad, and recently so has Japan. Outsourcing, however, results in a dilemma for manufacturers and even for government: high profits and sales seem to depend on foreign production, which is intrinsically out of the control of the home government.

Few major US corporations have not diversified abroad—successful firms such as IBM, GE, Wal-Mart, Microsoft, Intel, and others have invested heavily in plant and subsidiaries overseas. "Greenfield" investments by Japanese companies are characteristic in the United States, Europe, and China. Even defense departments do a share of their procurement overseas, though they seek to avoid dependence on a single supplier. Brooks (2005) argues that the most advanced nations in terms of growth and income could be those that are the most diversified in terms of overseas production.[3] Even China is becoming a major overseas investor, though more in the form of portfolio and money market investments than direct investments. As Chinese prices and costs rise, however, Chinese manufacturers will look for cheaper production sources in Bangladesh, Cambodia, or Pakistan. In more general terms, diversified economies with supply chains overseas might actually grow faster and maintain their industrial strength better than economies with production lodged at home. One perhaps does not want to make too much of this, but production supply chains did not exist in 1914 (see Brooks 2005). It does seem to be true, however, that foreign direct investment linkages between countries reduce the amount of conflict between them (see Rosecrance and Thompson 2003). Among the major powers today, these links are strong and becoming stronger. Economic interdependence might strengthen ties in the same manner that deterrence does, by giving each party a kind of "hostage" to hold to guarantee satisfactory behavior by the opposite number (see Gartzke 2003; Stein 2003).

Agglomeration Processes?

The study of international relations has, on the whole, favored the continued existence of a multiplicity of state units. Though empires occasionally emerged in China and India, attempts to establish one in Europe failed after the collapse of Rome. Economic and military influences appeared initially to militate on behalf of the continent's division into relatively small states, and neither pope nor holy roman emperor was able to construct an imperial dominion over all or most of Europe. The introduction of gunpowder after 1450 perhaps favored a greater combination of units, but new defensive techniques, waterways, and sea power helped to maintain the existence of relatively small states like Holland and Portugal against siege and invasion. Sea-borne trade gave coastal cities a livelihood that made them less dependent on the center of the state (see Fox 1971).

---

3. Brooks also argues that global production linkages probably make military conquest less likely and less effective: "I find that the globalization of production has greatly reduced the economic benefits of military conquest among the most advanced countries" (2005, 6).

Napoleon briefly appeared able militarily to aggrandize formerly independent units, but his political empire did not last. It first occasioned resistance in Spain, then evoked German and Russian proto-nationalism, which threw the invader out. Napoleon's liberal and legal reforms along the Rhine and elsewhere were not sufficient to support rule by his relatives in the tributary states of his empire.

Attempts by Hitler and Stalin to gain a great territorial empire also failed. Hitler ultimately conquered a territory whose prewar gross domestic product (GDP) exceeded that of the allies, but he could not organize that production toward military ends (see Overy 1995). Stalin, in contrast, was more cautious in attempting to realize his vast territorial ambitions, recognizing that further expansion into western Europe might jeopardize his gains at home. And Marxian historical materialism told him he would win in the long run anyway—he could afford to wait.[4]

The balance of power supposedly dictates the preservation of the multipolar order—countries are supposed to resist combination into larger units. Yet the balance of power permitted the reduction of the system to two major powers during the Cold War and the establishment of bipolarity. Now, it has adjusted to the existence of US unipolarity, at least in the military field. How can this be, given the assumption that power does not attract but repels? The answer, apparently, is that the balance of power does not operate uniformly: it is conditioned on the intentions of the parties, not on the amount of power they possess (see Walt 1987). There are, of course, many cases where strong states did not assert their power and where weaker states attempted to do so—power does not determine intentions. The United States, on the whole, has been exempted from pressures of the balance directed against it because its intentions have been either beneficent or locally confined. Even Manifest Destiny did not proclaim the United States' intention to conquer the Western Hemisphere or to arrogate Canada and Mexico. Today, therefore, a larger edifice of peaceful power could be created that would not generate pressures to balance

---

4. British diplomat Frank Roberts wrote back to the Foreign Office from Moscow in 1946: "Although Soviet Russia intends to spread her influence by all possible means, world revolution is no longer part of her programme and there is nothing in the internal conditions within the Union which might encourage a return to the old revolutionary traditions" (quoted in Hobsbawm 1996, 225).

against it. To avoid a balance-of-power response, however, such an agglomeration of power would have to include all or most of the major powers, and it would have to expand peacefully.

There has been no worldwide attempt at empire since the demise of the Soviet Union in 1991. US military efforts in Kosovo, Afghanistan, and Iraq—which some have deemed equivalent to imperial gains—have had indifferent success. Kosovo is tenuously presided over by international administrators and eyed by Belgrade, but it is winning de facto autonomy for its Albanian population. Afghanistan is still not pacified, and the movement of NATO troops to the south and Kandahar has not occurred without opposition. In Iraq, US and coalition forces have not put down resistance and confront a civil conflict.[5] Indeed, one might even construct a case that a possible effect of international processes today is to produce anarchy within previously consolidated states. Palestine is now divided between Fatah and Hamas. Southern Lebanon is ruled by Shi'ites, at least some of whom support Hezbollah. In the rest of Lebanon, Christians and Muslims have not come together to effect a strong new synthesis, and war and civil strife have reversed two decades of progress since the end of the Israeli occupation in 1982. Some believe that the trend of the future is to create "failed states" in which criminal or terrorist economic elements call the tune, defying a democratic consolidation. If this trend were to continue, the international system would observe not more or fewer states, but the creation of less effective ones (see Rosecrance and Stein 2006).

Yet, other powerful forces push in the opposite direction. The size and increasing integration of the international economy is dictating larger, not smaller, units.[6] The capital market can overwhelm any single country's

---

5. The three best studies of the Iraq War are Gordon and Trainor (2006); Ricks (2006): and Woodward (2006). For an overview, see Miller (2006).
6. Hobsbawm (1996, 277) observes:

> [A]n increasingly transnational economy began to emerge especially from the 1960s on, that is to say, a system of economic activities for which state territories and state frontiers are not the basic framework, but merely complicating factors. In the extreme case, a "world economy" comes into existence which actually has no specifiable territorial base or limits, and which determines or rather sets limits to, what even the economies of very large and powerful states can do.

stockpiles of foreign exchange.[7] As long as national currencies exist, countries in Asia, Latin America, or eastern Europe can run out of spare change, and they have periodically done so. Russia defaulted in 1998, Mexico in 1982 and 1994. Malaysia, Thailand, and Indonesia were forced to their knees when they could not pay their debts in hard currencies in 1997–98 (see Arthur 2000). South Korea was pressed to devalue and open up its economy as well. Even China and Hong Kong—with large reserves—shivered during the monetary outflow. Larger agglomerations of power or larger currency unions would prevent this.

Perhaps even more important, production linkages for modern industry have meant in practice that a single country or even a single continent is not large enough to guarantee low-cost production or high-return sales. Unless firms can operate in several continents and different national jurisdictions, they cannot be sure of remaining competitive against other multinationals. Multinationals take funds and goods into an economy, and they rapidly take them out, depending on conditions in the country. If taxes are too high, if tariffs prevent sales, if interest rates or inflation rise, money might leave for more receptive locations. Hedge funds move assets seamlessly between markets, but the affected governments and local economies might suffer.

Another uncertainty that might contribute to the need for "largeness" is "economies of scale." In some industries with high barriers to entry, the number of efficient producers might limited. In civil aircraft, perhaps automobiles, finance, insurance, software, pharmaceuticals, and other technical realms, there might be a limit on the number of competitive firms: in civil aircraft, it is two firms; in autos, it might be fewer than ten; in microprocessors or handheld computers, it might be four or five. Even the conventional military industry is becoming concentrated. In the United States, military firms have already consolidated. In Europe, EADS and BAE are big, and soon might become so in the United States. Holland has four major economies-of-scale complexes—ING-Barings, Philips, Lever, and Shell—but what does a country do if, like Mexico, it does not

---

7. If the US dollar remains a major international currency, however, US holdings of reserve currencies cannot be limited. They could always be printed, but with inflationary effects.

possess a single one? Is it any surprise that Mexican labor seeks to migrate to the United States? How many economies-of-scale industries does Canada possess? It is not surprising that Canada invests heavily in US firms or that Canadian labor and brainpower migrate to the United States. Even China lacks economies-of-scale industries. During a recent trip to China, I was asked, "Does that mean we in China would have to import military systems from you if we were going to attack you?" And my answer was, "Yes!"[8] Many Chinese firms (and not just military producers) will need links with established western and Japanese corporations in order to penetrate world markets. New Chinese auto producers probably will not be able to operate abroad alone. In this way, links between economies facilitate links between states.[9]

Contemporary Geopolitics

We could be moving into a novel system in which geopolitics helps us understand the long-term result of attempts at international governance. In the 1890s, Alfred Thayer Mahan propounded the "influence of sea power upon history": Britain's ability to dominate coastlines and trade routes gave it an intrinsic advantage over strictly "land powers," which were unable to export autonomously overseas. Shipping was the best means of transport, for both economic and military strategy.

This conclusion, however, was challenged in 1905 by Halford Mackinder, who saw the development of continental—especially Russian—railways as substituting an efficient land route for sea linkages. Russian railroads would bring development and trade to previously landlocked areas and industrialize the Heartland of the world. Railways would also permit rapid military mobilization of troops and matériel. This ability to dominate land, he argued, would substitute for the past influence of seapower, which

---

8. Stephen Brooks (2005, 11) notes: "[C]onsider what would happen if a great power were to go it alone in defense production in the current environment. Any state that pursues this course will not have leading-edge military equipment and will thus be in a weaker position to pursue revisionist aims."

9. Some have spoken of "econo-states" or "market states" as the hybrid model that is now emerging.

could rule only the sea coasts. In Mackinder's terms, "Who rules the Heartland [central Asia and Russia] rules the World Island [the continent of Eurasia]. Who rules the World Island rules the World."

This conclusion, in turn, was challenged in 1944 by Nicholas Spykman. He argued that there were two great contending bases of power in world politics: the Heartland and what he called the Rimlands, which constituted the coastal and offshore island economies of Europe, Britain, India, and Japan. Dominance of the Rimlands ultimately would convey the greatest world power. Open to the sea, Rimland countries would control worldwide trade and access to world markets, which, in turn, would govern the relative pace of development of major powers.[10] Of course, as we know historically, the Rimlands were never united. In World War II, Rimland powers were at war with one another, with the United States and western Europe fighting Germany and Japan, and it was a temporary alliance with the Heartland country of Russia that made victory possible for one Rimland camp (the United States and its allies) over the other.

A question for the future, however, is the possibility that the Rimland powers might increasingly come together economically and perhaps politically. This possibility was first sketched in the 1970s by Edward Whiting Fox, who envisioned the riverine, island, and oceanic world cohering along trading lines against the more landlocked interior. Some such connection could be in process today as European, US, and Japanese firms bestride the world, in competition but also in cooperation with one another for markets, raw materials, and access to capital. Indeed, as Jones (2000), Brooks (2005), and others have pointed out, one part of the Rimland becomes strong only by virtue of investing in the production of another part, and foreign direct investment interpenetration is now greater than it has ever been.

If the Rimland were to cohere economically, what would its impact be? Garton Ash (2004) makes the case that European and US interests with

---

10. Spykman (1944) wrote: "The Rimland of the Eurasian land mass must be viewed as an intermediate region situated...between the Heartland and the marginal seas. It functions as a vast buffer zone of conflict between sea power and land power. Looking in both directions, it must function amphibiously and defend itself on land and sea."

regard to the Middle East and Asia are closely aligned, if not identical.[11] German chancellor Angela Merkel called for a Trans-Atlantic Free Trade Area in her visit to Washington in 2006. Katzenstein (2005) notes that "Rimland" regionalism has been porous, open to penetration by trade, investment, and capital flows between regions, and that European and Far Eastern regions remain open to US influence and foreign policy priorities.[12] Steil and Litan (2006) argue that currency linkages—euroization, dollarization—between regions can bring continents together and diminish economic and financial crises.[13]

The key unanswered question, however, is whether any deeper association of Rimland nations would provoke opposition from those excluded. The role of China here is critical, because it could act either from its Eurasian (Heartland and Middle Kingdom) perspective or from its Asian coastal orientation. It has landlocked portions (Xinjiang and Tibet) and vibrant coastal provinces (Guangdong, Dalian, Fujian) that are each representative of characteristic and different attitudes. Which perspective would govern China's response? One could argue that its coastal perspective has, in historic terms, only recently come to the fore. Clearly, China remains divided on the issue.

If the Rimlands—in the first instance consisting of Japan and Europe —were to come together more closely together, the greatest danger to the

---

11. Garton Ash (2004, 122) points out that, in 2000, US firms had some US$3 trillion of assets in Europe, while European firms had about US$3.3 trillion of assets in the United States.

12. Katzenstein (2005, 247) writes:

   Germany and Japan, in brief, are core regional states that supported the purpose and power of the United States. In the second half of the twentieth century that conversion gave porous regionalism its dual political significance in the American imperium: as a buffer against an overweening United States when its power seemed to rise too fast, and as a support for an overtaxed United States when its power appeared to decline too much.

13. They write: "The long term answer…is to rid the world of unwanted currencies. Having a national money is not only becoming less and less useful as the world becomes more and more interconnected economically and financially, but it is becoming more destabilizing" (Steil and Litan 2006, 165).

United States would come from "the possibility that the Rimland regions of the Eurasian land mass would be dominated by a single power." Much more likely would be a consolidation of Rimland strength, with the United States as the core. How would China and Russia regard such a tripartite combination?

The most extreme contrariety in world politics would stem from a three versus three alignment of power: the United States, Europe, and Japan versus China, India, and Russia. This scenario seems wholly unlikely, however, for a variety of reasons. India is democratic, China is not. Russia historically has been much closer to India than to China, and the Shanghai Cooperation Organisation would not change this outcome appreciably. Russia is a raw materials power, while both India and China are short of key resources, particularly natural gas and petroleum. China has plenty of capital, but until recently neither Russia nor India has had enough. All three countries have large populations that, in time and with economic development, will be able to buy the output of their home industries. China's middle class is between 300 and 400 million people, India's is more than 200 million, while Russia's approximates 100 million. The dependence of each of the three powers on the rest of the world apparently could decline as wealth increases. They will not have to follow strategies of export-led growth forever.

On the other hand, the inner fastnesses of Eurasia do not offer the most propitious market or source of technology for any of the three. Russia made the huge mistake during the Cold War of cutting itself off from foreign capital and technology, thereby foreshortening its economic growth. It paid a price then, and does not wish to pay it again. In the past 20 years, both India and China have emerged from periods of introversion in which they protected nationalized industry and essentially renounced exporting abroad. India experimented unsuccessfully with import-substituting industrialization, while China, under the Great Leap Forward and the Cultural Revolution, sought to produce all its necessities at home. A trade bloc or even a currency union that brought together only India, China and Russia would hardly be satisfactory to any of the three. Russia orients toward Europe and seeks foreign investment. China directs its attention to both Europe and the United States. India increasingly seeks trade with the United States and Europe. Economic interdependence among the three

Figure 1: *Linkages among Great Powers, 2014*

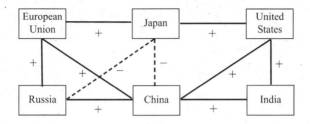

Heartland parties would be low. Moreover, as Figure 1 indicates, the cross-cutting linkages among the three Rimland powers would be strong, but would not give rise to bipolar antagonism with Russia, China, and India. In fact, the opposite would be true: US and European ties with both China and India would be positive, and only Japan would react in a mixed fashion to Russia and China.

Contrast today's configuration with the largely bipolar alignment of 1914 (Figure 2). As recently as 1901, Germany had been an erstwhile associate of Britain. However, the Haldane mission's failure to produce an Anglo-German naval accommodation and British military staff talks with France moved the 1904 Anglo-French entente closer to an outright alliance, and Britain increasingly viewed Germany as a threat to itself and the empire. In an attempt to offset the Anglo-French entente, Germany tried in 1905 for a sudden rapprochement with Russia, but relations between the two powers deteriorated thereafter. Germany saw Russia as a long-term threat. Russia believed, correctly, that Germany (backing Austria) had prevented it from gaining a strategic position at the Bosporus and the Dardanelles, the straits separating the Black Sea and the Mediterranean, to compensate for the loss of Bosnia. Russia had conceded three times (1908, 1909, and 1912), but would not do so again. In short, as Figure 2 shows, the structure of the 1914 alignment contained few cross-cutting cleavages to mitigate conflict.

Another important difference between the alignment in 1914 and a potential standoff between Heartland and Rimland powers today is the huge economic disparity between the two. The GDP of the three Rimland agglomerations today is about US$33 trillion (EU $13 trillion, the United

Figure 2: *Linkages among Great Powers, 1914*

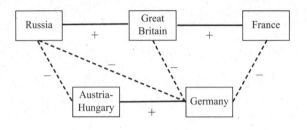

States $12 trillion, Japan $8 trillion), or more than half of Great Power GDP in world politics; in contrast, the combined GDP of Russia, China, and India, at best, equals that of Japan alone.[14] Under these circumstances, China and India, needing access to developed technology, would be attracted to associating themselves with the dominant economic complex of Rimland states, thereby reversing the balance of power. Power would begin to attract, bringing at least China and India into the dominant economic complex. Russia might be less tempted to do so because its abundant raw materials would provide a temporary sanctuary from the need to combine with other states.

Concerts Then and Now

The Concert of Europe that functioned from 1815 to 1848 was based on solidarity designed to prevent another great war like the Napoleonic Wars, which might lead to social and political revolution in the as-yet-unreformed states of Europe. War became tolerable once again (after 1854) only when it was proved that it could be both short and limited in its social effects. After the revolutions of 1848, conservatives in Austria, Russia, and Prussia also had to find means to ensure their positions domestically, and nationalism based on military success was one way of doing so.

Not all conservatives could hum this strain successfully, however, and only Bismarck succeeded with such a strategy—although Louis Napoleon

---

14. Britain, France, and Russia had no such dominance in 1914.

Figure 3: *Linkages among Great Powers, 1830–1848*

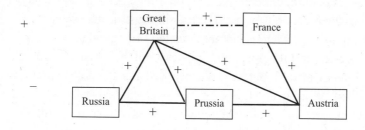

briefly benefited in France after the conservative *revanche* of 1849. But the key to Concert success before 1848 had been ideological agreement: Great Powers should not act militarily against each other but should use only proxies, and their machinations should not disrupt the fundamental repose of Europe. As Figure 3 shows, links between Britain and France, however ambivalent, did not prevent favorable ties with the rest of Europe. Britain prevailed in these alignments since its ties with the Three Eastern Courts were far stronger on territorial grounds than were those of France.

Britain and France had closer relations after the revolutions of 1830, raising the possibility of consolidating the Liberal Two against the Conservative Three. Both Russia and Britain, however, were still interested in restraining France. The Belgian Revolution in 1830, which brought independence from the Netherlands, raised important questions, as there was a chance Belgium might unite with France. Since neither Britain nor Russia would stand idly by as this happened, it was critical to confirm Belgium's independence and neutrality, free from Great Power influence. This was accomplished by 1833.

French policy also sought an outlet in the Middle East, where Napoleon had made some of his initial conquests. When Mehemet Ali, viceroy of Egypt, challenged the sultan of the Ottoman Empire, France supported Ali while the Russians and British supported the sultan. Ali's forces made some inroads in Syria, but this resulted only in a four-power ultimatum that closed the Bosporus and Dardanelles to foreign powers when the Ottoman Empire was at peace. British secretary of war Lord Palmerston then sent a fleet to interpose itself between Egypt and its temporary vassal, Syria. The French thought briefly that they could reverse this stand. But Palmerston rejoined that France would soon lose its ships, its colonies, and its commerce, and as for Mehemet Ali—he would be chucked into the Nile. Squadrons from Russia, Austria, and Britain arrived in the Levant, and Sir Charles Napier defeated the Egyptians in what was to become Lebanon. French prime minister Adolphe Thiers mouthed the threat of another war scare but was soon deposed and the more conservative François Guizot reinstated. All five Great Powers agreed to the final settlement of the Straits Convention. Mehemet Ali was sent back to rule Egypt during his lifetime and the sultan regained control of his dominions.

Britain and France, the Liberal Two, generally looked at things from a common ideological standpoint, but political influence often interposed to divide them. It did so in the Middle East and on the question of whom the Spanish queen would marry. France wanted one of its own, an *Orléanist*, while Britain offered a Coburg candidate the French opposed. The question was resolved when the queen married the duke of Cadiz, a vapid Bourbon whom neither the French nor the British liked but were willing to tolerate.

The secret of the Concert of Europe was not overweening ideological or territorial solidarity, but common opposition to those who would disrupt the peaceful settlement of Vienna. All European monarchs (and statesmen) distrusted one another, but they feared conflict even more. In each case, three or four cabinets agreed to prevent disruption by the Belgians, the Spanish, or Mehemet Ali, then the other holdouts came on board. Before 1848, at least, the Concert of Europe dared not risk another war between Great Powers, and would act to prevent one by disciplining any unruly party.

A concert of Great Powers in the twenty-first century would offer a number of similarities with the nineteenth-century Concert of Europe. Today, "terrorism" takes the place of "revolution" as the *bête-noire* of the Great Powers; so also does the further spread of nuclear weapons. In both cases, the Great powers are willing to act together to prevent them and deal with their consequences. In addition, there are positive elements to Great Power cooperation today that did not exist two centuries ago. As we have already seen, two things bring countries together: common goals that can be achieved only in tandem, and common opponents—states or movements—that can be opposed effectively only by cooperative action. Middle Eastern Islamism is a focus of worry and opposition among Great Powers today, including China. The possible spread of nuclear weapons occasions common attitudes and action against North Korea and Iran.

More positively, economic growth can be achieved only if each major power plays its part in the globalized economy. It is important that those countries that get out of balance should be allowed to find their feet and should enjoy the support of the system until they do. One speaks perhaps too much of the "primacy" of the United States. Clearly, however, non-hegemonic stabilizers—the EU, Japan, China—have assumed the role formerly played by the United States and have provided liquidity to countries in trouble, including the United States itself. Without the felicitous intervention of these new stabilizers—propping up the dollar and keeping US interest rates low—US economic growth would have ground to a halt. In David Lake's term, "supporters" have emerged to pre-empt the role of the hegemon. If China can prevent it, there will be no "hard landing" for the US economy, since China would also be grievously affected.

In addition, there are production linkages between major countries today that did not exist in 1914. Much of US production is "outsourced" to overseas nations and labor forces. The same is true for Europe and Japan. War between current concert members—even if it were somehow successful—would capture only the headquarters of key industrial combines; it would not necessarily aggrandize their producing units, which exist elsewhere. The rapid movement of factors of production from one geographic area to another mitigates any attempt to achieve a military monopoly of manufacturing. Capital moves faster than any army.

The effectuation of a new concert of powers would mean more than just reform of the UN Security Council. As Michael Lind (2006, 181) writes,

> Any attempt to institutionalize a concert of great powers in a formal organization like the UN Security Council is destined to fail. The world is too fluid. The relative power of particular countries is always changing, as a result of different rates of economic growth and population growth as well as changing political systems and foreign policies. If the great power concert is institutionalized, then fading great powers will cling to their institutional position while resisting the admission of new, rising great powers.... Even if the UN Charter were amended to admit new great powers as permanent members of the Security Council, the roster would probably be obsolete by the time the process of amendment

was complete. The unrealistic idea of a formal, institutionalized great power concert ought to be abandoned in favor of an informal consultative concert whose membership can change overtime.

In effect, the institutionalization of a Great Power concert takes place in different organizations. Each regional or functional club draws in the Big Five or Big Six in, say, Europe or the Far East in different ways—for example, in finance or political regulation. It is their participation in a variety of decisionmaking organizations that brings Great Powers together and that legitimizes and represents their common interests in a variety of international contexts. If a given roster does not solve problems effectively, new members (like India or China) are brought in to remedy the difficulty. It is their recognition of the need to have each other at the helm of international events that solidifies their rule.

This need to have all the Great Powers represented in international councils is similar to that which impelled the Concert of Europe's success. By bringing the erstwhile revolutionary France back into the system of states—by granting Paris a "voice" in the councils of the world—the Concert of Europe prevented French "exit" into revolutionary isolation. The welcome accorded France then is similar to current endeavors to welcome China into a new concert of "stakeholder" nations. In Paul Schroeder's words, the technique involved "not ... forming a blocking coalition against it but ... bringing the dangerous power within a restraining alliance or partnership" (1989, 145).

Conclusions

The international system is not easy to govern. There is a "democratic deficit" in political structures, in that all nations do not have an equal role in charting strategy for international institutions. But there is also a "democratic surplus," in that smaller and weaker nations are probably overrepresented in decision making. They have an influence in the UN Human Rights Commission and elsewhere that does not reflect their ability actually to accept or carry out decisions. They do not have the resources to be responsible guarantors and protectors of the international body politic. If terrorism and the spread of nuclear weapons are to be prevented, the Great

Powers will have to stop them. No one else can do so. The Great Powers, acting together, also have unparalleled legitimacy. They can act on behalf of regional constituencies in the Americas, Asia, Africa, and Europe. Their very agreement is testimony to the existence of a wider, interregional accord. In future, consensus among the Great Powers will be necessary not only to constitutionalize and limit the actions of the United States, but also to achieve common purposes for a larger agglomeration of the peoples of the world.

References

Abernathy, David. 2000. *The Dynamics of Global Dominance: European Overseas Empires, 1415–1980.* New Haven, CT: Yale University Press.

Arthur, W. Brian. 2000. "Myths and Realities of the High-Tech Economy." Presentation to Credit Suisse First Boston Thought Leader Forum, Santa Fe, NM, September 10.

Bhagwati, Jagdish. 2005. *In Defense of Globalization.* Oxford: Oxford University Press.

Brooks, Stephen. 2005. *Producing Security: Multinational Corporations, Globalization, and the Changing Calculus of Conflict.* Princeton, NJ: Princeton University Press.

Fox, Edward W. 1971. *History in Geographic Perspective: The Other France.* New York: W.W. Norton.

Garton Ash, Timothy. 2004. *Free World: America, Europe, and the Surprising Future of the West.* New York: Random House.

Gartzke, Erik. 2003. "The Classic Liberals Were Just Lucky." In *Economic Interdependence and International Conflict: New Perspectives on an Enduring Debate,* edited by Edward Mansfield and Brian Pollins. Ann Arbor, MI: University of Michigan Press.

Gordon, Michael R., and Bernard E. Trainor. 2006. *Cobra II: The Inside Story of the Invasion and Occupation of Iraq.* New York: Pantheon Books.

Hobsbawm, Eric. 1996. *The Age of Extremes: A History of the World, 1914–1991*. New York: Vintage Books.

Jones, Ronald W. 2000. *Globalization and the Theory of Input Trade*. Cambridge, MA: MIT Press.

Katzenstein, Peter. 2005. *A World of Regions: Asia and Europe in the American Imperium*. Ithaca, NY: Cornell University Press.

Kennedy, Paul. 2006. *The Parliament of Man: The Past, Present, and Future of the United Nations*. New York: Random House.

Keohane, Robert. 1984. *After Hegemony: Cooperation and Discord in the World Political Economy*. Princeton, NJ: Princeton University Press.

Lind, Michael. 2006. *The American Way of Strategy*. New York: Oxford University Press.

Miller, Steven E. 2006. "Mired in Mesopotamia? The Iraq War and U.S. Interests." In *No More States? Globalization, National Self-determination, and Terrorism*, edited by Richard N. Rosecrance and Arthur A. Stein. Boulder, CO: Rowman & Littlefield.

Overy, Richard. 1995. *Why the Allies Won*. New York: W.W. Norton.

Raiffa, Howard. 1982. *The Art and Science of Negotiation*. Cambridge, MA: Harvard University Press.

Ricks, Thomas E. 2006. *Fiasco: The American Military Adventure in Iraq*. New York: Penguin Press.

Rosecrance, Richard N., and Arthur A. Stein, eds. 2006. *No More States? Globalization, National Self-determination, and Terrorism*. Boulder, CO: Rowman & Littlefield.

Rosecrance, Richard, and Peter Thompson. 2003. "Trade, Foreign Investment, and Security." *Annual Review of Political Science* 6 (June): 377–98.

Schelling, Thomas C. 1978. *Micromotives and Macrobehavior*. New York: W.W. Norton.

Schroeder, Paul W. 1989. "The Nineteenth Century System: Balance of Power or Political Equilibrium?" *Review of International Studies* 15 (April): 135–53.

Spykman, Nicholas J. 1944. *The Geography of the Peace*. New York: Harcourt Brace.

Steil, Benn, and Robert E. Litan. 2006. *Financial Statecraft: The Role of Financial Markets in American Foreign Policy*. New Haven, CT: Yale University Press for the Council on Foreign Relations and the Brookings Institution.

Stein, Arthur A. 2003. "Trade and Conflict: Uncertainty, Strategic Signaling, and Interstate Disputes." In *Economic Interdependence and International Conflict: New Perspectives on an Enduring Debate*, edited by Edward Mansfield and Brian Pollins. Ann Arbor, MI: University of Michigan Press.

Walt, Stephen M. 1987. *The Origins of Alliances*. Ithaca, NY: Cornell University Press.

Woodward, Bob. 2006. *State of Denial: Bush at War, Part III*. New York: Simon & Schuster.

America and the Reform of Global Institutions

G. John Ikenberry

*   *   *

America is deeply ambivalent about international rules and institutions. In the decade after World War II, the United States was the leading architect and champion of global multilateral governance. It led the way in an unprecedented burst of global institution building—establishing the United Nations, the International Monetary Fund (IMF), the World Bank, the General Agreement on Tariffs and Trade (GATT), the North Atlantic Treaty Organization (NATO), and an array of other institutions and regimes. But the United States has also been deeply reluctant—today and at various moments in the past—to sponsor and participate in international agreements in areas as diverse as security, arms control, human rights, and the environment.

All sovereign states, to various degrees, are ambivalent about international rules and institutions. But the United States is the most powerful state in the world, so its ambivalence is unusually consequential for the functioning of the global system. Indeed, in recent years, America's reluctance ·

I gratefully acknowledge the helpful comments and suggestions of Alan Alexandroff and other members of the project. Andrew Moravcsik also provided valuable comments on an earlier draft.

to entangle itself in international rules and institutions seems to have grown, leading some observers to argue that, during the Bush years, the United States has essentially rejected its older postwar embrace of rules-based multilateral governance. Moreover, this new American resistance to such an approach is happening precisely when global multilateral institutions are weakening (see Ikenberry 2005b). Raising the stakes further, new sorts of global challenges are also emerging—such as climate change, contagious disease, and weapons proliferation—that call for added realms of institutionalized cooperation. So the "demand" for global rules and institutions is growing at the precise moment that the most powerful state in the system—and the previous underwriter of the multilateral governance system—is uncertain whether it is willing to help "supply" the needed rules and institutions.

This paper explores the logic and changing character of American foreign policy toward global rules and institutions. I try to make sense of US ambivalence toward rules-based international order. I also explore how shifts in the international system have altered the circumstances of and incentives for America's commitment to rules and institutions. Based on this analysis, I suggest ideas for a possible American agenda for strengthening multilateral governance.[1]

In the paper, I make four arguments. First, I outline a set of claims about why and how states use international rules and institutions; in doing so, I offer what might be called a "political control" explanation for institutions. In this view, rules and institutions are mechanisms that allow states to assert some control over their environment by rendering more predictable the policy actions of other states. In committing to operate within a framework of rules, a state agrees to circumscribe its policy autonomy or freedom of action—in various ways and to various degrees —so as to get other states to do the same. In other words, a state bargains away some of its policy autonomy to get other states to operate in more predictable and desirable ways, and the process is made credible through institutionalized agreements. The shifting incentives, choices, and circumstances

---

1. This paper builds on earlier essays, including Ikenberry (2003a, 2003b).

surrounding this "institutional bargain" help explain variations in state commitments to rules and institutions.[2]

Second, I argue that this same logic applies to powerful states, such as the United States. Indeed, a hegemonic state has a complex array of incentives—among others, to reduce its enforcement costs, to foster legitimacy, and to institutionalize a favorable international order for the long term—for using rules and institutions to shape its environment. But these incentives are not absolute: powerful states also have opportunities to shape their environment without making institutional or rules-based commitments. They can avoid and work around rules and institutions. They can act unilaterally outside institutionalized relationships or strike bilateral bargains directly with individual states. Critical to a hegemonic state's choice among these alternatives is the value it attaches to the efficiency and legitimacy of its "rule" over the international order—and its assessment of its future power position.

Third, I argue that long-term shifts in the global system have altered the incentives and circumstances that bear on America's hegemonic use of rules and institutions. The Bush administration has a specific ideological orientation and set of preferences toward multilateral institutions—which partly explains growing US reluctance in recent years to bind itself to global rules and institutions. But deeper forces are also altering the costs and choices the United States faces: the rise of unipolarity, the end of the Cold War, the erosion of norms of state sovereignty, and the shifting character of security threats are among the factors that are changing the logic of American hegemonic rule. Importantly, however, these changes cut both ways: the United States now has a more complex set of incentives and choices, and the types and mix of rules and institutions in the global system will have to be adjusted accordingly.

Finally, I argue that, if America does pursue a "renewal strategy" for international rules and institutions, it will need to accommodate itself to

---

2. In this view of state power and multilateralism, states do not seek multilateral agreements for idealist reasons. States are instrumental multilateralists. This is what Robert Kagan (2002) has called American-style multilateralism: "multilateralism is a cost-benefit analysis, not a principled commitment to multilateral action as the cornerstone of world order."

these new realities. Informal, bilateral, and domestic-centered governance arrangements will grow in importance—even as older-style multilateral government remains important in some realms.

I conclude the paper by identifying the most promising ways for the United States to make international commitments. These include:

- renegotiating the security alliance bargains;
- working through the "community of democracies";
- expanding informal and network-based cooperation among democracies and within a "community of democracies";
- building on the framework of the World Trade Organization (WTO); and
- recovering and updating America's public philosophy of liberal internationalism.

The critical question—the answer to which is still unknown—is whether the costs to American legitimacy and the erosion of institutionalized cooperation around which the United States asserts its hegemonic leadership are sufficiently advanced and costly to prompt the United States to return to more traditional rule and institution-based strategies.

States and International Rules and Institutions

Why do states—to the extent they do so—organize international relations around multilateral rules and institutions? The answer is that institutional agreements help states create a predictable and cost-effective environment in which to pursue their interests.

More specifically, international institutions are potentially useful to states in several ways. One is highlighted by neoliberal institutional theory —namely, that they help solve collective action problems by reducing the commitment uncertainties and transaction costs that stand in the way of efficient and mutually beneficial political exchange.[3] But institutions can also be seen as instruments of "political control." As Terry Moe (1990, 213) argues, "political institutions are also weapons of coercion and redistribution.

---

3. The paradigmatic statement of this functional view of institutions is Keohane (1984).

They are the structural means by which political winners pursue their own interests, often at the expense of political losers." A winning political party in Congress will try to write the committee voting rules to favor its interests. Similarly, in international relations, a powerful state will want to make its advantages as systematic and durable as possible by roping weaker states into favorable institutional arrangements.[4]

When a state makes an institutional commitment, it is agreeing to reduce its policy autonomy. Ideally, a state might want to remain unencumbered by international rules and institutional commitments, while operating in a global system in which all other states are bound to rules and institutions. But in order to get other states to make institutional commitments, states need to negotiate and offer restrictions on their own policies so as to achieve agreement.[5]

Thus, when deciding whether to sign a multilateral agreement, a state faces a tradeoff. In agreeing to abide by the rules and norms of the agreement, the state must accept some constraints on its freedom of action—or independence of policy making—in a particular area. In exchange, however, it expects other states to do the same. The multilateral bargain will be attractive to a state if it concludes that the benefits that flow to it through the coordination of policies achieved through rules-based

---

4. The notion that institutions can be used by states as mechanisms of political control starts with the neo-institutional view of the causal mechanisms at work. That is, institutions shape and constrain state behavior by providing value in terms of commitment and reduction of uncertainty or transaction costs. Political control is exerted through the manipulation of these causal mechanisms which alter the distribution of gains from institutional agreement.

5. The classic statement of the strategic use of commitment is Thomas Schelling (1960). Schelling (2006, vii) has recently restated the basic insight:

> Commitment is central to promises and threats, to bargaining and negotiations, to deterrence and arms control, to contractual relations. I emphasize the paradox of commitment—to a relationship, to a promise or a threat, to a negotiating position—entails relinquishing some options, giving up choices, surrendering opportunities, binding oneself. And it works through shifting the expectations of some partner or adversary or even a stranger of how one will behave or react.

constraints on policy choice are greater than the costs of its lost policy autonomy.

A state's willingness to agree to a multilateral bargain hinges on several factors that shape the ultimate cost-benefit calculation. One is whether the policy constraints imposed on other states (states B, C, D) by the multilateral agreement really matter to the first state (state A). If the "unconstrained" behavior of other states is judged to have no undesirable impact on state A, state A will be unwilling to give up any policy autonomy of its own. It also matters if the participating states are actually able to restrict their policy autonomy credibly. If state A is unconvinced that states B, C, and D can be constrained by multilateral rules and institutional agreements, it will not be willing to sacrifice its own policy autonomy. Likewise, state A needs to convince the other states that it too will be constrained. These factors are all continuous rather than dichotomous variables—so states must make judgments about the degree of credibility and relative value of constrained policies.

When states with highly unequal power make multilateral bargains, the considerations can be more complex. The more a powerful state is able to dominate or abandon weaker states, the more the weaker states will care about constraints on the leading state's policy autonomy. This is another way of saying that they will be more eager to see some limits and restraints placed on the arbitrary and indiscriminate exercise of power by the leading state. Similarly, the more the powerful state can actually restrain itself in a credible fashion, the more the weaker states will be interested in multilateral rules and norms that accomplish this end. When both these conditions hold—when the leading state can use its unequal power to dominate and abandon and when it can restrain and commit itself—the weaker states will be particularly eager for a deal. They will, of course, also care about the positive benefits that accrue from cooperation. From the perspective of the powerful state, the less important the policy behavior of weaker states the less the leading state will offer to limit its own policy autonomy. Likewise, the less certain the leading state is that weaker states can, in fact, constrain their policies, the less the leading state will offer constraints on its policy autonomy.

These considerations are helpful in understanding America's embrace of multilateral institution building after World War II. The United States emerged as the pre-eminent global power after the war. It cared greatly about the fate of western Europe and East Asia, both of which hung in the economic and geopolitical balance. It was willing to tie itself to these countries through various sorts of institutional agreements—to give up policy autonomy—to gain some leverage on their policy orientation and trajectory of political development. At the same time, these countries worried about American domination and abandonment, so they, too, were willing to enter into institutional agreements that entailed long-term commitments to an American-led international order. The credibility of these institutional commitments was facilitated by the democratic character of the states themselves as well as by other more specific steps, such as the stationing of American troops in both regions and the developing of complex sorts of institutional agreements.[6]

The logic is also helpful in explaining variations in America's institutional commitments to western Europe and East Asia. In the former, the United States pursued a multilateral strategy—with NATO as its anchor; in the latter, it pursued a series of bilateral security agreements with Japan, South Korea, and other southeast Asian states. In effect, the United States tied itself more tightly to Europe, embedding its power in a multilateral security order that involved extensive institutionalized restraints and commitments. In East Asia, however, the United States was not only more dominant than in Europe; it also wanted less out of the region. Thus, as a practical matter, in East Asia it was less necessary for the United States to give up policy autonomy in exchange for institutionalized cooperation. In western Europe, in contrast, the United States had an elaborate agenda for uniting the various states, creating an institutional bulwark against communism, and supporting centrist democratic regimes. These goals could not be realized simply through the brute exercise of power; to get what it wanted, America had to bargain with the Europeans, and this meant agreeing to restrain its exercise of power. In Asia, the United States did not have goals that were sufficiently important to "purchase" with an agreement to restrain its power. Bilateralism was the desired strategy because multilateralism

---

6. Two US moves, in particular, made a difference: it made asymmetrical short-term deals with other countries through, for example, the Marshall Plan and trade liberalization, and it entered into strong institutional commitments.

would have required more restraints on policy autonomy.[7] Put differently, the United States had much more unchallenged hegemonic power in Asia than in western Europe and, therefore, fewer incentives to secure its dominant position with international institutions.

Hegemony and Rules-Based Order

Why would hegemonic states—to the extent they do so—want to build international order around multilateral rules and institutions? When a state is sufficiently powerful to shape the organization of international relations, rules and institutions can serve quite useful purposes, becoming tools for managing international hierarchy. Again, however, costs, benefits, and trade-offs infuse the hegemon's calculations.

Rules and institutions can be useful to hegemonic states in three ways. First, they can reduce the costs of enforcement of hegemonic rule.[8] If a hegemon can get other states to buy into a set or rules and institutions, it does not need to spend its resources coercing other states into following them. The hegemonic state is, by definition, powerful, so it can engage in power struggles with subordinate states, most of which it is likely to win—it can dominate without the use of rules and institutions. In getting other states to operate within a system of rules and institutions, however, the hegemon reduces the time and energy it must expend to enforce order

---

7. Bilateral treaties tend to be easier for dominant states to translate their power into favorable agreements than multilateral treaties. Nico Krisch (2005, 390) explains:

    Bilateral negotiations are far more likely to be influenced by the superior power of one party than are multilateral negotiations, in which other states can unite and counterbalance the dominant party—*divide et impera*, as reflected in the forms of international law. The bilateral form is also more receptive to exceptional rules for powerful states. In multilateral instruments, especially *traités-lois*, exceptions for powerful parties are always suspicious and in need of justification, as manifest in, for example, the Nuclear Non-proliferation Treaty and the failed attempts of the US with respect to the ICC Statute....Bilateral treaties are thus a much easier tool to reflect and translate dominance than multilateral ones.

8. This insight is developed in Coasian regime theory; see Keohane (1984).

118 | G. John Ikenberry

and to get other states to do what it wants. By locking subordinate states into a rules-based order, it reduces its costs of enforcement (see Ikenberry and Kupchan 1990; Lake and Martin 1992; and Martin 1993).

Second, by agreeing to lead and operate within a rules-based international order, the hegemonic state enhances its legitimacy. In effect, it signals restraint and commitment—and this helps to strengthen the legitimacy of the hegemonic order. The assumption is simple: the more the hegemonic order has multilateral rules-based characteristics, the more likely other states in the global system will seek to join or cooperate with the leading state and to see the operation of the hegemonic order as legitimate in some fundamental sense. The more the hegemonic order has "imperial" characteristics—ruled by the leading state through the direct and coercive use of power—the less the order will be seen as legitimate.[9]

Third, if the system of institutional agreements has some degree of stickiness—that is, if it has some independent ordering capacity—the institutions might continue to provide favorable outcomes for the leading state even after its power capacities have declined in relative terms (see Krasner 1983; Keohane 1984). Institutions can both conserve and prolong the power advantages of the leading state. If leaders of a hegemonic state believe that their pre-eminent power position will last indefinitely—or even grow—the attraction of establishing an institutionalized order that will outlast the state's hegemonic zenith is less compelling. To the extent that the leaders see relative decline coming, however, incentives exist for building an institutionalized order with deep roots.[10]

---

9. Legitimacy refers to the normative quality of a political relationship. Legitimacy can be said to exist when actors—regardless of the underlying conditions of the relationship—see the terms of the relationship as normatively acceptable. The assumption, however, is that the normative acceptance of the terms of a relationship is related to the actual terms of the relationship. In this instance, the rules and institutions are assumed to have some actual impact on the way in which the superordinate and subordinate actors in the hegemonic relationship relate to each other—that is, it reduces the imperial characteristics of rule. Ultimately, however, legitimacy hinges on what states believe about the political relationship. For a discussion of the sources and character of legitimacy within international orders, see Clark (2005).
10. The logic of this argument is developed in Ikenberry (2001, chap 3).

But why would weaker states agree to be roped in? After all, they might calculate that it would be better to not lock themselves into an institutional agreement at a certain moment but wait until the power asymmetries did not favor the leading state as much. In fact, weaker states have two potential incentives to buy into the leading state's institutional agreement. First, in a noninstitutionalized relationship, lesser states are subject to the unrestrained and unpredictable domination of the leading state, so an agreement that also puts credible limits and restraints on the leading state's behavior would be welcome.

Second, a leading state that agrees to its behavior being circumscribed gives up some opportunities to use its power to gain immediate returns. In other words, with an eye toward longer-term gains, the leading state settles for fewer gains by operating within institutional rules and obligations than it could otherwise achieve with its brute power. But weaker states might also have reason to gain more sooner rather than later: the discount rate for future gains is potentially different for the leading and lesser states, which makes an institutional bargain potentially more mutually desirable. So the leading state is faced with a choice: how much institutional limitation on its own policy autonomy and exercise power is worth how much policy lock-in on the part of weaker states?

Several observations follow immediately from this discussion, all of which involve the "accommodation" of rules and institutions to the realities of state power. First, a hegemonic state will try to lock other states into institutionalized policy orientations while trying to minimize its own limitations on policy autonomy and discretionary power. This, of course, is the game that all states are playing. All states would like to be relatively unencumbered by rules and institutions, while operating in a global system where other states are tightly bound. So it would not be surprising to see the hegemonic state simultaneously agreeing to the creation of a set of institutionalized rules and seeking to exempt itself or minimize its own exposure to those rules.

Second, the hegemonic state will also attempt to make institutional commitments that grant it disproportionate influence or decisionmaking power. This is a basic characteristic of all the major postwar multilateral institutions the United States has championed. The IMF and World Bank give the United States and the other leading shareholder states weighted voting rights in their operation and governance. America's commitment to NATO carries with it the power of supreme command over the combined alliance forces—and within the organization, the United States is "first among equals." The United Nations Security Council also gives the United States and the other postwar great powers rights of membership and veto. In these various ways, the multilateral institutions specify rights and circumscribe obligations of the hegemon—thereby ensuring that the rules and institutions reflect, as much as constrain, hegemonic power.

Third, the hegemonic state can vary the "strength" of its commitments to rules and institutions. These different types or degrees of commitment run along a continuum from strong to weak in terms of their legally binding character. Strong commitments are manifest when the hegemon agrees to adhere to specific and explicit substantive rules or policy obligations. Weaker commitments take the form of less specific rules or policies, in which monitoring, compliance, and enforcement is less certain.[11]

Fourth, the hegemonic state can also offer "process" commitments rather than, or in addition to, substantive rules-based commitments. For example, the hegemon can agree to formal processes of multilateral consultation. In these instances, it is not, strictly speaking, giving up or reducing its policy autonomy, but it is agreeing to operate in an institutional environment in which other states have opportunities to influence what the hegemon does. The United States has made this a feature of its approach to hegemonic rule. Through NATO and other formal and informal arrangements, the United States offers "voice opportunities" to other states in exchange for their cooperation and acquiescence (see Ikenberry 2001, chap 3).

Finally, there are other ways—that, is, non–rules-based multilateral ways—in which a hegemonic state can make bargains with weaker and secondary states and thereby establish agreement over terms of international order. It can use its military capacity to deter or overturn security threats outside multilateral alliances. It can support the openness and stability of the world economy through unilateral measures, by opening its own market or coming to the rescue of other states. The hegemon can also

---

11. On institutionalized monitoring and enforcement as measures of regime strength, see Keohane (1984); Goldstein et al. (2001).

use the size of its economy—and the dependence of other states on it—to influence the policies of other states, through, for example, externalizing its own internal regulatory standards or sanctioning third parties who do not pursue similar policies toward target states.[12]

Importantly, the hegemonic state can also offer "services" to specific states through bilateral deals. As noted earlier, it is easier for powerful states to translate their dominance into bilateral than into multilateral treaties or agreements since the hegemonic state's bargaining advantages in bilateral negotiations are at least partially attenuated when it moves into multilateral venues. In such cases, the hegemon is able to use its power capacities to shape the character and functioning of the international order, and to do so without making binding multilateral institutional commitments.

In all these ways, the hegemon is confronted with cross-cutting incentives. Powerful incentives exist—efficiency, legitimacy, investment in future advantages—for a hegemonic state to establish and operate within a system of rules and institutions. Such a system can project and preserve hegemonic power as much as limit and reduce it. But the hegemonic state also has incentives—as do other states—to protect its policy autonomy and freedom of action. The specific incentives, tradeoffs, and choices shape the extent to which the hegemon makes commitments and binds itself to other states through rules and institutions—driven by attempts to get the benefits of multilateralism while minimizing the costs.

This perspective on hegemonic rule, however, leaves open the question of the value a hegemonic state attaches to the legitimacy of the overall global system. The model of state power and multilateralism presented here emphasizes the pragmatic or instrumental character of state choice. The implication is that a hegemonic state can pick and choose whether or not to act through multilateral rules and institutions. Each case is a matter of cost and benefit. At each moment of choice, this is probably true—but does the overall legitimacy of the hegemonic order decline if the leading state is selectively multilateral or only episodically multilateral? And what are the costs to the hegemon—in terms of cooperation and efficiency of

---

12. See Krisch (2005) for a discussion of the ways that a hegemon uses its domestic law as a tool for reshaping and introducing hierarchical characteristics into international legal arrangements.

rule—if the overall system declines in legitimacy? These are questions I return to in discussing the future of America's current ambivalence about rules and institutions.

Unipolarity and the Future of Multilateralism

How have shifts in the global system over the past decade, particularly the rise of unipolarity, altered the incentives, costs, and tradeoffs of America's acting through multilateral rules and institutions?

Two types of shifts are most relevant to the willingness of the United States to embrace rules-based multilateral agreements. One relates to the shifts in power disparities themselves, captured in the movement from Cold War bipolarity to American unipolarity. The other relates to the wider set of changes in the global system: unipolarity, the erosion of norms of state sovereignty, and the emergence of new security threats. As a result, American power itself has become a greater "problem" in world politics. The character of "rule" within the international system is being altered and American power is becoming harder to legitimate.

These contemporary shifts in the global system are tending to alter and to some extent erode the older postwar incentives that led the United States to build hegemonic order around rules and institutions. Old institutional bargains are being undermined or rendered out of date. Yet, these shifts are also creating new problems and dilemmas for the United States—in particular, a crisis in its authority as global leader—that are providing incentives for the establishment of new rules and institutions. Costs, incentives, and opportunities change, but the demand for rules and institutions does not disappear.

We can begin with unipolarity and its implications for multilateralism. Unipolarity happened almost without notice during the 1990s. The United States began that decade as the world's only superpower, and it had a better decade than the other major states. It grew faster than inward-looking Europe, while Japan stagnated and Russia collapsed. China has grown rapidly in recent years, but remains a developing country. America accounts for almost half of global expenditures on defense. No state in history has ever been more powerful and the international system has never been so dominated by one state. Interestingly, the United States did not fight a Great

Power war to become the unipolar state or overturn the old international order; it simply grew more powerful while other states sputtered or failed. This peaceful ascent to unipolarity probably has made the transition less destabilizing.[13]

First and foremost, the shift from Cold War bipolarity to unipolarity involved a shift in the power relations between the United States and other states. This shift has tended to increase the power advantages for the leading state, for a variety of reasons. First, the unipolar state has more discretionary resources because it no longer has a security peer competitor. Second, fewer external restraints exist on its exercise of power because it is not being balanced by other states. Third, weaker and secondary states no longer have an "exit" option—that is, the unipolar state has a near-monopoly on the global provision of security protection. Fourth, the unipolar state now has a more encompassing impact on the global system. Overall, if there is to be order and the provision of international public goods, the unipolar state needs to be involved in providing them. It is harder to "work around" the unipolar state than states in bipolar or multi-polar orders. Instead, other states must worry about whether or not the unipolar state provides public goods and exercises its power in ways that promote stability. These factors give the unipolar state added leverage in bargaining over global rules and institutions; at the very least, they help to explain why the unipolar state might seek to renegotiate older rules and institutions.[14]

But unipolarity also reduces some of the power advantages that the leading state had under conditions of Cold War bipolarity. First, weaker and secondary states are no longer threatened by a rival global power, so their need for security has declined, along with their security dependence on the unipolar state. To some extent, this has reduced the bargaining

---

13. On the measurement and character of unipolarity, see Wohlforth (1999); for general discussions of unipolarity and its consequences, see Kapstein and Mastanduno (1999) and Ikenberry (2002).
14. Obviously, the character and degree of American unipolar dominance varies across realms. The United States has overwhelming advantages in military power but its economic capacities are more widely distributed—indeed, in many economic respects, Europe is the equal of America.

advantage of the security-providing leading state. Second and more generally, the legitimacy of the leading state is less self-evident. In the eyes of weaker and secondary states, the leading state's exercise of power is not automatically seen as right or proper. Junior partners in a bipolar coalition see the leading state as a security patron and provider of order. In a unipolar order, the power of the leading state is less obviously good for the other states within the order.

We can capture these implications by looking at how the growing power of the leading state—the unipolar state—is altering the older institutional bargains. If power disparities grow too large, the leading state's interest in regulating the policies of weaker states through agreed-on rules and institutions might become more problematic. The unipolar state will have a lot of "bargaining chips" to play—that is, opportunities to offer restrictions on its policy autonomy in return for institutional agreements by other states—but it might not want to play them. It might not care as much about what other states do—that is, the attainment of the leading state's interests simply might not hinge as much as before on the policies of weaker and secondary states. Or the leading state can assert its influence and control over the policies of lesser states without resort to costly commitments to rules and institutions.

The shift to unipolarity has five important implications, in particular, for rules-based multilateralism. First, increased power advantages create opportunities for the leading state to recoup its policy autonomy. As power disparities grow, the leading state's security simply hinges less on the policies of other states. It can—or thinks it can—control its own destiny, so its willingness to pay the price of reduced policy autonomy goes down. For example, as the United States becomes the only state with a world-class military capability, it has fewer incentives to tie itself to and share decision making with alliance partners. Indeed, the disparities in their military capabilities have contributed to the loosening of binding security ties among America's postwar security parts.

Second, unipolarity creates incentives for weaker and secondary states to engage in "free riding," which undercuts multilateralism. If leaders of weaker and secondary states know that the unipolar state has incentives—based simply on its own preponderant position in the global system—to attend to security threats and to ensure the stability of the world economy, they in turn have incentives to free ride. The leading state will provide the public goods—security, stability, openness—with or without the help of other states. This has the effect of reducing the willingness of weaker and secondary states to agree to rules and institutions whereby they must share the costs and burdens of the provision of such public goods. (Indeed, for some state leaders, the optimal position might be simultaneously to consume the public good the unipolar state provides and to complain about the unipolar state's unilateral and highhanded behavior!)

Third, the erosion of common threats—associated with the shift from bipolar to unipolar order—alters the cost-benefit calculations on security cooperation, creating incentives for the leading state to pursue bilateral deals. Multilateral security cooperation seems to require some sense of a common threat[15]—as noted earlier, secondary and weaker states might not share the leading state's assessment of external threats. The effect is that each side of the old alliance partnership finds that it needs the other side less than before. For example, European states do not feel as dependent on the United States for security protection as they did in the past, and the United States is less reliant on an alliance partnership with Europe for its security protection. This has the effect of reducing both sides' incentive for making costly commitments to rules and institutions relating to security cooperation. It might also have some spillover effect on institutional bargaining in other areas, creating ambiguities and disagreements about who is providing what benefit to the system.[16]

Fourth, the unique global position the unipolar state occupies leads it to demand special status and exemptions from multilateral rules and institutions. For example, the United States cannot be party to the anti-land mine convention because its troops are uniquely deployed in harm's way—along the Korean demilitarized zone, for example. The United States also argues that it cannot sign the International Criminal Court treaty

---

15. At the very least, agreement on the presence of a common threat facilitates multilateral security cooperation.
16. For example, the United States thinks it is providing security and stability for Europe, in a general sense, by its global military role. Europeans are less willing to acknowledge this benefit. During the Cold War, costs and benefits were more readily apparent, facilitating institutional agreements.

because its global security presence makes Americans unusually vulnerable to politically inspired prosecutions. Thus, in a unipolar system, the leading state demands to be treated differently, which reduces its willingness to operate within multilateral rules and institutions.

Fifth, unipolarity creates more opportunities for the leading state to influence or control the policies of other states without committing itself to multilateral rules and institutions. The leading state's preponderance of power creates opportunities for it to push off "adjustment" onto other states. For example, when the United States sets its own domestic regulatory standards in some areas, it puts pressure on other countries and regions to adopt similar standards—it does not need to compromise its policy autonomy to get agreement from other states. Likewise, the United States can use its "market power" to influence or control the policies of others states—as, for example, when it imposes third-party sanctions on countries that do not adopt policies similar to those of the United States toward a target state.[17]

Taken together, power shifts create incentives to renegotiate institutional bargains—which does not necessarily reduce incentives for rules-based order, but only the specific equilibrium point of the institutional bargains that lay behind them. What can look like growing unilateralism on the part of the United States can also be seen as an attempt to forge a new set of multilateral agreements.

Along with the rise of unipolarity, a second profound shift is altering the way in which "rules" are established in the international system and making American power more contested and less legitimate: the erosion of the norm of Westphalian, state-centered sovereignty that was marked by the rising acceptance of international intervention in the internal affairs of states. In turn, this shift is providing powerful incentives for the United States to use rules and institutions to re-establish its authority as a hegemonic leader.

These shifts in the underlying character of the international system make American power—regardless of Washington's specific foreign policies

---

17. An example is the *Nonproliferation Act of 2000*, which outlines sanctions against countries and firms that supply weapons technology to Iran; in 2005, the act was expanded to include Syria.

—more worrisome to other states than in the past (see Ikenberry 2006). We have already explored the specific implications of unipolarity for multilateralism. But another, more subtle and potentially most consequential implication of the rise of unipolarity is the shift in the underlying logic of order and rule in world politics. In a bipolar or multipolar system, powerful states "rule" in the process of leading a coalition of states in balancing against other states. When the system shifts to unipolarity, this logic of rule disappears. Power is no longer based on balancing and equilibrium but on the predominance of one state. This is new and potentially threatening to weaker states, whether or not they are friendly to the leading power. As a result, the power of the leading state is thrown into the full light of day: unipolar power itself becomes a "problem" in world politics.

The erosion of norms of state sovereignty makes this problem worse. The gradual decline of Westphalian sovereignty is seen in the triumph of the postwar human rights revolution, an accomplishment we celebrate whenever we recall the Universal Declaration of Human Rights. The implication is that the "international community" increasingly is seen to have legitimate and expanding interests in what goes on within countries. In recent years, the threat of transnational terrorism has opened up states even more to outside scrutiny. Sovereignty is increasingly contingent, which has had two implications.

First, eroded norms of sovereignty have created a new "license" for powerful states to intervene in the domestic affairs of weak and troubled states. That is, the norms of state sovereignty have less "stopping power," and there are fewer principled and normative inhibitions on intervention. Second, however, the erosion of sovereignty has not been matched by a rise of new norms and agreements about when and how the "international community" should intervene. After all, who speaks for the international community?

This erosion of the norms of state sovereignty has ushered in a new struggle over the sources of authority in the international community, a struggle that, in turn, has been exacerbated by the rise of American unipolarity. After all, only the United States has the military power to engage systematically in the large-scale use of force around the world. Indeed, the two developments reinforce worldwide insecurity about American power: the United States is the only global political-military power, and the revolutions in human rights and transnational terrorism call forth new reasons why intervention—in the name of the international community or global security or hegemonic management—might be necessary.

Finally, the end of the Cold War eliminated a common threat that tied the United States to a global array of allies. In the absence of that threat, neither the United States nor its Cold War allies need each other as much as in the past. As a result, American power is less clearly tied to a common purpose, making that power less intrinsically legitimate or desirable in to other states and peoples.

These deep, long-term shifts in the global system have, in effect, made American power itself an issue and thrown into question the legitimacy of American hegemonic rule. This predicament brings us back to the changing costs and incentives that the United States might face as it makes choices about sponsoring and operating within multilateral rules and institutions. One implication is that other states now worry more about the credibility of the leading state's restraint and commitment, so they demand stronger and more binding institutional agreements. If these "costs" of lost legitimacy are sufficiently great, the desirability of organizing hegemony around rules and institutions might actually increase. In effect, the United States might find incentives to return to the logic it embraced in the earlier, postwar era—finding instrumental value in organizing international relations around multilateral rules and institutions in an effort, as before, to create efficiencies and reduce enforcement costs, legitimate its power, and lock in desirable rules and institutions for the long term.

The question, however, remains: how costly is lost American legitimacy and the associated decline in cooperation by other states? The answer is important, since the more costly it is, the greater the likelihood that the United States will embrace rules-based order even when it has the power and short-term incentives to act otherwise.

America and Global Institutions in the Twenty-first Century

If American leaders see the need to strengthen global rules and institutions and renew commitments to rules-based order, what steps would be most promising? A renewal agenda for global multilateral governance could include five types of initiatives.

Rebuild America's Alliances

One key initiative would be to update the old bargains that lay behind the postwar security pacts. In NATO—but also in the East Asian bilateral partnerships—the United States should agree to provide security protection to the other states and bring its partners into the process of decision making over the use of force. In return, these partners should agree to work with the United States—providing manpower, logistics, and other types of support—in wider theaters of action. The United States would give up some autonomy in strategic decision making, although this would be more an informal than a legally binding restraint; in exchange, it would get cooperation and political support from its allies. The United States would remain "first among equals" within these organizations and retain leadership of the unified military command. Alliance partners should agree to widen the regional or global missions in which they operate, and make new compromises over the distribution of formal rights and responsibilities.[18]

There are several reasons to begin with the renewal of security partnerships. One is that security alliances involve relatively well-defined, specific, and limited commitments, an attractive feature for both the leading military power and its partners. States know what they are getting into and what the limits are on their obligations and liabilities. Another reason is that alliances provide institutional mechanisms that allow disparities of power among partners within the alliance to be accommodated. Alliances do not embody universal rules and norms that apply equally to all parties—NATO, at least, is a multilateral body with formal and informal rules and norms of operation that accommodate the most powerful state while providing roles and rights for the others. Another virtue of renewing

---

18. The case for the renewal of NATO is made in Ikenberry and Slaughter (2006).

existing alliances is that, as institutional bodies, they have proved useful as "political architecture" across the advanced democratic world. The alliances provide channels of communication and joint decision making that spill over into the wider realms of international relations. They are also institutions with grand histories and records of accomplishment. Even though the United States is a unipolar military power, it still has incentives to share the costs of security protection and find ways to legitimate the use of its power. The postwar alliances—renewed and reorganized—are an attractive tool for these purposes.

Robert Kagan argues that, to regain its lost legitimacy, the United States needs to return to its postwar bargain with Europe by giving it some voice in American policy making in exchange for Europe's support of American decisions. The United States, Kagan says, "should try to fulfill its part of the transatlantic bargain by granting European some influence over the exercise of its power—provided that, in return, Europeans wield that influence wisely" (2004, 84). This is the logic that informed American security cooperation with its European and East Asian partners during the Cold War. It is a logic that should be renewed to help make American unipolarity more acceptable.

Strengthen the "Community of Democracies"

A second initiative would be to build agreements and commitments within the "community of democracies." The experience of the past century suggests that, for both practical and normative reasons, the United States is more likely to make institutional commitments to states that are democracies. Liberal democracies are governed by the rule of law and are open to scrutiny, so it is easier to establish the credibility of their promises and to develop long-term commitments to them (see Lipson 2005). But the values and identities that democracies share also make it easier for them to affiliate with each other and build cooperative relations among them. These shared identities were probably more strongly felt during the Cold War, when the United States was part of a larger "free world." Institutionalized cooperation between the United States and its European and East Asian partners is surely driven by shared interests—but it is reinforced by shared values and common principles of government. American leaders find it easier to rally domestic support for costly commitments and agreements abroad when the goal is to help other democracies and strengthen the community of democracies.[19]

In fact, in the last years of the Clinton administration, the United States led in the creation of a loose international gathering called the Community of Democracies, a group that continues to meet periodically at the ministerial level to support cooperative efforts at spreading and strengthening democracy around the world. This body and other gatherings of democracies are useful vehicles for infusing commitments to global governance institutions with the popular goal of democratic solidarity. When democracies make commitments to other democracies, they are not simply reducing policy autonomy; they are also strengthening the democratic community. These groupings of democracies can also be used within established international organizations, such as the United Nations, as coalitions that can help generate consensus and action.

Build on the WTO Framework

The World Trade Organization is probably the most successful global multilateral institution, certainly if measured in terms of the scope, depth, and growing global embrace of its rules and norms. Its trade rules—substantive and procedural—have been progressively expanded over the

---

19. Proposals exist for various types of groupings of democracies, some informal and consultative and others more formal and task oriented. For a proposal to create a "Concert of Democracies," see Ikenberry and Slaughter (2006). Ivo Daalder and James Lindsey (2004, B07) urge the creation of an "alliance of democracies" that would, to some extent, replace the United Nations as the source of cooperation and legitimacy for global security:

> Like NATO during the Cold War, the Alliance of Democratic States should become the focal point of American foreign policy. Unlike NATO, however, the alliance would not be formed to counter any country or be confined to a single region. Rather, its purpose would be to strengthen international cooperation to combat terrorism, curtail weapons proliferation, cure infectious diseases and curb global warming. And it would work vigorously to advance the values that its members see as fundamental to their security and well-being—democratic government, respect for human rights, a market-based economy.

decades, building on the postwar GATT agreement. States, including China and Russia, see membership in the WTO as critical to their economic development. The interests that states have in a global framework of trade rules and dispute settlement mechanisms are well established. This makes sense: as economic interdependence grows, the opportunity costs of not coordinating policies, within rules-based frameworks, grow relative to the costs of lost autonomy associated with making binding agreements. Shifts in power—and the rise of unipolarity—do not seem to have affected the incentives both powerful and weak states have in operating within the rules and institutions of the WTO system.

It follows that a strategy for renewal of global institutions should involve, at the very least, a commitment to maintain and build on the agreements and architecture of the WTO. This would certainly involve concluding the current Doha round of trade liberalization, which seeks to expand market opportunities for developing countries. Over the longer term, the WTO system might also be used to address wider global challenges. Robert Wright, for example, suggests making WTO membership and benefits conditional on the willingness of states to comply with arms control and nonproliferation monitoring and inspection agreements (Wright 2005). The idea would be to turn the WTO gradually into a body that conditions membership—and the benefits that flow from membership—on state commitments to openness, transparency, and the rule of law. These principles and standards certainly apply to trade, but they are also increasingly critical to the functioning of arms control and nonproliferation regimes in an era when the internal characteristics of states increasingly matter in security affairs.

Encourage Flexible Intergovernmental Networks of Cooperation

A great deal of regularized cooperation occurs in international relations outside formal organizations. Indeed, in recent decades, there has been a rapid expansion of informal intergovernmental networks. These networks link ministries and other governmental agencies in webs of consultation, information sharing, and policy coordination (see Slaughter 2004). These informal networks have several advantages over traditional formal multilateral organizations. They are more flexible and adaptable to shifting problems. They can form and reform, expand and contract, based on the needs of the moment. Beyond these functional advantages, intergovernmental networks can operate below the political "radar screen." They do not force governments to make hard decisions about how much policy autonomy to give up in exchange for how much policy cooperation from other states.

Traditional multilateral institutions have some advantages over informal intergovernmental networks. These formal institutions—and their official representatives—tend to be more accountable. Also, agreements rendered within these formal international institutions typically require ratification by parliamentary bodies, which helps to make the agreements more credible and durable. In various policy areas, however, these advantages might need to be traded off for the flexibility and practicality of networks.

Reclaim a Liberal Internationalist "Public Philosophy"

When, after World War II, American officials championed the building of a rules-based order, they articulated a distinctive internationalist vision of order that has faded in recent decades. It was a vision that entailed a synthesis of liberal and realist ideas about economic and national security and the sources of stable and peaceful order. These ideas—drawn from the experiences of the New Deal and two decades of depression and war—led American leaders to associate the national interest with the building of a managed and institutionalized global system. What is needed today is a renewed public philosophy of liberal internationalism that can inform American elites as they make tradeoffs between sovereignty and institutional cooperation (see Ikenberry 2005a).

The interwar years and the New Deal had a variety of impacts on American internationalism. The first was the importance newly attached to economics as such. Indeed, Truman's own understanding of the causes of World War II was nothing if not economically deterministic. Protectionism, trade blocs, and currency unions were the culprits. Another impact was the emergence of the view that, while open markets were good, they needed to be regulated and managed by government—left to their own devices, markets would end in calamity. At the international level, this meant the putting in place of regulatory and public goods mechanisms to guard against economic dysfunction or failure—and their spreading to other countries and regions. A third impact of the experience of the thirties and forties was that governments were now seen as obligated to ensure employment, economic well-being, and social security. In response, the United States needed to create a more facilitating international environment to make good on its economic security obligations. Finally, the progressive notions embedded in New Deal liberalism were brought forward into America's vision of an international order. The architects of the American order sought to do things in their day to make each succeeding generation more modern, prosperous, and secure.

The Depression and New Deal brought into existence the notion of "social security"—but the violence and destruction of world war brought into existence the notion of "national security." It was more than just a new term of art; it was a new and expansive internationalist notion of security. In earlier decades—and during World War I—the notion of "national security" did not really exist. The term most frequently used was national "defense," but this had the more restricted meaning of the protection of the homeland against traditional military attack. The new term and meaning emerged sometime during World War II; it captured the new vision of an activist and permanently mobilized state seeking security across economic, political, and military realms. "National security" required America to be actively attempting to shape its external environment—coordinating agencies, generating resources, making plans, building alliances, and laying the institutional groundwork.

What New Deal and national security liberalism brought to postwar American internationalism was a wider domestic constituency for liberal order building than in earlier eras. The desirable international order had more features and moving parts. It was more elaborate and complex. In several senses, the stakes had grown since the end of World War I: more had to be accomplished, more was at risk if the right sort of postwar order was not constructed, and more of American society had a stake in a successful American internationalist project.

American elites today need to recover this public philosophy of internationalism. It brought together liberal and realist strands of thinking and gave American leaders of the postwar era the ability to link American national security to the building of a rules-based international order. The restraint and the commitment of American power went hand in hand. Global rules and institutions advanced America's national interest, rather than threatened it. The alternative public philosophies that circulate today—philosophies that champion American unilateralism and disentanglement from global rules and institutions—are not meeting with great success. An opening now exists for an updating and rearticulation of America's postwar vision of internationalism.

Conclusion

Today, the global system is at a remarkable moment: the United States dominates the world as no state has ever done. At the same time, the political relations and institutional frameworks built over the past half-century for the organization of world politics have eroded. America is both partly responsible for this situation and a casualty of it. The United States has the capacity to dominate the world but not the legitimacy to rule. It has power but not authority.

In this paper, I have explored the logic of America's ambivalent embrace of rules-based international order and the shifting incentives and circumstances that shape its strategic choices about rules and institutions. Central to my thesis is the observation that disparities of power among states can provide incentives for states to establish rules and institutions among them. Weak states seek multilateral rules and institutions to circumscribe the exercise of power of the leading state, to curb its excesses and render it more predictable. A powerful state—even a hegemonic state —can use rules and institutions to create a congenial environment for the efficient promotion and protection of its interests over the long term. At the same time, a powerful state—certainly a unipolar one—has incentives and opportunities to avoid and work around rules and institutions. The logic cuts both ways, and the types and mix of international rules and institutions today reflect this changing reality.

How will the United States respond to its lost legitimacy as hegemonic leader? What can the United States do to re-establish its legitimacy and put its hegemonic order back on a solid footing? I argue that the United States needs to find ways to reassure other states of its intensions and to bind itself to the wider international community. If American power is to regain its lost authority, it will need to be reinserted in a reformed system of agreed-upon global rules and institutions.

The United States needs to send an unmistakable signal to the rest of the world—that it is again committing itself to promoting and operating within a rules-based international order. This was, after all, what the United States did after World War II, when it emerged as the pre-eminent global power and found itself in a position to shape the postwar global order. Truman and his colleagues created a far-flung liberal multilateral order and Cold War alliance system that fused American power to institutions and liberal purpose. The restraint on American power and the projection of American power went hand-in-hand.

True, a rules-based international order circumscribes the way power is exercised—and it would, to some extent, reduce America's autonomy and freedom of action. In return, however, the United States would buy itself a more predictable and legitimate international order. In getting other states to operate within a set of multilateral rules and institutions, the United States would reduce its constant need to pressure and coerce other states to follow its lead. If the United States were to make itself a global rule maker, other states would be concerned less with resisting American power and more with negotiating over the frameworks of cooperation. Today, American unipolarity is associated with the erosion of a global system of rules and institutions. This association is not inevitable. If the United States turned itself—as it did in the 1940s—into a rules producer, its authority would increase accordingly.

References

Clark, Ian. 2005. *Legitimacy in International Society.* Oxford: Oxford University Press.

Daalder, Ivo, and James Lindsey. 2004. "An alliance of democracies." *Washington Post*, May 23, p. B07.

Goldstein, Judith, Miles Kahler, Robert O. Keohane, and Anne-Marie Slaughter, eds. 2001. *Legalization and World Politics.* Cambridge, MA: MIT Press.

Ikenberry, G. John. 2001. *After Victory: Institutions, Strategic Restraint, and the Rebuilding of Order after Major Wars.* Princeton, NJ: Princeton University Press.

———, ed. 2002. *America Unrivaled: The Future of the Balance of Power.* Ithaca, NY: Cornell University Press.

———. 2003a. "Is American Multilateralism in Decline?" *Perspectives on Politics* 1 (3): 533–50.

———. 2003b. "State Power and the Institutional Bargain: America's Ambivalent Economic and Security Multilateralism." In *US Hegemony and International Organizations: The United States and Multilateral Institutions*, edited by Rosemary Foot, S. Neil MacFarlane, and Michael Mastanduno. Oxford: Oxford University Press.

———. 2005a. "Creating America's World: The Domestic Sources of Postwar Liberal Internationalism." Unpublished paper.

———. 2005b. "A Weaker World." *Prospect* 116 (November): 30–33.

———. 2006. "The Global Security Trap." Democracy: *A Journal of Ideas* 2 (Fall).

Ikenberry, G. John, and Charles A. Kupchan. 1990. "Socialization and Hegemonic Power." *International Organization* 44 (4): 283–315.

Ikenberry, G. John, and Anne-Marie Slaughter. 2006. *Forging a World of Liberty under Law: U.S. National Security in the 21st Century.* Final Report of the Princeton Project on National Security. Princeton, NJ: Princeton University, Woodrow Wilson School of Public and International Affairs.

Kagan, Robert. 2002. "Multilateralism, American style." *Washington Post*, September 13.

———. 2004. "America's Crisis of Legitimacy." *Foreign Affairs* 83 (2): 65–88.

Kapstein, Ethan, and Michael Mastanduno, eds. 1999. *Unipolar Politics: Realism and State Strategies after the Cold War.* New York: Columbia University Press.

Keohane, Robert, 1984. *After Hegemony: Cooperation and Discord in the World Political Economy*. Princeton, NJ: Princeton University Press.

Krasner, Stephen. 1983. "Structural Causes and Regime Consequences: Regimes as Intervening Variables." In *International Regimes*, edited by Stephen Krasner. Ithaca, NY: Cornell University Press.

Krisch, Nico. 2005. "International Law in Times of Hegemony: Unequal Power and the Shaping of the International Legal Order." *European Journal of International Law* 16 (3): 369–408.

Lake, David, and Lisa Martin. 1992. "Interests, Power, and Multilateralism." *International Organization* 46 (4): 765–92.

Lipson, Charles. 2005. *Reliable Partners: How Democracies Have Made a Separate Peace*. Princeton, NJ: Princeton University Press.

Martin, Lisa. 1993. "The Rational State Choice of Multilateralism." In *Multilateralism Matters: The Theory and Praxis of an Institutional Form*, edited by John Gerard Ruggie. New York: Columbia University Press.

Moe, Terry M. 1990. "Political Institutions: The Neglected Side of the Story." *Journal of Law, Economics, and Organization* 6 (Special Issue): 215–53.

Schelling, Thomas. 1960. *The Strategy of Conflict*. Cambridge, MA: Harvard University Press.

———. 2006. *Strategies of Commitment*. Cambridge, MA: Harvard University Press.

Slaughter, Anne-Marie. 2004. *A New World Order*. Princeton, NJ: Princeton University Press.

Wohlforth, William. 1999. "The Stability of a Unipolar World." *International Security* 24 (1): 5–41.

Wright, Robert. 2005. "The market shall set you free." *New York Times*, January 28.

Two Challenges to Institutionalism

Daniel W. Drezner

*   *   *

This century has seen no shortage of effort to think about how to improve the workings of global governance. The terrorist attacks of September 11, 2001, the Bush administration's unilateralist response, the blowback from this response, and the rise of China and India have all posed challenges to existing global governance structures. Within the academic study of international relations, institutionalists in particular have been prodigious in their efforts to build a better mousetrap on the global stage.[1] These efforts proceed from a distinguished and important theoretical policymaking tradition that focuses on how governments can cooperate in a world defined by anarchy. They build on the efforts of liberal internationalists responsible for the most significant international institutions operating today, including the North Atlantic Treaty Organization, the International Atomic Energy Agency, the World Trade Organization (WTO), and the International Monetary Fund (IMF).

I am grateful to Alan Alexandroff, Karen Alter, Ann Florini, Brink Lindsay, Sophie Meunier, Jennifer Mitzen, Jeremy Rabkin, Kal Raustiala, Gideon Rose, and Alex Thompson for comments on suggestions. This paper builds on prior work, particularly Drezner (2007a, 2007b).
1. See Ikenberry in this volume; Fukuyama (2006); Ikenberry and Slaughter (2006); Wright (2006); and Daalder and Lindsey (2007).

In light of this tradition, it is understandable that institutionalists would propose reinvigorating existing international organizations while buttressing them with additional rules, laws, and organizational forms. This kind of "renewal strategy," however, rests on a dubious foundation. Simply put, the world today poses a set of challenges that institutionalist theory has not previously considered. Institutionalists traditionally have been concerned with creating regimes when none previously existed. An emerging problem in global governance is the proliferation of nested and overlapping regimes. If institutionalists cannot cope with the politics of institutional choice, then policy makers should be wary of their advice.

This chapter looks at the origins of institutionalism in international relations, to see why today's challenges to global governance might lie beyond their paradigm. Two problems in particular bedevil the functioning of global governance structures: how to redistribute power among participating actors within international organizations, and how to manage nested and overlapping mandates between a growing number of international regimes. Unless and until institutionalists can devise governance solutions that avoid these problems, renewal strategies will be of little use.

Back to the Future:
Why International Institutions Matter

To understand the current challenges to institutionalism, it is worth reflecting why the paradigm considered international regimes to be important in the first place. In the debate that took place between realists and institutionalists a generation ago, the latter group of theorists articulated in great detail how international regimes and institutions mattered in world politics. Although this scholarly debate ran its course some time ago, the institutionalist logic permanently shifted the terms of debate.

The primary goal of institutionalism was to demonstrate that cooperation was still possible even in an anarchic world populated by states with unequal amounts of power.[2] According to this approach, international

---

2. See Axelrod (1984); Keohane (1984); Axelrod and Keohane (1985); Oye (1986); Baldwin (1993); Keohane and Martin (1995); Hasenclever, Mayer, and Rittberger

institutions are a key mechanism through which cooperation becomes possible. A key causal process through which institutions facilitate cooperation is by developing arrangements that act as "focal points" for states in the international system (Schelling 1960). Much as the new institutionalist literature in US politics focused on the role that institutions played in facilitating a "structure-induced equilibrium" within domestic politics, neoliberal institutionalists made a similar argument about international regimes and world politics.[3] By creating a common set of rules or norms for all participants, institutions help intrinsically to define cooperation while highlighting instances when states defect from the agreed-upon rules.

The importance of institutions as focal points for actors in world politics is a recurring theme within the institutionalist literature. Indeed, this concept is embedded with Stephen Krasner's commonly accepted definition for international regimes: "implicit or explicit principles, norms, rules and decisionmaking procedures around which actors' expectations converge in a given area of international relations" (1983, 2; see also North 1991, 97). More than a decade later, Robert Keohane and Lisa Martin reaffirmed that, "in complex situations involving many states, international institutions can step in to provide 'constructed focal points' that make particular cooperative outcomes prominent" (1995, 45).

By creating focal points and reducing the transaction costs of rules creation, institutions can shift arenas of international relations from *power-based outcomes to rules-based outcomes*. In the former, disputes are resolved without any articulated or agreed-upon set of decisionmaking criteria. The result is a Hobbesian order commonly associated with the realist paradigm.[4] While such a system does not automatically imply that stronger states will use force or coercion to secure their interests, the shadow of such coercion is ever-present in the calculations of weaker actors (see Carr 1939 [1964]; Drezner 2003).

(1996); and Martin and Simmons (1998). Though often conflated, the institutionalist paradigm is distinct from liberal theories of international politics; on this distinction, see Moravcsik (1997).

3. On structure-induced equilibrium, see Shepsle and Weingast (1981). For conscious translations of this concept to world politics, see Milner (1997); and Martin and Simmons (1998).

Most institutionalists agree that power also plays a role in the initial creation of rules as well.[5] They would also posit, however, that the creation of a well-defined international regime imposes constraints on the behavior of actors that are not present in a strictly Hobbesian system: institutions act as binding mechanisms that permit displays of credible commitment (Ikenberry 2000). In pledging to abide by clearly defined rules, Great Powers make it easier for others to detect noncooperative behavior, and powers that choose to defect will incur costs to their reputation. A codified regime, moreover, imposes additional legal obligations to comply that augment the reputation costs of defection (Abbott and Snidal 2000; Goldstein and Martin 2000).

Institutionalists and some realists further argue that, once international regimes are created, they will persist even after the original distributions of power and interest have shifted (Ikenberry 2000). As Hasenclever, Mayer, and Rittberger point out, because the initial creation of institutions can be costly, "the expected utility of maintaining the present, suboptimal (albeit still beneficial) regime is greater than the utility of letting it die, returning to unfettered self-help behavior, and then trying to build a more satisfactory regime" (1996, 187). Some realist scholars have acknowledged that international regimes will persist despite changes in the underlying distribution of power (Krasner 1983, 357–61). For smaller and weaker actors, institutions provide an imperfect shield against the vicissitudes of a purely Hobbesian order (Reus-Smit 2004).

By the late 1990s, most varieties of realists allowed that, at least at the margins, international institutions could contribute to rules-based outcomes,[6] while some realists have acknowledged the contributions made by neoliberal institutionalists. As Schweller and Priess observe, "institutions matter because even the most rudimentary actions among states requires agreement on, and some shared understanding of, the basic rules of the game" (1997, 10). In moving from an anarchical world structure to one with coherent international regimes, institutions could contribute to a shift away from Hobbesian outcomes in world politics.

---

5. Oran Young makes this point in an early article on international regimes (1980, 338).
6. The obvious exceptions here are structural neorealists and offensive realists; see Waltz (1979); and Mearsheimer (1994/95).

Why Rewriting the Rules Is Difficult

The institutionalist paradigm has been successful in challenging realist tenets, as well as in highlighting the ways in which international institutions can affect the likelihood of international cooperation. The current challenges to global governance structures, however, are essentially unrelated to this question. Policy makers are facing two significant puzzles that need solutions: how to reallocate power within existing international organizations and how to manage the proliferation of laws, rules, and organizational forms. It is far from clear whether institutionalism can offer the answers.

Powerful international institutions are the creation of powerful governments. In the short term, international regimes can persist despite shifts in the global distribution of power. If mismatches between governance structures and the distribution of power are allowed to fester, however, then those structures rest upon very shaky foundations. During the interwar years, for example, the United States was unwilling and Great Britain was unable to assume the responsibility for providing global public goods (see Kindleberger 1973; Frieden 2006). The result was a period of ineffectual global governance. For an even starker example, consider the end of the Cold War: every major Western-built institution enhanced its power and reach following the Soviet collapse; not a single international institution established in the communist world survived. Historically, global governance structures have not persisted long after the power of their originators has waned—even when the shift in the distribution of power has been peaceful.

The United States might be the current military hegemon, but it faces a possible power mismatch in the near future. The United States has already lost its status as the economic hegemon (Drezner 2007a, chap. 2), and future trends suggest shifts in other dimensions of power. Analysts in both the private and public sectors, for example, have posited the rise of the BRIC countries—Brazil, Russia, India, and China (see Wilson and Purushothaman 2003). The latter two countries, in particular, are emerging as economic and political heavyweights: both countries already possess a population north of a billion people, China holds over a trillion US dollars in hard currency reserves, India's high-tech sector is growing by leaps and bounds, and both countries, already recognized nuclear powers, have plans to develop blue-water navies. The National Intelligence Council, a US government think tank, projects that, by 2025, China and India will have the world's second- and fourth-largest economies, respectively (National Intelligence Council 2004). To be sure, there are risks to proposing global governance reforms based on future extrapolation—but these pale beside the risks of maintaining a status quo based on a distribution of power that is more than half a century old.

This tectonic shift poses a challenge to the US-dominated global institutions that have been in place for the past half-century. At the behest of Washington, these multilateral regimes have promoted trade liberalization, open capital markets, and nuclear nonproliferation, ensuring relative peace and prosperity for six decades—and untold benefits for the United States. But unless rising powers such as China and India are incorporated into this framework, the future of these international regimes will be uncomfortably uncertain. To its credit, the George W. Bush administration has recognized this fact. Its efforts to bring China and India into the concert of Great Powers, however, have yielded uneven results (see Drezner 2007b).

The problem is that, as difficult as it is to write the rules of global governance, it is even more difficult to rewrite those rules. Rewriting the rules of existing institutions is a thankless task that is attempted only when absolutely necessary. In world politics, power is a zero-sum game. By definition, empowering countries on the rise means disempowering countries on the wane. Any attempt to boost China, India, and other rising powers means that other countries will wind up with lower profiles and less influence within the affected international organizations. These nation-states will naturally resist any attempts at reform, stalling or sabotaging any changes in global governance.

In the present day, the resistors are the Europeans. In terms of both military prowess and economic might, France, Germany, and Great Britain were all more powerful in 1900 than in 2000. Since many of the key postwar institutions gave a privileged position to Europe, these countries are the inevitable losers in a redistribution of power to the Pacific Rim. Since they hold functional vetoes in many of these organizations, however, they can resist US-led changes.

Europe can count on many allies in resisting US reform efforts: developing countries on the periphery of the global economy will also resist losing what little influence they have in multilateral institutions. Beyond these countries, however, the Bush administration is in a quandary of its own making. The administration's penchant for unilateralism has elevated international suspicion about any proposal to alter the rules of global governance. Inevitably, US proposals arouse suspicion about US motives. Many countries and individuals will view reform efforts as an opportunistic attempt by the United States to free itself from multilateral strictures. Rising anti-Americanism across the globe creates an additional burden for governments to cooperate with the United States, by creating domestic political headaches for those who cooperate with the Bush administration.

Even if this barrier is surmounted, bringing rising states into a Great Power concert does not always lead to more agreement. Consider the present moment. One of the many stalemates paralyzing the Doha Round of multilateral trade negotiations is that the EU refuses to cut its agricultural subsidies any further unless the G20 countries agree to increase non-agricultural market access to their economies. Proposed reforms of the UN Security Council ran aground because the proposals emanating from the UN itself seemed impractical and the key players could not agree on which countries merit permanent membership. The larger the crowd in a negotiating green room, the less likely there will be consensus.

Historically, there have been successful efforts at global governance redesigns, but they have come at a staggering cost. As John Ikenberry points out in *After Victory* (2000), the principal efforts to craft "constitutional orders" have followed wars between major powers. These wars discredited the legitimacy of the old order and generated decisive shifts in the global distribution of power, allowing the victors to write the rules once the slate was wiped clean of pre-existing institutions.[7] The very good news is that the likelihood of such a Great Power war is remote; it also means, however, that the slate is not even close to being wiped clean.

---

7. Even then, as Ikenberry observes, the rules only took hold when there was a clear hegemon that was willing to bind itself to new institutions.

The Proliferation of
Global Governance Structures

One possible response to the sclerosis of existing global governance structures is to create new ones. In recent years, as Table 1 demonstrates, there clearly has been a steady increase in the number of conventional intergovernmental organizations, autonomous conferences, and multilateral treaties. The causes of this increase are varied: in some cases, economic globalization has increased "issue density" in world affairs, stimulating demand for new rules, laws, and institutions (see Keohane 1982; Drezner 2007a); in other instances, the "capture" of international institutional institutions by a powerful state or interest group has spurred the creation of countervailing organizational forms (see Mansfield 1995).

In a world thick with institutions, surmounting the transaction costs of policy coordination is no longer the central problem for institutionalists. Instead, the problem is now to select among a welter of possible governance arrangements (see Krasner 1991; Drezner 2007a). As Jupille and Snidal point out, "[i]nstitutional choice is now more than just a starting point for analysts and becomes the dependent variable to be explained in the context of alternative options" (2005, 2). The current generation of institutionalist work recognizes the existence of multiple and overlapping institutional orders.[8] The creation of new regimes—and the manipulation of old ones—can help rational actors cope with situations of uncertainty and complexity (see Rosendorff and Milner 2001; Koremenos 2005). For many issues and regions, more than one international organization can claim competency, a phenomenon Raustiala and Victor label as regime complexes: "an array of partially overlapping and nonhierarchical institutions governing a particular issue-area [and] marked by the existence of several legal agreements that are created and maintained in distinct fora with participation of different sets of actors" (2004, 279). Even those who stress the nonrational aspects of global governance agree that some actors engage in explicit efforts to foster strategic inconsistencies within a single regime complex (298).

---

8. Aggarwal (1998, 2005); Helfer (1999, 2004); Raustiala and Victor (2004); Jupille and Snidal (2005); Alter and Meunier (2006).

Table 1: *Growth in Global Governance Structures*

Type of International Regime	1981	1993	2003
International bodies	863	· 945	993
Subsidiaries or emanations of international bodies	590	1,100	1,467
Autonomous international conferences	34	91	133
Multilateral treaties	1,419	1,812	2,323
Total	*2,906*	*3,948*	*4,916*

Source: Union of International Organizations; available at Web site: http://www.uia.org/statistics/ organizations/ytb299.php.

Many scholars and practitioners have welcomed the proliferation of international institutions. The literature on regime complexes and the progressive legalization of world politics examines the extent to which these legal overlaps constitute a new source of specific politics and what strategies governments pursue to maneuver in such an institutional environment.[9] The editors of *Legalization and World Politics* observe approvingly that, "[i]n general, greater institutionalization implies that institutional rules govern more of the behavior of important actors—more in the sense that behavior previously outside the scope of particular rules is now within that scope or that behavior that was previously regulated is now more deeply regulated" (Goldstein et al. 2001, 3). At the same time, policy makers issue calls for ever-increasing institutional thickness.[10] In the final report of the Princeton Project on National Security, John Ikenberry and Anne-Marie Slaughter conclude:

> [H]arnessing cooperation in the 21st century will require many new kinds of institutions, many of them network-based, to provide speed, flexibility, and context-based decision making tailored to specific problems. This combination of institutions, and the habits and practices of cooperation that they would generate—even amid ample day-to-day tensions and diplomatic conflict—would represent the infrastructure of an overall international order that provides the stability and governance capacity necessary to address global problems. (2006, 27; see also Slaughter 1997, 2004)

9. See the citations in fn. 1.
10. For a recent example, see Daalder and Lindsey (2007).

The proliferation of international rules, laws, and institutional forms *might* lead to the outcomes that Ikenberry, Slaughter, and others predict. As regimes grow into regime complexes, however, there are at least four reasons to believe that the institutionalist logic for how regimes generate rules-based orders will fade in its effect. First, institutional proliferation can dilute the power of previously constructed focal points. Second, the existence of nested and overlapping governance arrangements makes it more difficult to detect opportunistic defections from existing regimes. Third, the creation of potentially conflicting legal mandates can weaken all actors' sense of legal obligation. Finally, the increased complexity of global governance structures places a disproportionate resource strain on poorer countries.

On the first point, the proliferation of regime complexes and decision-making fora leads to an inevitable increase in the number of possible focal points around which rules and expectations can converge.[11] The problem, of course, is that by definition focal points should be rare, otherwise it becomes more difficult to develop common conjectures. Indeed, in his original articulation of the idea, Thomas Schelling (1960) stressed that uniqueness was essential for focal points to have any coordinating power.[12] If the number of constructed focal points increases, then actors in world politics face a larger menu of possible sets of rules to negotiate. Logically, actors will seek out the fora in which they would expect the most favorable outcomes (see Raustiala and Victor 1994, 280; Busch 2007; Drezner 2007a, chap. 3). All actors will pursue this strategy, but institutional thickness endows Great Powers with a decided bargaining advantage. Because powerful states possess are more able to create, monitor, and sanction institutions, regime complexes endow them with additional agenda-setting

---

11. This is true even if newer organizational forms are created to buttress norms emanating from existing regimes. Actors that create new rules, laws, and organizations will consciously or unconsciously adapt these regimes to their political, legal, and cultural particularities. Even if the original intent is to reinforce existing regimes, institutional mutations will take place that can be exploited via forum-shopping as domestic regimes and interests change over time. For empirical examples, see Raustiala (1997a, 1997b); Hafner-Burton (forthcoming).
12. "Equally essential is some kind of uniqueness; the man and wife cannot meet at the 'lost and found' if the store has several" (Schelling 1960, 58).

and enforcement powers relative to a single regime (see Krasner 1991; Voeten 2001). For example, Hafner-Burton (2005) finds statistical evidence that human rights provisions in US and European preferential trade agreements have had a more significant effect on human rights performance than have UN human rights treaties. In this situation, the ability of the United States and the EU to shift fora away from the United Nations and into trade deals has allowed them to push for their preferred human rights standards—although, despite their similar overall intent, the specific rights they have pushed differ for domestic reasons (Hafner-Burton, forthcoming).

On the second point, the proliferation of international rules, laws, and regimes make it more difficult to determine when an actor has intentionally defected from a pre-existing regime. Within a single international regime, the focal point should be clear enough for participating actors to recognize when a state is deviating from the agreed-upon rules. If multiple, conflicting regimes govern a particular issue area, then actors can argue that they are complying with the regime that favors their interests the most, even if they are consciously defecting from other regimes. Consider, for example, the ongoing trade dispute between the United States and the EU over genetically modified organisms in food (see Drezner 2007a, chap. 6). The United States insists that the issue falls under the purview of the WTO—because the WTO has embraced rules that require the EU to demonstrate scientific proof that genetically modified organisms are unsafe. The EU insists that the issue falls under the 2001 Cartagena Protocol on Biosafety—because that protocol embraces the precautionary principle of regulation. The result is a legal deadlock, with the biosafety protocol's precautionary principle infringing upon the trade regime's norm of scientific proof of harm. It will be difficult to reconcile the legal norms contained within the WTO and Cartagena regimes.

Third, the legalization of world politics paradoxically can reduce the sense of legal obligation that increases the compliance of actors with international regimes. International law scholars argue that the principle of *pacta sunt servanda*, buttressed by the general norms and procedures of the international legal system, imposes important obligations upon states (Goldstein et al. 2001, 24–28). The proliferation of international law, however, can lead to overlapping or even conflicting legal obligations. If one posits an evolutionary model of institutional growth, such an occurrence can take place even if actors are trying to adhere in good faith to prior legal mandates. Once conflicting obligations emerge, so does the problem of reconciling the conflict. As Raustiala and Victor point out, "the international legal system has no formal hierarchy of treaty rules. Nor does it possess well-established mechanisms or principles for resolving the most difficult conflicts across the various elemental regimes" (2004, 300).[13] Because of legal equivalence, regimes can evade international laws and treaties that conflict with their current interests by seeking out regimes with different laws. Even if governments did not initially intend to act opportunistically when creating overlapping law, shifts in either the international environment or domestic politics can create political incentives for exploiting their existence.[14] Moreover, competing legal claims can create an institutional stalemate as states, international governmental organizations, and courts try to implement policies that lie at the joints of regime complexes (Aggarwal 2005; Alter and Meunier 2006). Politically, however, this situation privileges more powerful actors at the expense of weaker ones. When states can bring conflicting legal precedents to a negotiation, the actor with greater enforcement capabilities will have the bargaining advantage.[15]

Finally, and related to the last point, institutional proliferation increases the complexity of legal and technical rules. In such a complex institutional environment, more powerful actors again have the upper hand. Negotiating

13. The Vienna Convention on the Law of Treaties provides a limited set of norms regarding the hierarchy of law, but observed adherence to these norms remains unclear.
14. This problem is hardly unique to international law. In US politics, for example, different federal agencies with different mandates often conflict at the joints of a complex policy problem, which leads to obvious legal and bureaucratic battles. There is, however, at least one important difference between the domestic and international realms: in US politics, administrative law and administrative courts function as a means for adjudicating overlapping mandates, but at the international level, no concomitant body of widely recognized law exists.
15. A counterargument, however, is that legal obligations foster concerns about reputational costs if a state violates international law, although recent research suggests that reputational effects are more tightly constrained than previously thought (see Downs and Jones 2002; Press 2005; Tomz 2007).

the myriad global governance structures and treaties requires considerable amounts of legal training and technical expertise related to the issue area at hand. Although these transaction costs might seem trivial to great powers with large bureaucracies, they can be imposing for smaller states.[16] This is particularly true when dealing with regime complexes that contain potentially inconsistent elements. Navigating competing global governance structures requires a great deal of specialized human capital, a relatively scarce resource in much of the developing world.[17] It is less problematic for states that command significant resources.

Figure 1 displays the relationship posited here between institutional thickness and the prevalence of rules-based outcomes. In moving from a purely Hobbesian order to one with a single, well-defined international regime, there is a marked shift away from power-based outcomes to rules-based outcomes. As institutional thickness increases, however, the prevalence of power-based outcomes increases. Contrary to the expectations of global governance scholars and practitioners, after a certain point the proliferation of nested and overlapping regimes and the legalization of world politics actually contributes to more power-based outcomes.

A world of institutional proliferation turns the realist-institutionalist debate on its head. If it is possible for the major powers to shift policy from one forum to another, an institutionally thick world begins to resemble the neorealist depiction of anarchy. A Great Power like the United States has the luxury of selecting the forum that maximizes decisionmaking legitimacy while ensuring its preferred outcome. For example, in the wake of the financial crises of the 1990s, the G7 countries shifted decision making from the friendly confines of the IMF to the even friendlier confines of the Financial Stability Forum (see Drezner 2007a, chap. 5). If there are only minimal costs to forum shopping, and if different intergovernmental organizations promulgate legally equivalent outputs, then institutional thickness,

---

16. See Jordan and Majnoni (2002); Stiglitz (2002, 227); Reinhardt (2003); Drezner (2007a, chap. 5).
17. Some governments outsource their legal needs to Western law firms well-versed in international law. This mitigates the human capital problem, but replaces it with a budgetary problem.

Figure 1: *Institutional Proliferation and World Order*

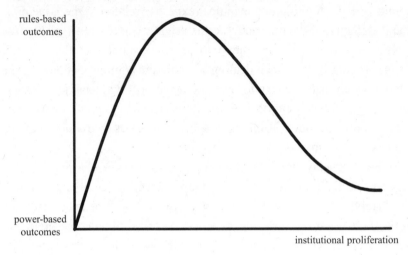

combined with low levels of viscosity, actually increases the likelihood of neorealist policy outcomes.

Policy makers and policy analysts in the United States have become increasingly aware of that country's ability to exploit institutional pro-liferation to advance its interests (see, for example, Brooks and Wohlforth 2005, 515). Richard Haass, director of policy planning in the State Depart-ment from 2001 to 2003, articulated the Bush administration's approach to global governance as "à la carte multilateralism." According to this doctrine, the United States would choose to adhere to some but not all international agreements to ensure that favored multilateral arrangements expand, rather than constrain, US options (Shanker 2001, A1; see also Haass 2001). Fukuyama explicitly endorses a forum-shopping strategy in promoting the idea of "multi-multilateralism" (2006, 158, 168).

The short-term gains of this strategy for the United States cannot be denied. The long-term effects on global governance structures are more troubling, since the United States is not the only country that will engage in this multi-multilateral strategy. So long as the United States maintains its hegemony, most of these efforts will yield little success. Rising powers in the developing world, however, are another story. These countries have already begun to create or revive alternative governance structures that bypass the United States (see Barma, Ratner and Weber 2007). In the past few years, dormant groups such as the Non-Aligned Movement have found new life, fueled by anti-Americanism. If India and China wanted to, they could make the future very discomfiting for the United States. China, in particular, has begun to create new institutional structures outside of the United States' reach. The Shanghai Cooperation Organisation, for example —consisting of China, Russia, and six central Asian republics, with Iran, Pakistan, and India as observers—is facilitating military and energy cooperation among its members. At its June 2006 Beijing summit, Iranian President Mahmoud Ahmadinejad proposed that the organization "ward off the threats of domineering powers to use their force against and interfere in the affairs of other states." The joint declaration from that summit appeared to endorse this sentiment, noting that, "[d]ifferences in cultural traditions, political and social systems, values and models of development formed in the course of history should not be taken as pretexts to interfere in other countries' internal affairs."[18]

Even though these challenges are currently at nascent levels, they can lead to a long-term tragedy of the institutional commons: institutional sclerosis plus institutional proliferation equals an increase in regime complexes contaminated with "organized hypocrisy" (see Krasner 1999; Lipson 2007), generating policies that are at odds with Great Power interests, decoupled from stated norms or so inchoate that they cannot be implemented or enforced. The likely policy response to this problem will be even more forum shifting. As the White House's March 2006 National Security Strategy explicitly states, "[w]here existing institutions can be reformed to meet new challenges, we, along with our partners, must reform them. Where appropriate institutions do not exist, we, along with our partners, must create them" (United States 2006; see also, more generally, Drezner 2007b). Other countries will adopt a similar approach. Yet, to paraphrase Montesquieu, useless regimes weaken necessary regimes. As more and more fora are created, each will find its legitimacy devalued by forum shopping. As states become willing to walk away from global governance structures that fail to advance their interests, all these structures will experience a decline in both legitimacy and effectiveness.

---

18. http://www.timesonline.co.uk/tol/news/world/middle_east/article675372.ece.

Conclusion

The institutionalist paradigm has a distinguished scholarly lineage, but it faces two empirical challenges. First, the distribution of power within international institutions is increasingly divorced from the distribution of power outside those organizations. To correct this mismatch, decision-making power needs to be reallocated within organizations such as the IMF and the UN Security Council. States in relative decline, however, will be reluctant to cede any formal levers of power, and there are a sufficient number of states in this situation to form a blocking coalition for reform of most prominent intergovernmental organizations.

One response to this institutional sclerosis has been a proliferation of international rules, laws, and institutional forms in world politics. A few institutionalists, some liberal internationalists, and many international law scholars posit that this trend will lead to a more rules-based world. This chapter suggests a contrary position—namely, that institutional thickness has a paradoxical effect on global governance. After a certain point, proliferation will shift global governance structures from rules-based outcomes to power-based outcomes—because proliferation can enhance the ability of Great Powers to engage in forum shopping.

This outcome leads to the second empirical challenge: the need for institutionalists to devise theoretical responses to the problems of the reform and proliferation of intergovernmental organizations. This will not be an easy task. The variables of concern in the study of regime creation seem less salient in looking at institutional choice. Any examination of the cohesion of international choices must recognize that, at some point in the past, the relevant actors were able to agree on a set of strategies such that cooperation was the equilibrium outcome.[19] This means that the costs of monitoring and enforcement could not have been too great. As Fearon observes, "there is a potentially important *selection effect* behind cases of international negotiations aimed at cooperation. We should observe serious attempts at international cooperation in cases where the monitoring and enforcement dilemmas are probably resolvable" (1998, 279; italics in

---

19. See Keohane (1984) for a verbal description of cooperation, and Bendor and Swistak (1997, 297–98) for a more technical description.

original). This selection effect implies that some factors affecting the origins of international cooperation are not as relevant for explaining the persistence of international regimes. For institutionalists, the challenges are clear; the solutions are not.

References

Abbott, Kenneth W., and Duncan Snidal. 2000. "Hard and Soft Law in International Governance." *International Organization* 54 (3): 421–56.

Aggarwal, Vinod, ed. 1998. *Institutional Designs for a Complex World: Bargaining, Linkages and Nesting*. Ithaca, NY: Cornell University Press.

———. 2005. "Reconciling Institutions: Nested, Horizontal, Overlapping, and Independent Institutions." Working paper, University of California at Berkeley. February.

Alter, Karen J., and Sophie Meunier. 2006. "Nested and Competing Regimes in the Transatlantic Banana Trade Dispute." *Journal of European Public Policy* 13 (March): 362–82.

Axelrod, Robert. 1984. *The Evolution of Cooperation*. New York: Basic Books.

Axelrod, Robert, and Robert Keohane. 1985. "Achieving Cooperation under Anarchy: Strategies and Institutions." *World Politics* 38 (Fall): 226–54.

Baldwin, David, ed. 1993. *Neorealism and Neoliberalism: The Contemporary Debate*. New York: Columbia University Press.

Barma, Naazneen, Ely Ratner, and Steven Weber. 2007. "A World without the West." *The National Interest* 90 (July/August): 23–30.

Bendor, Jonathan, and Piotr Swistak. 1997. "The Evolutionary Stability of Cooperation." *American Political Science Review* 91 (June): 290–07.

Brooks, Stephen, and William Wohlforth. 2005. "International Relations Theory and the Case Against Unilateralism." *Perspectives on Politics* 3 (September): 509–24.

Busch, Marc. 2007. "Overlapping Institutions, Forum Shopping, and Dispute Settlement in International Trade." *International Organization* 61 (October): 735–61.

Carr, E.H. 1939 [1964]. *The Twenty Years' Crisis*. New York: Harper and Row.

Daalder, Ivo, and James Lindsey. 2007. "Democracies of the World, Unite!" *American Interest* 2 (January/February): 34–44.

Downs, George, and Michael Jones. 2002. "Reputation, Compliance and International Law." *Journal of Legal Studies* 31 (January): S95–S114.

Drezner, Daniel W. 2003. "The Hidden Hand of Economic Coercion." *International Organization* 57 (Summer): 643–59.

―――. 2007a. *All Politics Is Global: Explaining International Regulatory Regimes.* Princeton, NJ: Princeton University Press.

―――. 2007b. "The New New World Order." *Foreign Affairs* 86 (March/April): 34–46.

Fearon, James A. 1998. "Bargaining, Enforcement, and International Cooperation." *International Organization* 52 (Spring): 269–305.

Frieden, Jeffry. 2006. *Global Capitalism: Its Fall and Rise in the Twentieth Century.* New York: W.W. Norton.

Fukuyama, Francis. 2006. *America at the Crossroads: Democracy, Power, and the Neoconservative Legacy.* New Haven, CT: Yale University Press.

Goldstein, Judith, and Lisa Martin. 2000. "Legalization, Trade Liberalization, and Domestic Politics: A Cautionary Note." *International Organization* 54 (Summer): 603–32.

Goldstein, Judith, Miles Kahler, Robert Keohane, and Anne-Marie Slaughter, eds. 2001. *Legalization and World Politics.* Cambridge, MA: MIT Press.

Haass, Richard. 2001. "Multilateralism for a Global Era." Remarks to the Carnegie Endowment for International Peace/Center on International Cooperation Conference, Washington, DC, November 14. Available at Web site: http://www.state.gov/s/p/rem/6134.htm.

Hafner-Burton, Emilie. 2005. "Trading Human Rights: How Preferential Trade Agreements Influence Government Repression." *International Organization* 59 (Summer): 593–629.

―――. Forthcoming. *Coercing Human Rights.* Ithaca, NY: Cornell University Press.

Hasenclever, Andreas, Peter Mayer, and Volker Rittberger. 1996. "Interests, Power, Knowledge: The Study of International Regimes." *Mershon International Studies Review* 40 (October): 177–228.

Helfer, Laurence R. 1999. "Forum Shopping for Human Rights." *University of Pennsylvania Law Review* 148 (December): 285–400.

―――. 2004. "Regime Shifting: The TRIPS Agreement and New Dynamics of International Intellectual Property Lawmaking." *Yale Journal of International Law* 29 (January): 23–47.

Ikenberry, John. 2000. *After Victory: Strategic Restraint, and the Rebuilding of Order after Major Wars.* Princeton, NJ: Princeton University Press.

Ikenberry, John, and Anne-Marie Slaughter. 2006. *Forging a World of Liberty under Law: U.S. National Security in the 21st Century*. Final Report of the Princeton Project on National Security. Princeton, NJ: Princeton University, Woodrow Wilson School of Public and International Affairs.

Jordan, Cally, and Giovanni Majnoni. 2002. "Financial Regulatory Harmonization and the Globalization of Finance." World Bank Policy Research Working Paper 2919. Washington, DC: World Bank.

Jupille, Joseph, and Duncan Snidal. 2005. "The Choice of International Institutions: Cooperation, Alternatives and Strategies." Paper presented at the American Political Science Association annual meeting, Washington, DC, September 1.

Keohane, Robert. 1982. "The Demand for International Regimes." *International Organization* 36 (Spring): 325–55.

———. 1984. *After Hegemony: Cooperation and Discord in the World Political Economy*. Princeton, NJ: Princeton University Press.

Keohane, Robert, and Lisa Martin. 1995. "The Promise of Institutionalist Theory." *International Security* 20 (Summer): 39–51.

Kindleberger, Charles. 1973. *The World in Depression, 1929–1939*. Berkeley: University of California Press.

Koremenos, Barbara. 2005. "Contracting around International Uncertainty." *American Political Science Review* 99 (November): 549–65.

Krasner, Stephen D., ed. 1983. *International Regimes*. Ithaca, NY: Cornell University Press.

———. 1991. "Global Communications and National Power: Life on the Pareto Frontier." *World Politics* 43 (April): 336–66.

———. 1999. S*overeignty: Organized Hypocrisy*. Princeton, NJ: Princeton University Press.

Lipson, Michael. 2007. "Peacekeeping: Organized Hypocrisy?" *European Journal of International Relations* 13 (January): 5–34.

Mansfield, Edward. 1995. "International Institutions and Economic Sanctions." *World Politics* 47 (July): 575–605.

Martin, Lisa L., and Beth Simmons. 1998. "Theories and Empirical Studies of International Institutions." *International Organization* 52 (Winter): 729–57.

Mearsheimer, John J. 1994/95. "The False Promise of International Institutions." *International Security* 19 (Winter): 5–49.

————. 2001. *The Tragedy of Great Power Politics.* New York: W.W. Norton.

Milner, Helen V. 1997. *Interests, Institutions, and Information: Domestic Politics and International Relations.* Princeton, NJ: Princeton University Press.

Moravcsik, Andrew. 1997. "Taking Preferences Seriously: A Liberal Theory of International Politics." *International Organization* 51 (Autumn): 513–53.

National Intelligence Council. 2004. *Mapping the Global Future: Report of the National Intelligence Council's 2020 Project.* Washington, DC: US Government Printing Office.

North, Douglass. 1991. "Institutions." *Journal of Economic Perspectives* 5 (Winter): 97–112.

Oye, Kenneth, ed. 1986. *Cooperation under Anarchy.* Princeton, NJ: Princeton University Press.

Press, Daryl. 2005. *Calculating Credibility: How Leaders Assess Military Threats.* Ithaca, NY: Cornell University Press.

Raustiala, Kal. 1997a. "Domestic Institutions and International Regulatory Co-operation: Comparative Responses to the Convention on Biological Diversity." *World Politics* 49 (Summer): 482–509.

————. 1997b. "States, NGOs, and International Environmental Institutions." *International Studies Quarterly* 41 (December): 719–40.

Raustiala, Kal, and David Victor. 2004. "The Regime Complex for Plant Genetic Resources." *International Organization* 58 (Spring): 277–309.

Reinhardt, Eric. 2003. "Tying Hands without a Rope: Rational Domestic Response to International Institutional Constraints." In *Locating the Proper Authorities,* edited by Daniel W. Drezner. Ann Arbor: University of Michigan Press.

Reus-Smit, Christian. 2004. *The Politics of International Law.* Cambridge: Cambridge University Press.

Rosendorff, Peter, and Helen Milner. 2001. "The Optimal Design of International Trade Institutions: Uncertainty and Escape." *International Organization* 55 (Autumn): 829–58.

Schelling, Thomas. 1960. *The Strategy of Conflict.* Cambridge, MA: Harvard University Press.

Schweller, Randall, and David Priess. 1997. "A Tale of Two Realisms: Expanding the Institutions Debate." *Mershon International Studies Review* 41 (May): 1–32.

Shanker, Thom. 2001. "White House says the U.S. is not a loner, just choosy." *New York Times*, July 31, p. A1.

Shanks, Cheryl, Harold Jacobson, and Jeffrey Kaplan. 1996. "Inertia and Change in the Constellation of International Governmental Organizations, 1981-1992." *International Organization* 50 (Autumn): 593–627.

Shepsle, Kenneth, and Barry Weingast. 1981. "Structure-Induced Equilibrium and Legislative Choice." *Public Choice* 37: 503–19.

Slaughter, Anne-Marie. 1997. "The Real New World Order." *Foreign Affairs* 76 (September/October): 183–97.

———. 2004. *A New World Order*. Princeton, NJ: Princeton University Press.

Stiglitz, Joseph. 2002. *Globalization and Its Discontents*. New York: W.W. Norton.

Tomz, Michael. 2007. *Reputation and International Cooperation*. Princeton, NJ: Princeton University Press.

Voeten, Erik. 2001. "Outside Options and the Logic of Security Council Action." *American Political Science Review* 95 (December): 845–58.

United States. 2006. Executive Office of the President. *The National Security Strategy of the United States of America*. Washington, DC. March. Available at Web site: http://www.whitehouse.gov/nsc/nss/2006/nss2006.pdf.

Waltz, Kenneth. 1979. *Theory of International Politics*. New York: McGraw Hill.

Wendt, Alexander. 1999. *Social Theory of International Politics*. Cambridge: Cambridge University Press.

Wilson, Dominic, and Roopa Purushothaman. 2003. "Dreaming with BRICs: The Path to 2050." Global Economics Paper 99. New York: Goldman Sachs. October.

Wright, Robert. 2006. "An American foreign policy that both realists and idealists should fall in love with." *New York Times*, July 16.

Young, Oran. 1980. "International Regimes: Problems of Concept Formation." *World Politics* 32 (April): 331–56.

International Institutions and Collective Authorization of the Use of Force

James D. Fearon

*   *   *

The authors of the United Nations Charter proposed that the organization should seek to "save succeeding generations from the scourge of war." Understandably, they had in mind avoiding world wars and other large interstate conflicts. Sixty years later, there have been hardly any "hot wars" among the militarily strongest states. This fortunate outcome probably has had less to do with the functioning of the United Nations system than with the perceived costs of interstate war in the nuclear age and with increasing doubts about the economic advantages of conquest.

The major threats to international peace and security today are radically different from those anticipated by the framers of the UN Charter. They also differ, broadly speaking, in the North and the South.[1] For the advanced industrial economies, the principal security threat in the coming

This essay draws heavily on a much longer paper, "Reforming International Institutions to Promote International Peace and Security" (Fearon 2006). I thank the International Task Force on Global Public Goods and its Secretariat for support for the research.

1. In this essay, I will take "security" to refer to freedom from risk of violent death, injury, or coercion at the hands of some organization. This is not, however, to rule out broader interpretations.

years will most likely be terrorists' use of weapons of mass destruction (WMD) in major urban areas (especially nuclear attacks). By contrast, for much of the rest of the world, the principal security threats will be internal war, state collapse, and consequent personal insecurity; violently abusive government; and, in some cases, risk of attack by strong states or neighbors.

How should these threats to peace and security be addressed in the next several decades? I argue that the UN system, or a redesigned or alternative system with similar basic commitments, is potentially more valuable for promoting peace and security now than it ever was during the Cold War. The main claim is that, given the nature of the security threats to the major powers and the relative absence of reasons for them to fight each other, there are greater gains to be had from a system for collectively authorizing and coordinating the use of force.

Whether the UN's members will be able to coordinate on reforms to improve the current system is another question, and a difficult one that would require a lot of speculation to try to answer. Instead, I focus first on making the case that the major security threats in the coming years will require multilateral coordination and authorization to handle effectively, and second on some of the major problems with the current UN system for authorizing the use of force. I analyze these problems by way of discussion of a normative question: if one could start over, from scratch, what would be the best institutional design for a UN Security Council-like body for authorizing the use of force in international politics? I then discuss the main obstacles and possibilities for moving the UN in this direction, closing with a brief discussion of alternatives to the UN.

Twenty-first Century Security Threats

The destructive power of a technologically advanced military, along with the deepening of democracy and international trade, has made the citizens of the major powers safer from attack and invasion than they have ever been before. Many of the benefits of peace among the major powers have extended to the smaller and militarily weaker states in the system as well, since they are less subject to annexation or direct control exercised by major powers playing "great games" or fighting wars with each other.

Nonetheless, the same technological advances that have helped bring about major power peace have created new security threats that will grow worse as technology improves and scientific knowledge spreads. Inter-*state* war is generally disfavored by weapons of mass destruction, but the horrific destructive potential of these weapons makes them attractive for terrorist use by nonstate or state-supported actors, and also a vastly greater concern. The risk of nuclear explosions in New York, Paris, London, Moscow, and other major cities is an existential threat for modern societies and economies. Further, because the knowledge will spread and the techno-logical ease of making WMD will grow over time, the threat is long run: it will remain long after al-Qaeda has disappeared.

The medium- and long-run threat of terrorist attacks with WMD gives the major powers a common interest in limiting the spread of nuclear weapons and in establishing an effective global system for controlling nuclear materials. It also increases the major powers' interest in the domestic politics of countries that have or could develop nuclear weapons. Highly opaque dictatorships with aggressive or erratic foreign policies are more frightening in a world with nuclear weapons and terrorist organizations. So are nuclear-capable states that seem at risk of political disintegration or whose officials engage in a lot of corrupt dealing.

In principle, the risk of WMD terrorism affects almost all states, but compared with other security threats it is a particular concern for the advanced industrial economies. In the rest of the world, the main security threats are quite different. Since 1945, at least 18 million people have died as a direct result of civil wars, almost entirely outside the economically most developed countries. This figure does not include the millions killed in one-sided massacres orchestrated by governments, such as those in Argentina, Cambodia, and Uganda under Amin. By comparison, about 3.3 million people have been killed in interstate wars over the same period.

In decreasing order of global severity, these three problems—internal war, mass killing by governments, and interstate war—represent the major security risks for much of the developing world.[2] They are also

---

2. Numbers of refugees and internally displaced persons, as well as levels of economic devastation, tend to be roughly proportional to numbers killed, so this is a reasonable first-cut indicator.

indirectly related to one of the early successes of the United Nations system: the promotion and management of mainly peaceful decolonization in Africa, Asia, and the Middle East. Initially, the UN Charter was signed by 51 countries in a world with about 60 independent states. Today, there are 191 members, half of which have gained independence since 1960. Decolonization has filled the international system with new states whose economies and administrative structures are often fragile and underdeveloped and that are especially prone to civil war and abusive rule (Fearon and Laitin 2003).

Why Unilateral Strategies Are Insufficient to Counter These Threats

Since a large portion of the international resources for addressing security threats, whether the Northern or Southern variants, inevitably will come from the rich states, it makes sense to start by asking why these countries have any need of multilateral cooperation to confront the threats at all. Why are unilateral policies not up to the task?

Regarding protection from terrorists' use of WMD, there is a range of unilateral strategies that states can and should pursue. These include hardening targets, improving border and port security, and putting effective emergency response measures in place, and doing all these while minimally compromising civil liberties.[3] But this is clearly not enough, and practically every other sensible response will require active multilateral or at least bilateral cooperation. Extensive coordination among states is required to gather intelligence on people and organizations who might be planning attacks; to control and monitor weapons materials; and to deal with problems posed by states that might be developing WMD and that might then be passed on or lost to individuals or groups intending to use them for terrorism.

---

3. Of course, international institutions might provide important assistance to states in undertaking such measures; see, for example, the agenda of the UN Security Council's Counter-Terrorism Committee, available at Web site: http://www.un.org/sc/ctc/.

The first task plainly requires international cooperation, although it is possible that bilateral exchanges might be a more effective strategy than a multilateral one. The second and third tasks will require intrusive measures ranging from expert monitoring teams to, in the limiting case, military intervention. A unilateral approach to these threats, however, is likely to be ineffective for several reasons.

First, there is the question of legal authorization. Unauthorized, unilateral action in this sphere signals strongly that it is *sauve qui peut* among states, which heightens incentives for weapons acquisition, which, in turn, undermines the goal of avoiding terrorists' use of WMD. If one state unilaterally demands access to another state's laboratories and reactor projects or unilaterally attacks a state to prevent its current leadership from developing WMD, then many countries might regard the option of secretly developing WMD to deter such attacks more attractive. By contrast, a multilateral process for authorizing intervention and intrusive inspections that proceeds according to rules could increase states' confidence that they will avoid being attacked at the whim of a stronger power. It would also reduce worries that neighbors or other states would develop WMD.

Second, multilateral cooperation is required to deal with the problems posed by "failed" or "collapsed" states. Among other problems, such states pose obstacles to the monitoring of weapons materials and their use. The control and monitoring of weapons materials is much harder if there are parts of the world not governed by any internationally recognized and responsible state apparatus, in which international monitoring and police work are infeasible. While it may be impossible for an organization actually to develop WMD (for example, to enrich uranium) in the chaos of a failed state, the options for trafficking in weapons materials or contraband to finance their purchase are excellent in these areas. Moreover, as the case of Afghanistan suggests, they might serve as recruiting or training grounds for terrorist groups.

Thus, in a world where the know-how to produce WMD is increasingly widespread, zones of anarchy pose a larger international security threat than ever before. Whether state collapse arises from years of destructive civil war or from an attack on a state perceived to be developing nuclear weapons, the major powers will have incentives to cooperate to help restore internationally responsible and domestically effective political orders.

The central security problem for the major powers can be summarized as follows: WMD imply, over time, a big increase in the "negative externalities" associated with both collapsed states and tyrannical rule in small countries that have some technological capability. The externalities are diffuse, potentially affecting many states, but the costs of dealing with them are concentrated. Unilateral military responses are likely to increase incentives for proliferation and to increase regional insecurities, worsening rather than reducing the problem in the long run.

This is a classic collective action problem, whose natural solution should tend toward multilateral arrangements to share the burden and avoid the escalation of insecurity that would follow from a unilateralist approach. In consequence, for the resource-rich Northern states to confront effectively the threat posed by WMD terrorism, they will need to cooperate in helping to address the central security threats of the developing world: civil war and widespread, government-inflicted human rights abuses.

The UN Security Council was mainly irrelevant for maintaining Great Power peace during the Cold War, and is not much needed for keeping peace between the major powers today. It is slightly ironic, then, that the UN system—whether in its current form or, preferably, reformed or even replaced by a new international institution with some core similarities— is such a natural forum for coordinating and authorizing international action to address these twenty-first century security threats.

For the several reasons mentioned above—nuclear weapons, democracy, trade relations among advanced industrial economies—the major powers have little reason to fear attack or invasion from each other. They have more to fear from WMD proliferation, WMD terrorism, and the consequences of state collapse and regional conflict in less-developed countries. To deal with these threats and problems effectively, the major powers will need international institutions that can function to authorize and coordinate the multilateral use of force, for several reasons.

In the first place, the function of *authorizing the use of force* is more important if more military interventions are to be expected in countries convulsed by civil war, and if the most dangerous cases of WMD proliferation sometimes require a credible threat of military intervention.

Second, the function of *mobilizing and coordinating peacekeeping operations* in civil-war-torn countries is more important now than during the Cold War. Further, the diffuse benefits but concentrated costs typical of intervention in such settings imply that international burden sharing through a UN-like body makes excellent sense.

Third, the function of *legitimating transitional governance arrangements while undertaking concrete steps to rebuild basic state capacities* in countries that have suffered state collapse due to war or invasion is more important than ever.

Finally, the function of authorizing and overseeing an international institution empowered to undertake more intrusive inspection and monitoring of possible WMD development within states is increasingly necessary.

Whether the UN in its present form is the best body to perform these functions is not clear. On the one hand, the thrust of what is required to meet the new international security threats runs against two premises of the UN Charter. The charter sought to regulate interstate relations, but not "internal" matters such as civil war and its effects, or national decisions about armaments programs.[4] And the charter conceived of the UN as an organization open to all states irrespective of form of government. I argue, however, that some of the new security challenges—such as preventing human rights abuses by governments and authorizing the use of force— might be better met by an organization whose membership is limited to democracies.

On the other hand, the UN Charter has proven a powerful yet flexible document, and it might be possible to find effective solutions to the new challenges within its basic structure. Later in this essay, I offer some suggestions about what might be done both within and outside of the UN system as it stands.[5]

---

4. Although Article 26 envisions that the Security Council will, with the help of the still-born Military Staff Committee, formulate "plans to be submitted to the Members of the United Nations for the establishment of a system for the regulation of armaments."

5. For a more detailed analysis of UN reform measures and possibilities, see Fearon (2006).

US Power and the Problem of Authorizing International Force

To a great extent, new thinking and calls for the reform of international institutions concerned with peace and security arise from concerns about the recent US-led interventions in Kosovo, Afghanistan, and Iraq. In a September 2003 speech to the UN General Assembly, then secretary-general Kofi Annan deftly captured the central dilemma. Referring to the George W. Bush administration's argument that pre-emptive attack to preclude a "state of concern" from developing WMD is justified by the dire consequences of WMD terrorism, Annan averred that

> [t]his [pre-emptive] logic represents a fundamental challenge to the principles on which, however imperfectly, world peace and stability have rested for the last fifty-eight years. My concern is that, if it were to be adopted, it could set precedents that resulted in a proliferation of the unilateral and lawless use of force, with or without justification. But it is not enough to denounce unilateralism, unless we also face up squarely to the concerns that make some States feel uniquely vulnerable, since it is those concerns that drive them to take unilateral action. We must show that those concerns can, and will, be addressed effectively through collective action. (Annan 2003)

Annan suggests that, on the one hand, unilateral military efforts to deal with the dangers posed by WMD proliferation and terrorism by strong states (the United States in particular) are likely to move the world farther into the "law of the jungle." If some states see the use of force as a permissible way to resolve regional disputes, then other states will worry about the use of force by neighbors, producing a spiral of arms build-ups, WMD proliferation, and military conflict. On the other hand, if the strongest states (again, the United States in particular) feel that they cannot adequately address their security concerns by working through multilateral institutions, they will go outside them.

It follows that a successful reform must strike a difficult balance. An institution that merely pronounces against actions that the most powerful state views as self-defense risks irrelevance. An institution that merely ratifies whatever the strongest state wants to do will be illegitimate. Either way, we would effectively have "the law of the jungle," not an approximation of the rule of law. An international institution for peace and security can foster the rule of law only if the strongest states see enough benefits to working through the institution in general that they are willing to submit to important collective decisions they do not like on some occasions.[6]

It is worth stressing that the problem here is how to create something new, not how to preserve something from being lost. During the Cold War, the strongest states frequently used force without Security Council authorization. Indeed, the Security Council was mainly an irrelevant international institution during that period. The problem is not how to preserve an institution that has maintained international peace and security through a legal process for 60 years, but how to adapt or change the institution to play this role for the first time.

What has changed to cause a new demand for a working system of the collective authorization of the use of force? During the Cold War, the superpowers' mutual fears of nuclear war somewhat tempered and restrained their use of force, which had the effect of reducing somewhat other states' worries about attack and control. In addition, for both technological and political reasons (including the success of the Nuclear Non-Proliferation Treaty), the major powers had less to fear from WMD proliferation and terrorism during the Cold War than they do now. What has changed is that the United States and possibly other major powers have new reasons to intervene abroad militarily, but lack the implicit checks and balances of the Cold War system.[7]

---

6. Or if the anticipation of an adverse collective decision in the international institution leads a strong state to act differently than it would without this implicit threat.
7. This is not to say that these checks were always effective, especially in Latin America and eastern Europe. Another important difference is that, during the Cold War, states could and did coordinate their positions on the use of force through the Cold War alliance systems. With these gone and no set of sharply divided alliance systems yet formed among the major powers, coordination efforts through the UN Security Council have become something of the default. See Voeten (2005), who argues that, since 1991, the Security Council has become a more legitimate institution than it ever was during the Cold War, and that the reason has to do with its use by major powers to coordinate their positions on the United States' use of force; see also Thompson (2006).

If We Could Start from Scratch ...

Suppose we could start over and design from scratch a body like the UN Security Council to issue authoritative resolutions concerning the use of force to address threats to international peace and security. What would such a body look like? What principles would determine its membership, and by what procedures would it make decisions?

The results of this exercise will be politically fanciful, since all manner of prior institutional forms, decisions, and interests sharply constrain what reforms are possible in practice. But a "from scratch" exercise is nonetheless important for grounding our sense of the direction in which specific reform proposals should head and for evaluating the merits of specific proposals that have been offered.

Following on the discussion above, a successful Security Council-like body needs to be both effective and legitimate.[8] To be effective, the institution must satisfy the principle that *decisionmaking power within the institution must reflect, to some significant degree, state military, economic, and persuasive power outside the institution* (call this principle 1). Otherwise, when there are conflicts over what should be done, the strongest states might ignore the institution's decisions and it will seem irrelevant. This axiom underlay Franklin Roosevelt's critique of the weakness of the League of Nations and the idea of creating a Security Council of major powers with veto rights in the first place. One major reason the UN system has been more successful than the League of Nations—for example, by preserving its structure and authority-in-principle despite stasis during the Cold War —is that the UN Charter tried to take account of this first principle.

Principle 1, however, is a necessary but not sufficient condition for efficacy. It was satisfied at least for the first part of the Cold War, but intense conflicts of interest among the Permanent Five (P5) nonetheless prevented the Security Council from playing much of a role in the maintenance of international peace and security. Effectiveness also depends on the perception of common interests among the Security Council powers,

---

8. The UN High-level Panel report (United Nations 2004, paras. 31–43) discusses related requirements under the headings of "effectiveness," "efficiency," and "equity."

although how much depends on the body's decision rules, as discussed further below.

One of the main obstacles to reform of the Security Council is that the veto power of the P5 reflects the distribution of international influence immediately following World War II better than it does the current distribution; understandably, there is great reluctance among the P5 to adjust the structure. Thus, an immediate and important implication of principle 1, and a "lesson learned" from the experience of the Security Council, is that the criteria for membership in an effective Security Council-like body ideally should be dynamic. That is, membership and voting criteria need to allow membership and influence in the institution to change as a function of shifts in the international distribution of power and influence.

For a Security-Council-like body's decisions to be viewed as legitimate —that is, that there is a widely perceived obligation to abide by its decisions—the institution should satisfy the principle that *all members should have some nontrivial influence, at least some of the time, on decisions taken, and that the membership should reflect in a broad sense the wider field of states and people that might be affected the body's decisions* (call this principle 2).

What criteria for membership and what voting rules could plausibly satisfy principles 1 and 2? Each of the criteria I discuss below has something to recommend it, but each fails in various ways. Accordingly, a mix of several criteria would be the best way to determine the parameters of an effective and legitimate Security Council-like body.

One State, One Vote?

The principle of sovereign equality enshrined in the UN Charter might be taken to imply "one state one vote," as in the General Assembly. This had a stronger justification when the UN was founded in a world of about 60 states, most of which were at least moderately large. Since decolonization, however, the rationale for this principle as a basis for allocating influence within a Security Council-like body—or indeed any international organization—has weakened considerably. From the 191 current members of the United Nations, one can form a majority of 96 votes from a group of countries that make up less than 3.6 percent of the world's population!

By sharp contrast, 50 percent of the world's population resides in the six largest states, an inconsequential fraction of the total UN membership if counted as one vote per state. Using this principle to allocate decision-making influence in an international institution grossly violates principle 1, the condition for effectiveness. It is also hard to justify on grounds of legitimacy (principle 2) or fairness, since it vastly overrepresents people in very small states.

The UN General Assembly's reliance on the principle of one state one vote is an important factor behind the perception that it is little more than a forum for empty debate and symbolic posturing: all votes are equal, but they count for almost nothing. Is it possible that a majority of states in the General Assembly might prefer a system in which votes were weighted by some measure of size, influence, or contribution, but in which, as a result, General Assembly votes could become consequential and influential?

Some form of weighted voting thus seems necessary to satisfy the condition for a Security Council-like body to be effective. But weighted how?

One Person, One Vote?

It could be argued that legitimacy is maximized by drawing on the democratic principle of "one person, one vote," and thus one should weight votes in the General Assembly by the state's share of world population. In an assembly of all 191 members, the states with the ten largest vote shares would be as shown in Table 1. Thus, China and India would control 37 percent of the votes (based on 2003 population figures), the top ten states would control 60 percent of the votes, and the remaining 40 percent would be divided in tiny shares among the remaining 180 states in the General Assembly.

Though clearly better on the legitimacy dimension than "one state, one vote," this criterion would also violate principle 1, the condition for effectiveness. Moreover, such a scheme assumes that all governments are equally good representatives of their citizens. As I discuss at length below, however, there is a strong argument that nondemocratic governments do not merit this assumption or the level of representation such a criterion would imply.

In addition, there is the practical matter of how to allocate vote shares weighted by population in a decisionmaking body that is much smaller

Table 1: *General Assembly Votes Weighted by Population*

Country	Vote Share
	(%)
China	**20.4**
India	16.7
United States	**4.6**
Indonesia	3.7
Brazil	2.9
Pakistan	2.5
Russia	**2.3**
Bangladesh	2.2
Nigeria	2.2
Japan	2.0
Total	60.0

Notes: Top ten in an assembly of 191; P5 in bold.

than an assembly of the whole (such as the Security Council). For example, if the body had the ten largest states as members, how would the remaining 40 percent of the votes be allocated among these ten—equal distribution? proportional to size? regional similarities or cultural ties? If the states on the council are understood as agents acting on behalf of those in states not represented on the council, then it is not clear by what principle one should assign agency.

Still, it must be allowed that any formula that does not give institutional standing to large segments of humanity would suffer on grounds of legitimacy (principle 2). Given that a large body, like the General Assembly, is likely to be ineffective at the crisis management that is central to the tasks of a Security Council-like body, this implies that at least some nonpermanent seats would be desirable in principle. Nonpermanent seats chosen by rotation, election, or some other rule would allow for representation to be distributed over large populations while retaining the form of an executive committee that could analyze, bargain, and act expeditiously (thus satisfying principle 1, on efficacy).

Influence as Measured by GDP?

Though hardly perfect, the size of a state's economy as measured by its gross domestic product (GDP) is the single best measure of power and influence on a broad range of international matters. The states with the largest economies necessarily exercise considerable power to "make things happen" through international collaboration, and they have considerable power to prevent things from happening if they do not agree among themselves or with others. A Security Council-like body could not be effective if it did not allow significant influence for the economically strongest states in the international system.

The increasing importance and scope of the G8 summits as an international institution illustrates this principle. Though the summits started as a forum for addressing international macroeconomic issues, the G8 increasingly address security affairs. Their most notable security initiative is the Global Partnership against the Spread of Weapons and Materials of Mass Destruction. But the G8 have also negotiated agreements, initiatives, and commitments on regional peace processes (Bosnia, Kosovo, the Middle East, central Africa), counterterrorism, landmines, and peacekeeping operations in Africa.[9] The forum has also served for political negotiations that have led to action in the UN Security Council. According to David Malone (2003), the Security Council Resolution that ratified and organized the end of hostilities between NATO and Kosovo (SCR 1244, June 10, 1999) was "actually negotiated within the Group of Eight forum."

If votes in a General Assembly of 191 members were weighted by contribution to the global economy, then the states with the largest vote shares would be those in the second column of Table 2. Thus, the United States would control about one-third of the votes, the top ten states would control three-quarters, and the top 15 would control 82 percent.[10] For an executive committee of 10 to 25 members (rather than an assembly), there is again the issue of how to allocate the remaining vote shares among committee members. In this case, however, if the sole criterion were relative influence, the natural solution would be to allocate proportionally. This would yield the vote shares shown in the third column of Table 2 for a council of 15. Now, the United States and Japan would control about 55 percent of the votes on the council, while the western European states together would control about 28 percent.

Although such a scheme arguably would do well on the necessary condition for council effectiveness (principle 1), it would suffer on the grounds of legitimacy since only 55 percent of the world's population

---

9. For summaries of G8 initiatives and commitments, see the Web site: http://www.g8.utoronto.ca.
10. Using purchasing-power-parity-adjusted figures, rather than GDP, in Table 2 gives rather different results, but also makes no sense here since we are trying to measure economic influence rather than to make welfare comparisons.

Table 2: *UN Votes Weighted by Economic Size*
(shares based on GDP in 2002, in constant US$)

Country	General Assembly of 191	Security Council of 15
	(percentage of vote)	*(percentage of vote)*
United States	**32.7**	**39.8**
Japan	12.6	15.3
Germany	6.2	7.6
United Kingdom	**4.9**	**6.0**
France	**4.5**	**5.5**
China	**4.0**	**4.9**
Italy	3.7	4.5
Canada	2.2	2.7
Spain	2.1	2.5
Mexico	2.0	2.4
India	1.6	2.0
South Korea	1.5	1.8
Brazil	1.4	1.7
Netherlands	1.3	1.6
Australia	1.3	1.6
Total	82.0	99.9

Source: Data on GDP are from the World Bank.
Note: P5 in bold.

would be represented on a council of 15, while Africa, the Middle East, and eastern Europe would be wholly unrepresented.

There is, moreover, a deeper problem with the rationale behind this scheme. The argument for representing power and influence is pragmatic: without the major powers, an international institution risks irrelevance. But to produce resolutions on the use of force that have legitimacy, some kind of principled justification for the body would be helpful and perhaps even necessary. Could the G8 vote on whether force was permissible in various international crises? Yes, and perhaps this could help legitimize the use of force by indicating agreement among the major powers. But it would be far better to have an institution established by some kind of initial consent among a broad spectrum of countries, whose founding principles would make it more than an explicit major power club.

Influence as Measured by Military Might?

Total military spending correlates strongly with total GDP across countries, but the correlation is not perfect. There can be little doubt, however, that military capability is an important factor in determining a state's influence in matters of international peace of security (for good or ill). So, at least on grounds of effectiveness (principle 1), one could argue for putting some weight on relative military capability for membership and decisionmaking power in a Security-Council-like body.

The argument is, however, weak. Such a criterion would create an incentive for militarism, which is contradictory to the very purpose of an international institution aimed at fostering peace and security. It is already a source of great trouble that some states' leaderships believe that producing nuclear weapons is a necessary condition or a valid claim for becoming a permanent member of the UN Security Council. (Given that the P5 are exactly the five nuclear weapons states recognized in the Non-Proliferation Treaty, they may perhaps be forgiven the confusion.) So, not only would this criterion suffer on legitimacy grounds for the same reasons as representing economic might alone would, it would also be dubious on purely pragmatic grounds.

Size of Contribution to the UN?

A principled justification that would have the effect of heavily weighting the votes of the major powers in the General Assembly is the size of their contribution to the UN. Such a criterion would make influence partly a matter of choice: if you want more influence, contribute more.

A highly attractive feature of this criterion is that it would provide an incentive for states to support the international institution. Lack of resources has been a persistent problem in the UN system. The UN Charter provides for the suspension of General Assembly voting rights of states that do not pay their dues for two successive years, but these provisions tie influence within the organization only weakly to the level of support a state provides and can be avoided even while a state runs up massive arrears. Imagine a scheme whereby voting weights within a Security Council-like body are based on states' contributions to the organization, averaged over the preceding three or five years. This could give states a powerful incentive to make financial support of the organization a priority.

What would voting weights look like under this scheme? It is impossible to say since we do not know how much states would choose to contribute.

But we can make some guesses based on current UN dues and voluntary contributions.

UN activities are financed by state payments to three major accounts: the regular budget, the peacekeeping budget, and voluntary contributions (typically to specific agencies, such as the UN High Commissioner for Refugees or UNICEF). "Capacity to pay" has long been the main principle behind assessments for the regular and peacekeeping budgets, meaning that a country's total GDP is used as the baseline. Since the UN's beginning, however, its members have accepted the principle that poorer countries should pay at a lower rate, leading to a "low-income offset" scheme that reduces the dues for countries with per capita incomes below the world average. Members also agree to cap the maximum share of any one state's contribution to the UN budget at 26 percent, although this was reduced to 22 percent in recent negotiations. The second column of Table 3 shows how voting weights would be allocated in an assembly of 191 based on the official assessment scale for 2003.

Not surprisingly, given the rule for computing dues, this scheme would give results similar to those from basing voting power on economic size. The United States' voting weight here, however, would be quite a bit less than its share of the global economy, due to the budget cap agreement. Moreover, because of the low-income offset, the relatively rich countries—particularly Japan and Germany—would gain more voting weight than their proportion of world GDP. China and India, by contrast, would have markedly less voting power if they chose to contribute at their current assessed levels, due to the low-income discount built into the current scheme.

One might obtain a better estimate of what states actually would choose to contribute by looking at what they now contribute voluntarily to UN agencies (see Table 4). Somewhat surprisingly, in light of congressional intransigence on US contributions to the regular UN budget, the United States already contributes close to its share of global GDP and more than its budget-capped 22 percent on regular dues. We would also see a large increase in the influence of the Nordic countries and the Netherlands, which are big voluntary supporters of the organization.

Basing voting weights on contributions to the organization would have two major advantages. First, it would provide a principled justification for a rule that is likely to satisfy the condition for effectiveness (principle 1).

Table 3: *UN Votes Weighted by UN Dues*

Country	Vote Share	GDP as a Share of World GDP
	(%)	*(%)*
United States	**22.0**	**32.7**
Japan	19.6	12.6
Germany	9.8	6.2
France	**6.5**	**4.5**
United Kingdom	**5.6**	**4.9**
Italy	5.1	3.7
Canada	2.6	2.2
Spain	2.5	2.1
Brazil	2.2	1.4
Netherlands	1.7	1.3
South Korea	1.7	1.5
Australia	1.6	1.3
China	**1.5**	**4.0**
Russian Federation	**1.2**	**1.1**
Argentina	1.2	0.3
Total	84.8	79.8

Source: United Nations System, Chief Executives Board for Coordination.
Note: Top 15 in an assembly of 191; P5 in bold.

It would seem fair in this context that those who contribute more should be granted more say. Second, it would provide good incentives for contributing to global public goods. On the downside, one can criticize this criterion on grounds of legitimacy (principle 2) for its not being likely to represent large portions of humanity. There is also the reasonable question of what constitutes a "contribution" to international peace and security, which should be weighed in the formula for deciding influence.

Size of Contribution to International Peace and Security?

One can conceive of contributions to the UN (or like body) narrowly, in terms of monetary or in-kind payments. But states that send their soldiers on peacekeeping missions surely also make a major contribution, even if they are paid. And states and organizations—such as the United States and the North Atlantic Treaty Organization (NATO)—that supply military planning and logistical services for peacekeeping operations also make a contribution. For that matter, if the United States and other major powers

Table 4: *UN Votes Weighted by Voluntary Contributions to UN*

Country	Vote Share	GDP as a Share of World GDP
	(%)	*(%)*
United States	**31.3**	**32.7**
Japan	10.6	12.6
Netherlands	7.3	1.3
Norway	6.4	0.6
Sweden	5.8	0.8
United Kingdom	**5.5**	**4.9**
Denmark	5.4	0.5
Germany	4.1	6.2
Canada	3.7	2.2
Switzerland	2.7	0.8
Italy	2.5	3.7
Australia	2.1	1.3
France	**1.7**	**4.5**
Finland	1.7	0.4
Brazil	1.3	1.4
Total	92.1	73.9

Source: United Nations System, Chief Executives Board for Coordination; see the Web site: http://ceb.unsystem.org/hlcm/programmes/fb/financial.situation.htm, table 8.

Notes: Top 15 in an assembly of 190; P5 in bold.

The total size of voluntary contributions from the richest states is very large, sometimes greater than their assessed dues. At least in the US case, one reason for greater congressional willingness to make voluntary contributions is that Congress can negotiate the specifics of the use of money, whereas regular dues to the UN are unrestricted funds. In-kind contributions to some voluntary agencies are also common. The United States contributes massive amounts of food to the UN's World Food Program, but this is basically the unloading of subsidized and protected US farm production. For humanitarian purposes, it would be far better to lower First World agricultural protection and subsidies to "level the playing field" for Third World farmers.

suddenly were no longer willing to confront aggressive cross-border attacks, we would likely see a great deal of regional violence as some minor powers attacked smaller neighbors. Is this not a contribution to international peace and security? What about the protection of international sea lanes by various large navies or the contributions of states' national development agencies? One could go on, but all these arguably contribute indirectly to peace and security.

Even for a hypothetical exercise, it is too fanciful to imagine how the international community could agree on a scheme that took into account all such "contributions." The one measurable and clearly justifiable element in this list is states' contribution to peacekeeping forces. Countries that are willing to put their soldiers at risk for international peace should be recognized by more than pay. Indeed, under current circumstances, if they are compensated only by pay, the arrangement begins to have an unpleasant mercenary flavor, whereby rich countries appear to pay soldiers from very poor countries to undertake dangerous peacekeeping jobs.[11] There is a strong argument on grounds of legitimacy that those who contribute soldiers to peacekeeping missions should gain in representation within the council that decides on their deployment.

Type of Government?

The only plausible principled justification for basing the organization of a UN-like body on states is that states are the best and most capable representatives of their citizens, whose welfare is the ultimate end of the institution.[12] If that is so, then there is a strong argument that a government that does not truly represent its population, in the sense of not having been elected out of a free and fair democratic process, should not have full or perhaps any representation in the international institution.

The UN Charter speaks of "[w]e the peoples," and Article 56 obligates members to promote "universal respect for, and observance of, human rights and fundamental freedoms for all without distinction as to race, sex, language, or religion." In slight contradiction, the charter also explicitly conceives of UN members as states, and specifies that "[n]othing contained in the present Charter shall authorize the United Nations to intervene in

---

11. During the Cold War, when most peacekeeping operations concerned monitoring ceasefire lines between states, as opposed to complex operations in civil-war-torn countries, soldiers wearing the UN's blue helmet came mainly from middle powers, often those with high income per capita. Since the end of the Cold War, this has changed markedly. Most peacekeeping troops now come from very poor countries. See the Brahimi Report (UN 2000) and Fearon and Laitin (2004).

12. The preamble to the UN Charter begins by saying that the purpose of the organization is to save "succeeding generations," not states, from "the scourge of war"; to affirm "fundamental human rights" and the "dignity and worth of the human person"; and to promote "social progress and better standards of life." This interpretation of the ends of the institution seems to have become increasingly accepted over time, as evidenced by, for example, ICISS (2000) and UN (2004).

matters which are essentially within the domestic jurisdiction of any state" (Article 2.7). Certainly, the charter does not distinguish among domestic political regimes that would be more or less fit for UN membership. Rather, the only question seems to be whether the state is willing to accept the principles of international interaction outlined in the charter. Thus, the proposal to make membership or voice in a Security Council-like body conditional on a state's observance of democracy at home is at odds with the current UN Charter, even if there might be a slight opening for the idea through the door of "human rights" and fundamental freedoms.

Nonetheless, on grounds of legitimacy, the argument is quite compelling.[13] Moreover, there are good reasons to believe that limiting membership to certified democracies could have important practical benefits and advantages for effectiveness as well. Most of all, making membership or voice contingent on electoral democracy would provide a powerful incentive for states to maintain or move toward to democracy. In recent years, compelling examples have emerged in eastern Europe, where democratic "conditionality" in the European Union and its related institutions has exerted strong and generally positive effects.

If one thinks democracy is a good form of government, this would be a good thing by itself. But it would also be a good thing for the promotion and maintenance of international peace and security, for at least three reasons.

First, a substantial body of scholarship finds that democracies are much less likely to fight wars against each other (see, for example, Russett and Oneal 2001).

Second, one of the major security threats of the past 60-odd years, mass killing by governments, is much less likely to occur in democratic regimes. Civil wars are less likely in established democracies, and the levels of violence and killing appear to be lower in the civil wars that do occur

---

13. In defense of an organization open to all states, one might maintain that electoral democracy is not the only form of government that can properly represent a nation's citizens, either because some governments always know better than citizens what is good for them or because citizens might approve of nondemocratic government. The first suggestion, however, denies the premise of human equality in the UN Charter and so is even more radical than the proposal for democratic membership. The second could be revealed only by holding free and fair elections at regular intervals.

in democracies.[14] Thus, the creation of an international institutional incentive for democracy and democratic consolidation could make a major contribution to reducing all three major security threats that afflict most of the world's population.

Third, democracies are apt to be less secretive and more willing to abide by the international rule of law—and thus with international regimes for the monitoring and control of WMD. In general, stable democracies are much less of an international threat on the WMD front than are narrowly held dictatorships. The spread of democracy, therefore, could lessen former UN secretary-general Annan's central concern about unilateral pre-emptive attacks by the United States or other major powers that are worried about WMD proliferation and aid to terrorists.

Indeed, whether or not it would be politically feasible to make democracy a condition for membership or voice in a UN-like body, reforms of existing international institutions should consider ways to promote democracy as a matter of promoting international peace and security. Democratic transitions can be dangerous for various reasons, but in the long run it is a hard to see how the main security threats of the coming century could be well addressed except in a world of stable democracies.

Although the normative and practical arguments for making democracy a condition for membership or voice are strong, one could pose reasonable objections on grounds of effectiveness (principle 1). Under any serious criteria for "democracy," China would not be admitted to or would have little voice in a Security Council-like body. Yet China holds 20 percent of the world's population and is a major power. Moreover, while the world's largest economies are democracies (except for China), about 40 percent of the world's population lives in countries that are not democratic by standard measures (another 20 percent in addition to China).[15]

---

14. Whether electoral democracy causes a state to have a lower risk of civil war is not clear; it could be that established democracies tend to be wealthier, and that high income reduces the odds of civil war. On democracy and casualties in civil war, see Lacina (2004).

15. This estimate is derived by coding as "democratic" those states that scored more than 5 on the Center for International Development and Conflict Management's Polity IV index for 2002; see the Web site: http://www.cidcm.umd.edu/inscr/polity.

On the plus side, then, making democracy a condition for membership or voice in a UN-like institution could provide powerful incentives for democratization and for the consolidation of democratic gains. Moreover, successful democratization could be a necessary condition for the promotion and maintenance of international peace and security in the twenty-first century. These advantages, however, could come at the short- or medium-run cost of increased conflict with the dictatorships that would be excluded from the institution.[16]

Starting from Scratch: Summary and Conclusions

States are the most capable representatives of the people whose welfare is the end of international peace and security. Thus, it still makes sense to base an international institution dedicated to this end on states as members. At the same time, however, since states are wildly unequal in terms of their population and their ability to affect and contribute to international peace and security, basing an international institution like the UN on the principle of "one state one vote" is a prescription for irrelevance. Indeed, because so many states comprise such a tiny fraction of the world's population, "one state one vote" as the main basis for decision making in an international institution is not just impractical but unethical.

On grounds of both legitimacy and effectiveness, then, some form of weighted voting and/or elected nonpermanent membership status would be desirable in any new UN-like institution (and especially in a security Council-like body). Votes should be weighted by criteria that are dynamic in the sense of being able to reflect changes in the international distribution of population and influence. Without this, the international institution will not be robust to international change.

Several plausible dynamic criteria exist for weighting influence within an international institution—in particular, population, economic size, contribution to the institution and to peacekeeping forces, and democratic government. (Military size or nuclear status are also commonly suggested criteria, but these create the wrong incentives and should not be incorporated

---

16. These costs might be mitigated by providing for associate membership or by retaining an organization with universal membership while shifting funding and program action to an international institution of democracies.

in any reform scheme.) None of these criteria by itself would enable an institution to perform well on both effectiveness and legitimacy grounds, · though each has some advantages for one or the other end. Therefore, if we could start from scratch, it would be desirable to base influence and perhaps membership in a Security Council-like body on a mix of state characteristics, combined by some formula.

One can also turn around these general considerations and use them to identify the major pluses and minuses of the UN's current design. Most obviously, the criteria for UN Security Council membership are not dynamic as far as the Permanent Five are concerned. Given the international changes over the past 50 years, this has led to a situation where some major powers that contribute a great deal to the institution have considerably less formal power than others in the Security Council or are sometimes not represented there at all. Moreover, vetoes arguably give some or all of the P5 more influence than would be optimal in a weighted scheme along the lines I have suggested. As a result, the Security Council in its present form is less effective and legitimate than it might be.

Outside the central problem of the P5 and the veto, the use of non-permanent seats chosen by regional groupings has managed with some success to spread representation on the Security Council around a large number of countries. At the same time, the system has managed to give "weight" (in terms of time on the Council) to relatively more influential states that contribute a lot to the institution. Figure 1 shows the percentage of time each member state has spent on the Security Council since 1945 (or since its independence) against country GDP. The P5 are in the upper right corner. Notice that some of the main aspirants for permanent status have done relatively well in terms of time spent on the Council under the system of choice by regional groupings. This suggests that greater Security Council legitimacy and possibly effectiveness could be gained by a reform that: increased the number of nonpermanent seats; increased the length of at least some nonpermanent seat terms; and added dynamic and appropriate criteria that nonpermanent Council members would need to satisfy.[17]

---

17. One such proposal was developed by the UN High-level Panel Report (UN 2004) and is discussed in more detail in Fearon (2006).

Figure 1: *Time on UN Security Council since 1945*
(or Independence), Selected Countries, by GDP

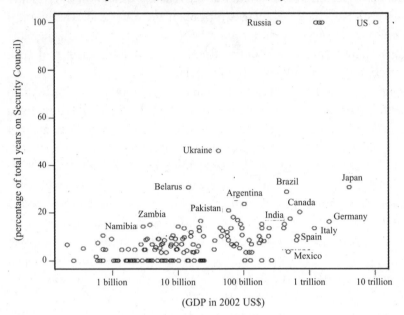

(GDP in 2002 US$)

Current thinking on UN reform focuses on the Security Council and for the most part ignores the General Assembly. This reflects the largely correct perception that the Council is an important and sometimes effective body, while the Assembly is not. But it would be a mistake to ignore Assembly reform. One way to make the Assembly a more effective body would be to change its voting rules so that votes are weighted by a state's contribution to the organization. It is even possible that the Assembly membership, or a large fraction of it, could come to see such a reform as desirable: what is the use of equal voting power (by state) if votes count for nothing?[18]

18. In the mid-1980s, the UN faced a financial crisis stemming in large measure from a US congressional bill that "stipulated that one-fifth of US dues were to be withheld until the General Assembly and the specialized agencies adopted the practice of financially weighted voting on budget matters" (Luck 2003, 42). The crisis was resolved with an agreement that budgetary decisions would require consensus, thus keeping formally within the "one state one vote" system but reducing the ability to get anything done.

There is a strong argument that making democracy a condition for membership or voice would be both ethically desirable and practically important in order to promote international peace and security in twenty-first-century conditions. But the UN as currently conceived cannot accommodate this. The UN could, of course, take various actions to promote democracy when member states (especially those on the Security Council) are so agreed—and they have done so with surprising frequency since the end of the Cold War. But to get the major international benefits of making democracy a condition for membership or voice, a refounding would be necessary.

Founding a New United Nations

Though it is clearly a radical proposal, founding a new United Nations would be easier and more feasible than one might first imagine. As Tables 3 and 4 suggest, a handful of advanced industrial democracies provide almost all the financial support for the current UN system—the top five contributors supply close to two-thirds of the total UN budget. If they agreed among themselves to withdraw from the organization, the UN could not survive for lack of resources, reduced effectiveness, and possibly loss of legitimacy as well.

To found a new institution, the set of major powers withdrawing from the old UN would need to convene international conferences to negotiate a new charter and to invite a new membership to join an institution that would take over or adapt many of the central functions of the UN. With broad enough international assent, it would not be necessary to start entirely from scratch. Parts of the UN system, such as various specialized agencies, could be incorporated or adapted wholesale.

The most ambitious departure a new United Nations could make would be to restrict full membership to electoral democracies. As I argued above, making democracy a condition for membership or voice might be essential for maintaining international peace and security in the long run. There is also a powerful argument on grounds of legitimacy—that the people of the world merit, for the first time, a United *Nations* rather than a de facto United *Governments*.

The main institutional innovation this would require is a credible international agency for monitoring and certifying elections. The criteria for deciding which states were democratic enough to join (or to gain a share of the vote or representation on a Security Council-like body) would have to be relatively objective and verifiable. The agency would be empowered to observe and monitor election practices inside member states and those that aspire to join, and to report on how they fare relative to a set of mutually agreed standards. The agency would report to a relevant council or committee of the new institution, which would make membership decisions.

The seeds for such an agency are already planted and growing in international institutions, including in the current UN. The UN's Department of Political Affairs already provides extensive assistance and expertise in setting up electoral systems and elections in new democracies. Several international groups—including the Carter Center, the Organization for Security and Co-operation in Europe, and the Organization of American States—provide election monitoring services that play an increasing role in legitimizing new regimes as democratic or discrediting them as dictatorial. Whether or not radical restructuring of international institutions is undertaken, the idea of developing a core international institution for the construction, monitoring, and certification of democratic elections has great appeal.

The other major innovation desirable in a new UN would be to ground decisionmaking influence in dynamic criteria that reflect the diversity of the world's population, the distribution of economic and political influence, and states' choices about how much to contribute to the organization. Were radical reform possible, weighted voting should be the norm in a new General Assembly. Weighting by financial and peacekeeping contributions would be the easiest to implement, the most justifiable, and the most likely to yield a body that had both legitimacy and the potential to matter. With an assurance of greater influence on average, the major powers might be willing to grant more powers to a new General Assembly than the old one has, which, in turn, might be attractive to a coalition of the current membership.[19]

---

19. Weighted voting in a new General Assembly would pose no barrier to states that choose to use their votes for symbolic politics, which certainly have their

The design of a new Security Council would pose thornier problems. There would be no point in constructing a new UN unless the new Security Council was also governed by some scheme of weighted voting, as in the World Bank and the International Monetary Fund (IMF), rather than the current system of vetoes for the P5. But why would the current P5 (or the democracies among them) agree to give up their vetoes for weighted voting in a new and untested institution? This is where this scenario looks particularly politically infeasible, at least under current international conditions.

Veto power is desirable because it allows a state to block resolutions condemning its use of force, resolutions in favor of the use of force it does not approve of, and sundry other resolutions it might find annoying or unhelpful. Veto power also gives a state enormous leverage in bargaining over the content of resolutions that do pass. Thus, the current P5 would be willing to trade veto power for weighted voting only if the cost of losing a vote on the use of force were to decline or if weighted voting were to make the new Council so much more productive and useful on average that occasional losses would be judged worthwhile.

Consider how the cost of losing a vote on the use of force might be reduced. The charter for a new UN could specify that states have the right to use force in self-defense and that, in the end, states must judge for themselves what constitutes self-defense in their particular case. The point of Security Council-like resolutions on the use of force would not be to "make international law," but to offer an authoritative statement of international opinion on the justification for force in particular circumstances. Council resolutions would then matter by influencing how the international community of states would react and respond to the use of force. States would have an incentive to gain support of the Council on the use of force, insofar as this would confer a sense of legitimacy and broader international support and assistance.[20] But a resolution saying that the

---

place. Nothing would stop members from introducing resolutions destined for defeat but designed to embarrass opponents or make them uncomfortable by voting them down.

20. Consider an analogy from international monetary affairs. Private lenders often condition their behavior on whether the IMF has entered into an arrangement with a state that is experiencing balance-of-payments problems, even though the IMF does not formally "make law" about who can lend to whom, when, and where.

justification for force was weak and that the Council did not approve would not have the status of a "binding" obligation.

De facto, this is how the current system already operates, except that Security Council resolutions are understood to be binding in some hypothetical sense of international law. My reform would formally weaken this hypothetical sense of legal obligation, which, in any event, has been routinely violated, to the detriment of the UN's legitimacy and authority. Such a reform could also make the veto less valuable to its possessors and so make them more willing to contemplate a possibly much more productive Security Council based on more permissive decisionmaking rules.[21]

The current P5 might also be more willing to move toward a weighted voting scheme if the average benefits of international cooperation through a Security Council-like body were to increase for these states. Veto power protects a state from resolutions that it dislikes intensely. But the veto system also means that resolutions that are beneficial to many states are sometimes blocked. The more often this occurs—which depends on the average benefits available from international coordination through a Security Council-like body—the greater is the attraction of majority or supramajority rule rather than a veto system.[22] Put differently, vetoes protect their holders from bad outcomes, but at the expense of reducing average council effectiveness. If international change were to increase the value of international cooperation or if Council members came to learn that, on average, the advantages of cooperation outweighed the cost of occasional losses, then moving toward majority or supramajority rule would become more appealing and feasible.[23] This is arguably part of the

---

21. It is ironic and curious that the US politicians and pundits who are most dismissive of the UN's authority are also the most strongly opposed to considering any plan that would weaken US veto power in the Security Council. If the United States "needs no permission slip" to use force, as some have put it, then why insist on having a veto?

22. Maggi and Morelli (2006) consider a model of voting in international institutions that formalizes this tradeoff.

23. When interests are perfectly coincident, the specific decisionmaking rule (veto, majority rule, weighted majority rule, and so on) does not matter, since cooperation will occur regardless. When state interests are often strongly opposed, a veto system is more desirable. In between, weighted majority rule is more attractive.

story behind the EU's gradual moves toward weighted majority voting in its Council of Ministers.

Despite some signal failures, the UN Security Council was a much more productive and effective body for organizing international cooperation on security matters in the 1990s than ever before. There were structural reasons for this change. The major powers that dominate the Security Council are less ideologically opposed than during the Cold War, and they share interests in addressing diverse bad consequences of terrorism, state collapse, and civil war in various regions. It is conceivable—though, I grant, not at all likely in present circumstances—that a bargain could be struck on weighted voting in a new Security Council based on the combination of downgrading the hypothetical "binding status" of Council resolutions and increased average benefits for international coordination on terrorism, peacekeeping, post-conflict reconstruction, and (perhaps) the control of WMD.

It is obvious that disbanding the current UN and reconstructing a new international institution for the promotion of international peace and security would be an extremely ambitious political project. At a minimum, it would require a major US diplomatic initiative—which would be impossible with the current administration and probably the next one as well—and strong support from Japan, India, Brazil, and several major European powers. Nonetheless, the project could well be taken up in the coming decades, as a result of the poor functioning of the current system together with a coalition of major powers and a US administration that sees international institutional overhaul as a political winner at home.

Going Outside the UN

Even if such a major project is not feasible, serious and significant UN reform is probably impossible without implicitly threatening a more radical reconstruction or the construction of alternative institutions. If member states believe that the status quo is the default option, then 60 years' growth of myriad interlocking status quo interests will make genuine restructuring to solve the new problems of international security impossible. To get serious action within the UN, it will almost surely be necessary to threaten to go outside it.

The G8, for example, has several features that could make it a natural and effective alternative to the UN Security Council. Excepting Russia, this is a group of the economically largest democracies in the world whose heads of state meet annually to discuss and sometimes coordinate action on a broad range of global problems. Though their meetings began in the late 1970s as a forum for macroeconomic coordination, in recent years the G8 have initiated programs on nuclear materials and nuclear security, HIV/AIDs, and peacekeeping in Africa, among others. By expanding its membership to the largest democracies in the world by population, rich or poor—bringing in, for example, India, Indonesia, Brazil, Mexico, South Africa, and possibly Nigeria—a G15 or G20 could represent a large portion of the world's people. At the same time, it would comprise many of the most economically and politically influential states in the world (notably excepting China). With the addition of a permanent secretariat and some rules on voting to approve or disapprove of the use of force, such a larger grouping could evolve into an international institution with a number of the desiderata for global governance discussed above. And, of course, one could argue whether international peace and security might be better served overall by opening the organization to nondemocracies.

Other alternative international fora could also develop non-legally binding procedures for expressing approval or disapproval of the use of force. NATO can play essentially this role—and has done so in Kosovo and Afghanistan. Some argue for a "community of democracies," a new international organization that would admit only certified democracies as members. The point would be to create an alternative international forum for deliberation and endorsement or condemnation of proposals to use force in the name of international peace and security. Such declarations would not have "the force of international law," for what that is worth, but they would signal degrees of international assent and thus add to or subtract from the legitimacy of various acts.

If there are alternative international institutions for legitimating and coordinating the use of force, will there be problems with "forum shopping" by states looking for the easiest way to get approval for what they want to do? In this particular domain—agreement or disagreement on the use of force—it is not clear to me that forum shopping would have particularly bad consequences. The United States could always try to put together a "coalition of the willing," but in terms of legitimation this is only as good as the coalition and the motivations its members have for joining it. The pressure on the UN to reform to keep its business depends on the quality of authorization provided by alternative institutions. The higher that quality the more effective and legitimate those alternatives will be—and thus good for addressing the new security threats. So it is not clear that the possibility of forum shopping would make for worse outcomes in this sphere than if the UN Security Council were to remain "the only game in town."[24]

Conclusion

One of the most striking—and strikingly unnoticed—changes in international relations since 1991 concerns alliance politics among the major powers. In brief, there practically are none, or at least none of the traditional variety.

Open up almost any diplomatic history of Europe for any period between 1648 (or even before) and 1945 and one will find the principal subject matter to be either the fighting of wars or the maneuvering of leaders to make or counter some military alliance. Alliance politics were deadly serious and at the heart of foreign policy because military alliances were critical to aggregating power for self-protection or conquest. Conquest of one Great Power by another was entirely possible.

By contrast, in a nuclear world, it is hard to see how the military conquest of one Great Power by another would be possible or even what the point of conquest would be among democracies that face low trade barriers with each other.[25] Since 1991, we have not seen any scramble among the

---

24. Drezner (2006) argues that greater possibilities for forum shopping favor powerful states, which have more resources than weak states to use to shop around for the forum likely to get them the best deal. This might be so, but on the issue of collective authorization, the quality of the "good" depends very much on the forum, and it is not clear that the existence of an alternative forum implies a reduction in the average quality of all fora.

25. Democracies have little positive economic reason to attack another democracy if they expect they would extend the same rights to the population of the conquered territory that their citizens currently enjoy. Democracies can, however,

major powers to forge new military alliances to protect themselves from possible invasion by other major powers. NATO has turned for the most part into a provider of peacekeeping troops and an iffy source of insurance for some (non-nuclear) eastern European states against the return of an aggressive Russia.

Instead of being preoccupied with the question of which major power might ally with which for a possible major war, the security affairs of the governments of the strongest states have focused on civil wars in minor powers and their consequences, on terrorism, on some regional conflicts among minor powers, and on nuclear proliferation among minor powers. I argue that the main security threats to the major powers are likely to continue to arise from these sources in the coming years, as are the principal security threats in the South—though with much more weight on civil war and abusive rule and less on nuclear proliferation.

With less to worry about from each other and with common interests in addressing dangers arising from state collapse, terrorism, and WMD proliferation, the strongest states have more reasons for, and fewer obstacles to, multilateral cooperation on matters of security. In particular, they have stronger grounds for working out a better system for collective authorization and coordination of the use of force. Failure to do so would allow the increasing unilateral use of force to work against the long-run goals of limiting nuclear proliferation and, indirectly, nuclear terrorism. Failure would also mean less than optimal collective action to address civil war and its negative externalities.

A better international institution for authorizing the use of force would not have permanent members. Instead, membership would depend on a mix of criteria, including economic size and the extent of a state's contribution to the UN or a UN-like organization. Decisions would be made according to a weighted voting scheme, as in the World Bank or the IMF. Arguably, membership would be limited to democracies, and the institution would have a system for assessing democratic practice in its membership. This would make the institution more legitimate by making

---

have a positive economic reason to fight a dictatorship, since changing the regime to a democracy could lower the cost of defending against possible invasion by the dictatorship. See Fearon (2007).

it representative of people rather than states, and it would provide stronger incentives and ability to move more states toward becoming functioning democracies. In the long run, it is hard to see how we could deal effectively with the dangers of WMD terrorism and nuclear blackmail except in a world of stable democracies.

We know from long experience that UN Security Council reform—and serious UN reform in general—is an extremely difficult proposition. However, the UN is highly dependent on a small number of states for its finances. Under a different administration and in somewhat different international circumstances, a motivated United States might be able to organize a coalition to force major UN reform. Short of such a major initiative, the United States and other major powers could seek to develop alternative international institutions—perhaps through an expanded G8—for coordinating action and programs on international security matters.

References

Annan, Kofi. 2003. Address by the Secretary-General to the UN General Assembly, New York, September 23.

Drezner, Daniel W. 2006. "Regime Proliferation and World Politics: Is There Viscosity in Global Governance?" Paper presented at the Annual Meeting of the American Political Science Association, Philadelphia, August 31–September 3.

Fearon, James D. 2006. "Reforming International Institutions to Promote International Peace and Security." In *Expert Papers: Peace and Security*. Stockholm: Secretariat of the International Task Force on Global Public Goods.

———. 2007. "A Simple Political Economy of the Democratic Peace." Stanford University. Unpublished paper.

Fearon, James D., and David D. Laitin. 2003. "Ethnicity, Insurgency, and Civil War." *American Political Science Review* 97 (1): 75–90.

———. 2004. "Neotrusteeship and the Problem of Weak States." *International Security* 28 (4): 5–43.

ICISS (International Commission on Intervention and State Sovereignty). 2001. *The Responsibility to Protect*. Ottawa: International Development Research Centre.

Lacina, Bethany. 2004. "Why Civil Wars Come in Different Sizes." International Peace Research Institute, Oslo. Mimeographed.

Luck, Edward C. 2003. "American Exceptionalism and International Organization: Lessons from the 1990s." In *US Hegemony and International Organizations*, edited by Rosemary Foot, S. Neil McFarlane, and Michael Mastanduno. New York: Oxford University Press.

Maggi, Giovanni, and Massimo Morelli. 2006. "Self-Enforcing Voting in International Organizations." *American Economic Review* 96 (4): 1137–58.

Malone, David M. 2003. "US-UN Relations in the UN Security Council in the Post-Cold War Era." In *US Hegemony and International Organizations*, edited by Rosemary Foot, S. Neil McFarlane, and Michael Mastanduno. New York: Oxford University Press.

Russett, Bruce, and John Oneal. 2001. *Triangulating Peace: Democracy, Interdependence, and International Organizations*. New York: W.W. Norton.

Thompson, Alexander. 2006. "Coercion through IOs: The Security Council and the Logic of Information Transmission." *International Organization* 60 (1): 1–34.

United Nations. 2000. Panel on United Nations Peace Operations. *Report*. (Brahimi Report). A/55/305-S/2000/809. New York. August 21.

———. 2004. High-level Panel on .Threats, Challenges, and Change. *Report*. A/59/565. New York. December 2.

Voeten, Erik. 2005. "The Political Origins of the UN Security Council's Ability to Legitimize the Use of Force." *International Organization* 59 (3): 527–57.

Multilateralism on Trial: From the 2005 UN Summit to Today's Reality

Ferry de Kerckhove

*   *   *

Interdependence is an accepted fact. It is giving rise to a great yearning for a sense of global purpose, underpinned by global values, to overcome challenges, global in nature. But we are woefully short of the instruments to make multilateral action effective. We acknowledge the interdependent reality. We can sketch the purpose and describe the values. What we lack is capacity, capability, the concerted means to act. We need a multilateralism that is muscular. Instead, too often, it is disjointed, imbued with the right ideas but the wrong or inadequate methods of achieving them. None of this should make us underestimate what has been done. But there is too often a yawning gap between our description of an issue's importance and the matching capability to determine it.

— Tony Blair, Davos, Switzerland, January 27, 2007

After the Iraqi debacle at the United Nations and the ensuing crisis of confidence both in and at the UN, Secretary-General Kofi Annan's initiative of asking a high-level panel of distinguished, independent, yet influential personalities to look at "threats, challenges and change" in the world rekindled hope in the institution's capacity to redeem itself. Much hype ensued, leading to the Leaders of the World Summit in New York on the occasion of the UN's sixtieth anniversary and, eventually, to the "delivery" of the now somewhat infamous Outcome Document of September 2005 (United Nations 2005).

Initially, the Outcome Document was intended to become the new normative charter for the Third Millennium; in fact, it wound up enshrining the full range of conceptual and ideological oppositions that characterize today's global commons. In this paper, I try to convey that, while attempts to reform the UN *en profondeur*, not unexpectedly, have more or less failed, the process has led more durably to a fundamental questioning of multilateralism as an effective mechanism to resolve the threats, crises, and conflicts of this day and age, whatever their origins. Yet, we know "instinctively" that, in the long run, only multilateral solutions, backed by political will, can handle modern-age crises and looming threats—climate change immediately comes to mind.

While 2005 was supposed to be the year of reform of multilateral institutions, 2006 marked the return of geopolitics with a vengeance, highlighting weaknesses and even the apparent obsolescence of the international institutions that 2005 was supposed to rebuild or reform. Less than a year after the World Summit, UN reform efforts withered, leading to a perception that multilateralism was failing, despite the extraordinary work of a host of other, more specialized multilateral institutions whose only "weakness" comes from a lack of political traction to lead the world to focus on today's new challenges.

Indeed, because of the multifaceted nature of the threats we face, insecurity appears more dominant today than at the worst time of the world of nuclear bipolarity. Or is it that the comfortable knowledge of mutually assured destruction during the Cold War days was more bearable than today's uncertainties from within our societies and from without our borders? Questions we now need to ask today's world leaders include: what are the new problems that existing institutions are failing to address? what are the alternatives? For Canadians in search of reassurances, what role can their country play in rekindling faith in the multilateral system, and what initiatives can it introduce to tackle the problems, both short and long term, that affect the planet? These questions confront policy makers on a daily basis, and their efforts should be treated with as much respect as the problems are intractable, or so it seems.

The Summit of 2005

La critique est facile, l'art est difficile, the French saying goes. Yet it should be recognized that, at the UN, 2005 was very much the year of ideas. The December 2004 report of the High-level Panel on Threats, Challenges and Change (United Nations 2004) had provided the intellectual framework for reform, but the framework then became a battleground. With debate raging along conventional lines—the North-South divide, the G77 developing countries and the Non-Aligned Movement, in their New York-style time warp, versus the rest (mostly developed countries)—and with anti-US sentiments fueled somewhat by the tough talk of US ambassador John Bolton, the feeling grew of a missed opportunity, underscoring how necessary reform was and still is.

What explains the mixed result, at best, for such a major endeavor? Evidently, after the Iraq debacle, Secretary-General Annan felt the need to rekindle faith in the United Nations. Some observers, such as Bruce Jones,[1] have argued that the secretary-general was gambling that the Iraq crisis had provoked such a crisis of confidence in the organization and in the relationships between the Security Council's traditional Western allies that it might generate the kind of transformational agenda that the world witnessed in 1945. Unfortunately, the gamble, assuming it was one to start with, failed. In fact, it was not the first attempt at a grand reform scheme for the UN. Kofi Annan himself, upon taking up the reins at the UN, launched a crusade with the release of the 1997 paper *Renewing the United Nations: A Programme for Reform*, prepared by Maurice Strong (United Nations 1997). In the end, however, this ambitious project did not deliver much change. And it demonstrated again how difficult it was for the international community to live up to Strong's contention that "[t]he concept of national sovereignty has been immutable, indeed a sacred principle of international relations.… What is needed is recognition of the reality that … it is simply not feasible for sovereignty to be exercised unilaterally by

---

1. Bruce Jones, professor and co-director of the Center on International Cooperation, New York University, oral presentation to the Department of Foreign Affairs and International Trade, Ottawa, 2006.

individual nation-states, however powerful" (Strong 1997, 2). How true this still rings a decade later!

Things started well in 2005. The report of the High-level Panel on Threats, Challenges and Change—the first document from the UN entrails that could nearly qualify as a best-seller—had just been released, and it provided an idealistic vision of a better world. Panel members had had the courage to go beyond the lowest common denominator and provide an integrated perspective on threats, none of which was hierarchically superior to another: poverty was as much a threat as weapons of mass destruction. The report had three complementary themes: freedom from fear, freedom from want, and the right to live in dignity, the latter to be obtained through the rule of law, the enshrinement of the concept—sacrosanct to Canadians—of the Responsibility to Protect, and full respect for human rights. To achieve this vision, the panel provided for a formidable program of reform of the management processes and institutions of the United Nations.

In his seminal document, *In Larger Freedom*, Kofi Annan (2005) renewed the panel's commitment to a vision of the world that, unfortunately, had all the qualities of an *image d'Épinal*—of the too-good-to-be-true variety, a beautiful vision for the World's Federalists, perhaps, but not for the harsh realism of Forty-seventh Street and First Avenue. And disillusion rapidly set in as negotiations commenced on a summit declaration for the UN's sixtieth anniversary. For a lot of UN delegates, one of their most profound disappointments had to be the rejection, throughout the negotiations, of the very idea that all of mankind had to come together to work as hard on security issues as on fostering development and eradicating a series of ills that knew no frontiers.

The complementary nature of global threats should not have pitted defenders of a stronger international consensus on security issues against those who saw development and renewed economic commitments as a summit's only valid outcome. Yet it was also clear that, initially, the 2005 summit had been conceived as an interim assessment of what the international community had achieved in implementing the Millennium Development Goals. Even valiant attempts by the High-level Panel to address development issues could not entirely disguise the fact that—as the title of its report (*A More Secure World*) indicated—its principal focus was on security. To observers from the South, the panel was imbuing *ab initio* the negotiations with a clear Northern perspective or bias. Notwithstanding the positive report of a team led by Jeffrey Sachs (UN Millennium Project 2005), this was probably the single most important reason the "grand bargain" did not quite work out as Kofi Annan had anticipated, as he, in fact, diverted the summit's original purpose to a loftier goal that ultimately proved unattainable.

The second, although more debatable, reason for the failure pertained to the "poison pill" of Security Council reform, which pitted different sets of players than the traditional North-South cleavage. Initially, the High-level Panel had not been particularly keen on tackling an issue that had been divisive since the first expansion of the council in the mid-sixties from 11 to 15 members, but only in the number of nonpermanent members. It seems, however, that Secretary-General Annan was adamant that the issue be covered in the panel's report, arguing—not incorrectly, according to most—that the reform of UN institutions would not be complete without changes in the world body's *primus inter pares* institution. In so doing, however, Annan wound up stacking more odds against a successful outcome. Indeed, apparently at his insistence, as he wished to leave a legacy of reform and had always shown sensitivity to the role of large powers in a fragmented world of more than 190 nations, the High-Level Panel came up with two constructs for Security Council reform. One, model A, called for an increase in both permanent and nonpermanent categories; the other, model B, suggested an increase only in the non-permanent member category, yet with some enjoying longer stints than others. Legend or rumor has it that Annan clearly preferred model A, but he never expressed it formally.[2] The result was that, at a time when unity among UN members should have been the primary objective, ferocious and divisive debates on Security Council expansion between the supporters of model A—led by India, Brazil, Germany, and Japan—and those that, under the banner of

---

2. I discussed this issue with both Stephen Stedman, research director of the High-level Panel, during a Ditchley Conference in 2005, and UN assistant secretary-General Robert Orr at a meeting in Spain of the Friends of UN Reform in early 2006. Both are outstanding personalities, even if they differ in their interpretations.

"Uniting for Consensus," wanted to fight against the already discriminatory setup of the post–World War II order and supported infinite variations of model B penalized the whole process of negotiations of the summit's outcome document.

The Outcome Document of the 2005 World Summit (United Nations 2005) has been the subject of numerous evaluations (see, for example, Heinbecker and Goff 2005; Malone 2006). Many are of the glass-half-full/half-empty type, with emphatic condemnations of the text's obvious failings, such as its lack of any reference to impunity, disarmament, or the International Criminal Court, and its tempered salutations to encouraging commitments regarding the enshrinement of the Responsibility to Protect (referred to as R2P), the creation of a Peacebuilding Commission, and the transformation of the Human Rights Commission into a new Human Rights Council. Subsequent negotiations did provide for progress in all three areas on an institutional basis: R2P was the subject of a Security Council resolution, the Peacebuilding Commission now exists, and the new Human Rights Council has started debating.

Anyone with any illusions that the spirit in which these reforms would happen would reflect an attitudinal change on the part of member countries quickly found, however, that the good old split between the G77 and the rest of the world would prevail—with a New York twist. Now, the implementation of the normative framework provided by R2P is being resisted by most of those countries that had been pushed into accepting the concept, and it is unlikely to be invoked formally in the near future, Darfur notwithstanding. For its part, the Peacebuilding Commission includes too many players, and is hard pressed to select a crisis it can manage—Burundi, at first blush the most amenable, is proving to be a very tough nut to crack. Meanwhile, the Human Rights Council managed to reduce its membership only from 56 to 47 and its early debates soon resembled those of the discredited commission it replaced.

In a way, the 2005 Outcome Document, as vilified as it has been, represents the logic of international realism's taking over from a generous, unfortunately unduly idealistic, vision of tomorrow's world. The downside of the debate is that it has tended to underscore the failings of the UN rather than extol its successes, to focus endlessly on the frustrations and inactions of the organization—on Darfur, for example—while forgetting the formidable work it has carried out in such places as the Democratic Republic of Congo.[3]

Still, there are many who lament the UN's poor record in management reform, underscored by the failure of a grand bargain launched by US permanent representative John Bolton, supported by several developed countries, who imposed a six-month budget cap on the organization that was to be lifted only in exchange for commitments by the G77 to a series of reforms, including mandate review, oversight, streamlined personnel policies, and so on. Eventually, the cap was lifted, even though only limited progress was registered on management reform. For their part, the developed countries managed to limit their commitments to development assistance to US$50 billion, a far cry from the 0.7 percent of gross national income called for by the Millennium Development Goals and that only a few countries actually deliver. Moreover, despite the terrorist attacks of 9/11, expectations of a major change in the area of counterterrorism—such as a comprehensive convention on terrorism—were also short changed.

In fact, the lesson of the whole process is that, in New York more than anywhere else, the crystallization of the North–South divide is matched only by an amazing level of hostility toward the United States, which Mr. Bolton did not help attenuate, however right he was 99 times out of 100 on substance. The US-engineered financial crisis in mid-2006 endeared him to no one, further fueling G77 resentment for what the group sees as a gross pro-Israel bias on the part of the United States. Even countries that are close allies of the United States in different situations, frameworks, and organizations mutate into "spoilers" at the UN. In the end, on paper, the normative framework of the United Nations clearly was enhanced, but both institutional fatigue and failed implementation brought the organization not much farther than it had been prior to the lofty exposition of the High-level Panel's prescriptions.

---

3. For its part, Canada put a lot of effort into ensuring a successful outcome for the 2005 summit; it also campaigned at all levels for R2P, including a series of prime ministerial phone calls to key leaders prior to the opening of the UN's sixtieth anniversary meeting, and provided the High-level Panel with a range of proposals pertaining to the concept of human security, which has yet to acquire a UN-sanctioned definition.

2006: Back to Strategic Reality

Evidently, the multiplicity of crises haunting the international arena did not stand idle, awaiting the summit's results. Plagued with conflict situations from Darfur to North Korea, via Afghanistan, Iran, the broad Middle East, Haiti, and Lebanon, with—as an increasingly stark and dangerous background—the incipient civil war in Iraq, the key players on the planet were returning to the strategic reality, leaving behind as unfinished business the broad objectives of UN reform. The most recent report on the reform process—that of the High-level Panel on System-Wide Coherence (United Nations 2006b)—aimed to establish how the UN system can respond most effectively to the global development, environmental, and humanitarian challenges of the twenty-first century. The report should have been welcomed as the coronation of the reform process; instead, it could find itself relegated to dusty shelves—although there are signs that the new secretary-general, Ban Ki-moon, might give it prominence in his huge work program for 2007, assuming the international agenda allows him to do so. And then there is report fatigue…

The immensity and diversity of the security problems confronting the planet is mind boggling. They defeat any attempt to rank them according to their salience, importance, or danger. The risk of nuclearization of a growing number of less and less reliable or stable countries competes gingerly with environmental degradation and other ills of similar ilk. The new and highly legitimate fixation of the international community, governments, and civil society alike with fragile and failed states underscores the growing realization that world security depends more on protecting against these festering nests of terrorism and instability than on military power and traditional defense capacities. Yet, mostly due to the perennial debate between sovereignty and impunity, the world is not prepared to agree on the normative framework required to deal with the problem, and has hardly adopted measures to deal effectively with the causes and effects of such failures. International frustrations with Sudanese president Omar al-Bashir's unending wavering, until recently, on allowing a hybrid UN-African Union mission to replace the poorly equipped and ill-prepared African Union force and bring peace to Darfur—or at least to end the savage brutalization of hundreds of thousand people there—

demonstrate amply the need for a new paradigm on sovereignty, under-pinned by the concept of the Responsibility to Protect. Yet, despite the procrastination that for so long frustrated the transfer of military forces in Darfur, no one, including the United States, questions the relevance of the UN in the crisis—quite the contrary![4] The real challenge, however, is to set up an implementation mechanism. What should troops on the ground do? That is the test of "results-based multilateralism."

Although there is no full consensus on the exact number of fragile and failed states at any given moment, the mere fact that the figure often referred to hovers around 40, or more than 20 percent of the membership of the UN, underscores the overall fragility of the international system. Thus, the present focus on these states expresses far more than a simple feeling of guilt on the part of the beneficiaries of globalization toward those left behind or of former colonial powers that realize that decades of independence have not compensated for the fundamental ills of colonial-ism—including artificial boundaries, the displacement of people and livelihoods, and their poor record of building civil societies. It actually reflects a legitimate fear that the gains from globalization and growth could be thwarted by a wave of increasingly uncontrollable crises.

Afghanistan

Afghanistan represents a particular challenge, in that it is a UN-mandated military operation pitting NATO forces—including a courageous Canadian contingent fighting in the most dangerous area, itself a reflection of the peculiarities of the situation—against a real force that actually was in power in most of the country for a good number of years. That force, while partially defeated by US forces in 2001, had little difficulty regroup-ing and reorganizing in subsequent years; today, it can resupply itself almost at will both in and outside of the country.[5]

---

4. The United States ably supported Canada's efforts to promote the Responsibility to Protect, and has demonstrated an equal eagerness to find a way to imple-ment it in Darfur.
5. There is, indeed, a consensus that the Taliban, in the early days of their creation, benefited from major equipment, training, and weapons support from the government of then-prime minister Benazir Bhutto. Tariq Ali (2007)

The author witnessed first hand the power and authority exuded by the Taliban, as well as the fear they inspired in the local population. He could not fail to note, however, that, although the atrocities they perpetrated on their own people were beyond the wildest imagination,[6] deeply resented, and profoundly repulsive as an instrument of control, their religious, ideological, and "moral" mindset or frame of reference unfortunately correlated to a considerable extent with the general traditional attitudes, beliefs, and perspectives of the local population, particularly in the Taliban-controlled southern stronghold of Kandahar and notably regarding the role of women in society and their education.[7] Therefore, defeating the Taliban is not only essential to ensure that the kind of assistance which really makes a difference is provided—that is, a kind of reconstruction that does not alter fundamentally the country's social fabric[8] but provides real improvements in livelihoods; it is the only way to ensure that progressive Afghans take over and establish new norms of behavior, particularly toward women, while respecting what makes the souls, spirits, and minds of Afghans—something that no Western input can achieve alone. Indeed, as a UN Security Council mandated mission, Afghanistan is not a Western-driven mandate. As Canadian prime minister Stephen Harper (2006) put

---

claims, "It was Benazir Bhutto's minister of the interior, General Naseerullah Babar, who, with the [Pakistani intelligence service], devised the plan to set up the Taliban as a politico-military force"; see also Rashid (2000). The author discussed this issue with General Babar in 1998, who made no attempt to deny it.

6. For a graphic and tragically realistic example, see Khaled Hosseini's remarkable novel *The Kite Runner* (2003).

7. This was the subject of a heated discussion I had in 1999 with the Taliban regime's number two, Mullah Hassan, then-governor of Kandahar, when he accused the West of wanting to remove the burka from their women, which was part of their tradition, to which I replied, "No, I only want them to have the choice of keeping it on or removing it."

8. The Canadian High Commission in Islamabad had a fund for Afghanistan that it used in cooperation with CARE to finance very small projects, in the order of $15,000 to $30,000, with major local impact, such as rebuilding a bridge across a small river to allow women to work in the fields without having to walk seven kilometres out of their way.

it, "if we fail the Afghan people, we will be failing ourselves. For this is the United Nations' strongest mission and, therefore, our greatest test. Our collective will and credibility are being judged. We cannot afford to fail." The stakes are incredibly high, particularly in terms of the success or failure of a major multilateral military engagement.

Iraq

Iraq is one area where the UN, barring electoral support engineered from Jordan, has been nearly totally absent since the tragic bombing of the UN office and the death of Sergio Vieira de Mello and a number of his colleagues on August 19, 2003. And yet, there is a consensus out there that, at some stage, the UN will have to be engaged with its programs and agencies. But no one knows when the conditions for initiating such a full-fledged involvement will be realized. It is the tragedy of so-called multilateralism *à la carte* that, when the real job of reconstruction needs to be done, the point of transition to the contributions of the UN and other conventional multilateral or regional organizations to the effort is extremely difficult to decide upon. More often than not, it follows on the failure of the early coalition's attempt to "solve the problem at hand." The Peacebuilding Commission was partly created to fill this gap, but the *ab initio* problem is that Iraq, more than any other crisis, was perceived as an "anti-UN engagement" in that it followed the Security Council's refusal to endorse the United States' proposed intervention—hence, Kofi Annan's dramatic call for UN renewal. The tragedy of the bombing of the UN compound in Baghdad put final paid to any real UN engagement for a long time. We now face a crisis that could define the next ten to twenty years of US engagement on the international stage, notably in the most volatile region of the world, the Middle East, with hardly any real UN-influenced fallback role, at least in the short run.[9]

---

9. Some scholars and diplomats argue privately that it is not so much a question of US involvement in Iraq and its failures that matters as the risk that a needed US intervention elsewhere in the world might not happen due to the political legacy of Iraq—reminiscent to a certain extent of the "Vietnam syndrome."

Nuclearization

Asian nuclearization, be it in Iran or North Korea, represents a different set of problems for the UN and for multilateralism in general. In fact, UN involvement, though highly laudable, is at best accessorial in that very little of the nuclear debate over the past 60 years has taken place at the UN—or, more accurately, the issue has been brought to the UN only once all decisions have been taken by the nuclear powers. Moreover, today's new approaches to control the "genie"—such as the proposed Fissile Material Cut-Off Treaty—have little to do with the UN. And it is not the recently agreed convention against nuclear terrorism, although part of the essential arsenal of the normative framework, that is going to change any of this. In fact, one would argue that the recent evolution in the nuclear relationship between the United States and India clearly demonstrates the need for an entirely new approach to nuclear issues in general and to non-proliferation in particular, including a recognition that the Non-Proliferation Treaty is at risk of never being reinforced, notably on the compliance side, or that as important a player as the United States, so it seems, will never sign the Comprehensive Test Ban Treaty.[10] While both Iran and North Korea are clear examples of countries that are ignoring the framework within which the nuclear debate has been carried out, there has been a crying need ever since the Indian and Pakistani tests of 1998 for a new paradigm to handle the necessary discriminatory provisions of the nuclear regime created at the end of World War II while ensuring that the seemingly unavoidable expansion in the number of nuclear powers does not lead to Armageddon and nuclear holocaust.

It is doubtful, however, that the UN will be the locus for the development of such a paradigm.[11] At best, it will be the place where any agreement among the expanding number of real players in the field will be legitimized

---

10. The US Senate's October 1999 rejection of the treaty seems to have sealed its fate for the foreseeable future.
11. The irony of the UN's seizing on North Korea is that, while the Security Council adopted a resolution calling for sanctions unless North Korea resumed discussions in the Six Party talks, once North Korea eventually agreed to resume talks, no subsequent resolution of the Council canceled the earlier sanctions.

under the guise of universality. Similarly, although the legal threat of the use of force pursuant to a Security Council resolution was once an effective deterrent of interstate conflicts, it is clear that countries with weapons of mass destruction (WMD)—nuclear, chemical, or biological—are hardly amenable to threats of use of force, as demonstrated by both North Korea and Iran.[12] It is also clear that the multilateral structure tasked with fostering measures to alleviate the menace posed by WMD—the Geneva-based Conference on Disarmament—has demonstrated its total incapacity to look at each component of WMD *sui generis*, failing to recognize they are different from one another and deserve to be treated separately, rather than held hostage to one another.

Lebanon

The jury, with 20/20 hindsight, remains divided on the UN and Lebanon. Some argue that the UN intervened too late—as Kofi Annan himself deplored.[13] Others claim it is a typical success from a UN standpoint, with a cessation of hostilities, a force in place, and specific measures to alleviate the crisis and address its root causes. But no one can deny the fact that the UN got involved in a decisive way, and that any delay came from the decisionmaking process in the Security Council. Of course, the United Nations Interim Force in Lebanon (UNIFIL) pre-existed the crisis, making it simpler to provide for reinforcement, although the resumption of hostilities changed entirely the context of the mission, as the existing UN force was incapable of taking any active measure. Hence the call by the Security Council, a month later, for the end of hostilities and the strengthening of UNIFIL's forces within an expanded mandate and the creation of a "buffer zone." This was far from easy to achieve, and involved a typical set of negotiations among the five permanent members of the Security Council.

---

12. Unless some regional power were to attempt an operation similar to the 1981 attack on Iraq's Osirak nuclear facility, but such an act would hardly qualify as legal and would be terribly dangerous, although some might regard it as legitimate.
13. As Annan said, "All members of this Council must be aware that this inability to act sooner has badly shaken the world's faith in its authority and integrity"; see http://www.un.org/Depts/dpko/missions/unifil/background.html.

Hostilities, at least, ceased, a peacekeeping force was installed, and reconstruction started. A real sense of fragility remains, however, and Kofi Annan's remarks bear remembering:

> In order to prevent a resurgence of violence and bloodshed, the underlying causes of conflict in the region must be addressed. Other crises cannot be ignored, especially in the occupied Palestinian territory, as they are all interlinked. Until the international community insists on a just, lasting and comprehensive peace in the Middle East, any one of these conflicts has the potential to erupt and engulf the entire region.[14]

It is no surprise that the Security Council continues to follow closely the situation in Lebanon, evidently deeply concerned about a potential deepening of the political crisis there that could lead to a further destabilization of the region. Unfortunately, that is where the UN cannot achieve much. It cannot operate on multiple planes or dimensions, which the Middle East quagmire certainly offers, particularly when it is impossible to achieve a consensus among key players. However, in creating a commission to investigate the assassination of Prime Minister Rafik Hariri in February 2005 and in continuing to envisage the possible creation of an international tribunal to bring its perpetrators to trial, the UN is contributing on an ongoing basis to peace and stability in Lebanon.

Haiti

Haiti represents, first and foremost, a case of missed opportunities. In 1994, in an amazing precedent, the Security Council authorized the use of force to change a member state's government and, through the Uphold Democracy Operation, succeeded in both restoring Haiti's democratically elected government and stemming emigration, thanks to planned political, military, diplomatic, and humanitarian activities. Yet the end result was very much what then Canadian prime minister Paul Martin described to the General Assembly in 2004: "[A]s we have seen in Haiti, all the aid in the world will have only a fleeting effect if a country does not have functioning

---

14. See http://www.un.org/Depts/dpko/missions/unifil/background.html.

public institutions. We must build countries' governance capacities and take the time to do it right." In 1998, David Malone contended that "[i]n Haiti … unsettled political conditions, weak management of economic policy, and public indifference to electoral processes underscore how little the [Security Council], even buttressed by bilateral and multilateral donors, can do to affect political and economic outcomes, no matter how large its investment in resources and effort has been" (Malone 1998, 184). Today, all the efforts the international community is making in Haiti, one hopes, will prove Malone wrong. But it will take considerable time, energy, and sustainable commitments that might not always be present. It also means, as recent developments have partly confirmed, that it has been finally recognized—both inside Haiti and within the international community—that the ultimate deal is regime change, not simply an electoral process. This needs to be enshrined multilaterally and universally, over and beyond the work of the UN's stabilization mission in that country.

Beyond Geopolitics

All these crises, one way or another, demonstrate the limits of the UN. It is not so much a case of pinpointing failures as of recognizing that there are many crises beyond the UN's capacity to resolve unless there happens to be a "transcendental" willingness to do so, which seldom obtains. While we have seen a growing "competition" to universality by coalitions of the willing, such coalitions alone are incapable of providing sustainable solutions to crises unless they are accompanied by a legitimating process that only universal or recognized regional organizations can provide. And therein lies, today as ever, the perennial value of the UN, warts included. But is this enough for tomorrow's world?

While the ongoing crises occupy capitals, organizations, and embassies all over the world, there is a growing sense that these are very much legacies of the past and that, however dangerous each of them might be, they blind us to much more fundamental problems that loom in the future but whose contours we can already perceive or recognize. For example, the Bulletin of the Atomic Scientists recently pushed the hand of its Doomsday Clock closer to midnight as a result of climate change. "Global warming poses a dire threat to human civilization that is second only to nuclear weapons," said Bulletin executive director Kennette Benedict (2007). In fact, when looking at the whole process of the 2005 summit, one could wonder if we have not focused unduly on the issues pertaining to a post–World War II era as opposed to the problems of the third millennium, if we have not worked from the perspective of a dated framework and obsolescent institutions. This might be due to the fact that the foundation of our universal multilateral institution is the legitimate use of force, a trademark that might have little coinage in terms of the emerging issues. It could also explain why the UN has such a poor record on the development agenda: the Monterrey consensus notwithstanding, there is no enforcement mechanism for development.[15]

This is not to say that established institutions such as the UN do not focus on new or emerging issues, just that they do not generate the same commitment or have as much salience as "the old games" countries play. The long-term importance of the issues discussed is often inversely proportional to the attention they elicit beyond a small number of informed officials and scientists. A quick look at the various committees that form the backbone of the UN demonstrates the breadth and variety of concerns, but any reference to the Economic and Social Council (ECOSOC) draws a tedious yawn. Yet, issues under ECOSOC include forestry, biodiversity, desertification, biotechnology, and information and communications technology, to name a few. The fundamental problem remains that politics does not square well with long-term crises, which are dealt with not at all or only at the margins, without political buy-in or traction. Or, more precisely, even when there is a heightened consciousness at the national level of the critical importance of an issue—even if not directly related to peace and security or human rights and democracy—at the level of the global commons, there is not enough consensus to create the necessary "takeoff" effect. Thus, institutions tasked with following such events have a faint resonance on major political radar screens.

Furthermore, we still seem to be living under the illusion that we can continue to ignore or neglect problems that are either long term or

---

15. The Monterrey consensus is the landmark global agreement between developed and developing countries, in which both recognize their responsibilities in key areas such as trade, aid, debt relief, and institution building.

unpredictable, such as a tsunami—although, in the latter case, measures were taken fairly rapidly after the December 26, 2004, tragedy to enhance the capacity to predict or react to such an occurrence. Yet, although natural catastrophes can have a huge impact, an increasing number of man-originated catastrophes in the making are both probable and predictable and likely to have an impact just as large. And therein lays the dichotomy between universal salience and multilateral atrophy, despite warnings to the contrary, such as that given by Kofi Annan in one of his last speeches (2006), in which he aptly described the world we now have to contend with,

a world where deadly weapons can be obtained not only by rogue states but by extremist groups; a world where SARS or avian flu can be carried across oceans, let alone national borders, in a matter of hours; a world where failed states in the heart of Asia or Africa can become havens for terrorists; a world where even the climate is changing in ways that will affect the lives of everyone on the planet. Against such threats as these, no nation can make itself secure by seeking supremacy over all others. We all share responsibility for each other's security, and only by working to make each other secure can we hope to achieve lasting security for ourselves.

Some examples will illustrate how right Kofi Annan's parting words were.

Polar Ice Melting

There are numerous examples of man-made or "derivative" catastrophes waiting to happen or in the process of occurring. For instance, the melting of the polar ice might or might not be entirely due to climate change but the results are already quite predictable, according to specialized institutions. A few years ago, the Arctic Council and the International Arctic Science Committee launched an international project aimed at evaluating and synthesizing knowledge on climate variability, climate change, and increased ultraviolet radiation and their consequences. The report presented at the Fourth Arctic Council Ministerial Meeting in Reykjavik in 2004 highlighted the worldwide implications of Arctic warming:

- Melting of highly reflective arctic snow and ice reveals darker land and ocean surfaces, increasing absorption of the sun's heat and further warming the planet.
- Increases in glacial melt and river runoff add more freshwater to the ocean, raising global sea level and possibly slowing the ocean circulation that brings heat from the tropics to the poles, affecting global and regional climate.
- Warming is very likely to alter the release and uptake of greenhouse gases from soils, vegetation, and coastal oceans.
- Impacts of arctic climate change will have implication for biodiversity around the world because migratory species depend on breeding and feeding grounds in the Arctic. (ACIA 2004, 10)

While the Arctic Council is certainly a respectable institution, which counts Canada among its membership and which is indeed focusing on critical issues affecting the High North, it is not a multilateral institution that has a major influence on decisions taken regarding the issues it brings to the table, unless it is combined with a much larger *prise de conscience* at a planetary level—which might be in the making.

Global Warming

When it comes to global warming, the single most important international covenant the international community has partially committed to is the Kyoto Protocol to the United Nations Framework Convention on Climate Change, a 1997 amendment to an existing international treaty on climate change, which assigns to signatory nations mandatory targets for the reduction of greenhouse gas emissions. Its objective is the "stabilization of greenhouse gas concentrations in the atmosphere at a level that would prevent dangerous anthropogenic interference with the climate system." Yet, other than by a small group of countries that excludes nonsignatories such as China and signatories that have not ratified the protocol, there is little stabilization in sight.

Despite the urgency of the climate change crisis, some scientists have called our collective inability to internalize its significance the largest marketing failure ever. Yet we have now reached, one hopes, the stage where the debate is no longer on global warming itself—it is happening for all to see[16]—but on its impact and how to mitigate it. Indeed, our global energy consumption is unsustainable.[17] The real issue is: have we reached a point of no return and, if not, how can we avoid it? The Intergovernmental Panel on Climate Change (IPCC) Fourth Assessment Report (2007b) presents a dramatic a picture of the situation, including a forecast, for certain models, of a possible global warming by 2 degrees or more between now and 2050, which some scientists consider to be that very point of no return in terms of impacts and perturbation to the overall climatic system of the planet. The IPCC's report highlights scientific, technical, and socioeconomic information relevant for the understanding of climate change, its potential impacts, and options for adaptation and mitigation, the latter two seemingly offering the only glimmer of hope through carbon sequestration schemes at a much higher level of technology.[18]

The IPCC (2007a, 8–11) also provides chilling evidence of the effects of climate change:

[In Africa,] by 2020, between 75 and 250 million people are projected to be exposed to an increase of water stress due to climate change. If coupled with increased demand, this will adversely affect livelihoods and exacerbate water-related problems.

Agricultural production, including access to food, in many African countries and regions is projected to be severely compromised by climate variability and change. The area suitable for agriculture, the length of growing seasons and yield potential, particularly along the margins of semi-arid and arid areas, are expected to decrease. This would further adversely affect food security and exacerbate malnutrition in the

---

16. As even US president George W. Bush recognized in his latest State of the Union message, when he referred to the serious challenge of global climate change. In fact, it is amazing to note that, even since I began writing this paper, the political salience and traction of climate change have grown exponentially, in no small part due to the combined impact of the reports of the International Panel on Climate Change and Al Gore's increasingly credible and profoundly resonant message.

17. The International Energy Agency (2006, 1) notes that "fossil-fuel demand and trade flows, and greenhouse-gas emissions would follow their current unsustainable paths through to 2030 in the absence of new government action."

18. See the Web sites: www.grida.no/climate; www.ipcc.ch; and www.worldwatch.org.

continent. In some countries, yields from rain-fed agriculture could be reduced by up to 50% by 2020....

[In Asia,] glacier melt in the Himalayas is projected to increase flooding, and rock avalanches from destabilised slopes, and to affect water resources within the next two to three decades. This will be followed by decreased river flows as the glaciers recede.

Freshwater availability in Central, South, East and Southeast Asia, particularly in large river basins, is projected to decrease due to climate change which, along with population growth and increasing demand arising from higher standards of living, could adversely affect more than a billion people by the 2050s....

As a result of reduced precipitation and increased evaporation, water security problems are projected to intensify by 2030 in southern and eastern Australia and, in New Zealand, in Northland and some eastern regions. Significant loss of biodiversity is projected to occur by 2020 in some ecologically-rich sites including the Great Barrier Reef and Queensland Wet Tropics....

Nearly all European regions are anticipated to be negatively affected by some future impacts of climate change and these will pose challenges to many economic sectors. Climate change is expected to magnify regional differences in Europe's natural resources and assets. Negative impacts will include increased risk of inland flash floods, and more frequent coastal flooding and increased erosion (due to storminess and sea-level rise). The great majority of organisms and ecosystems will have difficulties adapting to climate change. Mountainous areas will face glacier retreat, reduced snow cover and winter tourism, and extensive species losses (in some areas up to 60% under high emission scenarios by 2080)....

By mid-century, increases in temperature and associated decreases in soil water are projected to lead to gradual replacement of tropical forest by savanna in eastern Amazonia. Semi-arid vegetation will tend to be replaced by arid-land vegetation. There is a risk of significant biodiversity loss through species extinction in many areas of tropical Latin America....

[In North America, w]arming in western mountains is projected to cause decreased snowpack, more winter flooding, and reduced summer flows, exacerbating competition for over-allocated water resources....

In the Polar Regions, the main projected biophysical effects are reductions in thickness and extent of glaciers and ice sheets, and changes in natural ecosystems with detrimental effects on many organisms including migratory birds, mammals and higher predators. In the Arctic, additional impacts include reductions in the extent of sea ice and permafrost, increased coastal erosion, and an increase in the depth of permafrost seasonal thawing....

Small islands, whether located in the tropics or higher latitudes, have characteristics which make them especially vulnerable to the effects of climate change, sea level rise and extreme events.

Deterioration in coastal conditions, for example through erosion of beaches and coral bleaching, is expected to affect local resources, e.g., fisheries, and reduce the value of these destinations for tourism.

Sea-level rise is expected to exacerbate inundation, storm surge, erosion and other coastal hazards, thus threatening vital infrastructure, settlements and facilities that support the livelihood of island communities.

The scientific evidence presented by the IPCC has provided further ammunition to former US vice-president Al Gore's warning on climate change and his call for action:

Many scientists are now warning that we are moving closer to several "tipping points" that could—within as little as 10 years—make it impossible for us to avoid irretrievable damage to the planet's habitability for human civilization. Each passing day brings yet more evidence that we are now facing a planetary emergency—a climate crisis that demands immediate action to sharply reduce carbon dioxide emissions worldwide in order to turn down the earth's thermostat and avert catastrophe....

Because, if we acknowledge candidly that what we need to do is beyond the limits of our current political capacities, that really is just another way of saying that we have to urgently expand the limits of what is politically possible. (Gore 2006)

A much more solid multilateral framework is bound to emerge at some stage. But will it be too late? Will there be a real coalescence of nations? Will there be a truly multilateral common thrust, be it at the UN or elsewhere, to make a real difference? Or will it unfortunately have to await some catastrophe, man made but of a magnitude similar to that of the December 2004 tsunami, to seize public opinion worldwide? How many Katrinas will it take?

The multilateral debate, while increasingly focused, continues to meander around institutional issues such as the creation of a United Nations Environment Organization to replace the voluntarily funded UN Environment Programme. Though legitimate, this debate seems to be at cross purposes with the more fundamental objective of imperiled humanity's tackling the looming environmental crisis. It should be recognized, however, that new UN secretary-general, Ban Ki-moon, is decidedly taking on the issue of climate change, referring to the UN as the "natural arena" for an issue such as climate change that requires "concerted and coordinated international action," and stating that he is "strongly committed to ensuring that the United Nations helps the international community make the transition to sustainable practices" (Ban 2007).[19]

Political traction there is, but, as the French say, *il y a loin de la coupe aux lèvres*. Meanwhile, other challenges to the global commons continue to solicit multilateral responses that the international community is unlikely to provide with equal vigor.

Water

The international community has recently benefited from the publication of the latest Human Development Report by the United Nations Development Programme (UNDP), *Beyond Scarcity: Power, Poverty and the Global Water Crisis*, which underscores the whole point of this paper:

> Unlike wars and natural disasters, the global crisis in water does not make media headlines. Nor does it galvanize concerted international action. Like hunger, deprivation in access to water is a silent crisis experienced by the poor and tolerated by those with the resources, the technology and the political power to end it. Yet this is a crisis that is holding back human progress, consigning large segments of humanity to lives of poverty, vulnerability and insecurity. This crisis claims more lives through disease than any war claims through guns. (2006, 1)

Indeed, the cost is all the more worrisome when one considers the number of yearly victims of small arms and light weapons: more than 350,000.

---

19. In his keynote address to the UN conference, "Global Warming: Confronting the Crisis," Ban (2007) stressed the effect of climate change on developing countries and spoke of the need to reframe the debate to recognize the "inextricable, mutually dependent relationship between environmental sustainability and economic development." While he stopped short of referring directly to climate change as a security issue, he referred to upheavals resulting from environmental changes as likely drivers of war and conflict in the future.

While the report underlines that "the scarcity at the heart of the global water crisis is rooted in power, poverty and inequality, not in physical availability" (UNDP 2006, 2), it also recognizes that water is indeed becoming a rare commodity and that many aquifers are being depleted at a rate that prevents their natural replenishment. Moreover, technology will not offer cheap alternatives: desalinization is a costly and inefficient process.

Some nongovernmental organizations argue that access to water should be a fundamental human right, while international financial institutions make the case for increasing privatization of water—although at present, hardly more than 5 percent of world water resources is privatized.[20] One can hardly say that, over and beyond recognizing the quality and value of the UNDP report and paying lip service to the Millennium Development Goal on water, the international community has demonstrated a global commitment to eradicating the effect of the unavailability of water on poverty. Yet, the battle for access to water could loom closer once its uneven distribution starts seriously affecting the developed world. When that happens, a belated consensus might emerge on the creation of a multilateral institution capable of addressing the "right to access to water" issue in a cooperative mode.

---

20. The Center for Public Integrity (2003) notes:

> The explosive growth of three private water utility companies in the last 10 years raises fears that mankind may be losing control of its most vital resource to a handful of monopolistic corporations. In Europe and North America, analysts predict that within the next 15 years these companies will control 65 percent to 75 percent of what are now public waterworks. The companies have worked closely with the World Bank and other international financial institutions to gain a foothold on every continent. They aggressively lobby for legislation and trade laws to force cities to privatize their water and set the agenda for debate on solutions to the world's increasing water scarcity. The companies argue they are more efficient and cheaper than public utilities. Critics say they are predatory capitalists that ultimately plan to control the world's water resources and drive up prices even as the gap between rich and poor widens. The fear is that accountability will vanish, and the world will lose control of its source of life.

Vanishing Fish Stocks

Canada has been at the vanguard of mobilizing the international community in the fight against overfishing and marine resource depletion. In fact, Canada played a leading role in the development of the United Nations Fish Agreement (UNFA), which was adopted in August 1995 by a UN conference and which entered into force in December 2001, following ratification by the thirtieth UN member state. The agreement provides

> a framework for the conservation and management of straddling stocks and highly migratory fish stocks in high seas areas regulated by regional fisheries organizations. It provides for the obligation to use the precautionary approach and the ecosystem approach when managing these fisheries on the high seas. It obliges States to minimize pollution, waste and discards of fish. It reiterates obligations of States to control the fishing activities of their vessels on the high seas. The most innovative aspect of the Agreement is the right of States to monitor and inspect vessels of other state parties, to verify compliance with internationally agreed fishing rules of regional fisheries organizations such as the Northwest Atlantic Fisheries Organization...and the International Commission for the Conservation of Atlantic Tunas.... Finally, UNFA provides a compulsory and binding dispute settlement mechanism to resolve conflicts in a peaceful manner. (Canada 2004)

This is all well and good, but fish stocks continue to fall. As then-prime minister Paul Martin said at a May 2005 international fisheries conference in St. John's, Newfoundland and Labrador,

> Experts the world over agree that [the condition of the world's fisheries and oceans] is one of the major environmental crises facing us today. Countless stocks have fallen to historic lows. Some are being quickly driven to the brink of extinction. And it's becoming more and more difficult for our fishers to make a living from the ocean. Canada certainly isn't alone in facing this challenge. The United Nations estimates that more than 52 per cent of the world's fisheries are already fully exploited; that 24 per cent are either overexploited, depleted or barely recovering; that 30 per cent of the world's catch comes from illegal, unreported and unregulated fishing. In some regions, fleets are catching up to three times more than permitted levels. And this at a time when stocks have dwindled to a pittance.

This issue remains the subject of conferences, as well as calls for the implementation of the 1995 UN Food and Agriculture Code of Conduct for Responsible Fisheries,[21] which has led to the establishment, so far, of four international plans of action that are voluntary instruments applying to all states and entities and to all fishermen. Nothing revolutionary! And although the world average quantity of fish remains stable at some 16 kilograms per person, growing inequalities in distribution again disproportionately affect the poor in Africa and other underdeveloped regions of the world. It seems, however, that this is not enough to mobilize the international community or for a truly effective multilateral solution to emerge.

Marine Pollution

Water resources are deeply affected by marine pollution, both land and sea based. Marine pollution is generally the purview of scientists, but one institution that has a significant impact in the struggle against marine pollution is the International Maritime Organization (IMO), which is responsible for preventing pollution by ships. The most important convention regulating and preventing such pollution is the 1973 International Convention for the Prevention of Pollution from Ships, which covers accidental and operational oil pollution as well as pollution by chemicals, goods in packaged form, sewage, garbage, and air pollution. An important tool in its arsenal is the Intervention Convention, which affirms the right of a coastal state to take measures on the high seas to prevent, mitigate, or eliminate danger to its coastline from a maritime casualty. Similarly, the 1990 International Convention on Oil Pollution Preparedness, Response and Co-operation provides a global framework for international cooperation in combating major incidents or threats of marine pollution. The IMO is also responsible for the management of the 1972 Convention on the Prevention of Marine Pollution by Dumping of Wastes and Other Matter. While these conventions are admirable, it is still a race against time, and ships carrying flags of convenience remain a threat to the marine environment.

---

21. See the Web site: http://www.fao.org/fi.

Nuclear Power

It is fascinating to note the effect that the staggering rise of oil prices in recent years has had on rekindling faith in nuclear energy. Yet, the cloud hovering above the expansion of civilian nuclear development, as evidenced by the Iran saga, is clearly the unrealized military temptation, as well as the risk of proliferation. One should contrast this growing concern —which is looked at mainly in international organizations such as the UN or the International Atomic Energy Agency (IAEA)—with the fact that nuclear power meets only 2 percent of world demand for energy. Clearly, there is room for expansion for new, safer nuclear plants, but such expansion will be accompanied by a parallel expansion of concerns. Meanwhile, Chernobyl continues to haunt environmentalists and those who know about other nuclear reactors that remain at the threshold of risk, IAEA inspections notwithstanding.[22] Indeed, if a new paradigm regarding nuclear development is not elaborated at the multilateral level, the risk of some nuclear catastrophe, civilian or military, will rise exponentially. It is far from certain that the existing Non-Proliferation, Arms Control and Disarmament regime, including the Treaty on the Non-Proliferation of Nuclear Weapons, is up to the challenges—particularly that of the potential spread of nuclear weapons to new states and to nonstate actors. Furthermore, questions remain about the eventual "adaptation" of existing nuclear doctrine in the wake of the US-India nuclear cooperation agreement, which, if carried through, is likely to be emulated by other nuclear "haves."[23] One could

---

22. The irony, for instance, of Pakistan's nuclear test—and its earlier failure to live up to international peaceful nuclear energy use—is that Canada's Atomic Energy Company was not allowed to work on the maintenance of the Karachi-based KANUPP, the oldest CANDU nuclear power reactor currently in operation, which it built several decades ago, thus increasing the risk of an accident to occur.

23. In a June 14, 2006, letter to the US Congress, the Federation of American Scientists noted:

> The Non-Proliferation Treaty, backbone of international efforts to stop the spread of nuclear technology, is crumbling and needs to be replaced with a new international framework—one that reflects dramatic changes that have occurred in the 30 years since the treaty was written. New

envisage additional ad hoc mechanisms, including multilateral fuel assurance mechanisms and new controls on sensitive technologies to enhance the peaceful uses side of the equation. The experience acquired with existing mechanisms—such as the Proliferation Security Initiative, the Global Partnership, and the Global Initiative to Combat Nuclear Terrorism—should help. This is, however, an area in which it will be increasingly difficult to bring about international order through existing multilateral institutions, despite the outstanding job done by the IAEA, until some of the fundamental issues posed by Iran and North Korea are definitely resolved. Yet it cannot await further nuclear tests.

Renewable Energy

With all the talk these days about energy supply and long-term availability, renewable energy is back on the agenda. Although great strides have been made in the field—wind, solar, new heating systems, biofuels—and with increasingly competitive prices on the market, the bottom line remains the same: today, the world consumes more fossil fuels than it did 15 years ago. Moreover, despite a substantial increase in the use of non-hydro renewables, they will not exceed 5 percent of total energy consumption by 2030, with wind and bioenergy in the lead (Clerici 2004). Despite the uneven world distribution of strategic resources, and although consumption areas do not correspond to production areas, the developed world continues to rely on fossil fuels to meet its own needs even as it encourages the developing world to foster the development of renewable energies. Thus, the International Energy Agency—although it has had a clear and expanded mandate since its creation after the first oil crisis of the 1970s to foster balanced energy policy making—is unlikely to generate enough international commitment to its triple "E" focus on energy security, economic development, and environmental protection to make a real difference. Indeed, the fundamental issue with respect to renewable energy remains market-driven investment, as opposed to continued subsidies.

---

agreements must preserve the strength of the current treaty and increase international participation. Bilateral, ad hoc agreements such as the one just announced with India undercut US and world security.

A new bargain is required among international monitoring institutions, national regulatory agencies, and private investors.

Other Current and Looming Crises

The World Economic Forum (2007) has categorized ongoing or looming crises along five potential fault lines, with varying mechanisms in play to alleviate the impact—or, to use Arthur Stein's excellent typology of institutional adaptation: palliative, corrective, or transformative (see elsewhere in this volume). A number of such crises have already been mentioned in this paper, but a few more deserve mention (see also United States 2004b).

The Economic Front

One would think that, in the developed world at least, enough economic institutions exist to absorb major shocks. Yet uncertainties remain.

Further oil price shocks or energy supply interruptions. Recent events have clearly demonstrated that institutions such as the Organization of the Petroleum Exporting Countries (OPEC) can be more corrective in limiting fluctuations than in addressing quantum leaps in price levels that then tend to ratchet. In fact, OPEC can be as much a source of shocks as palliative. Meanwhile, western European countries in quest of energy supply reliability have questioned recent Russian gas supply practices. While Canada is becoming a major energy player, distance still prevents it from being an alternative beyond the US market.

The US current account deficit or a fall in the US dollar. The size of the US deficit is such that, although both the monetary policies of the Federal Reserve and the economic and fiscal policies of the US government ultimately can exercise a considerable influence in either palliative or corrective terms, there is a growing sense that transformative reforms are required, notably on agricultural subsidies to redress the fundamental structural imbalance of the US economy. While the resilience of the US economy continues to marvel, it is increasingly doubtful that, were a major crisis to happen, the Bretton Woods institutions as presently constituted—including an International Monetary Fund (IMF) in disarray—would be able to correct the course taken by the major economies of the world sufficiently rapidly to avert a major recession.

A Chinese economic hard landing. At a time when experts call for truly transformative reforms to global economic institutions,[24] a hard landing by the Chinese economy would have an impact at least comparable to, and most probably worse than, the Asian financial crisis of the late 1990s. It is not sure that existing institutional mechanisms would suffice to offset the impact of such a collapse. The recent minor collapse of the Chinese stock market had quite an impact on world markets, even though it was essentially a policy-driven correction, partly reversed thereafter. G8 unity in applying remedies to face a major crisis would be hard to establish. Indeed, although the contentious issues in conventional reform talks of the Bretton Woods institutions are those of voice and representation, the real short-term issues are the IMF's recurring and increasing yearly deficits and, more broadly, the mandates of both the World Bank and the IMF, which are under increasing questioning in changing circumstances— hence the existing uncertainties about the overall systemic capacity to forestall a major economic collapse.

Food crises. Interestingly, in the early days of development economics, hunger and famine were lamented as part of the vicious circle of poverty, yet today the issues are malnutrition and overproduction, neither of which is sufficient to mobilize a committed North to South movement, the UN's Millennium Development Goals notwithstanding. The World Food Programme is responsive to food crises, but it is not equipped to deal in the long run with chronic food shortages, such as those in North Korea. More and more developed countries are reviewing their aid programs and,

---

24. The fundamental argument is that major international institutions such as the World Trade Organization, the IMF, and the World Bank have been "emasculated." Yet, as Woods (2007, 5) argues, "Without effective international institutions, there is a real risk that the global economy will descend into accidents, chaos and gridlock."

while the OECD's Development Assistance Committee continues, year in, year out, to argue policies and programs, a feeling of unease is beginning to plague the development literature. Elsewhere in this volume, Paul Collier denounces what he sees as the diagnostic flaw underpinning international assistance policy:

> [T]o date the OECD's response to these problems has been one of deep-rooted inadequacy. First, OECD countries have failed to diagnose the problems correctly, wrongly perceiving them as being essentially about poverty reduction, rather than the more profound and intractable issue of divergence. In fact, it would be possible to eliminate absolute poverty, even as divergence became yet more pronounced. Divergence is driven by a constellation of distinct problems: unviable countries, the dysfunctional politics of resource wealth, the difficulty of breaking into global markets ..., and the menace of outright state failure as countries implode into conflict.[25]

The Environmental Front

In addition to climate change and reduced access to freshwater, natural catastrophes—often with an indirect causal relationship to humanity's abuse of Mother Nature—include Katrina-style tropical storms, earthquakes, and inland flooding (as happens regularly in Jakarta and has become the "natural" lot of Dhaka). Clearly, such disasters require an entirely new regime of emergency measures with as few palliative features (such as merely repairing dykes) as possible and an emphasis on corrective and innovative measures in construction technology and relocation policies. Natural disasters have been discussed multilaterally within the UN International Strategy for Disaster Reduction. Yet, notwithstanding its lofty goals—building disaster-resilient communities by promoting increased awareness of the importance of disaster reduction—its work has not generated the kind of investment that would establish a planetary vision

---

25. In a private setting less than two years ago, a senior EU official in charge of development assistance confided that he wondered when development assistance had ever made a difference—a *cri du coeur* if ever there was one!

of not just disaster relief but disaster prevention. Indeed, it has become common practice to denounce *ab initio* the UN's incapacity.[26]

Public attention also could be drawn to the triple threat of chemical, biological, and radiation contamination, thus possibly mobilizing nation-states to act collectively and multilaterally, because of the planetary dimensions of such threats and their "glocal" impact. Industrial accidents such as those in Chernobyl and Bhopal or shipping tragedies such as that of the *Exxon Valdez* are but precursors of events that could multiply all over the world. Effective instruments aimed at minimizing the risks or consequences of accidents do exist,[27] yet a considerable number of important countries have not adhered to them. Furthermore, transformative reform is required in terms of hazardous waste production, waste management, recycling, and, even more important, consumption management. Again, at stake here is the conscience of nations and their populations, which must hold their governments accountable.

The Geopolitical Front

Although I have already covered most geopolitical threats or challenges, it is worthwhile contrasting the extensive networks of cooperation created to thwart terrorism per se with the limited number of multilateral cooperative instruments developed to manage the variety of consequences that might stem from a terrorist attack—for example, along the lines of the post–9/11 anthrax scare in the United States, which created a collective psyche of

---

26. A serious article in the Science and Technology section of *The Economist* (February 24, 2007, p. 92) referred to a group of astronauts "lobbying the UN to put asteroid-impact planning on the agenda. However, given the glacial pace at which the organisation moves, this may not provide a good enough emergency response."

27. For example, the Basel Convention on the Control of Transboundary Movements of Hazardous Wastes and Their Disposal, the 1996 Protocol of the 1972 London Convention on the Prevention of Marine Pollution by Dumping of Wastes and Other Matter, the 1998 Rotterdam Convention on the Prior Informed Consent Procedure for Certain Hazardous Chemicals and Pesticides in International Trade, and the 2001 Stockholm Convention on Persistent Organic Pollutants.

fear (see Harvey 2004). Instead, each nation intends to manage as best as it can. Even the post-Chernobyl trauma was handled mostly on a national scale, with international assistance pouring in to help victims but not to develop multilateral management and prevention scenarios. There is, of course, extensive consultation among like-minded countries, but their varying degrees of sophistication of emergency preparedness have not led to the kind of civilian coordination that one could find, for instance, in the consultation and joint planning exercises that NATO fostered under military hypotheses during the Cold War. Still, the US National Response Plan under the aegis of the Department of Homeland Security certainly has a clear sense of the fault lines, as indicated in Box 1.

On the other hand, transnational crime has taken such a proportion that, if we are to share the perspective of US under secretary for global affairs Paula Dobriansky (2001), "the urgency of the world crime problem has elevated the issue to a priority position on the international agenda." The list of crimes is overwhelming: terrorism, human trafficking, drug trafficking, contraband smuggling, people smuggling, fraud, extortion, money laundering, bribery, economic espionage, intellectual property theft, and counterfeiting, cybercrime. The 2000 United Nations Convention against Transnational Organized Crime is the main international instrument in the fight against this scourge. The UN Office on Drugs and Crime salutes the convention as "the recognition by Member States of the seriousness of the problem as well as the need to foster and enhance close international cooperation in order to tackle those problems." Supplementary instruments include the Protocol to Prevent, Suppress and Punish Trafficking in Persons, especially Women and Children (2003) and the Protocol against the Smuggling of Migrants by Land, Sea and Air (2004). Work also continues on all these issues through working groups on international cooperation and technical assistance. While impressive, the normative framework is at best playing catch-up on a problem that seems both to feed and be fed by the underground and not-so-underground networks within failed and fragile states. Indeed, in the face of increasingly sophisticated money-laundering schemes, a further withering away of the sense of public good, and the thriving of mafias and fiscal paradises, there is a sense that the race might be lost.

Box 1: *The US Department of Homeland Security's Incident Annexes*

- The **Biological Incident Annex** describes incident management activities related to a biological terrorism event, pandemic, emerging infectious disease, or novel pathogen outbreak.
- The **Catastrophic Incident Annex** establishes the strategy for implementing and coordinating an accelerated national response to a catastrophic incident.
- The **Cyber Incident Annex** establishes procedures for a multidisciplinary, broad-based approach to prepare for, remediate, and recover from catastrophic cyber events impacting critical national processes and the national economy.
- The **Food and Agriculture Incident Annex** describes incident management activities related to a terrorist attack, major disaster, or other emergency involving the Nation's agriculture and food systems.
- The **Nuclear/Radiological Incident Annex** describes incident management activities related to nuclear/radiological incidents.
- The **Oil and Hazardous Materials Incident Annex** describes incident management activities related to certain nationally significant oil and hazardous materials pollution incidents.
- The **Terrorism Incident Law Enforcement and Investigation Annex** describes law enforcement and criminal investigation coordinating structures and processes in response to a terrorist event.

Source: United States 2004a.

The Societal Front

Health pandemics have exploded on the international radar screen. The sensitization started with SARS and continues today with avian flu. AIDS, too, ignoring more and more national borders, expands at a high rate, attracting large amounts of philanthropic funding. A lot of credit goes to the World Health Organization (WHO) for its work on major health crises and epidemics. Not surprisingly, as a multilateral, UN-based institution, WHO receives considerable voluntary contributions from many UN member states, highlighting a trend whereby those organizations deemed to be performing well receive funding additional to their statutory contributions, while those organizations that developed countries regard as too politicized or under "undue" influence of developing countries are starved

of supplementary funding. Of itself, this dichotomy is bound to affect negatively many attempts to unite the world in quest of sustainable remedies
to long-term crises and problems. Interestingly, there is also a North-
South divide in the health field, with the North focusing on chronic diseases while the South's attention is understandably on infectious diseases.

Somewhat related to health, but also to a series of social ills, is the
phenomenon of urbanization. As a Canadian government Web site notes,

> Since 1950, the percentage of the world's population living in urban
> areas has increased from 30% to nearly 50%. By 2030, that number is
> expected to reach 60%. This dramatic shift in population density has
> created a range of serious issues, including water, sanitation, shelter,
> urban poverty, HIV/AIDS and urban governance.[28]

The Third World Urban Forum, held in Vancouver in 2006, attracted
more than 10,000 people of good will and concluded with a host of commitments, yet we are still at an early stage of effective action accompanied
by appropriate means and corollary funding. One of the observations in
the Forum's final report says it all: "'Beautiful speeches, awful reality'—
the Millennium Development Goals are not having an impact on the
ground in many countries" (UN Human Settlements Programme 2006, 4).

It is interesting to note that, while immigration has always been
viewed as an issue to be addressed in some kind of multilateral framework, the politics of immigration are such that there is a strong reluctance
to have any grouping of countries take formal decisions on immigration
matters. The High-level Dialogue of the General Assembly on International
Migration, held in September 2006 at UN headquarters in New York, may
well have been the culmination of years of debate in the General Assembly
about how to address international migration and its interrelations with
development, but it was clear that no resolution or commitment would
emerge from it. In fact, the response to the secretary-general's proposal of
a global forum emphasized that, were it to take place, it "should be informal, voluntary, and led by Member States operating in a transparent and
open manner. It would not produce negotiated outcomes or normative

---

28. See Western Economic Diversification Canada, "World Urban Forum;"
available at Web site: http://www.wd.gc.ca/ced/wuf/default_e.asp.

decisions, but it would promote closer cooperation among Governments" (United Nations 2006a, 16). Clearly, the focus would be on promoting practical, evidence-based measures to enhance the benefits of international migration and minimize its negative impacts. A planetary issue it is, but the range of policies and concerns are such that any formal multilateralization of the debate through bodies such as ECOSOC would be vetoed by a number of countries.[29]

The Technological Front

While no one wishes to get carried away with sagas such as depicted in Dan Brown's *Digital Fortress* (1998), there are serious concerns about the risk of a breakdown of critical information infrastructure. Recent stories of Internet hackers, viruses, and worms have fostered an array of countermeasures developed more in parallel than jointly by countries reliant on information and communication technology. The World Summit on the Information Society averted the politicization—or, as some have described it, the "UN-ization"—of Internet governance by ensuring it would remain as it is, entrusting only a voluntary multilateral mechanism to review potential problems. Yet it is clear that the threat of a collapse in world communication systems, compounded by the possible emergence of risks associated with nanotechnology, remains an untested paradigm, with few coordinated advance response mechanisms—multiple redundant systems notwithstanding. But so far, the private sector, in coalition with the most technologically advanced national, public institutions, appears far better equipped than any international or multilateral entity to deal with major communication security crises. The International Telecommunications Union, however, provides marginal yet indispensable cyber security support through assistance to the development of national and regional policies in the field.

---

29. Although Canada prides itself for a successful immigration policy, including a polite dismissal of the European concept of "integration" in favor of the softer and somewhat evanescent apology of "multiculturalism," most Canadians are not aware that more than 80 percent of new immigrants go to the country's four largest cities. So much for regional distribution of the Canadian population! The pressures on cities are significant, particularly in terms of their infrastructure.

Ineffective Multilateralism or Nonexistent Political Will? The Example of Doha

Despite WTO director general Pascal Lamy's efforts to rekindle faith in, and work on, the Doha Round of world trade negotiations, it is clear that only the political will of the world's leaders can generate a true commitment to resolving the fundamental issues in play. Indeed, as German finance minister Peer Steinbrueck said in Melbourne in November 2006, "I'm not optimistic the Doha talks could restart because it's like playing pickup sticks: the first one who moves, loses. So no one is going to move."

At the 2006 meeting of the Asia-Pacific Economic Cooperation (APEC) group of countries, leaders emphasized that reviving the stalled Doha Round—as opposed to a US-proposed regional free trade agreement —would be their top priority. Yet, not much has come out of that priority, for several reasons. First, the quasi-existential row between rich nations on farm subsidies has yet to subside, even though such subsidies drive down world food prices, to the detriment of Third World countries. Second, in this day and age of global imbalances between saving nations (China, Japan, the oil-producing countries) and borrowing nations (principally the United States)—which the G7 finance ministers and heads of central banks committed in 2006 to resolve—the fate of the developing world seems to pall compared to the tenuous balancing act between the single-minded pursuit of export growth by the broad range of emerging and increasingly rich countries and the surprisingly continuous flow of capital to the United States. Together, these trends continue to ensure global growth and partial stability despite the evident imbalances, so that there is little incentive to alter the foundation of the system.

As a result, statements such as those of APEC leaders that "[t]he consequences of the failure of the Doha Round would be too grave for our economies and for the global multilateral trading system" ring somewhat hollow. Changing hegemonic patterns—with the ascendancy of China and, more generally, the so-called BRIC countries (Brazil, Russia, India, and China)—are far more salient than a trade round in which, on one side, inflexibility appears to many to be the rule and, on the other, the revisiting of established arrangements concluded in earlier rounds seems to constitute the starting block. Today, despite calls for new proposals to bring the stalemated global trade liberalization talks to a successful outcome by the end of 2007, it is clear that the North-South divide not only remains as strong as ever on Doha but also that the countries of the South are questioning more than ever the world's overarching economic, financial, and trade architecture even as they clamor for the right to join and to participate fully in its decisionmaking processes.

Conclusion

Where does all this leave us, in a world where, more than ever, multilateral solutions seem required, but where the rejuvenation of multilateral frameworks seems stifled and political will stymied?

Fundamentally, it has to do with the complexity of today's world. To the constant emergence of new geopolitical paradigms has to be added a continuous series of new challenges that affect traditional perceptions and conventional wisdom.[30] Interactions between phenomena are occurring in different spheres and different spaces, and correlations often lead to confusion rather than enlightenment: intellectual hierarchies are falling as fast as political supremacies. What is lacking in this day and age seems to be a capacity to synthesize new realities. One of the effects of globalization, for example, is a retrenchment in opposition to that very process—a rediscovery of the local, of traditional guiding values: a sense that, although national institutions might respond in the short term to essential needs,

---

30. The crisis in Darfur is a clear example of an intractable issue that defies logic and rational solutions. Part of the series of civil wars that have plagued the Sudan since independence, it has hugely complex ethnic, religious, territorial, colonial, economic, political, and social underpinnings. While its roots might go back to Ottoman rule, its emergence relates to the taking up of arms by the Sudan Liberation Army and the Justice and Equality Movement against the government in 2003, to which Sudanese president Bashir retaliated by arming Arab militia—the feared Janjaweed—to eliminate the civilian tribes in the region believed to be supporting the rebellion. When Bashir added climate change as a cause of the crisis, his comment was dismissed as a distraction from the real, root causes of the conflict. Now, of course, the UN secretary-general has endorsed the claim, which has become part of the series of Darfur-related problems! See International Crisis Group (2006).

they are as powerless to protect against unbridled competition as they are incapable of transcending to the international level to meet the broader challenges facing humanity. Every major crisis enhances the feeling of impotence: Iraq demonstrates the futility of raw military power; Iran is a live laboratory of contrasts between an ancient civilization and sophisticated culture and a fringe, theologically inspired regime that befuddles even the specialist; Russia wishes to regain its past stature but in so trying raises the angst of many an observer; China is both admired for its economic prowess and feared nearly at the level of the unconscious, rekindling fantasies of the "yellow peril"; Afghanistan remains on the brink of returning to the dark ages of the Taliban, despite a formidable coalition desperately trying to prop a nascent democracy; North Korea continues to play with our collective nuclear nerves while remaining as backward as a country can be; Palestine's roadmap to peace is ever more clouded by distrust and violence; Darfur underscores the distance between collective will and Westphalian, state-centered sovereignty, the UN Security Council notwithstanding.

Samuel Huntington's (1993) pronouncement on the "clash of civilizations" was initially related to a broad definition of culture, not specifically to a conflict between Islam and the West. Yet, since September 11, 2001, despite the repeated rejections of the claim by a large number of people, political leaders, and scholarly personalities—who often appear motivated less by conviction than by a desire to dispel its potential consequences—Huntington's contention that the West is pitted against a Confucian-Islamic coalition has inspired an unsympathetic fixation on Islam: a unimodal, often narrow-minded rejection of orthodox or conservative concepts of Islam, often confused with fundamentalism, as if the latter only existed in Muslim expressions of faith.

It also provokes a rightful, profound abhorrence of terrorism, unfortunately mostly considered as an aberration of Islam rather than as a societal aberration with religious overtones, often politically dictated. Proposals for a dialogue of civilizations have come from a variety of quarters. Indeed, as the UNESCO Web site puts it,

> In a world where no country is entirely homogenous, demands for recognition of different ethnicities, religions, languages and values are increasingly arising. There is an urgency of developing a sense of respect

for the Other that will provide a basis for mutual understanding, friendship and learning. Cultural diversity and heritage are vectors of identity and tools for reconciliation. Based on UNESCO's Constitution and the various resolutions adopted by the Executive Board and General Conference, the promotion of dialogue in the service of peace—in order to build "peace in the minds of men"—is one of the main themes of UNESCO's mission. Globalization and the emergence of new contemporary challenges and threats to humankind make the need for dialogue among peoples ever more topical. A principal objective of a dialogue is to bridge the gap in knowledge about other civilizations, cultures and societies, to lay the foundations for dialogue based on universally shared values and to undertake concrete activities, inspired and driven by dialogue, especially in the areas of education, cultural diversity and heritage, the sciences and communication and media.[31]

President Seyed Khatami of Iran was the first to suggest such a dialogue, and his proposal was eventually rekindled by Spain at the time of the 2006 UN summit. Yet, full wind has not yet caught the sails of this issue, which, though fundamental, has still to be properly defined if we are to avoid a needless discussion of faith or, even worse, comparative faiths as opposed to their possible impact on perceptions of reality and on reality itself.

The failure to address the new issues that call for rededicated multilateral institutions capable of taking the long view and driving the collective implementation of long-term remedies and that ignore the Westphalian state and its idiosyncrasies has spanned a new phenomenon: global social insecurity. The phenomenon is further fueled economically by an increasingly merciless competition, now compounded by a forceful technological race, the crisis of outsourcing, the implacable law of the market, and the growing inequalities brought about, so it is perceived, by free trade and economic liberalization.

Corporate fraud, flawed corporate financial reports, and excessive corporate earnings have convinced many that modern society is as defective nationally as it is incapable internationally of alleviating the plight of

---

31. UNESCO, Bureau of Strategic Planning, "Dialogue among civilizations"; see Web site: http://portal.unesco.org/en/ev.php-URL_ID=37084&URL_DO=DO_TOPIC&URL_SECTION=201.html.

the poor. A dim picture of inequality, deep inequities, and profound injustice emerges. As Baruch Lev (2003, 27) puts it:

> Investors' confidence in the quality and integrity of corporate financial reports has been seriously shaken. The ever-increasing procession of headlines about fraudulent earnings, inflated asset values and understated liabilities reported by erstwhile leading companies—the likes of Enron, Tyco, WorldCom, Xerox and a host of lesser household names, all audited by major accounting firms—suggests systematic deficiencies in the accounting standards and governance systems that generate financial information of public companies, not to mention in the regulatory systems overseeing them.[32]

World Economic Forum chairman and founder Klaus Schwab has said (2006) that the world is at a critical juncture in history and that we urgently need a better understanding of how the management of global interdependence works. He adds that "we need a better general understanding of how different people, different countries and different regions deal with each other." He further claims that "we are in the midst of a revolution" and witnessing a "changing power equation," with "vertical, command and control structures...being replaced by horizontal networks of social communities and collaborative platforms." More critically, he states that "our institutions and systems of global governance are disintegrating." Even more aptly from the perspective of multilateralism, he attributes the disintegration to the fact that "our global institutions and governance structures were built on the concept of the nation states, mainly designed to protect national interests but fostering no sense of global trusteeship." Yet, the number of global challenges that have to be faced simultaneously

---

32. These trends are increasingly worrying to the business community, as exemplified by the Washington-based Committee for Economic Development, which notes (2006, 1):

> The highly visible accounting scandals that surrounded the collapse of Enron, WorldCom and several other major companies—together with the revelation of fraud and other acts of malfeasance by corporate executive —have aroused public outrage, called into question the values and ethics of business leaders, and undermined the public's confidence in public companies.

in our dangerous and complex world would call for a much more powerful global stewardship. Schwab laments the decay of structures like the UN and the Bretton Woods institutions, and he quotes the unresolved crises I have been reviewing here. And his final point underscores the whole debate on institutional reform: "all reforms based on just prolonging the paradigms of the past will fail."

The United States has been assailed for allegedly practicing "unilateralism" in its foreign policy, yet it is a fiction. Even though "multilateralism à la carte" was coined by a member of the US administration, Richard Haass, it is an easy cliché that cloaks the limits of what is possible for any country having to decide if it can entrust its future to an international organization on which it exercises no more than 1/192 of influence. Sovereignty looks good from that ratio's perspective. What all authors on multilateralism are groping for is the pursuit of its Holy Grail, "effective multilateralism," or what is often referred to in Canada as "results-based multilateralism." In fact, there is no point in debating whether the United States is unilateralist or multilateralist, even if the trend varies from one administration to another. As Kim Holmes (2004), former US assistant secretary for international organization affairs, aptly said:

> we invest a great deal in the UN to make it an effective multilateral instrument. We would not do that if we thought it was going the way of the League of Nations. I would go so far as to say that, if we did not have international mechanisms like the UN to help us implement global responses to terrorism, nuclear proliferation, failed states, HIV/AIDS, or famine, we would spearhead efforts to create them.

The real idea is to develop a new concept of multilateralism that takes into account the more diffuse distribution of power, the emergence of the power of networks, which Schwab signaled and which eventually will move society from globalization to "planetization."[33] Idealists would argue that what is required is a transformation from a multilateral system at the service of national interests to a true system of world governance. This could again be the dream of World Federalists, but if we fail to espouse that dream, Schwab will be proven right. At the universal institutional

---

33. For a development of this concept, see de Kerckhove (1997).

level, the key question is whether the UN can transform itself to the point of becoming a world governance institution while retaining its essential characteristic as the only instrument legitimizing the resort to force (beyond the concept of self-defense). This is highly doubtful in today's fragmented world, ideologically and politically. Yet, this would be only a necessary condition, not a sufficient one. Indeed, there remains the crying need to tackle the fundamental issue of economic redistribution, which is the only passage to long-term growth. Today, while the Millennium Development Goals are a lofty purpose, even their achievement would not necessarily ensure redistribution or, as Paul Collier so aptly calls it, the reduction of divergences.

To a world in quest of its soul, there is little choice but to work on developing new policies, new channels, and new tactics to implement new norms, and to bridge divides with new capabilities. An old recipe, but, as Thomas Homer-Dixon (2007) says, "there are significant opportunities for renewal."

References

ACIA (Arctic Climate Impact Assessment). 2004. *Impacts of a Warming Arctic: Executive Summary*. Cambridge: Cambridge University Press.

Ali, Tariq. 2007. "The General in His Labyrinth." *London Review of Books* 29 (1).

Annan, Kofi. A. 2005. *In Larger Freedom: Towards Development, Security and Human Rights for All*. Report of the Secretary-General. New York: United Nations.

————. 2006. Farewell Address at the Truman Presidential Museum and Library, Independence, MO, December 11.

Ban Ki-moon. 2007. Keynote address to the United Nations International School Conference on "Global Warming: Confronting the Crisis." New York. March 1.

Benedict, Kennette. 2007. "Doomsday Clock moves two minutes closer to midnight." *The Bulletin Online*, January 18.

Brown, Dan. 1998. *Digital Fortress*. New York: St. Martin's Press.

Canada. 2004. Fisheries and Oceans Canada. "United Nations Fish Agreement (UNFA)." Backgrounder. Ottawa. May. Available from Web site: http://www.dfo-mpo.gc.ca/media/backgrou/2004/hq-ac45a_e.htm.

Center for Public Integrity. 2003. *The Water Barons: Introduction*. Washington, DC. Available at Web site: http://www.icij.org/water/default.aspx?act=ch&nsid=Introduction.

Clerici, Alessandro. 2004. "WEC Survey of Energy Resources 2004." Presentation to the World Energy Council. London. Available at Web site: http://www.worldenergy.org/wec-geis/congress/powerpoints/clericia0904.pps.

Committee for Economic Development. 2006. *Private Enterprise, Public Trust: The State of Corporate America after Sarbanes-Oxley*. Washington, DC.

de Kerckhove, Derrick. 1997. *Connected Intelligence: The Arrival of the Web Society*. Toronto: Somerville House.

Dobriansky, Paula. 2001. "The Explosive Growth of Globalized Crime." *Global Issues* 6 (2).

Gore, Al. 2006. "Global Warming Is an Immediate Crisis." Speech to New York University School of Law, September 18. Available at Web site: http://www.truthout.org/cgi-bin/artman/exec/view.cgi/64/22597.

Harper, Stephen. 2006. Speech by the Prime Minister of Canada to the UN General Assembly. New York. September 21.

Harvey, Frank. 2004. *Smoke and Mirrors: Globalized Terrorism and the Illusion of Multilateral Security.* Toronto: University of Toronto Press.

Heinbecker, Paul, and Patricia Goff, eds. 2005. *Irrelevant or Indispensable? The United Nations in the Twenty-First Century.* Waterloo, ON: Wilfrid Laurier University Press.

Holmes, Kim R. 2004. "Why the United Nations Matters to U.S. Foreign Policy." Speech to the Baltimore Council on Foreign Affairs. December 6.

Homer-Dixon, Thomas. 2007. Remarks to a conference sponsored by the Department of Foreign Affairs and International Trade. Ottawa. February 7.

Hosseini, Khaled. 2003. *The Kite Runner.* New York: Riverhead Books.

Huntington, Samuel P. 1993. "The Clash of Civilizations?" *Foreign Affairs* 72 (3): 44–57.

Intergovernmental Panel on Climate Change. 2007a. *Climate Change 2007: Impacts, Adaptation and Vulnerability, Summary for Policymakers.* Working Group II Report. Brussels.

———. 2007b. *Climate Change 2007: The Physical Science Basis, Summary for Policymakers.* Working Group Report I. Brussels.

International Crisis Group. 2006. "Getting the UN into Darfur." *Crisis Group Africa Briefing* 43. Brussels.

International Energy Agency. 2006. *World Energy Outlook 2006.* Paris.

Jones, Bruce. 2006. Remarks at the Department of Foreign Affairs and International Trade. Ottawa.

Lev, Baruch. 2003. "Corporate Earnings: Facts and Fiction." *Journal of Economic Perspectives* 17 (2): 27–50.

Malone, David M. 1998. *Decision-Making in the UN Security Council: The Case of Haiti.* Oxford: Clarendon Press.

———. 2006. "UN Reform: A Sisyphean Task." In *Canada among Nations, 2006,* edited by Andrew F. Cooper and Dane Rowlands. Montreal; Kingston, ON: McGill-Queen's University Press.

Rashid, Ahmed. 2000. *Taliban: Militant Islam, Oil and Fundamentalism in Central Asia.* New Haven, CT: Yale University Press.

Schwab, Klaus. 2006. "The De-Globalization of a Globalized World." London: Chatham House.

Strong, Maurice. 1997. "U.N. Reform." *eco-logic Powerhouse,* July/August.

UNDP (United Nations Development Programme). 2006. *Beyond Scarcity: Power, Poverty and the Global Water Crisis.* New York.

UN Human Settlements Programme. 2006. *Report of the Third Session of the World Urban Forum.* Vancouver, June 19–23.

UN Millennium Project. 2005. *Investing in Development: A Practical Plan to Achieve the Millennium Development Goals.* London; Sterling, VA: Earthscan.

United Nations. 1997. *Renewing the United Nations: A Programme for Reform.* Report of the Secretary-General. A/51/950. New York. July 14.

———. 2004. Secretary-General's High-level Panel on Threats, Challenges and Change. *A More Secure World: Our Shared Responsibility.* New York. December.

———. 2005. General Assembly. "2005 World Summit Outcome." A/RES/60/1. New York.

———. 2006a. Department of Economic and Social Affairs. Population Division. "The High-level Dialogue on International Migration and Development and Beyond." Background paper. New York. November.

———. 2006b. Secretary-General's High-level Panel on System-Wide Coherence. *Delivering as One.* New York. November.

United States. 2004a. Department of Homeland Security. *National Response Plan.* Washington, DC. December.

———. 2004b. National Intelligence Council. *Mapping the Global Future: Report of the National Intelligence Council's 2020 Project.* Washington, DC: US Government Printing Office.

Woods, Ngaire. 2007. *Power Shift: Do We Need Better Global Economic Institutions?* London: Institute for Public Policy Research.

World Economic Forum. 2007. *Global Risks 2007: A Global Risk Network Report.* Davos, Switzerland. January.

Facing the
Global Problems
of Development

Paul Collier

* * *

One of the most important problems facing the world today is the failure of Africa to develop. Concern about the nature of the problem usually focuses on poverty and mortality. In this paper, however, I attempt to shift focus by arguing that enlightened self-interest should propel the member countries of the Organisation for Economic Co-operation and Development (OECD) to take action to reverse the accelerating divergence of much of Africa from the rest of the world.[1]

I set out this argument in four stages. In the first, I restate the problem of African development as that of divergence rather than of poverty. In the second stage, I review four distinct bases for why citizens of OECD societies should care about Africa, and I again try to shift attention from the usual ethical basis for concern. In the third stage, I briefly make the case for enlightened self-interest in terms of the problems that divergence might generate for OECD societies. In the fourth stage, I prepare the ground for a discussion of actions the international community could take by arguing that, without external assistance, Africa's autonomous development is likely to be, at best, a slow process.

---

1. For a development of the themes in this paper, see Collier (2007).

In the second part of the paper, I turn to the question of what to do about Africa's lack of development. Here, I attempt to broaden the range of actions that are normally considered, arguing that the potency of aid has been overplayed relative to other instruments, some of which have been virtually ignored. I end by discussing how to coordinate these instruments, both between each other and among countries.

The Problem of Global Development and the Need for International Action

The problem of global development is usually seen as one of poverty. I think this is wrong, however, or at least dangerously inadequate. The focus on poverty is a political solution to a political problem facing the international development agencies, rather than a well-founded diagnosis of development challenges. The number of people in poverty globally, in fact, has been declining for around 25 years. If poverty is the problem, this is a battle we are winning, and globalization has quite dramatically been helping. The biggest decline in the numbers of people in poverty has been in China, which has globalized most successfully.

What Is the Global Development Problem?

The key development problem is not poverty, but divergence. By this I mean the tendency of a group of countries, now at the bottom of the world economy, to diverge from the rest of the world. This group is predominantly African, although not all African countries are part of it. Overall it contains about one billion people. Per capita incomes in this group have been roughly stagnant for the past three decades, whereas per capita incomes in the rest of the developing world have been rising, on average, at an accelerating rate. In the 1980s and 1990s, the per capita income of the bottom billion people diverged from that of the next four billion at around 5 percent per year, and is now only one-fifth of that of the latter group—that is, before we take into account the richest billion at all.

Whether absolute poverty is slightly rising or slightly declining in the countries of the bottom billion seems to me to be altogether secondary to this astounding rate of divergence, which, if it were to continue, would rapidly generate an unmanageable world. A sink of failure of one billion people in a world in which global information flows and advertising produce a convergence of aspirations is liable to produce implosive pressures in the societies at the bottom and a scramble for exit.

Divergence is fundamentally about the dynamics of inequalities among nations. But this fact has been neglected by all the development actors because it does not really fit their political agendas. Nongovernmental organizations (NGOs), most of which come from the political left within developed societies, are primarily interested in the internal distribution of income and power: their first preference is to reduce poverty through internal redistribution from the rich. The problem for development agencies such as the World Bank is that NGOs are the only constituency that has much enthusiasm for aid. Yet this constituency is deeply suspicious of growth, which it partly associates with "neoliberal" policies that some developed countries have adopted against the wishes of the left (see Collier and Dercon 2006). Hence, aid agencies have engaged the main potential constituency of support for aid through a focus on "poverty reduction." Such language, however, fudges the issue of whether poverty reduction is to be achieved through growth or redistribution. The most controversial research paper the World Bank has ever produced is "Growth Is Good for the Poor" (Dollar and Kraay 2001)—an astoundingly banal title that provoked the ire of NGOs because it links an acceptable objective, poverty reduction, with an unacceptable means, growth, thereby diminishing the main concern of the NGO left, which is not poverty reduction as such but redistribution.

If divergence, rather than poverty reduction, is the core development concern, then issues of internal redistribution within societies become quite minor. Divergence is inescapably about growth: it simply means that growth rates differ, and it can be rectified only by raising growth rates in the societies at the bottom. Whether or not growth is "good for the poor," it is the *sine qua non* of ending divergence.

The focus on poverty is fundamentally both divisive and anti-democratic. It is divisive because, in the societies of the bottom billion, typically nearly half the population is below the poverty threshold, and a discourse that focuses on poverty inevitably juxtaposes these people against the rest of society. Many societies of the bottom billion have a distribution of income fairly similar to that of many developed countries. The nonpoor are not, with a few exceptions, "rich"—indeed, virtually all distributions of income are broadly bell shaped.[2] The obvious concept to use in discussing a society with such a distribution of income is to focus on the large group of people in the hump of the distribution—whom one might most naturally describe as "ordinary." It is quite artificial to draw an arbitrary line right through the peak of the distribution and claim that those on one side are poor while those on the other are not.

The focus on poverty is anti-democratic because no democratic government can or should ignore the nonpoor majority. If the rich countries, rightly, encourage democracy in developing countries, they should not for the sake of consistency attempt to impose a value system that is inconsistent with democracy—or, indeed, with the political preferences revealed in the internal politics of their own societies. It is precisely because the NGO left does not like the outcomes of conventional democratic politics that it agitates that donors use their disproportionate influence in the poorest countries to promote an agenda of redistribution. This approach is an abuse of power and a neocolonial relationship.

Why Should Developed Countries Care about Divergence?

Why should people in the developed countries be concerned about what happens in developing countries? There are four distinct ethical positions.

The first is a sense of guilt, the basis for which is sometimes the affront of colonialism and sometimes the even greater affront of slavery. Guilt generates some sense of the need for restitution, so that the redistribution of income achieved through a transfer of aid is in some sense a right, remedying a wrong. Some obvious practical problems exist, however, with implementing such an allocation of aid. Even if one accepts the problematic notion of inherited guilt, which is problematic, the guilt is not distributed evenly among rich countries, and the wrong is not distributed

---

2. That is, the "hump" in the frequency distribution is left of center, with median income being below mean income.

evenly among poor countries. If the guilt is distributed among those countries that participated in colonialism and slavery, most rich countries, including Canada, would be burden free. In respect of slavery, Britain would be in the ambiguous position of having participated in the trade but then having been instrumental in closing it down. If the damage of colonialism is seen as broadly proportionate to its duration, India would receive around forty times as much compensation per capita as Ethiopia. In other words, guilt is liable to produce a pattern of redistribution radically at variance with current needs.

To my mind, however, the main problem with basing international concern on a sense of guilt is its consequences for the psychology of the recipient. The disproportionate power of rich-country mental models means that, if rich countries frame their concern in terms of guilt, then guilt will become the dominant mental frame in developing countries, where its counterpart is grievance. Yet a sense of grievance is incapacitating: it provides an alibi for failure and so belittles the autonomy of the actor.

The second possible ethical basis for concern about developing countries is a sense of the unfairness of grossly unequal outcomes. This concern differs from a sense of guilt in that it need not imply that the winners have committed any wrong; rather, it sees winners and losers as having participated on equal terms in a lottery that has produced unequal outcomes. We might ground this notion of unfairness in a quasi-Rawlsian concern for those who, for whatever reason, have fared worst.[3] From behind Rawls's "veil of ignorance," we might agree that a certain amount of insurance would be a good idea, but it is likely to fall far short of Rawls's own proposition of "maximin," whereby the economic order is run in such a way as to leave the worst off as well off as possible. In reality, nobody is that risk averse: we simply do not choose to run our lives so as to minimize the worst thing that can possibly happen to us. If a degree of insurance is something we all choose to have, then some *ex post* mechanism for redistribution is a way of retrofitting an institution

---

3. The philosopher John Rawls grounded his highly influential theory of social justice in notion of a "veil of ignorance": a system would be just if acceptable while ignorant of the place someone would occupy within the society; see Rawls (1971).

that we would have agreed on *ex ante* if we had had the chance to do so. The limit to this retrofitting of an insurance arrangement once outcomes are known, however, is that we also need to agree on the amount of coercion that is acceptable to enforce such redistributive insurance. Overwhelmingly, people have agreed that most of this power of redistribution should be at the level of the nation-state. People have also agreed that there should be many different nation-states—indeed, the decision about the number of nation-states is, implicitly, one about the limits of retrofitting insurance mechanisms.

This point can be seen most dramatically within the European Union, the world's most remarkable attempt to shift authority above the level of the nation-state. The typical EU member state takes around 40 percent of the income of its citizens and uses a considerable part of it for redistribution, sometimes directly and sometimes through the provision of public goods. By contrast, the central EU institution, the European Commission, takes only 1 percent of the income of the citizens of EU member states and redistributes almost all of it to citizens of the same country. In this, the EU is predominantly a mechanism for further internal redistribution within nation-states (essentially from consumers to farmers), rather than for redistribution between states. This is made explicit in, for example, the "British rebate," which caps the net contribution of the UK at a very modest level.

More generally, notions of redistribution on the basis of fairness rest on some quasi-insurance principle, and so are dependent on some sovereign institution's accepting to enforce the redistribution. It is, I think, incoherent to insist that each developing country should have complete national sovereignty, while also insisting on redistribution to developing countries on the basis of "fairness."

The third ethical basis for concern is compassion: a response to the misfortune of others out of recognition of a common humanity. Indeed, compassion is seen as so important that those who lack it are viewed as mentally flawed. The unfortunate do not have a "right" to receive compassion, but the fortunate can reasonably see themselves as having a duty to be compassionate: duties need not create rights as counterparts. One huge advantage of compassion is that, as a basis for resource allocation, it is automatically needs related: our compassion is directed to the needy. The great disadvantages of compassion are, first, that it is degrading to the recipient—nobody wants to be on the receiving end of charity, with its inevitable implication that the appropriate response is gratitude; and, second, that it is potentially fickle—compassion for the remote is likely to be at the end of the line of charity, and therefore highly sensitive to changes of mood and of circumstance. Compassion will always be important as a motivation for development action, but in practice it is likely to be radically unreliable, dependent on periodic waves of emotion.

The fourth ethical basis for concern is enlightened self-interest. Indeed, enlightened self-interest is barely "ethical" at all: it bypasses ethics, grounding action that helps others become aware that the action is also helping the actor. Enlightened self-interest does not create duties—one is always free to ignore one's own interest—but it does potentially create rights, this time belonging to the enlightened actor. Enlightened self-interest has the disadvantage of not being able to tap very readily into the huge pool of potential energy that morality constitutes: many citizens of rich countries want to do something that does not serve their own interest. Offsetting this disadvantage, however, are two massive advantages. The first is that a key criterion for assistance is effectiveness: whereas guilt-based provision is blind to its effectiveness, self-interest demands that resources work. The second advantage is that the recipient need not feel either aggrieved or grateful: the basis for any assistance is mutual advantage.

Assistance to the countries of the bottom billion is likely to be far greater if it is grounded on enlightened self-interest than on compassion. Indeed, if the motivation were self-interest, there is some presumption that sufficient resources would be made available to address the problem. One should, however, add the caveat that a problem with the presumption of adequacy is free riding among beneficiaries. Thus, while all the rich countries might benefit from reducing the divergence of the per capita incomes of the bottom billion, this benefit would be a public good for all of them, so that each individual rich country would have an incentive to stand aside and let others pay.

Such collective-action problems among rich countries need not be overwhelming—they are far easier to tackle than the provision of those genuinely global public goods that require the participation of very many countries. Rich countries have already implemented standardized approaches to overcoming collective-action problems by setting norms: the 0.7 percent target for aid budgets is one such, but there have been many others, including sharing the burden of military defense. I suspect that attaining the 0.7 percent target for aid has proved so problematic not because of the free-rider problem but because several important nations do not see poverty reduction as being in their self-interest and, further, do not see aid as being an effective means of poverty reduction.

Enlightened self-interest is possible only if the actor has a genuine self-interest. By far the most likely basis for self-interest is the fear that severe misfortune on the part of the potential recipient will have adverse consequences for the actor. If the spillovers are sufficiently adverse, their victim could have the right to rectify them: the owner of the smoky chimney that pollutes the neighboring laundry might find his freedom to pollute curtailed by public action. Thus, just as "fairness" invites some softening of the concept of national sovereignty, so does enlightened self-interest, though from a different perspective. With fairness, the prospective recipient needs to soften sovereignty in order to create the right to retrofit insurance institutions; with enlightened self-interest, the donor needs to soften sovereignty in order to create the right to redress adverse spillovers, which, in the language of economics, are called "externalities."

Externalities: Neighborhood Effects, Migration, and Weakest Links

Why is the divergence of the per capita incomes of the bottom billion so important for citizens of developed countries? The reason is that, if it continues, divergence will produce high costs not only for those trapped in impoverished societies but also for other societies.

One type of cost is spillovers, both to neighbors and to the world at large. Neighborhood spillovers occur with economic growth, with policy, and with conflict. Typically, if a country's neighbors grow at a rate of 1 percent, this raises growth in the country itself by around 0.4 percent. This is a favorable externality. Equivalently, if a whole region has low growth, this is partly because there is little growth to spill over. Hence, growth is a regional public good. Policy also spills over: if a region adopts bad policies, it is more difficult for any individual country to break ranks and pioneer different policies since it has no role models to follow. Finally, conflict spills over: a civil war in one country increases the risk of civil war in neighbors and reduces their growth substantially. Indeed, typically more than half the costs of a civil war are borne by neighbors rather than by the warring country itself. Costs of civil war also spill over to developed countries. For example, around 95 percent of the global production of hard drugs is in conflict-affected societies where civil war has created territory outside the control of any recognized government.

Another cost of divergence is the emigration it generates to developed countries. As developed countries raise barriers against immigrants, the flow of people is diverted into illegal trafficking. Illegal immigrants have few choices other than to earn their living through illegality, so that immigration becomes a major social problem for recipient societies. It is also a problem for the countries of emigration. Migrants tend to be not the poorest, but those with the most education and initiative. The societies of the bottom billion are thus losing precisely the people who are most needed to transform them. Evidence suggests that such emigration is accelerating, driven partly by the widening income gap between developed countries and the bottom billion societies, and partly by the growing population of migrants from these countries now living in the developed societies and so in a position to facilitate further immigration (Collier, Hoeffler, and Pattillo 2004). Even with this acceleration, emigration can never be on a scale sufficient to make a serious impact on the poverty problem of these countries: only a minority will be able to leave. But the exodus of the most talented minority reinforces the problems these societies face and, as I discuss below, there is evidence that they already lack a critical mass of educated people able to rethink national development strategies.

In addition to spillovers and migration, some global public goods face weakest-link problems. The most obvious is the eradication of disease. The last place on earth to eradicate smallpox was Somalia, in 1977. Had this effort been delayed until after the collapse of the Somali state in 1992, there would have been no prospect of disease eradication. In effect, state failure in one country would preclude the global eradication of a disease, so that all countries would have to keep on vaccinating. The potential costs in areas in which disease control is ineffective can be enormous, although they might not materialize until a serious pandemic hits, at which point the inability to control the pandemic in countries where the state is ineffective might make global containment infeasible.

Several other weakest-link problems concern crime and regulation. Territories outside the control of an effective government attract international crime since they provide a safe haven. As the criminal forces build up in such a society, they become the richest part of it, and so become a lobby for continued bad governance. More insidiously, governments with nothing to lose might exploit their sovereignty to sell ineffective but certified compliance with regulations in such a way as to undermine global regulation. A simple example is the registration of shipping: a substantial proportion of the world's merchant fleet is registered in Liberia, whose government requires far lower standards than do governments of other countries. Liberia is one of the most weakly-governed countries in the world, yet, bizarrely, it is the world's major exporter of governance services for shipping: it is, in effect, exporting bad governance.

For the developed countries, the spillover, migration, and weakest-link costs of the divergent per capita incomes of the bottom billion do not need to be enormous to warrant attention, but it seems self-evident that those costs will continue to grow if divergence is not tackled. During the Cold War, the developed countries devoted around 6 percent of their gross domestic product (GDP) to defense against the threat posed by the Warsaw Pact countries. The danger did not, in the end, materialize, and one could make a reasonable case that the defense expenditure was decisive in eventually eliminating the threat. The risks posed by divergence, however, are of a different nature than those faced during the Cold War. True, no single risk is as great as that of nuclear war, but among them are uncontrollable pandemics, unmanageable immigration, terrorism, international crime, and hard drugs. Do these risks warrant resources amounting to around 0.7 percent of developed countries' incomes? Benchmarked on the Cold War, this scale of resources does not seem excessive for such risks. Chauvet, Collier, and Hoeffler (2006) conservatively estimate that, if the growth rates of "failing states" were raised, and their risk of conflict reduced, to the norms for other developing countries, the payoff would be equivalent to 1 to 2 percent of the GDP of the entire OECD. Most of the payoff would accrue to neighbors because of the large adverse spillovers from a failing state next door. The payoff would be greater still if one factored in the global costs of terrorism and disease.

Thus, although the challenge of the bottom billion does not warrant the spending of resources on a Cold War scale, it does deserve far more than the current 0.7 percent target. These resources need not all be in the form of aid; common prudence arising from enlightened self-interest might be a more solid basis than compassion for collective action by the developed countries.

Will the Bottom Billion Develop Autonomously?

Prudent international actions make sense only if they are both effective and necessary. Before one can discuss how to make such actions effective, however, one should ask if they are even necessary. That is, can the bottom billion solve their own problems? Will they develop autonomously?

Over the past decade, donors have come to recognize the limits of externally driven policy reform. There is now broad consensus that a willing government is required for reform to be effective and sustained. But is the presence of a willing government both a sufficient and a necessary condition for development? And do strong autonomous processes exist within the society that will correct errors of policy and governance?

Is Reform Sufficient for African Development?

Throughout most of history, decent government has been sufficient to enable development. In Asia, decent government is achieving the most spectacular development ever seen, and it is also working to produce development in two small African countries: Botswana and Mauritius.

In Botswana, good government has harnessed the country's enormous diamond revenues for rapid growth. It has also enforced effective public spending by putting in place both an honesty hurdle (is the procurement corrupt?) and an efficiency hurdle (does the project offer the prospect of a satisfactory rate of return?) before public money may be spent. By enforcing these hurdles, the government of this landlocked desert country has managed to generate the highest sustained growth rate of GDP in the world.

In Mauritius, the task was very different. The island has no diamonds and, more generally, no bonanza for public spending. Instead, the government chose to encourage the development of the private sector—notably, the highly competitive garment and textile industries—by reining in the state, getting rid of tariffs, taxes, and regulation. The institutional device used, an export processing zone across the island, coincided with a stroke of good fortune that occurred in 1982. That year, the new Multifibre Arrangement gave Mauritius a textile quota, and Hong Kong businessmen, facing the end of their usual 15-year property leases when it became clear that the British colony would revert to China in 1997, began looking for another base of operations. Mauritius, with its textile quota and export zone, looked attractive, and the island soon experienced explosive growth. In just two decades, an impoverished sugar island was transformed into one with a per capita income of US$10,000.

Why have other African countries not followed these development paths? One-third of them are landlocked and resource scarce, and cannot emulate Mauritius or Botswana. Indeed, areas like Botswana or Mauritius are unusual. No more than 1 percent of the population of the developing world outside Africa lives in places with such characteristics, and there is, unfortunately, no way to bring such countries even to middle-income levels, let alone to those of developed countries. This does not imply that the situation is hopeless. Countries piggy-back on the growth of their neighbors—growing, on average, by 0.4 percent for every 1 percent growth by neighbors. Outside Africa, landlocked countries manage to organize their economies so as to achieve typical growth spillovers of 0.7 percent.

Africa's landlocked, resource-scarce countries are handicapped twice over. First, there is little growth to spill over into them because, for various reasons, more fortunately endowed neighbors have not made the most of their opportunities. Second, the landlocked have not organized themselves so as to benefit from such growth as is available; for them growth spillovers average a mere 0.2 percent.

Evidently, Africa is not sufficiently internally integrated: there are huge barriers to trade, partly a consequence of poor transport infrastructure, but mainly a problem of policy. Moreover, in implementing barriers, local officials are predatory, using roadblocks and breaking rules at personal discretion. Africa has a huge number of regional trade agreements. The problem is not a shortage of agreements; on the contrary, there are too many confusing and mutually inconsistent arrangements. Rather, the problem is that real political interests prefer high trade barriers, especially against neighbors.

In addition to piggy-backing on their more fortunate neighbors, resource-scarce landlocked countries might harness their abundant land and make a success of export agriculture. Here, however, they face three severe difficulties. First, with population growth, land is becoming less abundant and their comparative advantage in agriculture is deteriorating over time. Second, most are semi-arid, with climatic conditions that are both volatile and generally deteriorating over time, making them unreliable as sources of supply compared with other locations (meanwhile, reliability is increasingly valued as supply chains become more sophisticated and swift). Third, African agriculture is overwhelmingly small-scale, peasant production, a mode of operation that is at an increasing disadvantage in competition with the large farms that have become the norm in Latin America. Large-scale organizations are better able to raise finance cheaply, to keep up with technological innovations and related investments, and, above all, to guarantee that their sources of supply can be traced—an attribute increasingly necessary for success in European markets. Yet to transform African agriculture to a mode associated with colonialism and that has been in decline since the 1960s would be politically acutely difficult. Moreover, the recent expropriations in Zimbabwe are likely to have increased the perceived risks of investing in large-scale agriculture across the region. Evidently, although the problems of export agriculture are most severe for the landlocked, resource-scarce countries, many also apply to the more fortunately endowed countries.

If one-third of Africa's population is ruled out of developing to middle-income levels because their countries are landlocked and resource scarce, another third lives in resource-rich countries that potentially could emulate Botswana. The problem here, however, is governance. Globally, resource riches tend to detach government from the population and lead to a gradual erosion of checks and balances on government. In effect, government becomes free to spend money how it chooses; spending on public services is then seen as wasteful, since it benefits everyone rather than just the group in power. Of course, in an already-mature democracy, such as Canada or Norway, institutions are sufficiently robust to manage well the revenues from the discovery of natural resources. But in Africa, with the exception of Botswana, all the resource-rich countries very rapidly became autocracies, and even those that subsequently became democracies tended to lack the restraints on government common to a mature democracy.

Democracy can usefully be decomposed into two aspects: electoral competition and checks and balances. The former can be very readily established because the incentives to participate are so high—thus, even in Afghanistan and Iraq, it has been possible to get instant electoral competition. The process of establishing checks and balances, however, is quite different. To begin with, there are no private incentives to establish such institutions; indeed, the elite typically will wish to avoid them. They are public goods that take a long time to establish and are often rather low profile. An election is easily observed, whereas restraints on government are not. Hence, in instant democracies, the government remains free to embezzle, perhaps to use the proceeds to steal the election through patronage, bribing the electorate with its own money—though not with public goods, which are too indiscriminate to be cost effective for politicians who are self serving. Thus, uniquely among resource-rich societies, democracy as such worsens economic performance whereas checks and balances improve it (Collier and Hoeffler 2005). Since resource rents tend to erode checks and balances, the dynamics of these societies are conducive, not to autonomous development, but to deterioration.

The remaining third of Africa's population lives in coastal, resource-scarce economies that potentially could emulate Mauritius. For them, a scarcity of resources is in one sense an advantage, since an abundance of natural resources tends to make other exports uncompetitive. A resource-rich country could not emulate Mauritius.

To date, however, none of Africa's other economies has emulated Mauritius, and the most likely explanation is that of timing. In the early 1980s, when Mauritius was breaking into global markets, it faced relatively limited competition from other low-income countries. Competitors were still largely in the high-income OECD economies, where production was still profitable because radically higher labor costs were offset by radically lower costs of other factors of production arising from economies of agglomeration. That is, the economies that are generated when many similar firms locate in the same place so that, for example, among them they create a large pool of skilled labor and specialist suppliers. These agglomeration economies create a wall that excludes new entrants in other new locations. However, once labor costs become so massively different as to exceed this offsetting advantage, there is an explosive process of relocation. If the first firm can just be profitable in a new location, the second firm to locate there will be more profitable, and so on. This is what happened in Mauritius, and on a more dramatic scale across East Asia.

Why did firms not choose to locate elsewhere in coastal Africa at this time in the 1980s? Since there were plenty of good East Asian locations, it did not take much to push Africa off the shortlist. In francophone Africa, the CFA franc became severely overvalued, corrected only in 1994 by a 50 percent devaluation. Lusophone Africa was engulfed in civil war. In anglophone Africa, Tanzania and Ghana were engulfed in ruinous economic implosions as a consequence of extreme socialism. South Africa was in the throws of the struggle to end Apartheid. Kenya, following a bloody coup attempt in 1983, descended into intense ethnic politics in which private activity was vulnerable to political exploitation. In short, in Africa, only Mauritius offered a credible political environment.

By the time coastal Africa pulled out of these diverse nightmares, Asia had established the same sort of agglomeration economies the OECD had enjoyed. With both cheap labor and agglomeration economies, production in these locations was massively profitable. In the sectors in which Asia specialized, it rapidly wiped out OECD competition. Its more important consequence for our purposes, however, is that it wiped out the chance of entry by Africa. African wages are now generally down to Asian levels, driven by African poverty. Yet, even if African workers were to work for free, they could not compensate firms for the higher costs of production involved in the loss of agglomeration economies. Africa is locked out of these markets until wages in Asia rise to levels roughly comparable to those that prevailed in the OECD when Asia first broke into OECD markets. Even at current East Asian growth rates, this would take Africa several decades. Hence, the autonomous processes of globalization that were so benign for Asia are not going to be benign for Africa. Coastal Africa missed the boat: temporary policy mistakes proved to be permanently costly.

Is Reform Generated Autonomously?

A recent thesis suggests that failing states contain strong autonomous processes for improvement. Weinstein (2005) uses the example of Somalia to argue that, in post-conflict situations, even without external intervention there are pressures to build effective institutions. Somalia has indeed managed to build some local-level public services and to develop some private services, most notably telecoms. But Somalia comes much closer to being Africa minus government than Africa with new government.

Because so much regulatory intervention by African governments has been dysfunctional, Africa minus government is indeed able to support some private activities better than elsewhere on the continent. However, both the experience of Somalia and more far-reaching evidence on private market activity suggest that lawlessness is not conducive to economic development. Informal activities take place at a rudimentary level of cash-and-carry trade, and a small-scale trade develops based on insider networks. But network trade cannot scale up—as the network expands, the incentive for contract adherence becomes weaker, and at some point the trade collapses altogether (Dixit 2004). The sort of informal economic activity that is the only form of trade in Somalia and that predominates in the rest of the region is better seen as a desperate response to the lack of a functioning state than a hopeful sign of autonomous processes of growth. Informal activity does not evolve naturally into formal activity; it requires action by the state. Credit of all forms requires that firms be able clearly and uniquely to identify themselves and their location of business. This requires an effective process of registration. Assets require property rights. Reputation requires some form of collective memory of past transactions. Contracts require commercial courts. All these have broken down in Africa because there is little political gain from providing them. The benefits, though enormous, would be long term and nationwide, and there would be considerable costs to the insiders who benefit from existing arrangements.

In addition to facilitating private activity, an effective state needs to supply public services. This requires nonpredatory taxation and accountable systems of spending. There is considerable scope for both sides of this process to go wrong, and in Africa they have. Although collected revenue is usually modest, taxation often manages to be arbitrary with very high rates of leakage—a typical estimate is that around two dollars are collected for every dollar that gets spent. Taxation can discourage private activity even at such modest levels. Further, the tax base is typically very narrow because informality is feasible, so most entrepreneurs prefer to stay outside the tax net by remaining small. On the spending side, the evidence is yet more disturbing. Surveys of public expenditure reveal that, often, only a small part of the money released from a ministry of finance actually finds its way to its intended destination—in Uganda, the figure is 20 percent for nonsalary spending in schools; in Chad, it is only 1 percent for primary health clinics. In Africa, the normal mechanism of taxation to finance public services has largely broken down.

In principle, democracy might be sufficient to fix this problem. However, even in those states that are moderately democratic, the incentives for politicians to tax and spend effectively are weak. In the resource-rich states that account for around a third of Africa's population, governments do not need to tax citizens. As a consequence, there is little pressure to use public resources well. The natural resource rents are not seen as belonging to citizens, partly because these societies have not had such a concept (see Collier and Hoeffler 2005). The resources finance the politics of private patronage, rather than the provision of public goods. Even in the resource-scarce democracies, the high degree of ethnic diversity in most of Africa makes collective action for public service provision much more difficult (Collier 2001; La Ferrara and Alesina 2005).

Thus, although failing states are highly disadvantageous for most of their inhabitants, politically they are fairly stable equilibria. Indeed, the most likely way they are disturbed is through violence: coups and civil wars. Neither of these serves as a useful prelude to reform. Rather, they are development in reverse.

· A recent measure of the persistence of the typical failing state is that it takes on average around 60 years for such a state to attain a decisive and sustained escape (Chauvet and Collier 2007). Three factors contribute to such extreme persistence: low income, small population size, and low education. In effect, the very concept of reform is difficult for small, poor, uneducated societies. China and India once had policies every bit as bad as those in Africa, but their societies had a critical mass of educated people. A country such as the Central African Republic simply lacks the resident talent to undertake the necessary rethinking. It lacks the scale to support a financial press, which would be one natural medium for such discussion. As emigration of the skilled becomes more acceptable, both to recipient societies and to the families of those with the skills, the problem intensifies: the Central African Republic may never accumulate the resident critical mass of talent. Further, African countries have no neighboring role models. Successes are few, and information flows surprisingly from one African state to another. In Vietnam, in contrast, the elite could and did learn from the rest of East Asia. In Angola, the elite regard the country as absolutely unique; as a result, another 30 years of big oil revenues will probably leave it looking just like Nigeria does today.

In addition to these structural factors, high prices for commodity exports significantly and substantially reduce the chances of sustaining a policy turnaround (Chauvet and Collier 2006). This is probably because the impetus for reform among the elite comes initially from desperation at deteriorating conditions, while a windfall as a result of suddenly favorable external terms of trade reduces the pressure for change.

Autonomous Decline

I fear that a more realistic prospect than autonomous recovery is autonomous collapse. By collapse, I refer to civil war. The causes of civil war are now reasonably well understood.[4] Low income, low growth, primary commodity exports, a high proportion of young men in the society, and small population are all major risk factors. Africa has all of these characteristics. Each makes rebellion more feasible, and where it is feasible it is very likely to occur: some social entrepreneur will occupy the niche, although the agenda of the rebel group is unpredictable and could range from religious extremism to ethnic secession. Regardless of its agenda, civil war is persistent, on average lasting around seven years—more than ten times as long as an international war. Once over, there is around a 43 percent chance of reversion to conflict within the first decade.

---

4. See, for example, Collier and Hoeffler (1998, 2004); Fearon and Laitin (2003); Miguel, Satyanath, and Sergenti (2004); Collier, Hoeffler, and Rohner (2006).

The economic costs of civil war are enormous, typically leaving the economy around 20 percent poorer than had the war not occurred, and with a massive and highly persistent deterioration in health conditions. Around half of the costs of a civil war accrue after it has ended. The costs to neighbors are even larger collectively than the costs to the society itself. Thus, high-birth-rate countries that get stuck in poverty and dependence upon primary commodity exports are living dangerously.

Africa's civil wars are also dangerously secessionist: Eritrea split off from Ethiopia, leaving the latter country landlocked, yet without any remarkable improvement in the governance or peace of Eritrea. Southern Sudan is set to secede as part of its peace settlement. Africa is already divided into far more countries than either South or East Asia, despite its much smaller population. The more countries into which a region is divided the higher the risk of both civil and international war.

Hence, whatever autonomous processes of development might be present in these societies are offset by a clear and powerful process of autonomous decline, a problem I have termed the "conflict trap."

In view of the recent improvement in Africa's growth rates, one might reasonably question the thesis of autonomous decline. However, this improvement has been driven predominantly by the recent massive increases in the world prices of Africa's commodity exports; these high prices might not persist. More worryingly, even if they were to persist, the prognosis for African growth would remain unpromising. As a model by Collier and Goderis (2006) shows, in the typical African country, a 10 percent increase in the prices of its commodity exports increases GDP growth significantly for the first five years, rising cumulatively to a level 8 percent higher than it would otherwise have been. But then, even if commodity prices remain at their new higher level, things start to go wrong. Once all the effects on the economy have played out, GDP ends up not 8 percent higher, but 8 percent lower than it would have been without the improved export prices. Hence, unless political processes within Africa change radically from those prevailing in the past, even the new world of high commodity prices leads to a forecast of autonomous decline.

What Instruments Do We Have and How Should We Use Them?

Where does this leave us? I have tried to give a sense of five distinct problems facing African development that need to be confronted if international action is to be effective. I begin by summarizing them.

First, the terrible problem of landlocked, resource-scarce Africa is not very amenable to action. A harsh-sounding corollary is that the problems of the more fortunate neighbors need to be fixed first. Until that happens, a wide range of ameliorative polices may be appropriate for landlocked, resource-scarce countries, but these will not solve the development problem.

Second, countries are unlikely to turn around all by themselves: they need help to accelerate this process.

Third, the more likely autonomous process to play out is the eventual succumbing of poor and stagnant countries with rapidly growing populations to conflict. The current trend to resource discoveries in such countries actually increases this risk.

Fourth, the current importance of natural resource exports, combined with higher prices and more discoveries, is potentially Africa's major opportunity for development. However, the domestic politics of harnessing these resource rents is unpromising in the extreme. Nigeria, not Botswana, is the norm for the region.

Fifth, the coastal, resource-scarce economies face a daunting task in trying to emulate Asia. Manufactured markets are now dominated by countries with similarly low labor costs but radically greater agglomeration economies. Agricultural markets increasingly are being supplied by large business organizations, which are not acceptable politically to most African governments.

These unappealing conclusions constitute the true challenge that external actors need to confront in devising assistance strategies for the region. They warrant neither the fundamental optimism of the UN's Millennium Development Goals—that only a lack of money prevents the problem from being solved—nor the fundamental irresponsibility of those who dismiss external intervention as irrelevant or even counterproductive. Rather, they require some hard thinking across the full range of possible instruments the OECD countries possess. That is the agenda of this part of the paper.

Aid

Aid has attracted far more attention than is warranted by its likely efficacy. It has become highly politicized among OECD electorates, used by Europeans and Canadians to castigate the United States as "mean," by the left to castigate the right as "uncaring," and by the right to castigate the left as "naïve." It plays into precisely the mental frame of guilt-grievance that I have suggested is so massively dysfunctional for Africans themselves.

The statistical evidence on whether aid is good or harmful for African development is all over the place, but the median is that aid has small but positive effects (Doucouliagos and Paldam 2006). The underlying observations on which the statistical analysis is based reveal a scatter plot with no discernable dominant relationship. The most likely interpretation of this pattern is that aid has both some strongly positive and some strongly negative effects. But this produces a net outcome that is unclear and from which each side in the polarized debate can extract some statistical relationship in support of its political position. If, indeed, the net weak effect is the compound of offsetting effects, it is as important to discover where aid is counterproductive as to discover where it is effective. Aid needs to be shifted away from those situations where it is counterproductive, not merely from where it is useless.

I think there are two situations in which the evidence suggests that aid is significantly counterproductive. One is during incipient policy turnarounds from very poor policies and governance. Such a turnaround can be identified either by small but significant improvements already under way or by a change in the political leadership (such as the death of a president). These constitute political windows of opportunity for external actors. Unfortunately, it transpires that, in these situations, the provision of financial aid is significantly and strongly counterproductive: aid chills the impetus to reform. The result is reinforced by the previously noted result that an improvement in the price of exports has the same effect. Reforms are more likely to continue if the regime is squeezed for money.

A second situation in which aid is likely to be counterproductive is when the maintenance of a competitive real exchange rate is particularly important for development. Rajan and Subramanian (2005) make much of the effects of Dutch disease that aid generates.[5] Whether real-exchange-rate appreciation occurs as a result of aid and whether it is important are both contingent. Real-exchange-rate appreciation can be offset if the aid is spent on infrastructure that reduces the costs of the export sector, and if the expenditure itself has a high import content. Thus, the purchase of cranes for docks is likely to improve the competitiveness of exporters, but financing the salaries of primary school teachers is likely to reduce competitiveness. Whether competitiveness matters very much is itself contingent upon opportunities. The key group of African countries for which it matters is the coastal resource scarce, some of whom are ripe for an attempt to break into more diversified export markets. It would be ironic if aid targeted to such countries frustrated their best chance of development. One way around such a dilemma would be to make aid temporary—a surge in resources designed to fix up the export infrastructure over a short period—after which aid would be radically reduced, leaving the export sector with enhanced competitiveness.

Paradoxically, countries in both situations—early turnarounds and those with the potential for new exports—historically have been prone to receive "big aid." Incipient reforms attract donors desperate to support change and, since the countries most likely to succeed in penetrating export markets are those with the best policies, the increased tendency to link aid to good policies means that these same countries are the most likely to receive large aid programs.

In addition to these counterproductive consequences, aid has two adverse security implications. One is that around 11 percent of aid money leaks into military spending (Collier and Hoeffler 2006a). This is not a high rate of leakage, but in monetary terms it means that aid inadvertently finances about half of the typical African country's military budget. Further, evidence of neighborhood arms' races suggests that aid is fueling a regional public bad. The amounts involved are not enormous, but they imply that donors should be concerned to dampen military spending. The second adverse security consequence of aid is that it appears quite

---

5. "Dutch disease" refers to the appreciation of the exchange rate due to the export of natural resources and the resulting loss of competitiveness of other exports.

substantially to increase the risk of a coup d'état (Collier and Hoeffler 2006b). The most likely explanation is that aid increases the scope for rents that can be captured by a coup.

Just as there are clear situations in which aid is counterproductive yet still provided, so there are clear situations in which it would be productive but is not provided. For example, aid would be highly productive for growth in countries trying to cope with adverse terms-of-trade shocks, such as increases in the price of imported oil or declines in export prices (Collier, Goderis, and Hoeffler 2006). Aid can also be productive in countries that are experiencing incipient turnarounds. In such situations, where money is often counterproductive, large technical assistance programs can be highly effective in enhancing further reform. The most likely interpretation of this result is that, where the political will for reform exists, technical assistance helps to overcome the civil service's inability to implement it. To respond to such situations, development aid needs to be highly flexible, and organized along lines analogous to those of emergency relief. To date, however, the nearest approach has been an EU facility, Stabex, which was designed to help when export prices fell. Unfortunately, it released funds so slowly that the aid was actually pro-cyclical— arriving at times when export prices were high, rather than low—and thus counterproductive.

A third situation in which aid is atypically effective is in post-conflict situations, particularly during the middle of the post-conflict decade, when needs are still considerable but the capacity to spend money effectively has already improved somewhat. Paradoxically, although donors have been too slow in their provision of aid for terms-of-trade shocks and opportunities for technical assistance, they have been too swift in responding to post-conflict situations. Perhaps because peace is politically glamorous, aid arrives in large quantities in the first year of peace, then tapers off just as it is becoming useful.

Some evidence also exists of missed aid opportunities in failing states. Projects perform much worse in such environments, but it turns out that supervision is differentially effective in these conditions in increasing the success of projects. This is unsurprising: where government interests are most divergent from those of the donor, donor supervision is most likely to be useful (see Chauvet, Collier, and Fuster 2006). The implication is that, in failing states, donors should spend differentially high amounts on supervision. In fact, they do the opposite: donors' administrative budgets are lowest in precisely the environments in which resources are most necessary. There are many reasons for such a misalignment of resources, including the need to appear to be lean and efficient, with a low ratio of administrative expenses to disbursements; and the pressure to avoid the release of information that might lead to the cancellation of the project and, hence, to missed targets for disbursement.

These are important instances in which aid should be shifted from its current counterproductive use, and it is on this level that the aid debate needs to focus, rather than the "big politics" of meeting targets versus wasting money on crooked regimes. Yet, while aid is modestly useful and could be made more effective, it is unfortunately somewhat peripheral to the five major challenges I set out above. Consider them in turn.

First, landlocked, resource-scarce countries need their more successful neighbors to make the most of their opportunities. But aid to such countries has limited scope to trigger growth, because no clear, viable growth strategy exists to take them even to middle-income levels unless their neighbors do better than they have in the past.

Second, aid can assist turnarounds, but that requires technical assistance, not money; paradoxically, technical assistance is the least fashionable part of aid.

Third, aid can reduce the risk that a country will collapse into a syndrome of insecurity, most notably in post-conflict situations. But aid is evidently a weak instrument for this security problem. Aid even seems to worsen some aspects of the insecurity syndrome.

Fourth, the political problems associated with large natural resource rents evidently are not very amenable to aid. Resource-rich countries are, by definition, less in need of financial aid than other countries, though there may well be scope for technical assistance to the resource rich. Indeed, an essential aspect of Botswana's success has been its completely atypical willingness to rely heavily upon expatriate skills. The government used part of its resource rents to hire these skills, but where such a use is politically impossible, aid-financed technical assistance might be acceptable.

The final problem is the coastal, resource-scarce countries, which need to break into global markets. Aid has some part to play in support of this strategy, notably in pump priming export infrastructure. However, the problems generated by the Dutch disease are most acute in the context of a strategy of export diversification, and so the scope for aid is intrinsically limited.

Overall, if aid is the only instrument the OECD is willing to use, it is unlikely to be decisive in overcoming any of these five development problems. It can ameliorate living standards in the poorest countries by directly raising consumption above the level of income, but alone it is not very potent in raising income itself. Aid becomes considerably more potent as an instrument for growth and development, however, if it is combined with other instruments.

Trade Policies

The contrast between using aid to raise consumption directly and using it to raise the growth rate of income is paralleled by OECD trade policy. To date, the main focus of attention on trade policy has concerned agriculture, and the trade barriers and production subsidies that tend to reduce the prices of Africa's agricultural exports. Policy changes to raise those prices would raise Africans' income for given levels of production, but would also reduce the incentive to diversify into new exports. Yet, higher earnings from existing exports would have a Dutch-disease effect on potential exports analogous to the effects of aid. Thus, at least for the coastal, resource-scarce economies, a focus on agricultural exports might yield short-term gains in consumption, but only at the expense of the longer-term growth of income. In the event, the OECD agricultural lobby is too entrenched for significant progress to be made on this front and, at the time of writing, the Doha Round of multilateral trade negotiations looks to be a failure. As a result, the focal point for trade negotiations during the round has been both irrelevant to Africa's core long-term trade interest, which is diversification, and unrealistic.

What should the Doha Round focus on that would assist Africa's growth? Recall that global trade matters most for the coastal, resource-scarce economies. Here, the key problem is that Asia has developed economies of agglomeration and so is fundamentally more competitive than Africa: Africa has missed the boat. What is needed, therefore, is a trade policy that brings the boat back again sooner than if Africa has to wait for Asian wage levels to increase massively. The trade policy that can do that is preferences: Africa needs to be protected from Asia in OECD markets. Such a policy might sound fanciful. In fact, however, both the United States (with its *Africa Growth and Opportunity Act*, AGOA) and the EU (with its Everything But Arms agreement, EBA) already operate such schemes. Further, the OECD made a closely related offer of preferences in OECD markets at the Hong Kong stage of the Doha Round in December 2005.

Unfortunately, for different reasons, none of these schemes is very effective. By far the most effective is AGOA, which has raised African textile exports to the United States by more than 50 percent (Fraser and Van Biesebroeck 2005). In contrast, the EU scheme, EBA, has had no discernable effect. The Hong Kong offer was never implemented but would almost certainly have been useless. The devil in trade arrangements is in the details. Which markets are covered? Which products are covered? What is the time frame for the preference? Which countries receive the preference? What are the rules of origin of intermediate inputs used in production of the exports? I take these in turn.

Evidently, a satisfactory scheme would cover all OECD markets. Only the Hong Kong offer did this. AGOA is particularly handicapped because it covers only the United States, whereas Africa's natural market connections are with Europe.

The coverage of products should be as extensive as possible, but the essential core is a small range of labor-intensive manufactures on which OECD tariffs against Asian produce would remain significant—most notably textiles, garments, and footwear. The Hong Kong offer permitted OECD countries to exclude 3 percent of product lines from open access, which seems like a minimal limitation. Given the small number of products in which African countries could compete in OECD markets, however, it would have given OECD countries all the scope they needed to frustrate African export diversification.

AGOA and EBA differ markedly in the time frame of the preference. In AGOA, the preference lasts for three years at a time, and its key component, a waiver on rules of origin, is granted for only 12 months at a time. EBA, in contrast, has no time limits: it can continue to be ineffective for eternity. Twelve months is manifestly too short a horizon of market access to justify investment by exporting firms. Thus, for example, firms in Madagascar find it highly profitable to export garments to the United States, but they are unwilling to expand production because the investment needed for such an expansion would pay back only if the preferences were extended beyond the current limit. Yet, if 12 months is too short, an unspecified horizon such as EBA's is also dysfunctional. All trade preferences that are not fully compliant with the rules of the World Trade Organization (WTO)—which is the case with both AGOA and EBA—should have sunset clauses to make them more acceptable to other countries. Further, a sunset clause provides an incentive for African governments and donors alike to implement the complementary actions needed to diversify exports while the trade-preference window is open. A time limit thus facilitates coordination. A sensible time limit would be ten years.

Next, consider the countries that should receive preferences. AGOA is pan-African, whereas both EBA and the Hong Kong offer were limited to the least-developed countries. It is evident that those African countries best placed to break into global markets are those with the best policies, governance, and infrastructure, not the worst—that is, countries such as Senegal and Ghana. The least-developed countries, such as Liberia and Somalia, are in no position to take advantage of trade preferences. Hence, EBA and the Hong Kong offer were to a first approximation useless, as evidenced by the fact that EBA is so radically less successful than AGOA. A sensible approach would be to make the time-bound offer of a decade of preferences apply to those African countries that are not among the least developed. Then, after these countries have broken into global markets, the least-developed countries subsequently should get exclusive access, by which time they might be in a better position to make use of it.[6]

Finally, consider the complex matter of the appropriate rules of origin. If rules are too generous, then products could be produced in Asia, re-labeled in Africa, and sold in OECD markets, a process which would be

---

6. South Africa should be included in the scheme, as it is in AGOA, for two reasons. First, the country desperately needs extra job creation, given its very high rate of unemployment. Second, since South African firms are heavily engaged across the region, growth in South Africa has large spillovers to its neighbors.

useless for Africa. If, however, rules of origin are too restrictive, requiring very high domestic value added, the costs of producing within Africa would exceed the preference margin, rendering the scheme ineffective. The appropriate degree of required value added should be deduced from the typical proportions of value added found in recent successful entrants into global markets such as Bangladesh and Vietnam. These are the models for coastal Africa.

An OECD-wide super-AGOA along the lines proposed above would give several African countries the chance to emulate Asian development. Because African economies are so small relative to the global market, their becoming competitive even in a narrow niche of manufactures would increase enormously the scope for scaling up. In effect, the natural size of manufactured exports in these countries is either zero or infinity. The success of AGOA shows that, even without coordination with other policies, trade preferences can achieve a lot. However, an OECD-wide scheme has the potential for coordination both with aid and with the policies of African governments to ensure that an export strategy works (see Collier and Venables 2007).

Military Intervention

Overwhelmingly, the threats to security African countries face are internal: rebellions and coups. Africa's countries are ill-suited to the provision of security against rebellion. Defense is the classic public good, subject to economies of scale, and Africa simply has too many countries to reap these economies—most are too small to afford adequate defense. Defense against coups is even more difficult. In practice, those African governments facing the most severe risk of a coup try to buy off their own military by increasing spending on it. Thus, not only are African armies ineffective as protection against rebellion; they themselves constitute an important threat to legitimate government.

International military action in post-colonial Africa has had considerable successes and some failures. The most substantial success was the de facto security guarantee France provided the governments of francophone Africa until the mid-1990s. The guarantee came to an end partly as a result of the debacle in Rwanda, where France found itself uncomfortably close to defending a government that was embarking on genocide. The first manifestation of the change was the controversial decision not to put down a coup d'état in Côte d'Ivoire in December 1999. The French security guarantee was never explicit and it was never absolute, but it was supported by a string of military bases in Africa. Between 1965 and the mid-1990s, the risk of civil war in francophone Africa was less than one-third as high as might have been expected given the other characteristics of these countries (see Collier, Hoeffler, and Rohner 2006). In effect, potential rebels knew they were unlikely to win and so were discouraged from trying. Paradoxically, just after the French had abandoned the policy, the British introduced it for Sierra Leone. The civil war in that country was ended by a small British military intervention and the peace was maintained by a continued presence that ended only with the recent "over-the-horizon" ten-year guarantee of security for the incumbent government. The payoff to British military intervention in Sierra Leone has been spectacular: against a likely counterfactual of continuing civil war, a modest financial outlay has achieved a sustained peace.

One problem with security guarantees is that they cannot be unconditional. This indeed was the key to the unsustainability of the French strategy: France ended up supporting governments that were morally indefensible. An alternative to abandonment, however, would be to make military guarantees conditional upon certain basic rules of governance, a matter I discuss below.

A second context in which military intervention has been successful is in post-conflict peace building. Post-conflict situations in low-income countries are inherently dangerous. There is a high risk of reversion to conflict, and Africa has conformed to this pattern. The matter is currently very pertinent because several African civil wars have recently been settled. To date the international community has placed considerable reliance upon post-conflict political design, seeking to impose democracy and early elections. The statistical evidence is that there is no political fix for the problem of high post-conflict risks (Collier, Hoeffler, and Soderbom 2006).

Democracies are actually more at risk than autocracies. Elections during the post-conflict decade shift the risk from the election year to the subsequent year, with an overall increase in risk. Thus, post-conflict elections are radically ill-suited as milestones for the withdrawal of international peacekeeping forces. This has not stopped them being used for this purpose —for example, in the Democratic Republic of Congo, the second round of the elections was set for October 29, 2006, with European peacekeeping forces to withdraw on October 30. Faced with high risks, the typical post-conflict government chooses to maintain a large military—indeed, its post-conflict military spending looks much more like war than peace. While this is understandable, it is unfortunately counterproductive. Uniquely in post-conflict situations, domestic military spending actually significantly increases the risk of further conflict (Collier and Hoeffler 2006c). This is perhaps because the opposition interprets high military spending as a signal indicating that the government will renege on its commitments for inclusion and resort to repression.

Thus, the risk of further conflict is high, no magic political design will reduce it, and domestic military spending makes things worse. What are the solutions? In the longer term, economic recovery brings risks down, helped by aid as discussed above. Economic recovery takes time, however, so some other strategy is needed to contain risks during the post-conflict decade. The evidence is that international peacekeeping forces are highly effective in reducing risks: the more that is spent, the more the risks are reduced. Hence, external military force and aid are complementary. Without military force, aid is liable to be wasted as the country collapses back into violence before incomes have had time to grow. Without aid, military force would need to be semi-permanent because in a stagnant economy the risks remain high for well beyond the first decade.

A third area in which international military interventions and guarantees are useful is in protection against coups. Unfortunately, democracy does not appear to offer protection: low-income, slow-growth countries face significant risks that democracy does not reduce. Thus, to be protected from its own military, a government has no choice but to seek an external military guarantee. An international guarantee runs much less risk of triggering an international war than a guarantee provided by a neighbor. To give a practical example, in Togo, on the death of a long-serving president, the man's son promptly declared himself president. The African Union correctly described this as a coup and demanded an election. Unfortunately, the president's son staged the election and unsurprisingly won it. Evidently, what was needed was a temporary external military intervention following on immediately from the African Union decision, with external actors overseeing the elections and then withdrawing.

None of these three uses of international force should be particularly controversial. Indeed, over the past half-century, rich countries have used mutual security guarantees as the key instrument for their own security. Two considerably more controversial roles for external military intervention, however, involve the "duty to protect" particular populations from attack by their own governments and actively changing the regime of a government that flouts basic democratic practices. Following the disaster in Rwanda, the former is now advocated by the United Nations, but actions in Darfur have been extremely limited. The latter is a very distant prospect. However, these two controversial uses of international force, although they are glamorous and so attract a lot of attention, are not as important as the three less controversial uses and should not be allowed to inhibit them.

International military intervention has not been uniformly successful in Africa; indeed, it seems likely to face some inherent risks. The major disaster was the US intervention in Somalia. Following what in retrospect looks to be a relatively modest level of casualties, US forces were withdrawn. Since this ushered in 14 years of lawlessness that seems now to be in danger of evolving into a safe haven for terrorism, it is difficult to regard the decision as correct. Somalia's short-term lesson was that intervention was unwise; it took only months for this to lead to the genocide in Rwanda.

The difficulty with military intervention is political. In Africa, it is unpopular with the elites who like to preserve their abuse of power by protesting against "neocolonialism." Among development practitioners and NGOs, it is unpopular partly because the political left dislikes the military, and partly because military budgets fall outside the remit of development agencies and so compete with development budgets. Finally, it is even unpopular with the military itself: as one OECD foreign ministry official put it to me, "the defense ministry hates Africa." Africa is seen by the military as unglamorous and complicated.

Evidently, none of these reasons is legitimate. Despite these difficulties, however, international military intervention can be hugely cost effective, and can achieve objectives that cannot be reached by other instruments.

Standards for Governance

The final instrument available to international actors is to set standards of governance. Standards can range over a wide remit. For example, they can cover how banks in tax havens report deposits, how resource extraction companies win contracts, how arms are traded, and how African governments manage their budgets. Sometimes standards should be mandatory, carrying penalties for noncompliance; sometimes they should be voluntary. The bodies by which they would most appropriately be promulgated can also vary considerably.

The power of international standards should not be underestimated. Even when voluntary, they provide benchmarks around which reformers can coordinate, and they force the actors involved to make a clear signal one way or another: compliance or noncompliance. The most dramatic recent example of the power of international standards has been the transformation of eastern Europe as governments there attempt to comply with the *Aquis Communautaires* rules of the European Union. Another example was the effect of the Stability Pact rules of entry for the euro. In both cases, the promulgation of standards massively increased the perceived political costs of setting policies that were incompatible with them.

Standards for Companies That Operate in Africa

In Africa, standards could be used to improve the conduct of companies—particularly banks, resource extraction companies, and arms suppliers—that deal extensively there.

The key role of foreign banks in the context of Africa is as depositaries for capital flight, some of it the proceeds of corruption. Africa has a higher proportion of its private wealth held outside the continent than does any other region (Collier, Hoeffler, and Pattillo 2001, 2004). If these deposits faced a greater risk of exposure, capital flight would moderate; there might also be less incentive for corruption. The OECD has shown what is possible in its recent assaults of banking secrecy in order to trace terrorist finances. This is the agenda of the rich countries, though, not of Africa. Ordinary Africans need similar efforts applied to deposits made by rich Africans. Naturally, this will often not be a high priority among African elites. Moreover, the Swiss government's recent impeding of the repatriation from Switzerland of corrupt Nigerian deposits shows that such self-interest is not confined to African elites.

Transparency in international banking is one standard that should not be voluntary. The OECD countries have ample means of enforcing their banks' compliance, even those in tax havens—particularly recalcitrant banking havens can be threatened with changes in rules that would make their entire operations unprofitable. Instead of such drastic action, however, perhaps banks registered in OECD countries could be required not to enter into transactions with noncompliant banks. Such a rule would compel virtually all banks to comply.

Africa is in the midst of a financial bonanza from resource extraction. The last such bonanza, in the mid-1970s, was a disaster. There is some evidence that African governments have learned from past mistakes, but to reduce the risks of repetition, it is critical to change the behavior of resource extraction companies. Some progress has already been made through the UK government's Extractive Industries Transparency Initiative (EITI); to date, however, the initiative covers only transparency in reporting payments to governments. While this is a sensible place to start, it leaves four important areas for an expanded EITI, or EITI+. The first is the process by which exploration contracts are won. There need to be clear and precise rules governing competitive tendering, and commercial penalties for companies that participate in any award process that does not comply with these standards.

The second area that an EITI+ should cover concerns what the contracts say, and in particular how price risk is borne. At present, weak governments that can barely manage their budgets are exposed to highly volatile prices. Contracts should be designed that place more of the risk on the extraction companies.

Third, although revenue transparency is desirable, it is merely an input into expenditure transparency: governments that receive resource rents should be expected to meet adequate standards of budgetary transparency on the expenditure side. Such standards could only be voluntary, but they might nevertheless be potent. Citizens would be able to see how their money was being spent or to know precisely what aspects of budgetary mismanagement were preventing them from seeing how it was spent.

Transparency in spending is enormously important for resource-rich countries. Partly, public spending has to be the engine of growth in these economies because it is so substantial. Perhaps even more important, if spending is not transparent, public money is likely to get diverted into patronage politics. The real cost of corruption is not the waste of resources but the diversion of the democratic political process from its normal business of providing public goods to the politics of private patronage. Only transparency in spending can prevent this process, by making patronage politics unaffordable for political parties.

Fourth, revenues inevitably will continue to be volatile, so there is an urgent need for a simple international standard to smooth this volatility in the medium term. I give two examples of what happens in the absence of an international rule. In 2001, the new government of East Timor realized that it knew nothing about how to manage revenue volatility. Initially, it sent a team to Angola to learn what to do, a learning strategy that was not necessarily wise. In the event, it copied the Norwegian future generations fund, a strategy which is seriously inappropriate for a low-income country since it obviously should aim to build up capital domestically rather than financial assets in New York. The second example is the reform period in Nigeria introduced by the appointment of Ngozi Nkonjo-Iweala as minister of finance in 2003. Faced with an incipient oil bonanza, the minister designed a medium-term revenue smoothing rule, the *Fiscal Responsibility Act*. In 2006, she was dismissed from the government. Whether her rule will long survive her departure is an open question. The survival of the reform would have been more likely had there been an international norm for her to have adopted.

The final example of rules for companies concerns the arms trade. Small arms, notably the Kalashnikov AK-47 assault rifle, are considerably cheaper in Africa than in other regions (Killicoat 2006). This is indeed partly a consequence of ineffective governance. Arms are sucked into particular parts of Africa during conflict, then moved easily across borders that are not effectively policed. The United Nations now commonly imposes arms embargoes on many conflicts, yet a new study of the stock market prices of the companies that manufacture armaments and explosives (La Ferrara 2006) finds tentative evidence that it is non-OECD companies in places such as China and eastern Europe that break sanctions. The reason seems to be that embargoes depress the stock market prices of OECD armaments companies that have been trading with the embargoed country, but raise the stock prices of companies in non-OECD countries. In effect, embargoes are subject to a weakest-link problem in which free-rider countries profit from breaking the collective action. Various sanctions, some company specific and others country specific, exist to enforce these companies to comply, but enforcement works better with OECD companies since it places them at a disadvantage and so gives them an incentive to use their inside information to assist enforcement efforts against others.

Standards for African Governments

I now turn to standards that could apply to African governments. Some could be purely voluntary, while others could be linked to aid or external security guarantees through conditions. A sharp distinction should be drawn between policy conditionality and governance conditionality. The former has a track record of failure and is fundamentally at odds with building responsible government. When donors impose policy conditionality, it is unclear if governments or donors are responsible, which confuses the essential process whereby citizens hold governments accountable for their choices. In contrast, governance conditionality does not undermine accountable government but rather aims to reinforce it. Its objective is to require governments to be accountable to their own citizens rather than to external actors. Historically, this process of establishing accountable government has often required some form of external pressure. In Europe, the usual form of pressure was an external military threat that required high military expenditure. In turn, this required compliance with heavy taxation, the *quid pro quo* for which was accountability in government. No such external threat is going to operate in Africa, however, so it is both legitimate and expedient that other forms of external pressure be developed as substitutes. What aspects of governance should the international community seek to set as the minimum standard?

The first aspect concerns transparent budgets. Although transparent budgets are essential in resource-rich African countries, they are also highly desirable in other African countries. The dismal results from public expenditure tracking surveys show the extent of the problem. Accountability in public spending is not a simple matter. An effective system uses a combination of three different processes: top-down scrutiny, bottom-up pressure from end users of public services, and peer pressure among providers. The balance among these three processes appropriately changes depending upon the service involved. For example, the performance of doctors probably depends primarily upon the degree of peer pressure for the maintenance of professional standards. Many techniques, such as patient charters, parent representation on school boards, and league tables of performance, have been found to be effective for different services. What is needed is a compendium of such techniques organized as a desirable minimum set of standards. Evidently, such an approach could only be voluntary. However, by making a set of standards explicit, it becomes far easier for domestic lobbies and parliaments to demand action: pressure groups can coordinate around a common, certified agenda that is not owned by any one particular group and so does not advantage that group politically. An obvious form of conditionality would be to make budget support conditional upon such standards, an entirely legitimate goal since the essence of budget support is that the donor cede any control as to how the money is spent—it is simply part of the budget. If donor agencies do not insist on high and clear standards for budgetary processes, then they are failing to fulfill their fiduciary responsibility to their own parliaments when they support budgets that are not transparent. For example, in 2005, the EU provided €20 million of budget support to Chad at a time when a public expenditure tracking survey had found that less than 1 percent of the money released by that country's ministry of finance for health clinics reached the intended destination. There can be little doubt that the EU budget support found its way to financing the Chadian army, which was the government priority.

Another area where international standards should apply concerns free and fair elections. Democracy is often not sufficient for decent government, but in Africa it is likely to be a necessary condition. Africa is not like China, and its high degree of ethnic diversity makes autocratic regimes particularly dysfunctional. In an ethnically diverse society, an autocracy, invariably resting on the support of one particular ethnic group, has an overwhelming incentive to sacrifice the public good of growth for the narrow interest of redistribution toward the ethnic group in power. One new study (Ndulu et al. forthcoming) finds that around half of Africa's entire growth shortfall over the 1960-2000 period is attributable to a few policy "syndromes," or gross errors. At the root of these errors was the combination of extreme autocracy, which the authors classify as "rule by fear," combined with ethnic diversity. It was neither diversity nor autocracy in itself but the combination that was damaging. China can be successful with autocracy, but not Africa. Hence, compliance with the basic rules of democracy is important for African development. The obvious way to encourage compliance with free and fair elections is to make security guarantees conditional upon them. Had France done this in Côte d'Ivoire, it would have averted the current disaster there, because former president Henri Bedie probably would not have risked excluding rivals from the election.

A third, and controversial, area for international standards concerns the rights of foreign investors. Africa gets very little foreign investment other than for resource extraction. One reason is that the political environment is seen as very risky: property rights are insecure. The recent economics literature on development has placed enormous emphasis on secure property rights as the *sine qua non* of growth, yet Africa has the world's worst investor risk ratings. It now needs an approach that will enable it to live down its past—in effect, by-passing the burden of a bad reputation. An international standard for investor rights would do precisely this, benefiting most those countries whose weak reputations make it difficult for them to attract investors. The OECD recognized this need a decade ago when it proposed a Multilateral Agreement on Investment (MAI). The agreement came close to being adopted but was blocked by an alliance between crooked governments, such as that of Mugabe, and NGOs that wished to posture "support for the oppressed." Evidently, some African regimes would have signed up and benefited from the resulting investment, leaving regimes such as Mugabe's, which had intended to expropriate, to lose relatively from the agreement. Expropriation sounds appealing to the radical left, but it might not be to the advantage of African societies—indeed, a wise government would surrender the power to expropriate because it acts as a deterrent to investment. In the absence of a global investment standard, however, most African governments have promulgated their own national investment codes, which promise investors plenty of rights but lack credibility because they lack external enforcement. Perhaps enough African governments now see the advantage of enshrining investor rights in a supranational agreement that a further effort to launch an international set of standards for investors might not suffer the same fate as the MAI.

The final area for standards concerns post-conflict situations. Governments in these conditions should not be treated as if they were instantly fully sovereign. They are governments in the making, facing extremely difficult circumstances and with a poor record of success. They need large external finance and external security forces. In return, the international community has a responsibility to citizens who are providing the finance, to soldiers who are bearing the personal risks, and to the citizens of the country concerned, to ensure that the new post-conflict government does not make too many mistakes. The recent lesson of East Timor, in which an arrogant new government succeeded in going from independence to violent uprising in a mere five years, provides an object lesson in how not to manage a post-conflict situation. The UN's new Peacebuilding Commission provides the obvious forum for promulgating standards that post-conflict governments should be required to follow in return for peace keeping and aid. The standards should set out a path for the gradual evolution of government into a functioning democracy, complete with the accountable provision of basic services, over the horizon of a decade.

Standards are the least explored of the instruments available to the international community. In developed countries, standards have been heavily used—both the EU and the OECD abound in systems of peer group pressure. Indeed, the dominant trend of the past half-century among developed countries has been toward pooling and surrendering national sovereignty to achieve the national objectives of prosperity and security. These standards are not meant for low-income Africa, however, and are usually inappropriate. Similarly, the International Monetary Fund has focused heavily upon averting further financial crises in emerging-market, middle-income economies, but has neglected low-income Africa. The same is the case in trade policy: the General Agreement on Tariffs and Trade was a club for rich countries in which they negotiated mutually binding restrictions on sovereignty. Its expansion to the WTO has been a failure: African governments seek to stay out of pooled sovereignty arrangements. Overall, African governments have excess sovereignty in a wide range of areas, generally at the expense of their own citizens. Uniquely, while the rest of the world has been pooling and shedding national sovereignty to achieve national objectives, African governments have built up a practice of special and differential standards that inhibit the application of international standards.

Coordinating the Instruments

Each of the four instruments discussed above to promote African development has an area of potency, but their most striking feature is their scope for mutual support—for example, military coups are discouraged in Europe by the fact that a country ruled by the military would be excluded from membership in the EU. Coordinating the instruments, however, is no easy task. One problem is that some agency within each country has to be charged with the coordination. Another problem is a lack of coordination among the OECD countries themselves, since no one country is sufficiently large that it can achieve its national objectives without cooperation from other countries. I take these two tasks of coordination in turn.

Coordination among Instruments

The key problem for policy coordination on development is that each of the four instruments is the remit of a different ministry. Trade policy is evidently the remit of the ministry of trade. In practice, ministries of trade have learned to balance national protectionist lobbies against the goal of gaining access to foreign markets for the nation's exporters—in other words, policy is set within a mercantilist mental framework of bargaining. It is difficult to inject development priorities into this mental framework, however, and ministries of trade cannot be expected to take on these very different priorities just because of some general announcement: trade policy is negotiated across the bargaining tables of the WTO, while security policy is set by ministries of defense. Here, the mental frame is of external threats and mutual security agreements among allies. Ministries of defense in failing states are now adjusting to their new role, since that is so evidently likely to be their future, but such ministries have no tradition of involvement in development and are culturally distant from the development agencies and lobbies. Aid policy, in contrast, is in the hands of development ministries, but the main domestic lobby for aid is the NGOs, which have a very particular base on the left of the political spectrum, making the development discourse extremely lop-sided. In the UK, for example, no political party now supports domestic protectionism; over the past 30 years, the electorate has gradually come to understand the virtues of liberal trade policies. Yet the major British NGO Christian Aid is a passionate advocate of protectionism for Africa, a policy which would be immensely damaging. In effect, the dead protectionist debates of the 1970s within OECD societies have been exported to an African application. Moreover, the ability to formulate rationally based development policies against this background is becoming increasingly difficult—for example, UK politicians are reluctant to defy Christian Aid since they would lose some votes and gain none in return. Similarly, the skewed part of the political spectrum that is the constituency of support for Africa is suspicious of intervention, whether military or in the interests of governance, due to concerns about "neocolonialism" and "neoliberalism."

Standards of governance are even more problematic. Banking standards are the responsibility of central banks, not agencies with much interest in, or knowledge of, Africa. Armaments standards would come under the ministry of trade, while standards for companies in resource extraction would come under the ministry of industry. In each case, Africa is peripheral to the core interests of these ministries.

There seem to me to be two possible solutions to this severe coordination problem. The first would be to lodge responsibility for African development policy at the level of the head of government. Although this approach would have some major advantages—for example, it is how both the EITI and the Commission for Africa were launched—heads of government have many more pressing priorities than Africa, so their attention would be fitful at best.

An alternative approach would be to broaden the remit of national aid agencies so that they became genuine development agencies. In practice, the agency that comes closest to this approach is the UK's Department for International Development. The obvious advantage of this approach is that it would allow the development of a continuous pool of expertise that would integrate the different instruments. The approach would also have enormous difficulties. First, the budget of an aid agency that evolved into a development agency would still be dominated by the disbursement of aid, so the agency would be likely to continue to see aid as central to its role. Second, although the agency would control the aid instrument directly, it would not control any of the other instruments. Thus, for example, the cost of military security would continue to come out of the ministry of defense. Indeed, if the budget for military security were transferred to a development agency, the agency likely would favor spending the money on aid projects even over the provision of far more useful security. Further, in all OECD countries, development agencies are far down the political pecking order, implying that their influence over trade policy and banking regulations would be minimal—ministries of trade and central banks simply are not going to listen to advice from development ministries.

Although both approaches have their difficulties, there may be scope for a hybrid. It seems essential to have some continuous expertise that spans the four instruments, so expanding the remit of aid agencies is surely necessary. To give these agencies the political clout to span other ministries, however, requires the active involvement of the head of government. In effect, the head of government should also take on the role of minister of development, with the aid of some junior minister to deal with day-to-day business. Only a head of government can instruct other ministries to take development priorities seriously, but only a ministry of development can manage policy on an ongoing basis. Currently, heads of government routinely invade the domain of their foreign ministers. A head of government's having authority over an expanded development ministry would both formalize this process and ground the interest of the head of government in proper civil service support.

Coordination among Governments

Many of these challenges are too large even for a country like the United States, so the world needs international cooperation. This cooperation need not be global: there are simply too many countries with interests that are too divergent for global cooperation to be realistic except in a narrow range. Rather, what is needed is the cooperation of a group of countries that are sufficiently allied and sufficiently large to be effective. With four different instruments, it is not necessary for every participating country to do everything—there is some scope for specialization among the instruments. To some extent, coordination could be handled by ad hoc arrangements for each need, although such arrangements can be costly to put together and could have less scope for continuity. Continuity is helpful because it gives each member a reason for occasionally accepting agreements that are against its interest, in order to maintain the club and hence the possibility of other coordinated actions from which it will benefit.

The only collective groupings that are currently plausible are the Group of Eight (G8) largest industrial economies and the five permanent members of the United Nations Security Council (P5). The G8 potentially can be concerned with anything, but its continuity is limited and it conducts its business in a blaze of publicity that makes coherent policy difficult. It does, however, include almost all the important economies without the problems of free riders and weakest links. Africa is a natural topic for the G8, which is why it keeps appearing on the group's agenda. The problem with the G8 has not been a lack of concern but the poor quality of supporting analysis, designed for theatrical political domestic consumption rather than for its effectiveness. Presumably, what is needed is a prior degree of coordination among development ministries, each tasked with a broad remit of policies for African development rather than just with aid. Hence, the sequence would be, first, coordination of policies at the national level, then coordination among the G8 countries. To date, the attempt at international coordination without proper preparation of integrated policies has led to the mistaken privileging of aid as the core instrument of African development, and within aid policy to the posturing role of targets for its increase rather than for its effective redesign. The lack of serious policy foundations has enabled political leaders to grandstand, using Africa as an opportunity to say "I care."

The P5 has a more focused remit on security, which may be appropriate to address the problem of failing states in Africa. The recent creation of the Peacebuilding Commission directly under the Security Council considerably increases the potential for serious coordinated approaches to African development. However, the commission should not aspire to becoming yet another implementing agency—there are already manifestly too many such agencies. Rather, the commission should fill the gap in strategic thinking, linking the three instruments of aid, military security, and governance standards. Only trade policy does not fall naturally within its remit, but trade policy is not important as an instrument for failing states.

The different remits of the G8 and P5 suggest a possible division of focus between the two groups. The G8 might focus upon raising growth rates decisively through trade, aid, and standards of economic governance. The P5 might focus on preventing states from failing, through military security, aid, and standards of political governance. While such a division would miss some opportunities for coordination, the specialization would have offsetting advantages: each objective would be clear and more limited, and would fit naturally into the wider remit of each organization. The three supporting instruments would be sufficient for the G8 to achieve the objective of growth, conditional upon the P5's using its three instruments effectively to achieve its objectives.

Were it possible to be more ambitious than the two current groupings of the G8 and the P5, a somewhat larger grouping would have some advantages. China, although a member of the P5, is not in the G8, yet its cooperation is central to the new issues of economic governance in Africa, notably resource extraction. India is in neither the G8 nor the P5, yet it is also now a major player in the African region. There might thus be a case for tackling Africa's development issues through an expanded group such as the G20.

Conclusion

Africa faces acute problems. Yet to date the OECD's response to these problems has been one of deep-rooted inadequacy. First, OECD countries have failed to diagnose the problems correctly, wrongly perceiving them as being essentially about poverty reduction, rather than the more profound and intractable issue of divergence. In fact, it would be possible to eliminate absolute poverty, even as divergence became yet more pronounced. Divergence is driven by a constellation of distinct problems: unviable countries, the dysfunctional politics of resource wealth, the difficulty of breaking into global markets now that Asian economies are established, and the menace of outright state failure as countries implode into conflict.

Corresponding to a failure of diagnosis on the part of OECD countries has been a failure of concern. Divergence should alarm even the most hard-hearted citizen of an OECD society because it manifestly builds up trouble. Yet, the exclusive focus on compassion, unfairness, and guilt might well have been counterproductive in alienating the broad constituency that would normally recognize its own self-interest. Because the cause of development has been so firmly positioned as part of the more generalized protest movement against globalization, the political center has switched off or, worse, regards the whole international development agenda as misguided. For example, a UK opinion poll at the time of the Commission for Africa reported that a vast majority regarded development assistance as a waste.[7] The political territory that needs to be occupied is not unfamiliar: enlightened self-interest has been the basis for most global action. It is not necessary to take the patently false position that international terrorism is rooted in poverty in order to believe that continued divergence will be unmanageable. The marginalized will not literally kill us if we do not help them, but their actions and inactions will inadvertently impose a series of avoidable costs on the rest of the world. The unprecedented standards of living now attained in the developed countries in some respects introduce greater fragility into our social and economic order, so that dangers do not have to be catastrophic in order to be extremely expensive.

Given the OECD countries' mistaken diagnosis of Africa's problems and the failure to recognize self-interest as the major driver of action, it is unsurprising that the international response has been inadequate. A theatrical emphasis upon transfers of money and the resulting failure to target these transfers have crowded out more serious thinking about what could be done. In fact, the OECD countries have a powerful armory of instruments, most of which have been virtually unused. Aid is worthwhile, but it would be far more worthwhile if combined with these other instruments. Further, the polarized debate between supporters and opponents of aid has led to the neglect of intelligent reform of aid. Given the weak overall effects of aid to date, it seems very likely that some aid is counterproductive and

---

7. "Vast majority thinks aid is wasted, poll shows." *Daily Telegraph* (London), June 4, 2005, p. 1.

some is valuable. Establishing these distinct effects is made much more difficult, however, when each result is seized upon as demonstrating the case for one side or the other. In reality, both sides in this debate have ulterior political agendas.

Once the full range of development instruments is appreciated, there remains the enormous task of the practical politics of redesigning institutions to harness this potential. Long-neglected instruments need to be deployed, and all instruments need to be coordinated, both across ministries and across borders. It is an agenda that requires political energy, but it is also an opportunity for the exercise of political leadership and for civil society to put pressure on policy makers.

References

Chauvet, L., and P. Collier. 2006. "Helping Hand? Aid in Failing States." Oxford: Oxford University, Centre for the Study of African Economies. Mimeographed.

———. 2007. "What Are the Conditions for Turnaround in Failing States." Oxford: Oxford University, Centre for the Study of African Economies. Mimeographed.

Chauvet, L., P. Collier, and A. Fuster. 2006. "Supervision and the Performance of Projects: A Principal-Agent Approach." Oxford: Oxford University, Centre for the Study of African Economies. Mimeographed.

Chauvet, L., P. Collier, and A. Hoeffler. 2006. "The Cost of Failing States and the Limits to Sovereignty." Helsinki: World Institute for Economic Development Research.

Collier, P. 2001. "Ethnic Diversity: An Economic Analysis of Its Implications." *Economic Policy* 16 (32): 129–66.

———. 2007. *The Bottom Billion: Why the Poorest Countries Are Failing and What Can Be Done about It*. New York: Oxford University Press.

Collier, P., and S. Dercon. 2006. "Review Article: The Complementarities of Poverty Reduction, Equity and Growth: A Perspective on the World Development Report 2006." *Economic Development and Cultural Change* 55 (1): 223–36.

Collier, P., and B. Goderis. 2006. "Commodity Prices and Growth: Reconciling a Conundrum." Oxford: Oxford University, Centre for the Study of African Economies. Mimeographed.

Collier, P., B. Goderis, and A. Hoeffler. 2006. "Shocks and Growth: Adaptation, Precaution and Compensation." Oxford: Oxford University, Centre for the Study of African Economies. Mimeographed.

Collier, P., and A. Hoeffler. 1998. "On Economic Causes of Civil War." *Oxford Economic Papers* 50 (4): 563–73.

———. 2004. "Greed and Grievance in Civil War." *Oxford Economic Papers* 56 (4): 563–95.

———. 2005. "Democracy and Resource Rents." Oxford: Oxford University, Centre for the Study of African Economies. Mimeographed.

———. 2006a. "Military Spending in Post-Conflict Societies." *Economics and Governance* 7 (1): 89–107.

————. 2006b. "Unintended Consequences: Does Aid Promote Arms Races?" *Oxford Bulletin of Economics and Statistics* 69 (1): 1–27.

————. 2006c. "Grand Extortion: Coup Risk and Military Spending." Oxford: Oxford University, Centre for the Study of African Economies. Mimeographed.

Collier, P., A. Hoeffler, and C. Pattillo. 2001. "Capital Flight as a Portfolio Choice." *World Bank Economic Review* 15 (1): 55–80.

————. 2004. "Africa's Exodus: Capital Flight and the Brain Drain as Portfolio Decisions." *Journal of African Economies* 13 (2): 15–54.

Collier, P., A. Hoeffler, and D. Rohner. 2006. "Beyond Greed and Grievance: Feasibility and Civil War." Working Papers Series 2006-10. Oxford: Oxford University, Centre for the Study of African Economies.

Collier, P., A. Hoeffler, and M. Söderbom. 2006. Post-Conflict Risks." Working Papers Series 2006-12. Oxford: Oxford University, Centre for the Study of African Economies.

Collier, P., and A. Venables. 2007. "Rethinking Trade Preferences: How Africa Can Diversify Its Exports." *The World Economy* 30 (8): 1326–45.

Dixit, A. 2004. *The Economics of Lawlessness*. Princeton, NJ: Princeton University Press.

Dollar, D., and A. Kraay. 2001. "Growth Is Good for the Poor." Policy Research Working Paper 2587. Washington, DC: World Bank.

Doucouliagos, H., and M. Paldam. 2006. "Aid Effectiveness on Accumulation: A Meta Study." *Kyklos* 59 (2): 227–54.

Fearon, J.D., and D. Laitin. 2003. "Ethnicity, Insurgency, and Civil War." *American Political Science Review* 97 (1): 75–90.

Fraser, G., and J. Van Brieseboeck. 2005. "Trade Growth under AGOA." Working paper. Toronto: University of Toronto, Rotman School of Management.

Killicoat, P., 2006. "Cheap Guns: More War?" M.Phil. Thesis, Department of Economics, Oxford University.

La Ferrara, E. 2006. "Financial Markets and Conflict in the Developing World." Milan: Bocconi University. Mimeographed.

La Ferrara, E., and A. Alesina. 2005. "Ethnic Diversity and Economic Performance." *Journal of Economic Literature* 43 (3): 762–800.

Miguel, E., S. Satyanath, and E. Sergenti. 2004. "An Instrumental Variables Approach." *Journal of Political Economy* 112 (4): 725–53.

Ndulu, B., S. O'Connell, R. Bates, P. Collier, and C. Soludo. Forthcoming. *The Political Economic of African Economic Growth, 1960-2000.* New York: Cambridge University Press.

Rajan R., and A. Subramanian. 2005. "What Prevents Aid from Enhancing Growth?" Washington, DC: International Monetary Fund. Mimeographed.

Rawls, John. 1971. *A Theory of Justice.* Cambridge, MA: The Belknap Press.

Weinstein, J. 2005. "Autonomous Recovery and International Intervention in Comparative Perspective." Working Paper 57. Washington, DC: Center for Global Development.

Can the Trading System Be Governed?
Institutional Implications of the WTO's Suspended Animation

Robert Wolfe

*   *   *

Does the World Trade Organization (WTO) need to be fixed? The effort to launch and conclude the Doha Round of multilateral trade negotiations (formally the Doha Development Agenda) has stumbled from one ministerial conference to another. At the end of June 2006, after missing one self-imposed deadline after another, ministers from about 30 Member countries representing all the negotiating groupings went to Geneva to try to remove the impasse in the round. The discussions broke down without the issues

I appreciate the helpful comments of Miles Kahler, Arthur Stein, and the other participants in the Centre for International Governance Innovation's workshop on Global Institutional Reform, held at Princeton University, August 24–25, 2006. A version was also presented in September 2006 at CIGI'06, in Waterloo, Ontario. The analysis is informed by confidential interviews with WTO officials and national delegates in Geneva in September 2006. I also appreciate the suggestions of Steve Charnovitz, Manfred Elsig, Simon Evenett, Mats Hellström, Rod Macdonald, Peter Ungphakorn, and a number of officials. The support of the Social Science and Humanities Research Council of Canada for parts of this work is gratefully acknowledged, as is the research assistance of Jesse Helmer, Mathew Johnson, and Jill Webster.

even having been joined. Then, in July 2006, leaders at the annual G8 Summit of rich countries, meeting with some of their developing country colleagues in St. Petersburg, Russia, instructed their trade ministers to get the job done. They failed. The next day, the WTO's director-general, Pascal Lamy, recommended that the Doha Round be suspended. The daily work of the WTO, including its dispute settlement system, continued but the flagship negotiations were suspended until November, when Members agreed to resume "technical work." By spring 2007, Members had resumed full negotiations, but the prospects for a successful conclusion of this or any subsequent round seemed uncertain.

The WTO's difficulty managing a major renovation of the world trading system raises the question of whether the trading system can be governed. The question has implications for global governance generally, and for the management of negotiations in any large multilateral organization whose members must internalize the norms and practices of the system. No other organization faces a comparable problem of such a large and engaged membership, but if global governance continues to expand, others will.

The Doha Round is said to have collapsed in July 2006 because the Americans were unwilling to cut domestic subsidies, the Europeans were being coy about tariff reductions for "sensitive" farm products, and the Indians refused to be realistic about their own protectionist measures. Here, I neither discuss the political economy of this behavior nor offer a trade policy analysis of the merits of each position. Political "will" is an empty concept, but it is possible that the world's leaders did not take the tough decisions needed to advance the Doha Round because they were preoccupied in summer 2006 with the bombs that were going off in Afghanistan, Iraq, Gaza, and Lebanon, and with the worry about even bigger bombs in Iran and North Korea.

Rather than trying to explain the suspension of trade talks or the policy compromises that will be necessary to conclude the Doha Round, I ask whether the suspension signals the need for WTO institutional reform. Many people say it does. After the failed ministerials in Seattle and Cancún, Pascal Lamy famously described the organization as "medieval." "There is no way to structure and steer discussions amongst 146 Members in a manner conducive to consensus," he said, when still the European trade commissioner. "The decision-making needs to be revamped" (Lamy

2003).[1] If the WTO is a medieval organization, however, it might be because the world is, too, and there is no cure for that (Wolfe 2005). WTO Members are at vastly different levels of development, their political and legal systems are based on divergent premises, and while they are unequally penetrated by the social and economic forces of globalization, they must cope with overlapping regulatory domains. The WTO universe is certainly plural if not medieval, and the process for making legitimate decisions is inevitably untidy.

Given that untidiness, it is unrealistic to expect the WTO to be efficient in "making" new rules, but we can expect it to be effective in recognizing the emergence of new rules through the practices of the trading system. Since the multi-trillion dollar trading system is remarkably free of conflict, it seems that the WTO does indeed work rather well on a day-to-day basis. If the institutional edifice has a problem, it is that Members face great difficulty in undertaking needed renovations and new construction through negotiations, even as the organization goes about its daily work as usual. The WTO is in suspended animation. Would institutional reform help?

The question implies two familiar themes that run through this paper. The first is the hypothesis that the way in which *interests* are aggregated changes outcomes. A change in WTO procedures will not change the interests of an Iowa farmer, but a change in the decision rule—for example, the United States' adoption of the fast-track procedure with the *Trade Act of 1974*—will change how those interests can be mobilized. The second theme is that deliberation aids *learning* and the understanding of interests, which changes outcomes. If negotiation is all about interests, then the agenda is an institutional design choice: what must be in the Single Undertaking? are less-than-universal agreements appropriate? should there be differentiation among developing countries? If learning also matters, then collective decision making that engages all Members requires consensual understanding, deliberation that legitimates effective bargaining, and domestic resonance.

---

1. This widely shared concern with the functioning of the institution was a principal motivation when Lamy's predecessor commissioned a study by a consultative board of eminent experts on the future of the WTO. The analysis and recommendations on institutional design of the so-called Sutherland Report (Sutherland et al. 2004) have not been discussed within the WTO.

I begin with some theoretical considerations about power and participation in international negotiations. I then show that WTO decisionmaking principles have implications both for what is discussed (the agenda) and how (process). In the third section, I ask whether all of the WTO's diverse Members must be bound by every agreement. I then consider WTO modalities, followed by a discussion of the institutional design aspects of what the Single Undertaking, or the WTO agenda, must contain. After a brief discussion of the external legitimacy of the WTO, I turn to an examination of the negotiating process. In the conclusion, I return to the tension between interest and learning in the context of options for institutional reform.

Power and Participation in Negotiations

Once upon a time, the world was dominated by a hegemon, or so goes the familiar story. It is easy enough to see the General Agreement on Tariffs and Trade (GATT) of 1948 as a public good supplied by the United States alone, but by the 1960s the GATT could be seen as a bilateral agreement with Europe. That model was still a good approximation in the Tokyo Round of the 1970s, but it was clear from the roles played by Brazil and India in shaping the launch of the Uruguay Round in the 1980s that things had begun to change. Either power was shifting into new hands, or new forms of power had emerged. The Blair House accord between the United States and the European Union was necessary to conclude the Uruguay Round, but far from sufficient. It would still be foolhardy to pretend that any round would end before the United States and the EU are ready, yet they cannot force an outcome. It follows that the notion that the Doha suspension suggests the need for institutional reform rests on two interrelated assumptions about the changing nature of global politics. First, institutional reform is said to be needed to accommodate the rise of new powers (especially Brazil, India, and China). This structural assumption leads to consideration of what is "power" in this context, who has it, how much is enough, and how it can be exercised. The second assumption is that one manifestation of globalization is that every state now wishes to be an active participant in global governance, a change that requires a reordering of international organizations created in an earlier era.

Critical Mass in the WTO

Power is a problematic concept in international relations. Traditional definitions and the hierarchical classifications of actors associated with them are not always analytically helpful in the context of the WTO, but two types of power seem especially salient. *Compulsory power*, Barnett and Duvall (2005, 14–15) argue, "can be based on material resources, and on symbolic or normative resources." Not only states, but international organizations, firms, and civil society organizations have the means to get others to change their actions in a favored direction. The concept of *institutional power* is a reminder that the diffuse social relations that institutions shape can also constrain behavior. The challenge is identifying those two types of power at work within the WTO and knowing whether the structure of power facilitates or impedes governance.

Multilateral trade reform requires the supply of two collective goods: new rules and more open markets. No state alone can now supply either of these goods, but the systemic good of an open, liberal, multilateral trading system does not require collective supply by all 150 Members of the WTO, as long as the nondiscrimination norms are respected. But how many Members are needed to provide a systemic "critical mass"? The idea of critical mass implies that the relevant process—whether a nuclear reaction or the wide diffusion of a social norm—is sufficiently large to be self-sustaining. Many applications in social science derive from Mancur Olson's work (1965) on the provision of collective goods. While Olson is pessimistic about the possibility of cooperation, other scholars (for example, Oliver and Marwell 2001) explore the circumstances under which a group of sufficient size can be created to supply public goods.

Critical mass implies that markets that represent a significant share of global production and consumption should help to supply the systemic public good. Yet, if current material power determined the relative hierarchy of WTO Members, it would be hard to understand the list of countries that appear to play leading roles. The original Quad (the United States, the EU, Japan, and Canada) still includes the largest markets, but they can no longer supply systemic leadership alone. China, India, and Brazil are often mentioned as the most important new powers—although only China has entered the ranks of the top traders (see Wolfe 2006). These three are not powers on the scale of the United States, but they now have the collective strength to challenge the established order (Hurrell 2006).

The provision of the public good of new rules also depends on acceptance by participants in the trading system that the rules themselves are appropriate and legitimate, which suggests that critical mass must have another dimension. The coercive power of the largest markets is now limited both by the emergence of other significant markets and by equally powerful symbolic and normative claims based on justice for developing countries in general, but especially for the poorest. The rhetoric of development, which resonates strongly with the public in the North as well as the South, often provides developing countries with the "better argument" in public debate. Given the "forum effects of talk" (Mitzen 2005), large Members must take account of what the WTO community considers acceptable reasons for action, whether they seek to promote or resist trade liberalization. The leading developing countries, in particular, are attentive not only to their own domestic constituencies but also to audiences in other developing countries.

We now confront the implication of the assumption that institutional reform is needed to accommodate many new players in global governance. This part of the WTO picture, however, is complex and misleading. Consider, for example, that, although 99 countries nominally participated in the Tokyo Round, the WTO now has, with Vietnam's January 2007 accession, 150 Members that must be part of a consensus. At the same time, many Members either have no representation in Geneva or only a small, overworked mission that also handles UN agencies. At most, only 40 members (counting the EU as one) play significant roles in the services negotiations, and fewer than a dozen understand the technicalities of each of the 20 aspects of the agriculture negotiations. These capacity disparities did not matter in the Tokyo Round, because developing countries could simply opt out of the bits they did not understand or that seemed inapplicable. Since the end of the Uruguay Round, however, the WTO is a Single Undertaking: all Members must accept all the obligations, in principle if not in practice. Consensus now gives every Member the ability to slow the process down, a form of institutional power of which developing countries are increasingly aware. They are also increasingly aware of the need to participate, which has put stress on the ability of the WTO process to remain effective while becoming more inclusive and transparent. The new institutional power of developing countries has also changed the nature of the debate on the agenda: what must be discussed, even if there is not much WTO can do, and what cannot be discussed, even if the WTO offers a useful forum?

Clearly, critical mass has two dimensions: when all issues are lumped together and any Member can block consensus, institutional power must be joined to compulsory power to reach a successful outcome in negotiations. A bargain must satisfy Members whose market weight is sufficient to give effect to the deal, but it must also satisfy Members whose acquiescence is sufficient to give the deal legitimacy. Critical mass will differ on both dimensions in the Doha Round as a whole and in each negotiating area. A Member that dominates one domain might be willing to follow the lead of a like-minded Member in another. But that still requires each Member's knowing what action is needed, and then acting.

Agency in Negotiations

If compulsory power were the only dimension, standard political economy approaches to understanding the WTO might be sufficient, even if they do not readily account for symbolic or normative resources. Multilateral economic negotiations are often explained by such exogenous factors as the identifiable economic interests of participants or their domestic industries or the general political and economic context. Negotiation analysis, however, turns the standard approach on its head by looking, not at exogenous *structural* factors, but at variations in endogenous factors based on *agency*. In the significant stream of literature led by John Odell, analysts assess the effects of negotiation *strategies*, whether distributive (value claiming), integrative (value creating), or mixed (see Odell 2000). In this literature, "power" is sometimes seen as the ability to walk away from a negotiation—an idea captured in the technical term, the Best Alternative to Negotiated Agreement (BATNA). A strong BATNA gives the negotiator some leverage to avoid accepting an unwanted outcome, but is less helpful for achieving a desired outcome. While staying within a utilitarian framework, other analysts note that institutions shape and influence the bargaining process, or the context in which actors pursue their strategies

(Winham 2006). Indeed, the WTO's decisionmaking principles create specific opportunities for relatively weak states to use this institutional power effectively.

In utilitarian negotiation analysis, "negotiating" and "bargaining" are interchangeable terms referring to "a sequence of actions in which two or more parties address demands and proposals to each other for the ostensible purposes of reaching an agreement and changing the behavior of at least one actor" (Odell 2000, 4). In constructivist ideas about social learning, however, negotiations comprise both bargaining and learning (see Checkel 2001). Market conditions obviously have a major influence on determining issues, actors, and strategies in international negotiations (Odell 2000, chap. 3). If "traded services" were negligible, states would not create the General Agreement on Trade in Services (GATS); countries that are not large traders of such services might have little interest in such negotiations, while those with complementary export interests might be allies in negotiations, and so on. But actors first have to know that they have "interests," that "services" can be traded and are thus a subject for bargaining. Negotiating is first a process of learning, and learning requires participation.

In utilitarian theory, based on the bounded rationality assumption that actors pursue their objectives as best they can with the limited information available to them (Odell 2006, 9–11), analysts see learning as the acquisition of new information about the context of negotiations, which allows parties to aggregate their strength with that of other actors in order to affect ego-centric "gains" and "losses" for states or coalitions (Odell 2006). In other words, actors know their own BATNA but need information about the BATNA of others. In addition, by "learning," constructivists mean not only the acquisition of new information, but an *argumentative* or *deliberative* process in which an actor's understanding of self and others can change (see Risse 2000, 2005; Müller 2004). This view of negotiation is one in which parties gradually articulate shared interpretations of events, which come to define both the identity of the actors, including who is legitimate, and the way actors understand their "interest," while developing new consensual understanding of causal relationships (Haas 1990, 9, 23).

Why does learning matter? Take an example from the Tokyo Round, in which negotiating nontariff measures was difficult because, as Winham (1986, 88) reports, "they were largely undefinable, numerous, often concealed, and incomparable, and that their effects were unknown precisely but generally thought to be pernicious. Negotiators had to achieve an intellectual understanding of these measures before they could negotiate their removal." Yet, in the Tokyo Round, countries could simply ignore issues they did not understand. In the Doha Round, many issues are much more complicated, the many new significant players in the negotiations start with less shared experience and knowledge, and the Single Undertaking requires all Members to accept complex new obligations. Despite the many provisions for special and differential treatment, many Members have implemented only weakly agreements that require sophisticated domestic regulatory frameworks. A great deal of negotiating time has been devoted to finding ways to ease the burden of the Agreement on Trade-Related Aspects of Intellectual Property Rights (TRIPS), in particular. Members are understandably wary about accepting further new obligations they do not understand or that seem distant from their policy needs. Learning, therefore, seems an essential part of the process.

For negotiation analysis, therefore, the question is not, does the WTO provide good policy advice? or, what is the political economy of a compromise? but, is the institutional design appropriate? My hypothesis is that good institutional design that contributes to effective and legitimate global governance must facilitate both *bargaining* over known interests and *learning* through arguing and deliberation. The central institutional challenge is thus to square the circle of the formal equality of Members and the practical inequality of their willingness and capacity to participate. The challenge would be considerable even if it were seen only as a factor in bargaining and adjudication among Members; it is all the larger when the focus is on deliberation and learning. Moreover, it is not enough for the Geneva delegates to learn—officials and ministers in their home capitals must, too. Ministers cannot participate in every aspect of detailed negotiations, but inevitably they participate in debates at home about domestic policies that are increasingly subject to multilateral constraint.

By stressing the role of learning, I assume that the implementation of new rules is based on understanding and acceptance of new obligations. It is, moreover, a mistake to think that the WTO deals merely with trade policy as economic policy. Trade policy is about social relationships, changes in which are not decided on utilitarian grounds alone. If, as some observers claim, the difficulties of the Doha Round are associated with a trend toward increased public apprehension about globalization, then the WTO must do more than assure citizens and domestic officials that the organization is good for them—it must facilitate public deliberation about new obligations. That might the biggest challenge of all.

If this approach is the right way to consider the institutional implications of the suspension of the Doha Round, then some of the issues most often identified in the WTO reform literature, including the Sutherland Report, are not relevant. I do not think that evolutionary action will be displaced to disputes, and dispute settlement reform is neither essential in general nor necessary to end the suspense. Equally misguided is the view, with roots in legal positivism (Hart 1961), that, since the WTO "court" is so strong, it is essential to improve the weak "legislative" capacity of its "incomplete" legal system. Rather, as Rosendorff (2005) argues, the flexibility inherent in the system as it stands might be essential for the stability of the WTO. Nor are regional negotiations an alternative: most of the benefits that were and ultimately still are available through multilateral trade negotiations are not available in bilateral and regional negotiations; moreover, though proliferating, many bilateral deals are likely to founder on their inability to deal with the big issues that have slowed the Doha Round. Finally, while there may be a democratic deficit in the trading system, its locus is not in Geneva (see Wolfe and Helmer 2007).

The central question is, therefore: does the institutional design of the organization and the negotiating process affect the outcome? One way to get leverage on this question is to ask if a particular institutional design both structures *interests* and facilitates *learning*. Power has shifted in the WTO in ways that put great pressure on its institutional design. Assembling a critical mass of market power requires many more Members and must be complemented by a critical mass of institutional power. What are the implications of this shift in power for how the WTO makes decisions?

WTO Decisionmaking Principles

International relations scholars agree that global governance lacks centralized authority. Decentralized governance is inherently horizontal, which means that some institutional forms—including both hierarchical command

and simple majority voting—are not available for making decisions. This generic reality of global governance has an air of artificiality in the trading system, however, because, unlike some international organizations, the WTO is not an actor in itself.[2] The Final Act of the Uruguay Round, creating the WTO, is a contract among governments, not a constitution for a world polity. As a practical matter, Members are unlikely to implement provisions they do not accept, so consensus is fundamental. Since allowing 150 Members to pick and choose among the obligations they accept would undermine the system, the Single Undertaking is also fundamental.

In principle the WTO is indivisible, and it is the Single Undertaking that holds it together. In signing the Final Act, Members agreed that "the WTO Agreement shall be open for acceptance as a whole." The new agreement included all of the Uruguay Round agreements, as well as the revised agreements from the Tokyo Round, and Members could accept or reject it only in its entirety. In a famous phrase, in the WTO, "nothing is agreed until everything is agreed." This general principle, the Single Undertaking—which includes the norms of reciprocity, multilateralism, and nondiscrimination—had been enunciated in the Punta del Este Declaration of 1986: "The launching, the conduct and the implementation of the outcome of the negotiations shall be treated as parts of a single undertaking."[3] Now, the Single Undertaking and the practice of building major revisions of the agreements into a "round" go together. Although the General Council could take most decisions on the results of negotiations at any

---

2. Recent scholarship by both utilitarian (Hawkins et al. 2006) and constructivist scholars (Barnett and Finnemore 2004) seeks to understand international organizations as actors, usually by looking closely at international organizations as bureaucracies. This approach does not produce satisfying results when applied to the WTO, because the WTO has so little autonomy with respect to its Members.
3. The Tokyo Round declaration of 1973 had been subtly different: "The negotiations shall be considered as one undertaking, the various elements of which shall move forward together." In the end, this principle had no bearing on the outcome of that round (Winham 2006, 12). It can also be argued that once US negotiators were able to submit the results of the round to Congress as a single package under the "fast-track" procedure, they wanted other Members to be bound by a similar constraint (VanGrasstek and Sauvé 2006, 839).

time,[4] in practice a round is needed. And so is the Single Undertaking. No other mechanism, in an organization with such a large and diffuse membership, could ensure an appropriate aggregation of issues and participants or force Members large and small eventually to accept the best deal on offer. The Single Undertaking ensures "circular logrolling" or diffuse reciprocity (Keohane 1989): everybody has to offer a concession to one Member while receiving a benefit from another, like drawing numbers from a hat to assign holiday gift giving (see Barton et al. 2006, 149). The contributions have to be reciprocal in the aggregate, because each Member needs to, and can, contribute different things to an overall result.[5] Diffuse everyday interaction in the trading system might be the source of WTO law, but codification is now possible only with the Single Undertaking.

If the Single Undertaking is an essential characteristic of the WTO and the central institutional constraint on the Doha Round, consensus as the decisionmaking rule is its equally essential counterpart. The considerable extent of the WTO's legal obligations and the quasi-automatic nature of the dispute settlement system are possible only because of the political participation made possible by the consensus rule (Pauwelyn 2005). It would be pointless to have a vote that created obligations large and small sovereign states refused to implement. Consensus and the Single Undertaking simplify a complex process through forced tradeoffs, but logrolling is not necessarily based on internalized agreement or understanding. Just as holiday gift giving at the office depends on shared expectations and trust, so too does the Single Undertaking. It could not work under majority voting, and the need for consensus keeps everybody deliberating until a compromise emerges. Opportunities for deliberation are a chance to feel that you have been heard, which matters when trust is fragile.

It is surprising, in this light, how much attention the Uruguay Round negotiators devoted to crafting WTO voting rules and how much attention lawyers pay to those rules (see Van den Bossche and Alexovicova 2005; Ehlermann and Ehring 2005; Footer 2006), given the theoretical objections

---

4. And sometimes does—see WTO (2006c); see also Van den Bossche and Alexovicova (2005) on secondary law making.
5. On why a big package is needed in the Doha Round and what contributions the major participants need to make, see Schott (2006, 6).

to voting in multiparty, mixed-motive situations in the negotiation literature (Bazerman and Neale 1992, 154–55) and the practical reality that votes are virtually unheard of in most international economic organizations, let alone in the GATT/WTO system.[6] The Single Undertaking might require consensus as a practical matter, just as the successful conclusion of a round depends on a single vote in the US Congress under the fast-track-procedure. Otherwise, on what would WTO Members vote—on whether to include agriculture in the Single Undertaking, or on modalities for reducing domestic support before a vote on the formula for market access?

Practitioners and academics debate the implications of this analysis. Given the complexity of each issue, the Single Undertaking creates a high demand for consensual learning, which small delegations have trouble meeting. The problem is compounded because the linkages between, say, agriculture and services are not obvious, even for the largest delegations. Those who think the Single Undertaking a necessary mechanism wonder how to manage it; those who think it a straitjacket wonder how it can be relaxed.

Can the Single Undertaking Be Relaxed?

One response to the demands of the Single Undertaking would be to retreat into preferential or regional deals outside the WTO; indeed, many analysts see that route as inevitable if the Doha Round fails. Another response would be to argue that, although all deals should be under the aegis of the WTO, the Single Undertaking could be relaxed. Are less-than-universal deals feasible? Are some derogations from nondiscrimination acceptable, given the WTO's diverse membership? Three related issues

---

6. For a formal discussion of why majority voting is so rarely observed in international conferences and why "unanimity" (in their use, close to what the WTO calls "consensus") is the common decisionmaking rule, see Black et al. (1998, 180–82). On consensus in the UN system, see Sabel (2006). On how consensus in the Executive Board of the International Monetary Fund can mean informal signals from the holders of enough votes for a majority, see Woods and Lombardi (2006). On the long history of unanimity or *liberum veto* as a multilateral decision rule, and why the increase in majoritarian voting on merely technical matters is unlikely to displace efforts to persuade and find compromises on major international issues, see (Claude 1971, chap. 7).

arise: should there be more of what trade experts call "variable geometry"? would explicit differentiation help? and would plurilateral "clubs" be a better way to address some issues?

Variable Geometry

"Variable geometry," at the WTO, means that agreements articulate a universal principle to which all strive while allowing national implementation to differ. Indeed, the trading system depends on both *equal obligations* to ensure openness and *differential application* to accommodate national public administration. One can find many examples of such variable geometry in the WTO: in the Agriculture Agreement, for one, where tariffication and the rules on domestic support allow policy differences; in the GATS, for another, whose "specific commitments" are scheduled from the bottom up. The Basic Telecommunications agreement's "Reference Paper" contains principles whose implementation differ from country to country. But is more needed?

The Single Undertaking has had the consequence, not fully anticipated, that all obligations, whether or not they are appropriate to a country's circumstances or stage of development, apply to all WTO Members. At one level, this requirement simply hardens the "most-favoured nation" (MFN) rule, thus avoiding the political problem of a fragmentary system or one in which countries or groups of countries threaten to withhold favorable treatment from others. At another level, however, strict interpretation of the Single Undertaking makes it more difficult to maintain nationally distinctive policies or internal distributive bargains—at least for developing countries, which are coming late to the normative enterprise.[7]

Globalization can be described as the continuing expansion of the market, both in the greater diversity of things that can be exchanged and in the increased exposure of people and places to global markets. This phenomenon also affects the less skilled in poor countries, with predictable political consequences. The embedded liberalism compromise in

---

7. Whether demands for "policy space" are reasonable is another matter; see Page (2007).

international trade was about safeguarding free trade abroad by protecting the ability of the welfare state at home to redistribute the benefits of openness (Ruggie 1982). Developing countries, with less money and less administrative depth than the member countries of the Organisation for Economic Co-operation and Development (OECD), are still learning how to meet these challenges.

Most developing countries would benefit from more trade, but what sort of rules would help them, and at what cost? If their problems are primarily those of domestic governance, should regulatory changes identified by the WTO be at the top of their policy reform list? Some officials argue that a single set of rules for all Members is, in any event, impossible. But must recognition of this reality lead to a two-tier WTO, with two levels of obligation? Would it be better to have some formal recognition that a Member's capacity to take on rules should be linked to its stage of development? Or should there be a formal, unitary set of obligations, while allowing some rules to be "soft"—meaning subject only to surveillance—rather than "hard" ones subject to the dispute settlement system? Could the surveillance system also monitor all of a country's requests for special and differential treatment, with participation from other international organizations to ensure "coherence"? In short, consideration of variable geometry inevitably raises the hornets' nest of differentiation.

Differentiation

"Developing countries," in the WTO, vary considerably, from prosperous Singapore to poor Bangladesh. Often, the implicit assumption is that a developing country is any WTO Member not also a member of the OECD. The treaty, in fact, mentions "developing countries" only in the Preamble. "Least-developed countries" (LDCs) are defined in Article XI:2, but only as countries "recognized as such by the United Nations." In practice, countries designated themselves as "developing" either when the WTO was created or as part of their accession negotiations.

Some reform is surely needed, because the existing agreements and the Doha agenda are riddled with demands for special and differential treatment. The WTO is not helped by the blanket use of "developing country," as if China and Uganda should be thought of in the same way with respect to their ability to participate in negotiations or to undertake new obligations. (Similarly, the umbrella term "Global South" obscures more than it illuminates at the WTO.) The Doha declaration contains significant offers of technical assistance in many areas, but these efforts divert scarce WTO Secretariat resources away from support of the negotiations; those resources are, in any case, trivial compared with those of international organizations whose budgets are orders of magnitude bigger than that of the WTO (WTO 2006b).[8]

Differentiation is unpalatable for some developing countries, but LDCs in particular are neither able nor willing to discuss the obligations that should now be incumbent on Brazil and India, and that China is assuming as a result of its 2001 accession. Winham (2007) shows the more insidious ways in which a claim for assigning priority to "development" has undermined the inherently reciprocal basis of trade negotiations based on nondiscrimination. Special and differential treatment implies nonreciprocal concessions from OECD countries in favor of developing countries, with nothing offered in return. Now, concessions requested by OECD countries are resisted as illegitimate, and the possibility of mutually beneficial South-South bargains is not explored. It is hard to structure negotiations on this basis.[9]

The official developing country rhetoric, as expressed by India, is that all developing countries are equal. In the face of such unwillingness to debate general criteria, the emerging solution is unspoken differentiation. Indeed, much of the Doha debate is really about the criteria to distinguish

---

8. A separate problem is that giving the Secretariat two roles risks organizational tension if Members see a conflict between its providing impartial analysis one moment and assistance to a subset of Members the next. The favored Members might also come to mistrust the assistance if they see the Secretariat as guardian of WTO orthodoxy (Shaffer 2005).

9. One way forward would be for OECD countries to make unreciprocated concessions on duty free and quota free market access for the LDCs as a form of official development assistance. Concessions involving countries such as Brazil, India, China, and other large Members not eligible for such assistance could be offered on a reciprocal basis, while those countries, in turn, would be expected to offer nonreciprocal concessions to LDCs—as Brazil has already hinted it would do.

among three groups of Members: those to which all rules apply, those for which some requirements are relaxed, and those to which no new obligations will apply. LDCs will, in effect, get the "round for free," especially in the way that flexibilities are built into the Non-Agricultural Market Access (NAMA) proposals. The fact that this differentiation is emerging through negotiation is a good thing. The fact that it is unarticulated might obscure it from both developing countries themselves and their civil society supporters, which does not help deliberation about the merits of the round. In the same vein, the Doha reference to "less than full reciprocity in reduction commitments" for developing countries, which echoes language going back to the Kennedy Round, also confuses the issue. Assessing the balance of reciprocity in a negotiation full of incommensurable issues is technically so complex that it is best left to the eye of the beholder (see Hoda 2001). Rather than insisting on rights for developing countries in this way, a systematic differentiation principle might put the debate on a more positive footing (for one example, see Keck and Low 2005).

Plurilateral Deals

One way to give practical effect to variable geometry and differentiation is to hold negotiations under the WTO umbrella, in which only the eventual adherents to new rules would be permitted to participate. This approach has three variants: sectoral deals on goods; the new plurilateral collective requests on services; and "clubs" for new issues. All such deals depend on the critical mass concept discussed above.

It may be said that, when the proponents of a new agreement represent a critical mass, there might be no harm in proceeding with a less-than-universal deal. The critical mass concept facilitated the 1997 agreement on trade in basic telecommunications services, for example, though it is used more typically on goods. Canada and the United States have suggested that the technique might help advance sectoral negotiations. In their NAMA proposal, they state that

> critical mass represents a negotiated level of participation based on the share of world trade that interested Members determine should be covered in order for those Members to be willing to reduce rates in a given sector. If the sectoral [negotiation] succeeds, all participants implement reductions on an MFN basis so all WTO Members benefit. (WTO 2005b)

This approach ensures that Members with only a slight interest in a sector cannot block negotiations, yet the requirement to have a critical mass creates a high hurdle that prevents a small group from getting too far ahead of other Members. It has worked before: participants in the "zero for zero" sectoral deals of the Uruguay Round represented more than 70 percent of world trade in the sectors concerned (Hoda 2001, 38). But if this approach is perceived to be a way to exclude developing countries, it is doomed. In the Uruguay Round, the participation of developing countries in the market access sectorals was not needed, but the leading countries are now so large, and have such a large share of remaining market access barriers, that proceeding without them would be pointless. The poorest Members, in contrast, are allowed to opt out of the package anyway.

Both the notion of critical mass and the success of the 1997 telecommunications agreement are clearly part of the motivation for the second variant on the less-than-universal deal: the "plurilateral" negotiations on services (described in the next section, on modalities). Members participating in the collective requests are not plurilateral "clubs", however, because like the sectoral deals, the results will ultimately be part of the Single Undertaking.

In the third variant, "clubs" are typically proposed for new issues. A notable example is the Agreement on Government Procurement, one of the last relics of the Tokyo Round "codes." Robert Lawrence (2006) proposes a sophisticated set of criteria for considering when a subject might be suitable for a club-based negotiation within the WTO but outside the Single Undertaking. In addition to theoretical arguments that call into question the supposed tradeoff between broader and deeper agreements (see Gilligan 2004), I think that all of Lawrence's justifications ultimately fail on institutional grounds.

First, both the negotiation and the operation of clubs would be parasitic on limited WTO Secretariat resources. Second, only OECD governments are sure to have the national capacity to implement agreements in new areas, yet capturing these countries in new disciplines is rarely the point. Third, only the most advanced developing countries have the capacity even to participate in negotiations. Lawrence observes that everyone participated in the negotiations on the Tokyo Round codes, which means that "all had the ability to craft the agreement in a manner which reflected their interests." But developing countries did not participate much, and then ignored the codes, creating the problem the Uruguay Round tried to solve. Experience with the "Singapore issues" goes in the other direction: the issues were forced off the agenda at the 2003 Cancún ministerial and out of the work program, partly for tactical reasons, but mostly because many developing country Members could not cope with the additional negotiating challenges. Fourth, given the complexity of the WTO negotiating process and the pressures for both transparency and participation in restricted meetings, it would surely be foolish to include any Member in a club process that had no intention of accepting the results. Finally, if non-participants are significant actors in a domain, it might be unwise to proceed without their willing participation if it is hoped to attract their subsequent adherence.

All three plurilateral options are based on the critical mass concept and carry varying risks for both interest aggregation and learning. Where the critical mass threshold is high, a sectoral deal causes little difficulty. It would be unfortunate, however, if a sectoral or a plurilateral deal were to undermine the political dynamic of a round. Rounds work when negotiators can find tradeoffs between issues and countries—indeed, when negotiators can see the tradeoffs between import-competing and export interests within a given economy. The last element is quite important. It is hard to exert direct influence on protectionist forces in another country—a producer who wants to block imports has little reason to negotiate with foreigners. In the standard political economy arguments, therefore, the supply of protection is determined in domestic politics through bargaining between producer demand and political supply (Magee, Brock and Young 1989). But exporters are also participants in domestic politics and are interested in the market access that foreigners have to offer (Sherman 2002). Reciprocal bargaining allows foreigners to influence domestic politics, creating an incentive for exporters to trump protectionists in domestic ratification debates. For example, it would be a pity if the United States, by becoming part of a plurilateral club on a "new" issue, were to lose the lobbying power of businesses in support of a round that also included uncomfortable concessions on "old" issues. It would be equally unfortunate if a developing country dependent on a single commodity export were to participate in a sectoral deal, then lose interest in the rest of the round.

The argument against plurilateral deals goes beyond political economy or interest aggregation considerations to their effect on learning. The appeal of a two-speed system is evident, yet it risks excluding poor countries from the negotiations while creating norms that would be difficult to change later (Hoekman 2005). If the WTO is a central component of global governance, then there are no grounds for saying that its normative framework should apply only to some states or that only some states must or can be full participants in deliberations about its evolution. Moreover, with respect to the regulatory negotiating agenda (where much of the trouble lies), the essential task is to build appropriate regulatory capacity in developing countries, then to encourage those regulators to go to Geneva to learn, to advance their interests, and to take ownership of the WTO rules. If developing countries are exempted from participation in clubs, they will forever be trying to catch up, they will not be playing their part in the continual evolution of the system and in the development of consensual knowledge about the system, and they will continue to complain about having to implement rules they had no part in drafting.

I conclude that the Single Undertaking can be relaxed, but only slightly. Before considering what issues must be on the negotiating agenda, however, it is necessary to address *how* issues are negotiated, or "modalities" in WTO jargon.

The Importance of Modalities

Much of the Doha Round has been taken up with the modalities question, especially with respect to agriculture (Blandford and Josling 2006). I consider the question in three different domains: trade in goods, trade in services, and trade rules. I find that negotiations on issues included in the Single Undertaking can make more progress to the extent that the modalities are multilateral.

The first GATT negotiations were based on the procedures of the proposed 1948 International Trade Organization (ITO) treaty, which called for negotiations to be conducted on a product-by-product basis and specified that "[t]he requests for reduction of tariff on a product could be made in principle only in respect of products of which the requesting countries were individually or collectively the principal suppliers to the countries from which the concessions were asked" (Hoda 2001, 27). Negotiating on a "request and offer" basis among "principal suppliers" is multilateral only to the extent that the MFN principle extends the results to all participants, but it limits the interests of Members with large markets in negotiations with Members with small markets. Deals negotiated with "principal suppliers" do benefit small Members, which can act as free riders, but the practice also hurts them by limiting their ability to negotiate on subjects of greatest interest to them.

The possibility of a formula approach as an alternative was first discussed as early as 1953, but it was only in the Kennedy Round (1964–67) that it was agreed that the tariff negotiations for industrial products would be based on a plan of "substantial linear tariff reductions." Hoda (2001, 30) observes:

> Two main considerations led to the adoption of the linear approach. First, the item by item, request-offer method adopted in past negotiations, with its dependence on the extent to which the principal supplier was willing to reciprocate the reduction of duty in a particular product, had led to very small reductions which were in some cases worthless in commercial terms. Second, with the increase in the number of contracting parties the traditional method had become increasingly cumbersome and unwieldy.

And that was in the 1960s, when the trading system had fewer participants and covered fewer issues. The Tokyo Round of the 1970s continued the formula approach to market access. The Uruguay Round market access negotiations for goods were based on a mix of bilateral, sectoral, and formula approaches, but agriculture was formula based. The Doha NAMA and agriculture negotiations similarly must be formula based because of the increase in the number of active members: negotiations on thousands of individual tariff lines with two or three dozen significant trading partners is not feasible for any Member, however large.[10]

---

10. For a description of the technical complexities of the many formula approaches, see WTO (2003); see also Panagariya (2002); Francois, Martin, and Manole (2005); and Trebilcock and Howse (2005, 179ff). They can be designed to cut tariffs equally, to harmonize rates, or to cut high tariffs more than low ones. An

As a modality, a formula ultimately requires consensus, which allows a voice at the outset for any Member, however small, and which changes the institutional dynamic. These issues are traditional, and one might have thought they would be easily negotiable. But the legacy of the past, when developing countries were not major participants in shaping the rules, weighs heavily on a round in which everyone wants to be engaged. Here, too, the difficulty is that nobody wants to admit their country is no longer a "developing country," with all the attendant claims for special and differential treatment. The tariff rates developing countries actually apply are relatively high, and the legal rates that are bound in their WTO commitments are often higher still. A formula approach would lead to significant nominal cuts in their tariffs, yet some still have trouble seeing why cutting their tariffs from 120 percent to 60 percent is as fair, and as good for Doha's development objectives, as cutting a developed country's tariff from 3 percent to 2 percent (Nath 2007). The formula also might not deliver the desired results in specific sectors: efforts in early 2007 to break the logjam reportedly had aspects of "reverse engineering" as US negotiators tried to work backward from a desired outcome on an EU tariff for a specific commodity to the formula that would produce such a result.

It follows, then, that a formula can be too opaque—if, for example, it is hard to see how a formula on an agricultural issue would affect farmers. Yet a formula can also be too transparent. The successful formula negotiations of the past (see Winham 2007) were conducted between relatively like-minded developed countries, and the final deals were based on behind-the-scenes bilateral bargains. The advantage of the Uruguay Round market access approach was ambiguity: until the schedules were published, everyone at home who had not been privately briefed by the negotiators could hope that their interests had been protected. The disadvantage of the July 2004 Framework approach to modalities, the approach on which

---

example of the latter is the so-called Swiss formula: $Z = AX/(A + X)$, where X = the initial tariff rate; A = the coefficient and maximum final tariff rate; and Z = the resulting lower tariff rate at the end of the period (Goode 2003). The key is the coefficient, A. If the formula as a modality is agreed, then negotiations focus on the value of the coefficient and on whether some groups of countries or products should have a higher or lower coefficient than others.

negotiations foundered in 2006, is that once the coefficient is inserted into a formula, all domestic producers can calculate the effects on their interests. Those sensitive to imports can start to rally support for the designation of certain products as being too "sensitive" or "special" to be liberalized (ICTSD 2006) or for certain "flexibilities" to be exercised in their favor. Exporters watching this process at home might suspect that their hoped-for benefits in other markets are illusory. With a more transparent formula, forces wanting protection would be easy to mobilize, while those wanting liberalization might be demoralized.

Much less progress has been made on designing a truly multilateral modality for services, leading many sophisticated observers of the GATS negotiations to conclude that the bottom-up or "positive list" approach to scheduling commitments has failed and that it is time to find an analog to the "negative list" approach implicit in traditional tariff negotiations.[11] Through much of the Doha Round, observers have complained that the offers on the table are inadequate—an example of what happens with a positive list when new obligations apply only to things a Member explicitly puts on the table, as opposed to a negative list that would exempt from new obligations only those things the Member explicitly takes off the table. In an effort to change the calculus, the EU has proposed numerical targets for positive commitments as benchmarks, but with limited support. In fall 2005, attention turned to other "complementary" negotiating modalities.

One problem with a standard "request and offer" negotiation in services is that it is bilateral. In the periodic special sessions of the Council for Trade in Services, a given Member might have wanted to have bilateral meetings with as a many as 40 other Members. The physical impossibility of arranging so many serious meetings in a two-week period was compounded by the impossibility of ever having the right sectoral experts in the room for any one meeting. The more active members have always organized themselves in "Friends" groups—much of the negotiations for the 1997 telecommunications services agreement, for example, took place within the Friends of Telecommunications group. In effect, the Friends groups are networks of domestic experts who talk to each other about the

---

11. Curiously, OECD members stopped their secretariat from pursuing new approaches to services modalities. For early work see Thompson (2001).

regulation of trade in services. The groups do not include the Secretariat, and decide for themselves who can come to meetings. The challenge is finding a modality to make use of their expertise, a challenge complicated by the low level of participation by developing country experts in the groups.[12]

The answer was the plurilateral approach introduced in the Hong Kong Declaration (WTO 2005a). In early 2006, close to three dozen countries participated in the 21 collective requests under this provision. In the process, 15 or so Friends groups surfaced in a more transparent way than hitherto in order to prepare the requests, and then to meet collectively with representatives of the Members to which the requests were addressed. I assume that the Members making and receiving these collective requests represent an approximation of critical mass in the sector concerned. This change in modalities, in short, offers the promise of making services more negotiable, in part by enabling networks of officials who learn to see themselves in the trade context, and in part by offering a route out of the bilateral trap— even if it is still plurilateral, rather than fully multilateral. In striking contrast to the large numbers of active participants in agriculture, barely a dozen developing countries participated in any of the collective requests, and few of those made more than a couple of requests. The good news, in contrast, is that the developing country Members that received requests then engaged in the process, with many capital-based participants attending the subsequent meetings.

The problems in finding multilateral modalities do not afflict all aspects of the Doha Round. Trade rules and domestic policies began to

---

12. The low participation is not surprising, given, as Sauvé (2007, 12) observes,

the limited number of developing country services experts available for bilateral discussions in Geneva missions and in capitals; the negotiating imbalances that flow from the limited ability of most developing countries to formulate their own requests; significant asymmetries in negotiating-relevant information available to policy officials; and the more limited extent of stakeholder consultations and private sector engagement—and presence abroad—of service suppliers from developing countries. The extensive inter-agency coordination and external stakeholder consultation machinery required to make a success of services negotiations is simply lacking or inoperative in the vast majority of developing countries.

come to the fore in the Tokyo Round, but the decisionmaking structure was still pyramidal, with the largest players negotiating agreements among themselves, then discussing the results with others (Winham 1986). This "minilateral" process conserves negotiating energy, but makes it impossible for smaller countries to influence the results. Not surprisingly, therefore, most developing countries did not sign the minilateral Tokyo Round "codes." Many of the Uruguay Round agreements were explicitly designed as new understandings of GATT rules—for example, on subsidies. These aspects of trade negotiations are inherently multilateral, but the Single Undertaking makes this reality explicit. Once a domestic policy—for example, the definition of a subsidy or of antidumping—is changed, all trading partners can take advantage of the new rules, so bilateral negotiations on rules issues are rarely successful, and rarely needed. The Doha negotiations in both the Rules group and the Trade Facilitation group were suspended along with the rest, but these inherently multilateral negotiations had been making good progress to that point, with no modalities obstacles.

What Must the Single Undertaking Contain?

If the Single Undertaking can be relaxed, but only slightly, what institutional design criteria help to determine what it should contain? The WTO does not deal merely with simple tariffs at the border nor, at the other extreme, does it include every issue that might for some reason be subject to the dispute settlement system. The choices are made because some *interests* must be accommodated in the package, and they are made because some issues are suitable to the institutional features of the trading system while others are not.

Many observers have tried to articulate a basis for when the WTO should add new issues to its agenda. The argument that it is useful to bring a domain within the scope of the dispute settlement system is the easiest to reject. Some reform suggestions would have the WTO agenda become much broader; others would have it be narrower and more focused. The argument against broadening is similar to the one against seeing the WTO as a "development" organization, though usually advanced by different people. The WTO, it is said, should concentrate on commercial policy and nothing else. The argument has merit, especially if the WTO is to remain simple enough for all its Members to understand. And yet, if the WTO is to focus on the way commercial transactions transmit the externalities of domestic policy decisions across borders, it requires a pretty broad agenda. If the organization's mandate were more limited, would it still be interesting to the largest traders? And if it ceased being interesting to them, would it be interesting to anybody else?

The nature and handling of the agenda might well have affected the suspension of the Doha Round negotiations. The Doha Declaration was ambiguous in how it described the subjects for negotiation and discussion, with nobody sure what the eventual Single Undertaking would have to contain. Much of the work of the past five years has been about just that— that is, the agenda bargain is also about learning. The bargain on launching the round could be seen as a triangle: old issues involving physical trade (NAMA and agriculture, with some rules), new or intangible issues (services and the Singapore issues), and development, with something needed at all three corners (Wolfe 2004a). The essential objective for the Doha ministerial, therefore, had been to enlarge the negotiations envisaged under the Uruguay Round's "built-in agenda" (Ostry 1997). Agriculture and services alone were not enough for a round, and progress in negotiations in those areas seemed unlikely without the possibility of broader tradeoffs in a Single Undertaking. The ideal is a balanced agenda with horizontal linkages that create a strong internal dynamic of countries that want a deal, since tradeoffs do not come in one domain alone, even if balance is needed within each domain. The addition of NAMA plus rules (subsidies and antidumping) created the basis for a round, along with a political recognition of the requirement to take account of the needs of developing countries both in the texts and in technical assistance. What Ostry has called the "asymmetry" of the Uruguay Round "grand bargain" could not be ignored.

What is surprising in retrospect is how the original Doha triangle kept being reduced. The round had been slowed by the time it took to get the Singapore issues off the table; by so-far futile efforts to respond constructively to concerns about "implementation" of Uruguay Round commitments in favor of developing countries; and by demands to improve special and differential treatment. By late June 2006, observers were saying that success hinged on breaking the "iron triangle"—getting the United

States to make deeper cuts in its domestic farm subsidies, the EU to offer more agricultural market access by means of deeper tariff cuts, and Brazil and India to open wider their domestic markets for industrial goods. It is striking that the iron triangle did not include services, let alone development, and, in their last-ditch efforts, ministers never got past agriculture. Yet agriculture alone is not self-balancing, and tariffs alone are equally difficult.[13]

The Doha agenda might have been reduced so much in order to accommodate the interests of all Members, but it has also shrunk because some issues were institutionally unsuited to the WTO. Whether one thinks negotiating is synonymous with bargaining or requires learning, it is possible only if it engages national officials who have responsibilities in a domain, have the capacity to participate, and either know their interests or have the ability to learn about their interests. It also helps if economic and governmental actors perceive an international dimension to an issue—if they are, in fact, engaged with actors in other places, since law emerges from such interaction. Trade negotiators discover and codify the rules, but they do not engage in "rule making" out of whole cloth. The GATS is based on a sophisticated vision of the economy and the role of policy. Developing countries often do not understand the relevant sectors of their own economy or that of their trading partners well enough to make binding offers or sensible requests, because they cannot imagine the real effects of a policy change. These considerations lead me to conclude that issues should be added to the WTO agenda only if they satisfy certain criteria (see Box 1).

These criteria help to explain why the 1997 telecommunications services agreement was relatively easy to negotiate. Deliberation in Geneva can be part of how people come to see the changes under way, but it is the change in the sector that matters. Services negotiations cannot drive domestic policy change. Rather, in many developing countries, there is an endogenous dynamic for the regulatory reform of telecommunications. It affects a small number of economic actors, requires few trained officials,

---

13. For an economic analysis of the merits of a broad, but not too broad, agenda, see Levy (2005). His conclusion, however, misunderstands one aspect of the Single Undertaking: as a decisionmaking principle, it requires consensus before a new package can be agreed, so the problem of excluding nonsignatories from the benefits of a new agreement does not arise.

Box 1: *Criteria for Adding Issues to the Single Undertaking*

1. A potential new issue should be consistent with the broad WTO objectives of using trade liberalization to promote international order and global prosperity, but if it can be handled in another international organization, it should be.

2. It should be possible to negotiate in this domain using basic WTO norms and principles—especially with respect to reciprocity and non-discrimination.

3. The issue should be possible to negotiate using a multilateral modality that allows for variable geometry and differentiation.

4. WTO obligations, however intrusive, should apply to the sector when economic or policy externalities cannot be managed unilaterally—as when markets and territory do not readily align or when transaction flows are dominated by intra-industry trade.

5. The sector should have an industrial organization and regulatory structure that are changing in ways that make international obligations practical, in principle.

6. The issue should be amenable to negotiations that engage a transgovernmental network that is willing to see the WTO as a focal point for its work.

7. The potential new rules should address governments, not other actors who cannot be subject to WTO obligations, and should engage officials in each Member country who are able to see the relevance of the WTO.

8. While compatibility with multinational norms is essential, domestic implementation of the new rules should not depend on administrative law protections for foreigners that states have yet to extend to their own citizens

9. The possibility of new rules should first be addressed horizontally in existing WTO agreements, rather than vertically in a new stand-alone agreement; plurilateral deals are rarely appropriate

10. The issue should strengthen the Single Undertaking by adding new domestic supporters of the WTO.

---

and has highly visible benefits in increased investment in vital modern infrastructure. Endogenous regulatory reform makes it easier for a country to participate in exogenous multilateral negotiations.

By these criteria, the TRIPS agreement was a mistake. Similarly, sanitary and phytosanitary rules are problematic when they require a developing country to have a more sophisticated food inspection system than it might otherwise choose in order to comply with consumer preferences in OECD countries. Calling the new round the "Doha Development Agenda" was seen as foolishness by officials who think the WTO is not a development organization. They do not mean that trade is irrelevant to development—quite the reverse—but that development as a discrete activity is no business of the WTO. Since that position is not sustainable when developing countries make up a substantial majority of the Members, the question is how best to include development considerations on the agenda, given the limited utility of trade negotiations as a policy instrument for promoting development. The slow progress on this set of issues might signal the virtue of an exclusively horizontal approach to differentiation. Allowing "development" to be a vertical issue with its own negotiating body might have been then-director-general Mike Moore's greatest contribution to ending the sterile debates on "implementation" of Uruguay Round obligations after Seattle. In the long run, however, those issues should be dealt with systematically in the agreements where problems arise, by the experts concerned, leaving assistance to the competent international organizations.

Of the new issues within the ambit of the original Doha Declaration, trade facilitation readily satisfies the criteria I set out in Box 1. Competition policy, in contrast, is the most problematic, because international interaction among nascent competition authorities in developing countries is still limited,[14] and procurement officials usually have a domestic orientation. Consideration of two other original Doha issues—investment, now explicitly off the table, and the environment, nominally still in play—helps to illustrate the criteria.

Investment is already covered in the agreement on trade-related investment measures (TRIMs) and in the GATS, but the available modalities for explicit investment negotiations might be as much of an obstacle to including it on the agenda as opposition from developing countries. Sauvé (2006) concludes that, with respect to investment protection, the

---

14. Although the 1977 telecoms Reference Paper is a horizontal device that incorporates competition policy principles in a way that allows national variance in implementation.

need for recourse to investor-state dispute settlement rules out a role for the WTO. He also notes that, since two-thirds of aggregate foreign investment inflows and four-fifths of identified barriers to investment affect services, it follows that most of the relevant issues can be addressed horizontally in the GATS. Of the distortions that affect manufacturing investment, most are already covered by the TRIMs agreement or could readily be incorporated in the subsidies agreement. A WTO investment agreement might also address elements of the good governance agenda, but most of these issues are not suitable for WTO obligations.

Investment is now off the WTO agenda, and will not be put back on soon. The environment, however, still has both a committee and a Doha negotiating group. Where specific agreements have environmental implications, they can be addressed horizontally, as they are in many areas of the negotiations. But the WTO is not an environmental organization; it has no expertise in the area, it does not engage environmental officials, and its key norms are not especially suited to environmental issues. If the three paragraphs on the environment in the Doha Declaration result in anything specific, it will be last-minute window dressing (Halle 2006). Environmental worries are far from being a central concern of trade ministers, which means the issues bring little to the Single Undertaking. It is not that the environment does not matter, but that it costs a great deal of negotiating time and capital while obscuring the ability of regular work, and the dispute settlement system, to clarify the applicability of existing rules.

It follows that another way of thinking about the WTO agenda is to ask if an issue can or should be handled elsewhere. Many WTO agreements already show explicit deference to other organizations. It is now accepted, for example, that the WTO should consider the effect on trade of domestic regulations to prevent the spread of animal diseases, but leave consideration of how those regulations accomplish their intended goal to the expertise of the World Animal Health Organization.

The Trade Policy Review Mechanism (TPRM) presents an underused opportunity for such coherence. It is not a forum for discussion of formal WTO obligations, but could be a forum for deliberation and learning. A great deal of trade-related policy is not, or should not be, subject to WTO discipline—especially, perhaps, issues on the development agenda. It might be easier to achieve the necessary transparency and coherence with the broad objectives of the trading system, not through trying to craft formal, and contentious, rules, but through open discussion in the TPRM. Possible roles for the International Monetary Fund (IMF) and the World Bank in such a process are obvious. The International Labour Organization could also be asked to comment in a TPRM on how a country is doing on core labor standards, or the World Wildlife Fund on environmental issues. Collaboration with the UN Environment Programme would make sense on multilateral environmental agreements (Palmer and Tarasofsky 2007). Progress in developing international norms for cultural promotion, with a secretariat, could also become a part of TPRM consideration of trade-related cultural policy. In addition, Members should consider how to strengthen links between the TPRM and surveillance processes in other bodies. Deference to other organizations, international or domestic, could also mean what Nordstrom (2005) calls "outsourcing": making use of the greater analytic capacity of organizations such as the OECD and the World Bank.

In sum, I think that assessments of the existing agenda and proposals for additions must meet the substantive criteria in Box 1. What these criteria do not address, however, is process. The Single Undertaking and multilateral modalities allow any Member to have influence because agreement is subject to consensus. Simply blocking consensus is relatively easy in principle, but shaping an outcome is more complicated. Yet, even if the WTO had the right agenda, can its processes cope? Indeed, is the issue a more fundamental one of legitimacy?

Legitimate Engagement in the WTO

The trading system is not governable if it is not legitimate, but legitimacy for the regime as a whole does not require the same instrumental form at every node in the system. What goes on in Geneva is surely important, but so, too, is what goes on in national capitals, in the boardrooms of multinational corporations, and in the everyday practices of consumers and traders. To add to the complexity, insiders and outsiders frame the debate on legitimate engagement differently. Insiders frame it as "internal" or "external" transparency, defined by reference to events in Geneva. Outsiders frame it as part of the debate on whether global governance can be democratic, defined by reference to citizens. Given all the attention paid to external transparency, it is surprising how little of the literature on WTO reform focuses on internal transparency—the inverse of the attention negotiators devote to these issues. The two are clearly linked in the creation of a legitimate order (see Mitzen 2005). But they are also linked by many critics who see the WTO as undemocratic, arguing that civil society cannot properly participate in the organization and that many small countries are severely disadvantaged by the WTO's practices. I address internal transparency issues in the next section; here, I ask whether the external considerations help explain the suspension of the Doha Round or point the way to essential reforms.

The Doha Development Agenda confirmed the rhetorical importance WTO Members attach to the essential democratic values of transparency and participation. That commitment, however, is merely to make information available in Geneva while convincing citizens at home that the WTO is good for them. The fact that paragraph 10 of the Doha agenda, on transparency, is not a subject for negotiations signals the sensitivity of these issues for many Members, even though the public is not clamoring for more information or a greater role. Trade policy is not a highly salient issue for most people, and the 1999 "Battle in Seattle" never resonated much except as a strange case of street violence in the latte capital of the world (Mendelsohn and Wolfe 2001). The WTO is rarely front page news even in the business section. Still, the "permissive consensus" on trade policy remains robust, understood as the freedom to act that the public has traditionally accorded governments in this realm: as long as trade policy delivers prosperity without too much domestic disruption, the public is not interested in the details (Mendelsohn, Wolfe, and Parkin 2002; Wolfe and Mendelsohn 2005).

That does not, however, let WTO off the hook, even if it is doing relatively well at providing more information on the Internet and increasing access for nongovernmental organizations (NGOs) at ministerial meetings. But I do not share the views of some observers (for example, Esty 2002) that greater engagement of civil society organizations in Geneva is needed to provide more information to citizens at home. I do not see the merit of emphasizing public education about the facts and benefits of WTO "law" (Cho 2005), as if dispute settlement is the most important way the WTO affects its domain. I do agree, however, that having modest ambitions for the dispute settlement system helps legitimacy, what some scholars call "institutional sensitivity" (Howse and Nicolaidis 2003).

The familiar democracy frame is also inadequate because, in its obsession with Geneva, it does not consider the problem of support at home for new rules. For example, in the crucial stages of designing the proposed ITO in 1948, negotiators convinced each other but lost touch with currents of opinion at home. Their failure to prepare the ground was part of the explanation for the ITO's ultimate failure (Hampson and Hart 1995, 163). Thus, the Sutherland Report's focus on external transparency in Geneva, rather than on the responsibilities of national governments, missed the point: the legitimacy of the WTO has little to do with the few NGOs that pay it most attention. It is important to ask, therefore, whether the WTO has sufficient domestic resonance, whether the public, farm lobbies, business interests, and domestic officials in Europe, North America, and the developing countries are learning about what is at stake in the Doha Round. Transparency in Geneva and more engagement with civil society might not contribute to a more effective and legitimate WTO, but they do contribute to a more effective and legitimate national trade policy process (Charnovitz 2004). That domestic process must involve all of government, not just the trade ministry.

Transparency alone, however, is not enough. Internet access is now available everywhere, so people potentially affected by new WTO rules can easily find out if something is going on. If they lack deliberative opportunities, they might react negatively to proposals they do not fully understand.[15] One aspect of domestic consultations should be greater engagement of parliamentarians in the WTO and trade policy (see Glania 2004; Mann 2004; Shaffer 2004; Berg and Schmitz 2006), although the Australian experience leads to some skepticism about the ability of such involvement to mitigate a supposed "democratic deficit" (Capling and Nossal 2003). For developing countries, especially small ones, improving the trade policy process by introducing more and better consultation is a daunting task, but Members can learn from each other. Sylvia Ostry (2004) argues that the quality of the national trade policy process should be

---

15. On the value of domestic trade policy consultations, see Halle and Wolfe (2007) and the literature cited there.

considered in each Member's WTO Trade Policy Review. Transparency about the trade policy process can be as valuable as transparency in the process. The process matters because it helps Member countries and their citizens identify and capture the gains from trade. Using the TPRM to strengthen that process is not a grand scheme for improving the world, and it will not get the WTO or trade policy generally off the hook of demands to be more open and responsive to civil society concerns, but it is a small step the WTO can take, and one consistent with its principles and practices.

The caveat matters: increased transparency might hurt the WTO if it encourages posturing by negotiators and politicians. If constituents perceive a negotiation as purely distributive, they will be critical of a negotiator who pursues the possibility of an integrative outcome. Thompson (1998, 159) suggests that, given the natural desire to save face, "[n]egotiators who are accountable to constituents are more likely to maintain a tough bargaining stance, make fewer concessions, and hold out for more favorable agreements compared to those who are not accountable." US, European, and Canadian agricultural groups know exactly what is going on in Geneva at any moment and publicly instruct their negotiators on what is or is not acceptable, especially on matters as clear cut as a formula coefficient. The transparency that modern governance demands undermines the privacy essential for negotiations (Stasavage 2004). It might also undermine liberalization, or force protection into less transparent forms (Kono 2006). Nevertheless, transparency is essential for deliberation, and deliberation matters for democracy as well as learning. Deliberation is especially important whenever collective decisions allow burdens to be imposed on others, which demands "public deliberative processes through which reasons can be scrutinized, debated and either revised or rejected in light of the available evidence and argument" (King 2003, 39).

If deliberation matters at home for citizens, it also matters for their representatives in Geneva. The WTO provides a forum for the legitimation of a regime, in part, by providing opportunities for voice. These opportunities affect the possibility to defend interests, of course, but they are even more important for developing consensual knowledge and for the deliberation that makes effective bargaining legitimate. Do all Members have an effective voice?

Internal Transparency: The Negotiation Process

The general perception of WTO negotiations is of episodic ministerials at which all the work is done. Close observers know, however, that ministerials are the tip of an iceberg of diplomatic activity in and out of Geneva, and that developing countries have been increasingly insistent on having a voice in that activity. Whether the quality of that deliberation is adequate might bear on whether a better institution could have avoided the suspension of the Doha Round, given the same exogenous factors in the world political economy and the same negotiating strategies. Should the process be bottom up or text based? Do small group meetings advance negotiations or should all informal meetings be open ended? Should the chair select some Members to attend consultations, and if so, should they be the major players, the like minded, or the principal antagonists on a particular issue? When should ministers be involved? The issues in this section, therefore, concern who should negotiate and where.

Informality in the WTO

The WTO is a forum, not an "actor" in itself, and it is Member driven. Unlike the IMF or the World Bank, it has a tiny professional staff whose role is to serve as a Secretariat to the dozens of WTO bodies. The Secretariat can commission background papers, but negotiating proposals come from Members. The WTO is a place to talk, and the talking is done by representatives of Members: diplomats based in Geneva and officials from capitals, including ministers. Members talk at biennial ministerial conferences and in the Council for Trade in Services. They talk in regular committees that meet two or three times a year, in the negotiating groups that meet every four to six weeks, and in the dispute settlement body. They talk in hundreds of formal on-the-record meetings every year, and in many hundreds of more informal meetings (Wolfe 2004b). Some of these off-the-record meetings are held in the WTO building, others are held in the offices of delegations, or in Member countries. Box 2 is a first attempt to delineate the dimensions of all these meetings.

Such complexity creates practical problems for delegations and for efficient negotiations. Given the formal equality and practical inequality

---

Box 2: *Dimensions of WTO Meetings*

1. Formality
   a. official WTO meeting (mandated by treaty or rules of procedure)
   b. informal (multilateral: chaired by the chairperson of the regular body)
      i. plenary of any WTO body, including "transparency forum," announced by the chair
      ii. limited number of delegates per Member (technical experts)
      iii. small group (selected delegates meeting with the chair)
      iv. Green Room (20–30 heads of delegations) or Room F (20–30 delegates); Secretariat present
      v. "fireside chat" (20–30 delegates); Secretariat not present
      vi. bilateral (confessionals, where one delegation meets the chair)
      vii. friends of the chair (usually meetings of chairs called by the director-general)
   c. outside the WTO (not chaired by the chairperson of the regular body; Secretariat sometimes invited)
      i. bridge clubs
      ii. services expert groups (plurilateral)
      iii. mini-ministerials
2. Transparency
   a. documentation available to public, other members
   b. open to public (webcasting, NGO observers)/closed
   c. unofficial summary reports on WTO Web site
   d. official records (minutes)
   e. statement by the chair for the record, and circulated to Members
   f. informal reporting by club coordinators to Members not present (routinized transmission belt)
   g. no records

---

of WTO Members, the Sutherland Report notes "the need to streamline regular activity and reduce the burdens on small delegations" (Sutherland et al. 2004, 69), but then makes no recommendations on how to do so. In a Member-driven organization, a Member that lacks the capacity to be an informed presence at every meeting is at a disadvantage, but the alternatives are not obvious. On the one hand, disaggregation makes things simple while engaging distinct policy networks; on the other hand, aggregation

Box 2 - continued

3. Membership
   a. universal/plenary/open ended
   b. limited by/to
      i. geography
      ii. interest
      iii. principal antagonists
      iv. representatives of clubs
      v. size of room
4. Level
   a. ministers
   b. senior officials from capitals
   c. ambassadors
   d. Geneva delegation
   e. experts from capitals
5. Chair
   a. chosen by Members annually or for duration
   b. self-selected (ministerial conference and mini-ministerial)
   c. clubs:
      i. continuing (for example, Cairns, G33, G20, G10)
      ii. rotating (for example, African Group, LDCs, ASEAN, ACP)
6. Purpose (in negotiation mode)
   a. preliminary exchange of views
   b. arguing
   c. bargaining
   d. decisions (on process, texts, obligations)
7. Domain
   a. WTO/trading system
   b. negotiating round as a whole
   c. specific substantive areas
   d. process

into a smaller number of committees forces tradeoffs while reducing the number of meetings that small delegations have to cover.[16] When the number of active participants in multilateral trade negotiations increased dramatically in the 1980s, experience confirmed the well-understood proposition that the legitimacy gained by involving large numbers of participants

---

16. For a description of how the 15 Uruguay Round negotiating groups were reduced to four "tracks" as the round progressed, see Winham (2006).

comes at the expense of the efficiency associated with small numbers (Kahler 1993). No organization with 150 Members can find consensus on sensitive matters such as agricultural reform if all discussions must be held in public, in large groups, with written records. It follows that little real work is done in meetings that would be at the first level of formality in Box 2. Most of the negotiating groups meet for a week at a time, but in plenary session only at the beginning and the end of the week, and then only briefly, to record statements and decisions. For transparency, the groups also meet in informal plenary sessions that provide an opportunity for all Members to hear about the informal smaller group meetings that have been taking place. Much of the work, and associated controversy about internal transparency, surrounds the smallest groups—informal bodies with no recognized standing, limited membership, and no written reports.

Only the largest WTO Members can monitor and participate in all meetings. The United States does so easily. EU Members are represented by the European Commission. Perhaps fewer than half a dozen more Members—notably Canada and Japan—have the capacity to participate actively across the board. Other leading developed and developing countries participate more actively in some areas than others. At most, 40 delegations are significant players, a reality mentioned again and again by senior members of the Secretariat and by ambassadors, including from developing countries. Agriculture is the area followed most closely, yet only about 15 delegations really play, and the principal ideas come from fewer than ten. The institutional design issue becomes one of structuring a process whereby these few can get on with it without losing touch with the interests of the rest, and in a way that builds confidence in the process and the results. And all countries must find ways to aggregate their strength with others in negotiating groupings, an innovation that has contributed to the developing country sense that they are being heard. Box 3 is an attempt to list all the known groupings of recent years. Figure 1 shows the overlapping membership of the agriculture clubs.

The list in Box 3 raises a great many questions about negotiation groupings, or clubs, with respect to what they do and how they differ (Wolfe 2007). I define a club as a group of nations united or associated for a particular purpose, a definition that purposely evokes a looser form of association than the common tendency to see informal groups of states working within international organizations as "coalitions" (Odell 2006). The clubs that seem such an important part of the institutional design of the Doha Round have their roots in earlier GATT rounds—indeed, in long-established multilateral practices going back to the League of Nations. Three sorts of clubs are relevant for WTO negotiations. Clubs based on a broad *common characteristic* (such as a region or level of development) can influence many issues, including the round as a whole, but only weakly. Clubs based on a *common objective* (such as agricultural trade) can have a great deal of influence, but on a limited range of issues. *Bridge clubs* can be essential for breaking deadlocks, or for managing negotiations, often by building bridges between opposed positions.

The original Quad that met regularly at ministerial level from the end of the Tokyo Round in the 1970s through the lengthy Uruguay Round negotiations to the early days of the WTO has not met at ministerial level since 1999, but it still meets informally among Geneva delegates. Efforts to craft a compromise take place, as always, in bilateral EU-US meetings, but also in newer bridge clubs. The most structured groups (such as the Cairns Group of agricultural exporting countries) require high-level recognition in capitals, especially for subordinating national strategy to joint negotiating positions; they have formal coordination and decision-making procedures; sometimes meet at the ministerial level; and some-times have sophisticated analytical support. The least-organized groups are loose consultative mechanisms at the technical or delegate level, often requiring authority from capitals—but they matter in the larger dynamics of building consensus and in solving substantive problems. Some groups exist because of negotiating modalities. Some are "coalitions" designed to allow actors to aggregate their strength with other actors in order affect egocentric "gains" and "losses." Others facilitate deliberation, in which participants come to a new understanding of their interests and of the col-lective problem, which can lead to different outcomes.

The new groupings do not always help: it is hard to move any group off a position once adopted. The most prominent, the G20, barely agreed among themselves on agriculture, and not at all on other issues. They also failed to reach a common position on NAMA, so that the rump speaks in that part of the negotiation not as the G20 but as the NAMA-11, which lacks technical support and has not been a creative force in the negotiations.

Box 3: *Known Negotiating Groupings*

Common characteristic groups
  G90†   .
  ACP†
  African Group†
  LDCs†
  ASEAN†
  CARICOM†
  Small and Vulnerable Economies
    (SVEs)
  Recently Acceded Members
    (RAMs)
  Small Vulnerable Coastal States
    (SVCS)

Agriculture
  Offensive Coalitions
    Cotton-4†
    Tropical and Alternative
      Products Group
    Cairns Group (N/S)†
    G20 (S/S)†
  Defensive coalitions
    G10†
    G33†
    RAMs, SVEs

Non-Agricultural Market Access
(NAMA)
  NAMA-11†
  Friends of MFN
  Friends of Ambition in NAMA
  Hôtel d'Angleterre
  RAMs, SVEs

Rules
  SCVS
  Friends of Fish
  Friends of Antidumping
    Negotiations (FANs)

Environment
  Friends of environmental goods
  Friends of the environment and
    sustainable development

Trade facilitation
  Core Group/W142 group
  Colorado Group/W137 group

Textiles
  International Textiles and
    Clothing Bureau (ITCB)

Services
  G25
  ASEAN-1 (-Singapore)
  African Group, ACP, LDCs, SVEs
  Real Good Friends of GATS/
    Friends of Friends

  "Friends of…" (plurilateral expert
    groups):
  audiovisual, legal; architectural/
  engineering/integrated engi
  neering; computer and related
  services; postal/courier, including
  express delivery; telecommuni-
  ications; construction and related
  engineering; distribution; education; environmental services;
  financial services; online enter-
  tainment; maritime transport;
  air transport; logistics; energy;
  services related to agriculture;
  cross-border services (Mode 1/2),
  Mode 3, Mode 4,
  MFN exemptions

TRIPS
  African Group

Box 3 - continued

["Disclosure" group of developing countries?]
Friends of Geographical Indicators
Friends Against Extension of Geographical Indicators

Bridge clubs

Agriculture and NAMA
(principal antagonists):
G4 (US, EU, Brazil, India)†
G6 (add Australia, Japan)†

NAMA caucus

Services
Enchilada

General (deadlock breaking)
Oslo or Non-G6 (Canada, Chile, Indonesia, Kenya, New Zealand and Norway)
Quad (Canada, EU, Japan, US)
Dirty Dozen (Quad plus)
"senior officials" (25–30)
mini-ministerials† (25–30)

Notes:
1. † indicates groups that have met at the ministerial level during the Doha Round.
2. For a glossary of agriculture groups, see (WTO 2006a). The list in this document is based both on self-identified groups and on sets of Members that have submitted joint proposals at various stages of the negotiations. The Five Interested Parties (FIPs) group has ceased meeting in that form, as has, therefore, the FIPs Plus group. The agriculture Quint does not seem to have met for some time.
3. The Enchilada Group incorporates Members who once met as the Core Group and then the G15.
4. Certain regional (common characteristic) groups apparently no longer actively coordinate in WTO except occasionally on electoral or political issues, such as observer status: ALADI, Andean Group, Arab Group, APEC, CEFTA, GRULAC, Islamic Group, Mercosur, OECS, SADC, SAPTA, SELA.
5. The once-prominent Like-Minded Group (LMG) has not been active for many years. The status of the "informal group of developing countries" is not clear.

Experienced chairs lament that, in the old days, open dissent allowed them to ascertain the center of gravity of a negotiation more easily; now, people toe the line and say nothing. Less important countries do not even bother negotiating, or trying to understand the issues, because bigger countries take the lead. Developing countries draw on analysis from bodies such as the United Nations Conference on Trade and Development, the

Figure 1: *Overlapping Memberships in the Agriculture Clubs*

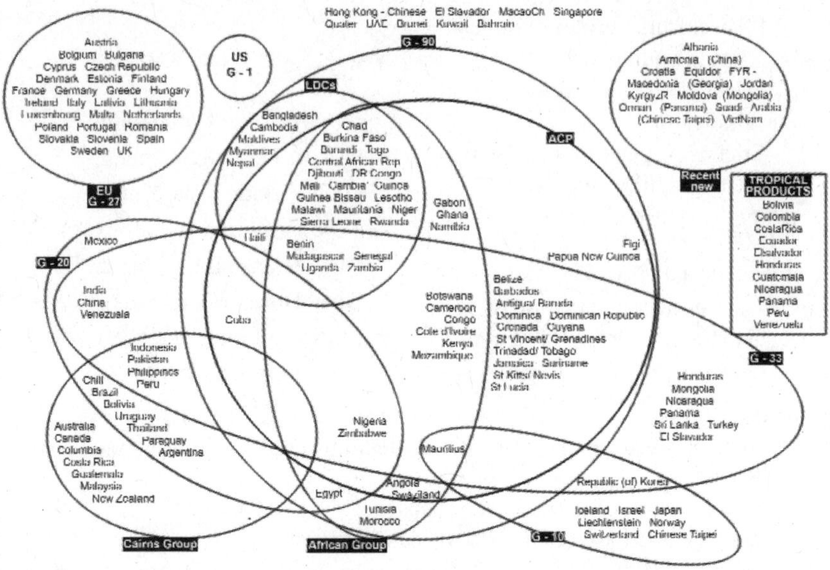

Source: International Centre for Trade and Sustainable Development; modified by the WTO Secretariat.

South Centre, and various NGOs, but these sources of expertise vary widely in quality, consistency, and ideology. None provides the kind of systematic consistent support that Brazil gets on agriculture from a think tank like the Instituto de Estudos do Comércio e Negociações Internacionais (ICONE) or that OECD countries get from their own bureaucracies.

The norms governing all this talk have been the subject of considerable reflection since the third ministerial conference, in Seattle in 1999, which clearly failed in part for institutional reasons (Odell 2002). Too many Members did not know what was happening, did not feel a part of the process, and did not see their issues being addressed. The difficulties were actually apparent at the WTO's first ministerial, in Singapore in 1996, but active procedural discussions among ambassadors in Geneva began only as part of the response to Seattle (WTO 2000), since that was the first WTO ministerial with something significant at stake. Moreover, Members had painfully to learn how to *prepare* for and *organize* a ministerial conference (Pedersen 2006). The two aspects are different. When the WTO became an Single Undertaking, everybody had to engage all the time, because every aspect of the negotiations might result in new obligations for every Member. But many developing countries were not accustomed to that level of intense participation in a ministerial conference; they did not know how to prepare, how to follow all the issues, or how to build alliances—and the result was a feeling of exclusion. Efforts since then have been directed to ensuring that traditional processes are transparent while not slowing everything down to the speed of the least capable Member.

WTO insiders understand the process as a series of nested "concentric circles." In the outer ring are official WTO meetings, mandated by the treaty or by the rules of procedure; these plenary meetings are held only for the record. In the next circle are informal plenary meetings of regular bodies, under their regular chairs, held mostly for transparency purposes. The real work is done when chairs meet with limited numbers of technical experts from Members, or when chairs invite small groups of key players to explore selected issues. If discussions reach an impasse, the response, adopted from the GATT, is to convene meetings of a restricted group of Members in a "Green Room," so-called after the color of the director-general's boardroom, where many such meetings were held at the invitation of Arthur Dunkel early in his term. At the 1988 Montreal ministerial, contentious issues were first discussed by small groups of officials, then by similar limited groups of ministers (see Croome 1995). This inner circle became controversial, however, only after the first WTO ministerial in Singapore, when a Green Room of 34 countries left all the other ministers loudly wondering why they had come. Contrite promises to ensure it would never happen again led to no changes (Blackhurst 1998, 2001), and the anger erupted at Seattle in 1999. The subsequent debate on internal transparency led to new procedural understandings—see the chair's report in WTO (2000). But developing countries were unhappy with the preparation and conduct of the Doha ministerial in 2001, when final compromises were again hammered out in a Green Room, leading to further debates about WTO procedures before Cancún.

The Green Room, therefore, refers to both a real place and a specific type of meeting, whether of ambassadors in Geneva and chaired by the director-general, of sectoral negotiators and presided over by the chair of a negotiating group (for example, in agriculture, Room F, if held in the WTO building, or Fireside Chats, if convened by the chair in his or her own offices in the absence of the WTO Secretariat), or of ministers at the biennial ministerial conference (the Chairman's Consultative Group in Hong Kong).

The original Green Room practice, carried into the WTO, reflects three negotiating realities: first, that informality is vital; second, that the largest Members, especially the United States and the EU, must always be in the room; and, third, that other interested parties should be engaged in the search for consensus. The key is "inclusiveness": including representatives of all Members and all interests; and "transparency": representatives in the room must fairly articulate the views of their club and expeditiously and comprehensively report on the deliberations; and the chair must fairly present any results when reporting on negotiations in plenary meetings or drafting documents designed to attract consensus.

Part of what the many groupings in Box 3 do, therefore, is to create a claim that one of their number should represent them in a meeting of the Green Room type. A Green Room—often 30 Members, but sometimes fewer depending on the issue or the conjuncture, with Members often represented by two or more ministers or officials—can be a large group for a negotiation, but all key players plus all groups must be represented if it is to be legitimate. In Green Room meetings of ambassadors or ministers, the Members of the original Quad are always represented, along with other leading traders, representatives of coalitions, and coordinators of the regional groups. Membership in a "bridge club" might be a function of a country's weight in the world or of its capacity to influence others (Malnes 1995), but smaller participants seem to be selected as a kind of "contact group" responsible for keeping others informed.[17] Although the procedure is controversial when used to advance negotiations, in Geneva it is used more often for transparency, and not always well—some chairs report difficulties in getting group coordinators to adopt a position or explain the situation to their group.

This unwritten process, based on rules everyone understands, works well enough. Since consensus is, and should be, the decision rule and since participants do not discover information about each other's preferences

---

17. For a discussion of this and other principles of delegation to small groups, see Kahler (1993, 320).

through iterated voting, they must have other structured forms of interaction to learn about the possibility of compromise. Most matters are settled informally because consensus forces actors to find a compromise instead of allowing a vote to decide a controversy. Paradoxically, however, a principle that advantages small Members also disadvantages them, because they are usually not part of small group informal meetings. Some NGOs and developing countries complain about such informal meetings, yet since they are a consequence of the consensus rule, the only alternative would be to insist on a formal vote. If the WTO worked this way, then the General Council would be like the UN General Assembly, where the developing country majority can win any vote it wants, but no issue of importance is ever on the agenda since the largest and most powerful Members never allow a significant issue to be decided in that way. The WTO would then need some sort of executive committee for all the reasons that the UN needs the Security Council. And as with the Security Council, all the real discussions would still take place in informal meetings among the principal players.[18] Creating some sort of standing consultative group— as the Sutherland Report, some governments, former officials, and many academics (including this author) have suggested—would not be an alternative. The Green Room would be replicated at a moment in time, but it would then be stuck in that formation like a fly in amber.

With the WTO's smorgasbord of issues and diversity of Members, clubs ebb and flow as the agenda evolves, which is one of the organization's great strengths—as is the ability of a chair to call a restricted meeting only when the issues are ripe. The effort to crystallize informal bodies that emerge organically might be needlessly divisive without accomplishing much. No group of Members should have to create negotiating obstacles only to get a representative in the room, and no Member should have to block consensus because it did not know what was going on.

Is a New Negotiating Forum Needed?

Judging by the paltry complaints about the Hong Kong ministerial, the effort to improve the negotiation process could be judged a success. And

---

18. On informality in other international organizations, see Sureda (2003); Prantl (2005).

yet the round was suspended six months later. As one senior official said, in all the procedural discussion, "[s]omewhere we forgot to negotiate." A constant refrain among negotiators, going back to before Cancún, is that there is lots of talk, but no negotiations are being joined. Over and over they observe ruefully that nobody can negotiate in public. Members lack a collective understanding of the difference between "technical" work, and isolating those matters on which a ministerial decision is needed. It is easier for ministers to endorse a difficult conclusion than to have to choose among alternatives. With the Green Room used mainly for transparency, is something else needed for negotiations? A representative Green Room or mini-ministerial might be too large to provide leadership, and the old Quad will never return. But some new grouping might be needed to conclude the Doha Round, and it might need to change either the *level* of participation or the *Members* involved.

The first approach to changing the level is to bump up thorny issues to heads of government. Former Canadian prime minister Paul Martin was convinced that an informal meeting of leaders could make a major difference on issues such as agricultural trade reform (Martin 2004). He received little support for the idea. Brazilian president Luiz Lula da Silva angled for months to have a summit devoted only to breaking the Doha logjam. He, too, received little support. In the event, on the margins of their St. Petersburg summit in 2006, the G8 leaders had a meeting with their five regular interlocutors (Brazil, India, China, Mexico, and South Africa), but managed only to tell their trade ministers to get the job done. The ministers then failed.

The effort to engage leaders is based on what people think they remember about the then G7 summit contributions to ending the Tokyo Round in 1978 and the Uruguay Round in 1993. In both cases, however, leaders did little more than ask the Quad trade ministers to meet in advance in order to present a report at the summit. At Tokyo in 1993, leaders were able to "endorse" the progress their trade ministers had made on market access; they then encouraged others to match it, which started the Uruguay Round end game (Hoda 2001, 37). The eclipse of the Quad at the ministerial level since 1999 might have limited the contribution the summit could make, since ministers were not in a position to meet to prepare the discussion. Leaders can force coordination within their own government if the lack of it is the obstacle to agreement. When networks of officials and ministers are fully engaged, however, can leaders add anything? Leaders could not solve the agriculture problem from the top.

The alternative approach to changing levels is to bump things down from ministers to officials. When Robert Zoellick (then United States trade representative) and Pascal Lamy (then EU trade commissioner) dominated the WTO, they sought intimate engagement in all aspects of the negotiations. Many negotiators believe that the organization has yet to recover from the effects of the "Bob and Pascal show." As former bureaucrats, Zoellick and Lamy imagined themselves capable of being their own chief negotiators, and they acted as super technocrats with no need for lesser officials. Their engagement required other countries to engage at the ministerial level, though few ministers other than Brazilian foreign minister Celso Amorim, also a former bureaucrat, could match them. One consequence was the evisceration of the Geneva process when attention shifted to the ministerial level. Now as director-general, Lamy prefers to engage with ministers, rather than ambassadors, which is why the Geneva Green Room is used mostly for transparency, not negotiation. One result of Lamy's apparent assumption that real negotiations take place only among ministers is that chief negotiators and capital-based senior officials do not participate in a continuing process that crosses issues and stitches things together.

Many officials now look at the July Framework of 2004, which relaunched negotiations after the Cancún failure, as a poorly prepared mistake. It is both too detailed and too vague, an overly transparent straitjacket. Many people can be blamed for the process that led to such a text, but a crucial aspect is the premature engagement of ministers who did not have the time or capacity to master all the detail. A perverse consequence of the belief that ministers can settle tough issues on their own is that the moment a mini-ministerial is announced, negotiations in Geneva grind to a halt while delegations wait for the politicians to pronounce. It might be useful for the director-general to travel to capitals, as he did during the winter of 2007, because political leaders are the ones who ultimately must make the tough compromises, but going over the heads of Geneva ambassadors might harm the round.

If changing the level of participation does not help conclude the Doha Round, changing the Members involved might. The Bob and Pascal show also starred Brazil's Celso Amorim and India's trade minister Kamal Nath.

These four tried to sort things out as a "new Quad," and failed. In 2004, they included Australia (representing the Cairns Group), in what became known as the "five interested parties," or FIPs. They next added Japan (representing the G10 group of agricultural importers), making a G6, which met frequently but without success. After the group's spectacular failure to resolve the modalities conundrum in summer 2006, it seemed they would never meet again. When the G4 started meeting again in 2007, they again aroused misgivings among excluded Members about a process outside the WTO that was not really multilateral.

The G6 failed in 2006, as did the G4 at their Potsdam meeting in June 2007, because none of them, and none of the groups they represent, could advance a systemic interest. The group contains the principal antagonists, but they are all publicly committed to their positions, which makes compromises difficult. The old Quad was more effective because one participant, Canada, was not a principal antagonist. Having listened to all the others, Canada was able to put possible compromises forward quietly among senior officials in a way that could advance the negotiations. Some negotiators think it is time, therefore, to change both countries and levels.

Two Uruguay Round events are precedents for changing the countries. The first is the "café au lait" process led by Switzerland and Colombia in 1986. Known as the de la Paix Group, after the hotel where they first met, this group advanced a compromise proposal on the arrangements and subjects for the Uruguay Round that was successful in part because the proponents shared, not specific negotiating objectives, but a commitment to the importance of the round itself. The group was reconstituted in June 1988 with an informal proposal that helped energize the process, partly because of its source, the seven Members Australia, Canada, Hong Kong, Hungary, New Zealand, South Korea, and Switzerland (Croome 1995). Now a group of six Members (Canada, Chile, Indonesia, Kenya, New Zealand, and Norway) are trying something similar. Senior officials, including chief negotiators and sectoral negotiators, met in Oslo in October 2006 to discuss key issues—NAMA and services, in addition to agriculture—that are blocking progress in the negotiations. None of the six belonged to the G6, but they represent many of the major different negotiating groupings at the WTO, North and South. Participants in the "non-G6" have tried not to attract attention to themselves with their subsequent meetings, making it too early to assess the eventual contribution the group might make.

Bottom-Up versus Text-Based Negotiations

The top-down desire of some Members to engage ministers collides with a different WTO pathology, the demand for a bottom-up process. During 2005, the jargon of WTO negotiators began to differentiate between "bottom-up" and "text-based" negotiations. The apparent opposition might seem odd, since in the end any successful negotiation focuses on some sort of text. The roots of the distinction are in the agreement on the organization of the Doha Round (WTO 2002, 4):

- Chairpersons should aim to facilitate consensus among participants and should seek to evolve consensus texts through the negotiation process.
- In their regular reporting to overseeing bodies, Chairpersons should reflect consensus, or where this is not possible, different positions on issues.

The implications of this agreement became clearer in the months before Hong Kong, when Members said that they wanted a "bottom-up" process, meaning that content had to come from the Members, not from a chair trying to guess what compromises might be acceptable. It was too soon, they said, to move to a "text-based" process.[19] Many Members praised the "bottom-up" process in Hong Kong, but that praise might indicate why nothing much happened at that ministerial.

The UN is often seen as a place to register positions. The WTO, however, is not analogous; it should be seen instead as a place to reach agreements on the rules for a global economy. UN practice, familiar to some developing country diplomats who have to cover all the Geneva-based international organizations, leads to misguided demands that all views be reflected in the negotiating texts, whatever the priority attached to them. The risk of such a process was obvious in Seattle, when Members whose

---

19. Members sometimes use a similar term for a different idea: that it can be harmful to draft a text in legal language before the negotiations are ripe.

views made it into the draft text did not want to give up something they thought they had already "won" and could not be seen to back down. Despite the protestations of developing countries and many NGOs (see Kaukab, La Vina, and Yu III 2004), there is no virtue in a text that reflects all the views expressed in the preparatory process, as long as that process allows sufficient opportunities for deliberation.

The formulation tactic of preparing an informal single negotiating text, usually in the chair's name, is a technique often used to stimulate a move toward consensus.[20] As John Odell (2005, 480ff) describes it,

> [t]he chair normally decides what to include in the text after considering Secretariat proposals and conducting extensive "confessionals" with delegations. The [single negotiating text] is meant as a vehicle for moving the large group toward agreement. It is informal in the sense that no delegation has approved it; it is an intermediate starting point for more talks if the parties accept it as such.

Without something on the table, and not realizing that support is limited, Members can retain ideas that have no hope of success.

Despite the many attempts to produce such focal points since the famous "Dunkel text" of 1991 (GATT 1991), chairs of WTO meetings are often criticized for submitting texts "on their own responsibility." It is worth recalling that 80 percent of Dunkel's text had been successfully negotiated before he tabled it, yet it was still rejected. In the most delicate areas, Members are not likely to thank a chair for proposing a formula coefficient. The "reference papers" that chairs prepared in April 2006 were immediately a subject of humorous derision for their hundreds of square brackets [denoting drafting not yet agreed], but they served to show how far apart delegations remained. Negotiators make more progress by adding to the text those things on which they agree than by trying to knock off encrustations of square brackets. Political engagement in trade negotiations is essential—indeed, having regular biennial ministerial

---

20. On the evolution of a single negotiating text in the Law of the Sea negotiations as a technique of "active consensus" and the consequent requirements for a skillful chair, see Buzan (1981).

conferences is one of the things that makes the WTO so much stronger than the GATT—but tough decisions must be well prepared for ministers with limited time and technical knowledge.

A related problem is the reluctance of negotiators in bargaining mode to reveal all their cards until others do, which limits everyone's ability to assess the size of the remaining gaps. If the chair is not allowed to draft a text, and Members cannot do it themselves, then the "bottom-up" process will lead from suspense to collapse. With the failure of the G4 to agree at Potsdam in June 2007, collapse seemed close. When this paper was completed in July 2007, it was thought that the revised modalities papers expected from the NAMA and agriculture chairs by the end of the month might well look like a chairman's text and might even include coefficients, but a prediction on whether these texts will help Members skirt the abyss is impossible.

Can the Trading System Be Governed without Institutional Reform?

If the WTO is medieval, it is because the world is, too. Is reform needed? The trading system works, and it is ruled by law. The only problem is renovation, and that is only a certain problem for those who lack patience (Wolfe 2004a). Finding a multilateral consensus among 150 participants on complex global issues will inevitably and properly be slow (Buzan 1981). Institutional design questions arise because it seems the world has changed, with power more widely dispersed and many more Members wishing, and needing, to play an active role. That power takes two forms, compulsory and institutional. Many more countries have such power, but power as such has not substantially changed. John Ruggie's (1982) central insight, derived from Max Weber, that system change depends on two forces, material power and legitimate social purpose, indicates why, in the current situation, one should expect to see change within the WTO but not of the WTO. The further assumption is that, although these changes might be due to exogenous structural forces that affect the interests of Members, their understanding of these interests is constructed in part through social interaction. The WTO constitutes who is a legitimate actor in its processes, but it is Members that constitute the WTO. Critical mass thus has two dimensions: on a given issue, the Members with the bulk of material power are essential players, yet they will be stymied if the process does not also have the legitimacy that comes with a critical mass of institutional power.

My titular question, therefore, has a curious answer. Would institutional reform have saved the Doha Round? In fact, in the WTO's typical organic evolution, it has so far. The organization as it was at Seattle in 1999 would never have launched the Doha Round, let alone carried it this far. More reform might be needed, but would-be architects should be cautious, following the advice of Ernst Haas, whose first maxim for designers of international organizations was to avoid fundamental constitutional revision in favor of the "self-designing" organization, in which states, secretariat, and NGOs can allow practices to evolve as circumstances change (Haas 1990, 201). Such humility requires institutional designers to know what they can alter at the WTO, and what they cannot.

The Single Undertaking and consensus in conjunction with ever more multilateral negotiating modalities shape the institutional environment that affects every Member's strategy. New rules apply to all, which means that voice matters: all want to participate. While exit is difficult for any country, any Member can deny consensus, in principle if not in practice. All this creates more roles for small groups and coalitions, and a common need for transparency. The logic looks something like Box 4.

What, then, is the flaw in the logic—is it the absence of a forum for bargaining, especially among senior officials, or is something else broken in the WTO? My hypothesis is that good institutional design that contributes to effective and legitimate global governance must facilitate both *bargaining* over known interests and *learning* through arguing and deliberation. Is WTO institutional design appropriate?

If negotiation is all about *interests*, then the agenda is an institutional design choice: what must be in the Single Undertaking? are less-than-universal agreements appropriate? should there be differentiation among developing countries? The criteria in Box 1 imply that the WTO agenda must be limited to issues that are consistent with the objectives and principles of liberalization, and that negotiating modalities should be based on multilateralism and reciprocity. New agreements can support change in the world economy, but only where networks of officials learn to see the WTO as relevant. New rules are easiest to negotiate as horizontal

---

Box 4: *The Logic of WTO Negotiations*

- Diverse issues and Members = Single Undertaking
- Single Undertaking = consensus, not voting
- Consensus = seeking compromise informally on every aspect of the package in a bottom-up process
- Complex issues = need for learning (ministers, officials, farmers)
- Multilateral modalities and 150 Members = small groups
- Multiple groups with unequal weights = need for informal but transparent coordination
- Coordination = Green Room-type meetings

---

amplifications of existing agreements, rather than as new vertical agreements. The criteria in Box 1 have to be met in assessing the existing agenda and proposals for additions. Some of these criteria relate to consistency with WTO norms—things Members cannot control or alter easily; others are about how interests can be aggregated into a deal.

It might be necessary to loosen the Single Undertaking straitjacket (variable geometry, differentiation), but only slightly. Early or partial harvests are a bad idea if they decrease pressures among Members to reach a deal. For example, the 2001 Doha package included a series of interim deadlines that aimed to build confidence by resolving issues of critical concern to developing countries, especially TRIPS and public health (Ismael 2005, 55). For some smaller developing Members, not fully understanding a round's dynamic, the receipt of such a package might have reduced their motivation to look for compromises on other issues. It follows that Members should see duty free/quota free access as part of the Single Undertaking: no country should get what it wants outside the Single Undertaking while remaining in a position to block inside.

If *learning* also matters in negotiations, then collective decision making that engages all Members requires consensual understanding, deliberation that makes effective bargaining legitimate, and domestic resonance. Is the complicated menu of institutional forms shown in Box 2 appropriate? Small, informal meetings can serve fundamental purposes, yet too much transparency too soon can kill frank discussions—and issues need to be ripe before ministers become engaged. The distinction between interests and learning has analytic utility, but if priority must be assigned, then constructivists think learning comes first. The agenda shapes a negotiation and alters the incentive structure, but the agenda itself emerges through discussion. After five and a half years, Members are still learning about what the Doha Single Undertaking must contain. It is better to build the agenda slowly and gradually. Members expected the Doha Round to be a quick sprint compared to the Uruguay Round, then flagellated themselves when it turned into a marathon. Their unnecessary haste might even have provoked some of the institutional reform debates, as some people began to think that things were moving too fast, that they were being railroaded.

The Doha Round's suspended animation notwithstanding, it would be a great mistake to think the WTO is finished. All the difficulties in the Doha negotiations, and all the tensions around Chinese textiles, European airplanes, and US genetically modified corn also notwithstanding, the trading system centered on the WTO is actually working rather well. It might not be efficient, but it is effective. What is striking about the WTO, whether Doha succeeds or not, is the enormous effort states are making to build on their common understanding of how the trading system hangs together, which shows how it shapes their self-understanding.

At the time of writing, no sensible person would confidently predict success or ultimate failure for Doha. Both are still possible, despite the expiration of the United States' "trade promotion authority" in mid-2007.[21] Nor would one confidently predict that the agriculture impasse is the last of its kind—that another just as severe, on an issue not yet properly joined, was not just around the corner. The broad political and economic climate might not be propitious for a deal. The political economy of the Single Undertaking might not be right. In short, a deal might not be attainable this time, even if the WTO were the ideal institution for the purpose. What is clear is that any successful outcome will require a text. If Members cannot find a way to negotiate one, Doha will fail. Lamy may yet release a consolidated negotiating text on the basis of texts prepared

---

21. Trade promotion authority is the current legal name for the fast-track procedure introduced with the *Trade Act of 1974*.

by the chairs of the negotiating groups, but he clearly hopes Members will do it themselves.

The complex WTO process to hammer out a Single Undertaking package for the round appears to have foundered on one issue: finding consensus on reforming global farm trade. That goal, however, is anything but simple. Any deal must accommodate the interests of large commercial farmers in Europe and Brazil as well as those of small rice farmers in the Philippines and dairy farmers in eastern Canada. The current process has emerged as a means to help everybody learn about the issues and the technical complexities of possible solutions. At its periphery, it includes consultations with farm organizations. At its core are discussions among a small group of Members on the elements of a compromise. But any compromise must go beyond farmers. Agriculture might have too many groups, while other domains might have too few either to aggregate interests or to facilitate learning. The mechanisms to ensure transparency are working, but deliberation might be inadequate, resulting in (or from) insufficient consensual knowledge about causal relations. Some, evoking the limited analytic capacity of developing countries both in Geneva and their capitals, call it the "knowledge trap": the round might simply be too complex for most Members to follow, analyze, and comprehend. It is a useful fiction to see "negotiations" as meaning meetings attended by ministers; it is also harmful. The WTO needs a more sophisticated conception of how negotiations should involve economic actors, national governments, senior officials, ambassadors—and ministers.

Procedural improvements by themselves will not solve intractable policy disagreements on major issues, nor can they substitute for the willingness of Members to engage in the give and take of negotiations. The WTO's decisionmaking *principles* might well be suited to the plural global polity, even if its *practices* must keep evolving. The lessons that GATT Contracting Parties learned in the Tokyo Round on how to negotiate domestic issues contributed enormously to the success of the Uruguay Round. Similarly, the lessons now being learned in the Doha Round—on how to manage negotiations on old issues within a different structure of power and how to ensure all Members participate in the process—might also pay off only in a subsequent round. Moreover, codification is not the agreement itself; the journey matters as much as the destination. Just as hundreds of Soviet and US officials learned how to manage their nuclear standoff during the Cold War, even if their thousands of hours of meetings resulted in a small number of agreements (Nye 1987), so the engagement of thousands of officials in the WTO process is shaping the collective management of the global trading system, even when revisions to the WTO treaty prove elusive.

References

Barnett, Michael N., and Raymond Duvall. 2005. "Power in Global Governance." In *Power in Global Governance*, edited by Michael N. Barnett and Raymond Duvall. Cambridge: Cambridge University Press.

Barnett, Michael N., and Martha Finnemore. 2004. *Rules for the World: International Organizations in Global Politics*. Ithaca, NY: Cornell University Press.

Barton, John H., Judith L. Goldstein, Timothy E. Josling, and Richard H. Steinberg. 2006. *The Evolution of the Trade Regime: Politics, Law, and Economics of the GATT and the WTO*. Princeton, NJ: Princeton University Press.

Bazerman, Max H., and Margaret Ann Neale. 1992. *Negotiating Rationally*. New York: Free Press.

Berg, Peter, and Gerald J. Schmitz. 2006. "Strengthening Parliamentary Oversight of International Trade Policies and Negotiations: Recent Developments in Canada and Internationally." PRB 05-68E. Ottawa: Parliamentary Information and Research Service. February.

Black, Duncan, et al. 1998. *The Theory of Committees and Elections*, rev. 2nd ed. Boston: Kluwer Academic.

Blackhurst, Richard. 1998. 'The Capacity of the WTO to Fulfill Its Mandate." In *The WTO as an International Organization*, edited by Anne O. Krueger. Chicago: University of Chicago Press.

———. 2001. "Reforming WTO Decision Making: Lessons from Singapore and Seattle." In *The World Trade Organization Millennium Round: Freer Trade in the Twenty-First Century*, edited by Klaus-Gunter Deutsch and Bernhard Speyer. London, New York: Routledge.

Blandford, David, and Tim Josling. 2006. "Options for the WTO Modalities for Agriculture." IPC discussion paper. Washington, DC: International Food & Agricultural Trade Policy Council. May.

Buzan, Barry. 1981. "Negotiating by Consensus: Developments in Technique at the United Nations Conference on the Law of the Sea." *American Journal of International Law* 75 (2): 324–48.

Capling, Ann, and Kim Richard Nossal. 2003. "Parliament and the Democratization of Foreign Policy: The Case of Australia's Joint Standing Committee on Treaties." *Canadian Journal of Political Science* 36 (4): 835–55.

Charnovitz, Steve. 2004. 'Transparency and Participation in the World Trade Organization." *Rutgers Law Review* 56 (4): 927–59.

Checkel, Jeffrey T. 2001. "Why Comply? Social Learning and European Identity Change." *International Organization* 55 (3): 553–88.

Cho, Sungjoon. 2005. "A Quest for WTO's Legitimacy." *World Trade Review* 4 (3): 391–99.

Claude, Inis L. 1971. *Swords into Plowshares: The Problems and Progress of International Organization*, 4th ed. New York: Random House.

Croome, John. 1995. *Reshaping the World Trading System: A History of the Uruguay Round*. Geneva: World Trade Organization.

Ehlermann, Claus-Dieter, and Lothar Ehring. 2005. "Decision-Making in the World Trade Organization: Is the Consensus Practice of the World Trade Organization Adequate for Making, Revising and Implementing Rules on International Trade?" *Journal of International Economic Law* 8 (1): 51–75.

Esty, Daniel C. 2002. "The World Trade Organization's Legitimacy Crisis." *World Trade Review* 1 (1): 7–22.

Footer, Mary E. 2006. *An Institutional and Normative Analysis of the World Trade Organization*. Leiden, Netherlands: Nijhoff.

Francois, J., W. Martin, and V. Manole. 2005. "Formula Approaches to Liberalizing Trade in Goods: Efficiency and Market Access Considerations. In *Economic Development and Multilateral Trade Cooperation*, edited by Bernard M. Hoekman and Simon J. Evenett. London, Washington, DC: Palgrave Macmillan; World Bank.

GATT (General Agreement on Tariffs and Trade). 1991. "The Draft Final Act Embodying the Results of the Uruguay Round of Multilateral Trade Negotiations." MTN.TNC/W/FA 20. Geneva. December.

Gilligan, M.J. 2004. "Is There a Broader-Deeper Trade-Off in International Multilateral Agreements?" *International Organization* 58 (3): 459–84.

Glania, Guido. 2004. "Various Approaches for Institutional Reforms within the WTO." *Aussenwirtschaft* 59 (1): 7–28.

Goode, Walter. 2003. *Dictionary of Trade Policy Terms*. Cambridge: Cambridge University Press for the World Trade Organization.

Haas, Ernst B. 1990. *When Knowledge Is Power: Three Models of Change in International Organizations*. Berkeley: University of California Press.

Halle, Mark. 2006. "Trade and Environment: Looking beneath the Sands of Doha?" *Journal of European Environment and Planning Law* 3 (2): 107–16.

Halle, Mark, and Robert Wolfe, eds. 2007. *Process Matters: Sustainable Development and Domestic Trade Transparency*. Winnipeg: International Institute for Sustainable Development.

Hampson, Fen Osler, and Michael Hart. 1995. *Multilateral Negotiations: Lessons from Arms Control, Trade and the Environment*. Baltimore: Johns Hopkins University Press.

Hart, H.L.A. 1961. *The Concept of Law*. Oxford: Clarendon Press.

Hawkins, Darren G., David A. Lake, Daniel L. Nielson, and Michael J. Tierney, eds. 2006. *Delegation and Agency in International Organizations*. Cambridge; New York: Cambridge University Press.

Hoda, Anwarul. 2001. *Tariff Negotiations and Renegotiations under the GATT and the WTO: Procedures and Practices*. Cambridge: Cambridge University Press.

Hoekman, Bernard. 2005. "Operationalizing the Concept of Policy Space in the WTO: Beyond Special and Differential Treatment." *Journal of International Economic Law* 8 (2): 405–24.

Howse, Robert, and Kalypso Nicolaidis. 2003. "Enhancing WTO Legitimacy: Constitutionalization or Global Subsidiarity?" *Governance* 16 (1): 73–94.

Hurrell, Andrew. 2006. "Hegemony, Liberalism and Global Order: What Space for Would-Be Great Powers?" International Affairs 82 (1): 1–19.

ICTSD (International Centre for Sustainable Development and Trade). 2006. "The Impact of Sensitive Products on Trade and Development." *Bridges* 10 (7): 3–4.

Ismael, Faizel. 2005. "A Development Perspective on the WTO July 2004 General Council Decision." In *Reforming the World Trading System: Legitimacy, Efficiency, and Democratic Governance*, edited by Ernst-Ulrich Petersmann and James Harrison. Oxford; New York: Oxford University Press.

Kahler, Miles. 1993. "Multilateralism with Small and Large Numbers." In *Multilateralism Matters: The Theory and Praxis of an Institutional Form*, edited by John Gerard Ruggie. New York: Columbia University Press.

Kaukab, Rashid S., Antonio La Vina, and Vicente Paolo B. Yu III. 2004. "From Cancún to Hong Kong: Lessons from the Fifth Ministerial Conference of the World Trade Organization." T.R.A.D.E. Working Paper 20. Geneva: South Centre.

Keck, Alexander, and Patrick Low. 2005. "Special and Differential Treatment in the WTO: Why, When and How?" In *Economic Development and Multilateral Trade Cooperation*, edited by Bernard M. Hoekman and Simon J. Evenett. London, Washington, DC: Palgrave Macmillan; World Bank.

Keohane, Robert O. 1989. "Reciprocity in International Relations." In *International Institutions and State Power: Essays in International Relations Theory*. Boulder, CO: Westview Press.

King, Loren A. 2003. "Deliberation, Legitimacy, and Multilateral Democracy." *Governance* 16 (1): 23–50.

Kono, Daniel Y. 2006. "Optimal Obfuscation: Democracy and Trade Policy Transparency." *American Political Science Review* 100 (3): 369–84.

Lamy, Pascal. 2003. "EU Trade Commissioner Press Conference Closing the World Trade Organization 5th Ministerial Conference (Cancún, Mexico)." PRESS03-028EN. Brussels: European Commission. September 14.

Lawrence, Robert Z. 2006. "Rulemaking Amidst Growing Diversity: A Club-of-Clubs Approach to WTO Reform and New Issue Selection." *Journal of International Economic Law* 9 (4): 823–35.

Levy, Philip I. 2005. "Do We Need an Undertaker for the Single Undertaking? Angles of Variable Geometry." In *Economic Development and Multilateral Trade Cooperation*, edited by Bernard M. Hoekman and Simon J. Evenett. London, Washington, DC: Palgrave Macmillan; World Bank.

Magee, Stephen P., William A. Brock, and Leslie Young. 1989. *Black Hole Tariffs and Endogenous Policy Theory: Political Economy in General Equilibrium*. Cambridge: Cambridge University Press.

Malnes, Raino. 1995. "'Leader' and 'Entrepreneur' in International Negotiations: A Conceptual Analysis." *European Journal of International Relations* 1 (1): 87–112.

Mann, E. 2004. "A Parliamentary Dimension to the WTO—More than Just a Vision?" *Journal of International Economic Law* 7 (3): 659–65.

Martin, Paul. 2004. "The Future of Global Interdependence." Address by the Prime Minister of Canada at the World Economic Forum, Davos, Switzerland. January 23.

Mendelsohn, Matthew, and Robert Wolfe. 2001. "Probing the Aftermyth of Seattle: Canadian Public Opinion on International Trade, 1980-2000." *International Journal* 56 (2): 234–60.

Mendelsohn, Matthew, Robert Wolfe, and Andrew Parkin. 2002. "Globalization, Trade Policy and the Permissive Consensus in Canada." *Canadian Public Policy* 28 (3): 351–71.

Mitzen, J. 2005. "Reading Habermas in Anarchy: Multilateral Diplomacy and Global Public Spheres." *American Political Science Review* 99 (3): 401–17.

Müller, Harald M. 2004. "Arguing, Bargaining and All That: Communicative Action, Rationalist Theory and the Logic of Appropriateness in International Relations." *European Journal of International Relations* 10 (3): 395–435.

Nath, Kamal. 2007. "Commerce and Industry Minister Addresses Oxford University on Future of World Trade Talks." New Delhi: Ministry of Commerce & Industry, Press Information Bureau. May 4.

Nordstrom, Hakan. 2005. "The World Trade Organization Secretariat in a Changing World." *Journal of World Trade* 38 (5): 819–53.

Nye, Joseph S. 1987. "Nuclear Learning and U.S.-Soviet Security Regimes." *International Organization* 41 (3): 371–402.

Odell, John S. 2000. *Negotiating the World Economy*. Ithaca, NY: Cornell University Press.

———. 2002. "The Seattle Impasse and Its Implications for the World Trade Organization." In *The Political Economy of International Trade Law: Essays in Honor of Robert E. Hudec*, edited by Daniel L.M. Kennedy and James D. Southwick. Minneapolis: University of Minnesota Press.

———. 2005. "Chairing a WTO Negotiation." In *Reforming the World Trading System: Legitimacy, Efficiency, and Democratic Governance*, edited by Ernst-Ulrich Petersmann and James Harrison. Oxford; New York: Oxford University Press.

———. 2006. "Introduction." In *Negotiating Trade: Developing Countries in the WTO and NAFTA*, edited by John S. Odell. Cambridge: Cambridge University Press.

Oliver, Pamela E., and Gerald Marwell. 2001. "Whatever Happened to Critical Mass Theory? A Retrospective and Assessment." *Sociological Theory* 19 (3): 292–311.

Olson, Mancur. 1965. *The Logic of Collective Action*. Cambridge, MA: Harvard University Press.

Ostry, Sylvia. 1997. *The Postwar International Trading System: Who's on First?* Chicago: University of Chicago Press.

———. 2004. "External Transparency: The Policy Process at the National Level of the Two Level Game." In *Doha and Beyond: The Future of the Multilateral Trading System*, edited by Mike Moore. Cambridge: Cambridge University Press.

Page, Sheila. 2007. "Policy Space: Are WTO Rules Preventing Development?" ODI Briefing Paper 14. London: Overseas Development Institute. January.

Palmer, Alice, and Richard Tarasofsky. 2007. *The Doha Round and Beyond: Towards a Lasting Relationship between the WTO and the International Environmental Regime*. London: Foundation for International Environmental Law and Development and Chatham House.

Panagariya, Arvind. 2002. "Formula Approaches to Reciprocal Tariff Liberalization." In *Development, Trade and the WTO: A Handbook*, edited by Bernard M. Hoekman, Philip English, and Aaditya Mattoo. Washington, DC: World Bank.

Pauwelyn, Joost. 2005. "The Sutherland Report: A Missed Opportunity for Genuine Debate on Trade, Globalization and Reforming the WTO." *Journal of International Economic Law* 8 (2): 329–46.

Pedersen, Peter Norgaard. 2006. "The WTO Decision-Making Process and Internal Transparency." *World Trade Review* 5 (1): 103–31.

Prantl, Jochen. 2005. "Informal Groups of States and the UN Security Council." *International Organization* 59 (3): 559–92.

Risse, Thomas. 2000. "'Let's Argue!': Communicative Action in World Politics." *International Organization* 54 (1): 1–39.

———. 2005. "Global Governance and Communicative Action." In *Global Governance and Public Accountability*, edited by David Held and Mathias Koenig-Archibugi. Oxford: Blackwell.

Rosendorff, B.P. 2005. "Stability and Rigidity: Politics and Design of the WTO's Dispute Settlement Procedure." *American Political Science Review* 99 (3): 389–400.

Ruggie, J.G. 1982. "International Regimes, Transactions, and Change: Embedded Liberalism in the Post-War Economic Order." *International Organization* 36 (2): 379–415.

Sabel, Robbie. 2006. *Procedure at International Conferences: A Study of the Rules of Procedure at the UN and at Inter-Governmental Conferences.* Cambridge; New York: Cambridge University Press.

Sauvé, Pierre. 2006. "Multilateral Rules on Investment: Is Forward Movement Possible?" *Journal of International Economic Law* 9 (2): 325–55.

———. 2007. "Towards Improved Negotiating Modalities in Services Trade." *Bridges Monthly* 11 (1): 12–14.

Schott, Jeffrey J. 2006, "Completing the Doha Round." Policy Brief 06-7. Washington, DC: Peter G. Peterson Institute for International Economics.

Shaffer, Gregory. 2004. "Parliamentary Oversight of WTO Rule-Making: The Political, Normative, and Practical Contexts." *Journal of International Economic Law* 7 (3): 629–54.

———. 2005. "The Role of the Director-General and Secretariat: Chapter IX of the Sutherland Report." *World Trade Review* 4 (3): 429–38.

Sherman, Richard. 2002. "Endogenous Protection and Trade Negotiations." *International Politics* 39 (December): 491–509.

Stasavage, D. 2004. "Open-Door or Closed-Door? Transparency in Domestic and International Bargaining." *International Organization* 58 (4): 667–703.

Sureda, Andrés Rigo. 2003. "Informality and Effectiveness in the Operation of the International Bank for Reconstruction and Development." *Journal of International Economic Law* 6 (3): 565–96.

Sutherland, Peter, et al. 2004. *The Future of the WTO: Addressing Institutional Challenges in the New Millennium.* Report by the Consultative Board to the Director-General. Geneva: World Trade Organization.

Thompson, Leigh. 1998. *The Mind and Heart of the Negotiator.* Upper Saddle River, NJ: Prentice Hall.

Thompson, Rachel. 2001. "Cross-Cutting ('Formula') Approaches to Multilateral Services Negotiations." In *Trade in Services: Negotiating Issues and Approaches*, edited by Julia Nielson and Pierre Sauvé. Paris: Organisation for Economic Co-operation and Development.

Trebilcock, Michael J., and Robert Howse. 2005. *The Regulation of International Trade*, 3rd ed. London; New York: Routledge.

Van den Bossche, P., and I. Alexovicova. 2005. "Effective Global Economic Governance by the World Trade Organization." *Journal of International Economic Law* 8 (3): 667–90.

VanGrasstek, Craig, and Pierre Sauvé. 2006. "The Consistency of WTO Rules: Can the Single Undertaking Be Squared with Variable Geometry?" *Journal of International Economic Law* 9 (4): 837–64.

Winham, Gilbert R. 1986. *International Trade and the Tokyo Round Negotiation.* Princeton, NJ: Princeton University Press.

———. 2006. *An Institutional Theory of WTO Decision-Making: Why Negotiation in the WTO Resembles Law-Making in the U.S. Congress.* Toronto: University of Toronto, Munk Centre for International Studies.

———. 2007. "The Doha Round and Its Impact on the WTO." In *The WTO after Hong Kong: Progress in, and Prospects for, the Doha Development Agenda*, edited by Donna Lee and Rorden Wilkinson. London: Routledge.

Wolfe, Robert. 2004a. "Crossing the River While Feeling the Stones: Where the WTO Is Going after Seattle, Doha and Cancun." *Review of International Political Economy* 11 (3): 574–96.

———. 2004b. "Informal Political Engagement in the WTO: Are Mini-Ministerials a Good Idea?" In *Trade Policy Research, 2004*, edited by Dan Ciuriak and John M. Curtis. Ottawa: Department of Foreign Affairs and International Trade.

———. 2005. "Decision-Making and Transparency in the 'Medieval' WTO: Does the Sutherland Report Have the Right Prescription?" *Journal of International Economic Law* 8 (3): 631–45.

———. 2006. "New Groups in the WTO Agricultural Trade Negotiations: Power, Learning and Institutional Design." CATPRN Commissioned Paper CP 2006-2. Guelph, ON: Canadian Agricultural Trade Policy Research Network. May.

———. 2007. "Canada's Adventures in Clubland: Trade Clubs and Political Influence." In *Canada among Nations 2007: Room for Manoeuvre*, edited by Jean Daudelin and Daniel Schwanen. Montreal; Kingston, ON: McGill-Queen's University Press.

Wolfe, Robert, and Jesse Helmer. 2007. "Trade Policy Begins at Home: Information and Consultation in the Trade Policy Process." In *Process Matters: Sustainable Development and Domestic Trade Transparency*, edited by Mark Halle and Robert Wolfe. Winnipeg: International Institute for Sustainable Development.

Wolfe, Robert, and Matthew Mendelsohn. 2005. "Values and Interests in Attitudes toward Trade and Globalization: The Continuing Compromise of Embedded Liberalism." *Canadian Journal of Political Science* 38 (1): 45–68.

Woods, Ngaire, and Domenico Lombardi. 2006. "Uneven Patterns of Governance: How Developing Countries Are Represented in the IMF." *Review of International Political Economy* 13 (3): 480–515.

WTO (World Trade Organization). 2000. "Minutes of Meeting Held on 17 and 19 July 2000." General Council WT/GC/M/57. Geneva: WTO. September 14.

———. 2002. "Statement by the Chairman of the General Council." Trade Negotiations Committee TN/C/1. Geneva: WTO. February 4.

———. 2003. "Formula Approaches to Tariff Negotiations, Note by the Secretariat." Negotiating Group on Market Access: TN/MA/S/3/Rev.2. Geneva: WTO. April 11.

———. 2005a. "Doha Work Programme." Ministerial Conference, Sixth Session, Hong Kong, December 13–18. WT/MIN(05)/W/3/Rev.2. Geneva: WTO. December 18.

———. 2005b. "Market Access for Non-Agricultural Products: How to Create a Critical Mass Sectoral Initiative." Negotiating Group on Market Access: Communication from Canada and the United States TN/MA/W/55. Geneva: WTO. April 20.

———. 2006a. "Countries, Alliances and Proposals (Agriculture Negotiations: Backgrounder)." Geneva: WTO. Available from Web site: http://www.wto.org/english/tratop_e/agric_e/negs_bkgrnd04_groups_e.htm; accessed November 2006.

———. 2006b. "Technical Assistance and Training Plan 2007." Committee on Trade and Development WT/COMTD/W/151. Geneva: WTO. October 17.

———. 2006c. "Transparency Mechanism for Regional Trade Agreements: Draft Decision." Negotiating Group on Rules JOB(06)/59/Rev.5. Geneva: WTO. June 29.

Slipping into Obscurity:
Crisis and Institutional Reform at the IMF

Eric Helleiner and Bessma Momani

*   *   *

What a difference a decade can make. Ten years ago, the International Monetary Fund (IMF) was seen as one of the most influential international organizations. Today, top policy makers warn that the IMF might "slip into obscurity" (King 2006, 3). A far-reaching debate about the IMF's future role and purpose is now under way. In the background to the reform debate is the perception that the IMF is losing its influence. Why are IMF reforms being demanded and who is supplying the reform ideas? Are the current reform proposals focused more on process issues or on changes in outcomes? Are they best described as palliative, corrective, or transformative? And how would the Fund be changed by these reforms?

This paper attempts to provide some tentative answers to these questions. In the first section, we argue that two developments are particularly important in explaining why IMF reforms are being demanded: the declining use of IMF loans to middle-income borrowers in the past few years and the increasingly critical view of US policy makers toward the institution since 2000. These developments have prompted Fund management, key

We would like to thank Daniel Bradlow, Miles Kahler, Steve Miller, Arthur Stein, and other participants of the Global Institutional Reform workshop for their helpful comments.

shareholders, and the concerned policy community to supply a number of reform proposals. In the second section, we seek to make sense of these numerous reform proposals, their efficacy, and limitations. The most politically prominent proposals include both process-oriented reforms that focus on governance issues and outcome-oriented reforms that address the Fund's performance. None of the prominent proposals can be described accurately as transformative; instead, the reform debate to date has focused more on proposals that are of the palliative and corrective kind. We conclude by briefly exploring future scenarios of reform implementation, potential roadblocks to reform, and the implications of the current crisis for scholarly debates about the IMF's role in global governance.

What Explains the Demand for IMF Reforms?

The IMF has waned in and out of a position of influence in the international financial system. It has also faced historical moments when its role and purpose have been seriously questioned, and it has adapted to new international economic circumstances. When the IMF was created at the 1944 Bretton Woods conference, it was meant to be at the center of global financial governance, yet US officials almost immediately sidelined it. After the late 1950s, the IMF began to assume a more important position in international financial affairs. This role was short lived, however. The Bretton Woods exchange-rate regime system broke down in the early 1970s, and the IMF's rationale became less clear. After the outbreak of the international debt crisis in the early 1980s, the IMF re-emerged with a renewed mandate that placed it at the center of international financial crisis management vis-à-vis developing countries. The Fund held its influential position in the international financial system through the 1990s, playing a lead role in advising post-communist states in their transition to capitalist economies. At the dawn of the new century, however, the IMF faces yet another crisis of legitimacy and purpose.

Declining Use of IMF Loans

Why are there demands for IMF reform today? One reason is that the use of Fund loans has been rapidly declining. While the IMF still has loans outstanding to dozens of low-income countries, three of its four largest borrowers—Argentina, Brazil, and Indonesia—recently announced they would repay their loans early and would not renew their borrowing from the Fund. Many countries in east Asia have also indicated their disinterest in using the Fund's financial assistance, and have been accumulating large reserves of foreign exchange to protect their countries from future currency crises. In total, the IMF's outstanding lending has declined from US$107 billion at the end of 2003 to US$35 billion in mid-2006 (Snow 2006).

As use of its loans declines, the IMF faces more than a loss of influence, utility, and legitimacy. The Fund's financial balance sheet is affected adversely because its organizational costs are financed by the interest and fees it charges on its loans. The early loan repayments have already triggered budgetary shortfalls for the institution. The IMF's financial woes were highlighted in May 2006, when Managing Director Rodrigo de Rato appointed an expert group to advise him on how to develop alternative sources of income. The importance attached to the task was evident from the group's high-profile membership, which included former US Federal Reserve chairman Alan Greenspan, European Central Bank president Jean-Claude Trichet, and People's Bank of China governor Zhou Xiaochuan.

The declining use of IMF loans is explained partly by the absence of large-scale financial crises in the past few years and partly by the increased availability of funding from private international financial markets for medium-income, "emerging market" countries. Private capital inflows to developing countries in 2005, for example, totaled US$491 billion, a figure that dwarfed IMF lending (World Bank 2006). In a sense, the Fund is returning to a situation similar to that of the 1970s, when its lending was increasingly marginalized by developing countries that had access to abundant private international lending.

The turn away from the IMF by many borrowing countries, however, may not simply be a temporary, cyclical phenomenon, to be reversed when private funding dries up or balance-of-payments crises recur. Instead, and more ominously for the Fund, the turn away appears to be more of a long-term, secular trend linked to the declining legitimacy of the IMF's advice and governance. Its advice has never met with universal approval, but opposition grew particularly intense after the East Asian financial crisis in 1997–98. Many in East Asia and elsewhere blamed the

Fund, not just for worsening the financial crisis, but also for acting as an agent of US interests by attaching intrusive conditions to its loans, as Washington favored.

In East Asian countries, an important rationale for the accumulation of foreign-exchange reserves is the desire to lessen future dependence on the IMF. (Another objective is the goal of preventing their exchange rates from appreciating.) This sentiment has also led East Asian countries to explore the creation of regional mechanisms for balance-of-payments financing. At the height of the East Asian financial crisis, the Japanese government famously put forward the first substantial proposal of this kind: an Asian Monetary Fund that would have offered an alternative source of funding unaccompanied by the intrusive, heavy-handed loan conditionality the IMF was imposing at the time. However, the proposed mechanism received wary reaction from some governments in the region, such as China's, which worried about Japan's intentions (see Lee 2006), and it was shot down by strong opposition from the United States.

Since the failed Asian Monetary Fund initiative, East Asian governments have been working incrementally toward creating a set of regional swap arrangements among monetary authorities, starting with the Chiang Mai Initiative of 2000. As initially implemented, the swaps posed little challenge to the IMF's role in the region—governments requesting more than 10 percent of the regional funds available had to have IMF programs in place. In 2005, however, the figure was raised to 20 percent and, as further changes of this kind appear likely, it seems that the Chiang Mai initiative will indeed work toward diminishing the IMF's role in the region. Similarly, the Asian Development Bank is also beginning to take on roles, such as surveillance functions, that the IMF traditionally performed. The momentum of creating and expanding alternate regional mechanisms in East Asia to avoid future dependence on the IMF appears to be accelerating.

Growing dissatisfaction with the IMF's advice also helps to explain the declining use of IMF loans in Latin America. The IMF's intellectual standing in that region was severely undermined by the Argentine economic collapse of late 2001. Argentina had been under the watchful eye of the IMF for ten years, and was widely seen as one of the IMF's "star pupils" in the region throughout the 1990s. Many saw the country's sudden economic crisis—rightly or wrongly—as evidence of the failure of the

IMF's free market-oriented ideas and its ability to warn of and predict looming crises. Policymakers in many of the left-of-center governments that have come to power across Latin America in the past few years have been critical of the IMF's advocacy of the "Washington Consensus."

Argentina's subsequent negotiations with the IMF under the administration of Nestor Kirchner also undermined the Fund's powerful image. Using the Fund's large financial exposure to the country as a source of leverage, the Argentine government succeeded in extracting further funding, with much looser conditions than the norm, and in segmenting its private creditors to its advantage (Cooper and Momani 2005; Helleiner 2005). In March 2004, Argentina and Brazil also agreed to adopt some common positions in negotiating with the IMF on issues such as primary budget surplus targets and the definition of government spending (Helleiner 2005). Their coordinated stance culminated in their near-simultaneous announcements in early 2006 of early repayments of all IMF loans—announcements that were widely portrayed across the region as a kind of boycott of, or declaration of independence from, the Fund.

Some governments in Latin America, like those in East Asia, have proposed regional financial facilities to replace the IMF. The most enthusiastic advocates of these regional proposals are usually those most critical of the IMF, its advice, and the Washington Consensus. Unsurprisingly, Venezuelan president Hugo Chávez has suggested the most ambitious of proposals: the creation of a *Banco del Sur* to serve the countries of Latin America exclusively and bypass the IMF.

Discontent with the IMF in borrowing countries is not restricted to Latin America and East Asia; it has also been intense in other regions, particularly sub-Saharan Africa, where the intrusive conditions attached to IMF loans and the neoliberal nature of IMF policy advice have attracted many critics. Facing large debts and lacking the access to capital markets available to their Latin American and East Asian counterparts, however, most sub-Saharan African governments have found it difficult to cut their financial dependence on the IMF. Without the tool of "exit," sub-Saharan African governments have been restricted to using the tool of "voice." Their voice, however, has attracted much less attention in debates about the future of the IMF—not least because of the nature of IMF governance structures, which, as we discuss below, restricts the influence of these smallest quota holders.

In short, the decline of Fund legitimacy in the eyes of potential IMF borrowers has been a precipitating factor behind the declining use of IMF loans. A key reason that countries are demanding reform of the IMF today is potential borrowers' dissatisfaction with the Fund, a development that has hurt the IMF's own finances. Reforming the IMF to restore its legitimacy, some believe, is a way of bringing borrowers back to the Fund and reasserting the Fund's place in global financial governance.

US Criticism of the Fund

The IMF faces calls for reform not just because many potential borrowers are turning away from it, but also because of increasing criticism it receives from many of the countries that act as creditors to the institution. Criticism from nongovernmental organizations (NGOs) in northern countries, often in alliance with their counterparts in the South, has focused on the social, political, and environmental costs of IMF lending programs in debtor countries. The fact that the Fund has felt compelled in recent years to engage more systematically with northern and southern NGOs is clear evidence of these groups' growing influence. Although these critical voices have contributed to the crisis of legitimacy the Fund faces, their actual impact in changing IMF policies and behavior is the subject of considerable scholarly debate.

What is clearer to judge is the impact of recent criticism from the IMF's chief creditor: the US government. Throughout the 1990s, the Clinton administration supported IMF efforts to address financial crises with large-scale rescue packages, beginning with the 1994 Mexican crisis through to the 1997–98 East Asian crisis. In contrast, the Bush administration has taken a different view and course, as many of its leading officials have sought actively to constrain the Fund's influence. This US policy shift has contributed significantly to the IMF's diminishing role in global finance in recent years.

Ironically, some of the increasing US skepticism of the IMF has come from policy makers of a free market or "neoliberal" persuasion. During the second half of the 1990s, many neoliberal US policy makers were highly critical of the IMF's bailout lending, arguing that such large-scale rescue packages distorted proper market signals and encouraged reckless lending by international investors. To address this "moral hazard" problem, Fund critics felt it was necessary to scale back—or even to end altogether—the practice of providing international bailouts. Such a shift in dealing with financial crises, Fund critics argued, not only would change market expectations but also "bail in" foreign private creditors by forcing them to accept sovereign defaults and debt restructuring at the outset of a crisis.

Even before the Bush administration assumed office, these arguments for a new approach to sovereign debt crises had prompted the IMF to push more actively for "private sector involvement" during South Korea's financial crisis in 1998 and subsequent crises in Ecuador, Pakistan, and Ukraine through 1999 and 2000 (Blustein 2001, ch.7, 9). Nevertheless, it was the election of George W. Bush that substantially boosted the new "bail-in" approach. Key officials in the Bush administration were convinced of the moral hazard critique of IMF bailouts, including then treasury secretary Paul O'Neill and his under secretary for international affairs, John Taylor (Suskind 2004, 173, 175, 243–44). As a professor at Stanford University, Taylor had called for the IMF's abolition on moral hazard grounds: "It should be abolished, I agree. And I'd like to do it slowly in a way that takes some of the talents there and use it in a more effective way" (quoted in Helleiner 2005, 967).

Opposition to large-scale IMF bailouts similarly came from the US Congress, which had been increasingly critical of the IMF since the 1994 Mexican crisis. Congressional opposition grew during the 1997–98 East Asian crisis, when the Clinton administration asked Congress to approve a US$18 billion increase in IMF funding. At the time, the IMF's resources had been severely depleted by a number of large-scale bailouts. The funding increase passed the Senate, but it was much less popular with House Republicans, including prominent figures such as House majority leader Dick Armey and chair of the Joint Economic Committee James Saxton. Some Republicans were influenced by the moral hazard critique of IMF bailout packages, while others were driven by a more general distrust of multilateral institutions and a desire to save US taxpayers' money. In the end, the funding proposal passed, but subject to certain provisions that notably included the establishment of a congressional commission to review US policy toward the IMF and other international financial institutions. The so-called Meltzer Commission—headed by Allan Meltzer, a conservative economist who had advocated abolishing the IMF in the mid-1990s (see Meltzer 1995)—published its report in March 2000 recommending a dramatic scaling back of the IMF's activities (United States 2000). Many of the commission's recommendations were supported by key Republicans in Congress, who have continued to welcome the advice of Meltzer and other commission members throughout the Bush administration.

The views of Bush administration officials and members of Congress have contributed to the recent diminution of the IMF's global role and influence. In the Bush administration's first months in office, officials publicly signaled their intention not to bail investors out of future sovereign debt crises. In late 2001, they found an opportunity—in the context of Argentina's dramatic financial crisis—to translate their words into action (or, more accurately, inaction). After initially backing an IMF loan to Argentina in August 2001, the Bush administration refused to support further IMF assistance when Argentina failed to meet IMF targets, a decision that acted as one of many catalysts of that country's massive financial crisis in December 2001. When Argentina defaulted on its loans—marking the largest sovereign default in history—the United States refrained from supporting any IMF intervention in the crisis, defending its approach on the grounds of stopping moral hazard. During the subsequent lengthy negotiations over the 2002–05 period to restructure Argentina's massive debt, Bush administration officials also undermined the IMF's bargaining power at some key moments—much to the consternation of other creditor governments (Helleiner 2005).

Throughout the Bush administration's tenure, political support for new IMF funding has also been less forthcoming. Indeed, during the debate in 2004 and 2005 about how to fund the cancellation of the debts of what are referred to as Heavily Indebted Poor Countries, US officials actively sought to force the IMF to bear the brunt of the costs, particularly through its Poverty Reduction and Growth Facility (PRGF), a lending facility to low-income countries that the Meltzer Commission had recommended be abolished to get the IMF out of the business of long-term development assistance to poor countries. The message appeared clear: the IMF's lending programs for poor countries had become too ambitious, and the Fund should accept responsibility for its past bad lending decisions (Helleiner and Cameron 2006).

US policy makers have also opposed the expansion of the IMF's mandate at some critical instances. Perhaps the most important such moment was the debate between 2001 and 2003 about the creation of a Sovereign Debt Restructuring Mechanism (SDRM).[1] The Argentine crisis highlighted that, if the IMF was to refrain from large-scale bailout lending, there would be more defaults by sovereign debtors. To make debt restructuring more orderly, the IMF's deputy managing director Anne Krueger suggested in November 2001 that the Fund set up a SDRM to legitimize sovereign debt defaults and prompt private foreign creditors to join debt-restructuring negotiations. Krueger, a free market US Republican, had been appointed only a few months earlier with the strong support of the Bush administration and was less supportive of IMF bailouts than had been her predecessor, Stanley Fischer. She felt, however, that the post-bailout world had left a "gaping hole" in the international financial architecture that the IMF should fill (Krueger 2001, 1).

Krueger's proposal generated enormous attention and gained the tentative support of treasury secretary Paul O'Neill and that of officials in Canada, the United Kingdom, and a number of other European countries. The proposal also encountered powerful critics, however, including the international investor community, which preferred a more market-oriented approach, and some emerging market countries—most notably Mexico and Brazil, which worried about its impact on their ability to borrow from private markets. Particularly important, though, was criticism from US officials such as Taylor and prominent Republican members of Congress. A key source of opposition within some US policymaking circles was the belief that the SDRM would reinforce the power of the IMF. As Congressman Jim Saxton put it, Krueger's proposal represented another example of IMF "mission creep," and it "would have the effect of compensating the IMF for the reduction in its influence arising from a more restricted policy towards international bailouts" (Saxton 2002).

When O'Neill left as treasury secretary in December 2002, Krueger lost a key supporter, and the SDRM proposal was taken off the table at the

---

1. This section draws on Helleiner (2006).

IMF's April 2003 steering group meeting of the International Monetary and Financial Committee. If the SDRM had succeeded, it would have left the Fund at the center of the governance of sovereign debt crises in the post-bailout age. As we discuss below, however, the failure of the initiative represented an important turning point for the IMF: the Fund was being assigned a more marginal role in the governance of international financial crises.

What Kind of Reforms Have Been Proposed?

With critics in many parts of the world and a shrinking set of borrowers, the IMF's future in global governance is uncertain. Some opponents of the Fund—on both the left and right of the political spectrum—would like to see it abolished, and regard its current vulnerability as a political opportunity to push for this outcome. But international organizations rarely die. Reform is the more common fate, and the IMF certainly has experienced its share of transformations during its 60-year history. What are the most politically prominent proposals for reform today? In what direction might these proposed reforms take the Fund?

Governance Reforms: The Quest to Re-establish Legitimacy

Among those advocating reform of the IMF, there is near-universal agreement that a top priority is an overhaul of the Fund's governance. This focus reflects the widespread sentiment that the Fund is facing a serious crisis of legitimacy that can be addressed only by creating governance structures that are more open to the voices of those disaffected with the institution and more reflective of changing political and economic realities.

Chairs and Shares

Perhaps the issue highest on the agenda of those advocating IMF governance reform is the reallocation of quotas (and, thus, votes) and the composition of chairs on the IMF's Executive Board. Already, at a number of moments in its history, the IMF has seen such changes take place to reflect changing political and economic realities. At the IMF's founding, for example, the United States' share was more than 30 percent of total votes; today, after numerous adjustments, that share is 17 percent. Similarly, the Executive Board started with 12 executive directors; the five largest contributors were assigned a single seat each and other members were represented by constituency groups. Today, however, the number of executive directors has risen to 24, and single-country constituencies have been added for Saudi Arabia, China, and Russia.

It is worth highlighting that these changes generally reflect political bargains, rather than technical economic arguments. In the current debate, considerable attention has been devoted to various economic calculations when making arguments for changes to specific countries' relative positions. This attention is understandable, but its importance should not be overstated. Historically, economic calculations for countries' relative quotas and executive director seat allocations were used only after the fact to justify decisions already made on political grounds (Momani forthcoming).

Given the crisis of legitimacy the Fund faces, the political circumstances would seem ripe for a major reallocation of "chairs and shares." Indeed, Managing Director de Rato has effectively highlighted the importance of seat reallocations by backing a two-stage process to address governance reform. In the first stage, Fund members attending the September 2006 annual meeting in Singapore endorsed ad hoc quota increases for at least four countries—China, South Korea, Mexico, and Turkey—whose existing shares were particularly out of line with their growing economic significance.

The agenda and timeline for the second stage have been left more open ended, but are to be decided through 2007. Asian governments are calling for a more systematic redistribution of quotas and seats on the Executive Board in order to boost their region's share. The economic case for this reform is clear, and underrepresentation of Asian economies in the IMF has been well documented (see Rapkin and Strand 2003). The political case is equally compelling, since it is the drift of Asian countries away from the institution that poses one of the most serious threats for the Fund. Importantly, US policy makers have backed calls for an increase in Asian voting weight, although they have also called for a rationalization of overall Executive Board representation (Snow 2006).

Supporters of developing countries have also argued for enhancing low-income country votes and voice at the Executive Board. Evans and Finnemore (2001) note that the combined vote of all 80 low-income countries that qualify for the Fund's PGRF amounts to roughly 10 percent, while that of the ten largest industrialized countries is 52 percent. Democratizing the IMF, some argue, requires the board to better reflect the Fund's main clients and frequent users—that is, borrowing low-income countries.[2] Former executive director Cyrus Rustomjee (2004), who represented the sub-Saharan constituency, also suggests that enhancing developing members' voice in IMF decision making would translate into loan conditionality that better emphasized long-term economic growth. Critics of the Washington Consensus add that having more developing countries on the board would allow them to better resist "pressure to liberalize" and to press for more staff recruitment from such countries (Birdsall 2003, 12).

In formulating ways to enhance developing countries' influence on the Executive Board, Ariel Buira, former executive director and head of an agglomeration of member countries known as the Group of 24, suggests developing a new quota formula that would use purchasing power parity (instead of market exchange rates) and population as factors for adjusting gross domestic product in the calculation of countries' respective quotas (Buira 2002, 2003).[3] This would not, however, change representation of less populous and relatively poor countries in sub-Saharan Africa. To give them more votes, it would be necessary to restore the importance of "basic votes": as an equalizing measure, all members of the IMF were allocated 250 votes when the institution was founded. But these votes have not been changed since, and their significance has diminished over the years from their original level of 11 percent of total votes to approximately 2 percent

---

2. Kelkar, Yadav, and Chaudhry (2004, 740) argue that restoring basic votes would help enhance the perceived legitimacy of the Fund in developing countries. For a cautionary note on the limits of this democratization argument, however, see Birdsall (2003), who argues that many low-income countries are not developed democracies and their presence on the Executive Board might not be representative of their many disenfranchised citizens. Similarly, Kahler (2006, 266) adds that the IMF should not be compared to national parliaments, but treated as a "delegated authority" and compared to judiciaries or central banks.

3. Camdessus (2005) also thinks that population deserves more weight.

today because of the entrance of new members and quota increases. Managing Director de Rato has responded positively to the idea of increasing basic votes. African policy makers are also pressing for the creation of an additional third seat on the board because of the heavy workload of the existing two executive directors.[4]

Any effort to assign more votes and Executive Board seats to emerging market and low-income countries, of course, would mean relatively lower shares for other countries, a kind of reform that past history suggests would be politically difficult to undertake. Throughout the 1970s and 1980s, for example, efforts of Japanese policy makers to increase substantially their quota share met with considerable resistance from the existing powers, which would have lost relative voting shares. The prospect of a major shift today seems even more dim, since an overall increase in IMF quotas is unlikely given the United States' clear opposition to such a move. In the past, the reallocation of voting shares usually took place in the context of quota increases—that is, countries did not see their absolute quota reduced but rather their relative share.

Still, many argue that the push for closer European integration provides a unique window of opportunity for substantial change. Those who call for reform of the IMF's "chairs and shares" tend to agree that European chairs are overrepresented on the Executive Board; indeed, members of the European Union appoint or play a major role in selecting 10 of the 24 directors. This distribution of seats in favor of Europe might have reflected that region's economic and political weight in the early years of the Fund's history. Today, however, there is a clear economic shift away from Europe to emerging market economies that puts Europe's pre-eminence at the board in doubt. Both consolidation of the European Union and its adoption of a common currency further support calls for a more consolidated European representation. Truman (2006) proposes a relatively straightforward method of consolidation: countries that are not members of the European Union should not be members of EU-led constituencies, while Ireland, Spain, and Poland should join EU-led constituencies. This change would reduce the number of EU or potential EU executive directors by three or four.

---

4. "First Multilateral Consultation to Focus on Global Imbalances," *IMF Survey*, June 26, 2006, p. 196.

A more radical proposal would be to consolidate the members of the European Union or perhaps just the euro zone into one seat (Camdessus 2005; Bini Smaghi 2006), which some US policy makers have noted would provide a means of increasing the number of seats for other regions.[5] There is also support in Europe for the idea. The European Central Bank's Lorenzo Bini Smaghi, for example, argues that consolidating the chairs of euro-area countries into one effective seat would actually enhance EU voting, power, and voice on the Executive Board (2006). Former German executive director Fritz Fischer adds that a consolidated EU seat would even help in efforts to harmonize European foreign policy and should be actively pursued (2006; for a critique see Dabrowski 2006). The European Parliament has also endorsed the idea of consolidating EU seats, and has called on its members to "work towards a single voting constituency" (European Parliament 2006, 4).

There is, of course, some European resistance to these proposals. Some outside Europe also worry that a reduction in European influence might undermine the region's commitment to the institution. It is worth highlighting, however, that the opposite could also result. If the European Union consolidated its vote under the existing quota distribution, its quota would be the largest in the Fund, a fact that might give it new influence and interest in the institution.

To ease European resistance, it might be worth considering changes to IMF decisionmaking rules. At present, the Executive Board, using a simple majority, decides most day-to-day issues, but special majorities are required for a number of important changes to governing issues. During the mid-1970s, US resistance to having its share reduced to below 20 percent in order to have more votes allocated to Japan and Germany was softened by an agreement to raise the threshold required for qualified majority votes from 80 percent to 85 percent. Today, a similar change—or an alteration of the kinds of issues required for qualified majority voting—might help to address European concerns. It might also help to provide a greater voice for poorer countries (Woods 2006, 210).

---

5. See the comments by Tim Adams in "First Multilateral Consultation," *IMF Survey*, June 26, 2006, p. 105.

Beyond Chairs and Shares

Despite the attention given to "chairs and shares," their importance should not be overstated. The IMF's Executive Board, after all, rarely takes votes and usually operates on a "consensus" basis. Insiders also report that the board's chair, the managing director, often plays a dominant role in board discussions. The kinds of changes to chairs and shares that are likely to find enough support are also likely be rather limited.[6] In this context, some analysts suggest that other governance reforms might, in fact, be more significant in enhancing the Fund's legitimacy (see Kenen 2006). A number of these alternatives also have the benefit of being easier to implement politically.

One of the most important ways to enhance legitimacy would be to modernize the Fund's procedure for selecting the managing director, a procedure that remains trapped in a time warp of the 1940s. Since the Fund was created, European members and the United States have conspired to allow Europe to nominate its head, while the United States nominates the president of the World Bank. This process remains unchanged, even as other international institutions have developed more transparent, merit-based, and inclusive mechanisms for selecting their heads. Fund reformers call for the process to include candidates selected on merit as well as elections without citizenship restrictions (Ostry and Zettelmeyer 2005, 17). Former managing director Michel Camdessus has also urged the United States and Europe to forgo their "privileges" in choosing the Fund's leadership; he proposes instead opening up the leadership selection process to allow for competition, arguing that this would help enhance organizational and external legitimacy (2005, 11). Kahler (2001, 92–98), however, cautions against an overly transparent and competitive process, which he says could lead to deadlock, as the case of selecting the head of the World Trade Organization has demonstrated. Instead, he recommends "a process of restrained competition" in which minimum qualifications would be agreed upon, search committees would establish a qualified list of possible

---

6. As Mervyn King has put it, a comprehensive deal to rearrange chairs and shares "will be extremely difficult to reach" (2006, 14).

candidates, and national governments would narrow down the list to a veto-proof shortlist of nominees.

Strong normative arguments exist in favor of democratizing the process; clearly, however, the hesitation of US and European political capitals to forgo their "privileges" remains a key obstacle. To initiate such a change, Kahler (2006, 265) suggests that members who want to change the status quo should "withhold their support" for a candidate selected by the Europeans and the Americans in the next search for a managing director unless a process of competition and meritocracy is used.

Another set of important reform proposals concerns the functioning of the Executive Board. Lombardi and Woods (2006b) argue that reallocating chairs might be less necessary if improvements could be made to the constituency system, which pools votes and shares into one elected executive director. They observe that constituency members who do not hold a chair on the board have less voice and voting power in the organization, because chairs do not cast split votes and often reflect the will of their own capitals. This leaves many IMF members unable to have their voices heard on the board in an effective manner. Lombardi and Woods recommend enhancing the capabilities of chairs and improving their accountability to constituency members.

A number of proposals have also been made to enhance the ability of the Executive Board to provide the kind of strategic political direction that might improve the IMF's legitimacy among its member country governments. As King (2006) has highlighted, executive directors are currently engaged primarily in time-consuming micromanagement of the Fund's activities. The board meets several times a week, and directors are left swimming in a mass of detailed paperwork; in 2004 alone, they were given 70,000 pages of material to absorb and they generated another 10,000 pages themselves. Directors also do not always have the political weight in their own countries to go much beyond repeating the official positions of their governments on various issues. Indeed, they are not even fully accountable to national governments in the way that an ambassador is, and it is the Fund that pays their salaries (Momani 2004; Woods 2006, 192).

In King's view and that of Bank of Canada governor David Dodge (2006), the Fund would be better served by a nonresident board (as John Maynard Keynes had suggested when the Fund was established) that would meet infrequently—perhaps six to eight times per year—and that could be made up of more senior officials from member governments (see also Kelkar, Chaudhry, and Vanduzer-Snow 2005). Such a reform would enable the board to assert its authority more decisively on big-picture issues in a way that ensured that the Fund's strategic direction better reflected the preferences of its member governments.

A nonresident board would, of course, provide the Fund's managing director and staff with greater independence in their day-to-day operations, which could affect perceptions of the IMF's legitimacy in a couple of ways. Freed of direct political oversight over day-to-day affairs, IMF staff would be better able to offer more dispassionate advice on key issues facing member governments, thus bolstering the credibility and authority of the Fund's "surveillance" role—staff would be less apt to resort to "clientism." Such a reform might also enhance the Fund's role in prescribing conditionality—staff might be better able to resist the kind of micromanaging of conditionality by the United States that appeared to take place during the Asian currency crisis.

The other possible effect on perceptions of the IMF's legitimacy is that, without the day-to-day watchful eye of the Executive Board, Fund staff might prescribe more intrusive conditionality and take fewer considerations of political economy into account when devising loan programs. In this vein, the Executive Board ensures that IMF staff do not prescribe conditionality that is deemed politically damaging to member states (see Momani 2004). A more technocratic-based IMF might reduce the Fund's perceived legitimacy if borrowing member states were pressured to accept more intrusive and politically impractical conditionality.[7]

A more ambitious proposal to reform the functioning of the Executive Board comes from Michel Camdessus. Instead of altering the board's mandate in King's way, Camdessus calls for the creation of an IMF "council," meeting perhaps four times a year, that could assume responsibility for strategic decision making. As he notes, the creation of such a council was, in fact, endorsed at the time of the 1976 Jamaica amendment

---

7. King (2006) acknowledges that this reform would have to be accompanied by mechanisms to keep the managing director and staff accountable. He suggests that an Independent Evaluation Office could help in this task.

of the IMF Articles of Agreement. Camdessus suggests that the council—whose membership he leaves unspecified—could replace the advisory International Monetary and Financial Committee, which has become more of a communiqué-writing body than a creative decisionmaking forum. Under Camdessus's proposal, the existing Executive Board would remain in place, but it would focus on more technical issues in ways that would help to keep management accountable. Kenen (2006) goes even further to suggest that the Executive Board be transformed into a 16-member managing board of experts who would not represent governments but would be nominated by the managing director, with consideration given to the differing interests of the members, and would work without weighted voting.

A further proposal to increase the Fund's legitimacy among developing countries is to reform the recruitment, training, and deployment of its staff. Evans and Finnemore (2001) argue that such a reform could play a major role in enhancing both the voice of developing countries in the Fund and their sense of ownership of the institution. They suggest a range of reforms, including allocating more support staff to developing country executive directors and drawing more on people with "hands-on" knowledge of concrete circumstances in developing countries.

Other analysts have also been particularly critical of the IMF's narrow base of recruitment (see Momani 2005b). Camdessus, discussing the IMF staff's "cloning syndrome," argues that the Fund would "benefit greatly in selecting for their dialogues with officials facing the complexities of political life, staff members with national experience, or a broader culture in social studies than the one that is generally required for their recruitment" (2005, 9).

One noteworthy feature of the debate on reforming IMF governance in the past year or two has been the relative absence of proposals seeking to involve NGOs more formally in IMF decision making. Proposals of this kind were popular in the wake of massive societal protests against the IMF and other international economic institutions during the late 1990s and early 2000s (see Scholte 2002; Thirkell-White 2004). To enhance its relations with civil society and the NGO community, the IMF has become more transparent in its publications, including the release of more staff reports and Executive Board documents, though only after a five- or ten-year embargo. Many have argued that this is not enough, however, and that, for the IMF to be credible and accountable, it should release Executive Board votes and minutes immediately. Proposals have also been made to establish more formal linkages between the IMF and NGOs, such as the creation of an IMF ombudsman and an IMF-NGO liaison committee (Bradlow 2006).

At the current political conjuncture, the IMF reform debate has shifted to one that is more traditionally state-centric, no doubt reflecting the fact that the nature of the challenges to the IMF have shifted. Today, attention is devoted increasingly to the goal of re-establishing the Fund's credibility and legitimacy in the eyes of those national governments that have drifted away from the institution. The chances of transformative change have diminished, however, as states increasingly participate in and guide the process and are often more reluctant to redistribute power in the organization.

The IMF's Performance: Refocusing Its Activities

Although governance reforms are clearly fundamental to restoring the IMF's global standing, many also argue that reform of the Fund's performance is also important to its future. Particularly prominent have been calls for the IMF to strengthen its surveillance role and to redefine its lending and crisis-management roles.

Refocusing on Surveillance

When the Fund was created in 1944, its architects hoped the institution would draw attention to the financial needs of the world economy as a whole and discourage countries from returning to the "beggar-thy-neighbor" economic policies of the 1930s. In the 1970s, the IMF was given a formal mandate to engage in "surveillance" of member countries' policies (Pauly 1997). In the current context, many see surveillance of financial sector policies, exchange rates, and capital accounts of both systemically important countries and emerging market economies as a key Fund function. Indeed, many argue that the surveillance role should now be seen as the central *raison d'être* of the institution.

Fund officials have supplied a number of reform proposals to expand and enhance IMF surveillance. The current managing director, Rodrigo de Rato, has argued for increasing Fund surveillance by targeting the monitoring of systematically important countries and global capital markets' vulnerabilities. To accomplish this, de Rato has merged the International Capital Market Department and the Monetary and Financial Systems Department to create what he calls a "single centre of excellence."[8] The Fund has recently argued that surveillance is the organization's comparative advantage over financial institutions and domestic governments because it can provide impartial analysis (Ragan 2006).

To improve surveillance, the IMF research department's Ostry and Zettelmeyer (2005, 8–9) suggest that the Fund end its ambiguous evaluation of member states and instead openly rate members on their overall performance in a publicized "report card." The report card would also determine the level of financing a country could receive, as an added measure to preventing crises. Edwin Truman also supports such a reform, calling on the IMF to start "naming and shaming" its members, including systemically powerful countries such as the United States (2005, 13). To date, Truman argues, the IMF has been soft on member states that have not followed its advice in formal (Article IV) consultations, an approach that harms the international economic system while systemically important countries remain insulated from crisis. The Fund, Truman argues, needs to act more like an "umpire" rather than just an "adviser" or "lender" (45). This would require the Fund to get specific about countries' wrongdoings and to detail how to correct errors. Bank of Canada governor David Dodge has reiterated this suggestion, urging the IMF to become an "independent, impartial umpire, ready to call out countries that break the rules" and recalling Keynes' hope that the Fund would engage in "ruthless truth-telling" (Dodge 2006).

Some Fund staff have expressed concerns about this kind of umpire role, arguing that it might compromise the Fund's ability to act as trusted advisor to governments. One difficulty, according to Michael Mussa, former head of IMF Research, is organizational. He notes that staff act one day as "social worker," sympathetically prescribing conditionality, then the next day as "tough cop," enforcing rules of conduct perceived to be for the benefit of the economic community (2002, 67). Mussa suggests that staff are

---

8. "First Multilateral Consultation," *IMF Survey*, June 26, 2006, p. 51.

under pressure to appease country officials, with whom staff work closely, producing watered-down bilateral surveillance reports. Kahler (2006, 267) suggests that one way to insulate staff from such pressure would be to release bilateral Article IV surveillance reports immediately after consultations end. Both Mussa (2002) and Kahler (2006) go so far as to suggest some bureaucratic reorganization to separate surveillance work from area departments, thereby removing the tendency to produce watered-down assessments and chummy IMF-government relations. Ideally, an independent IMF surveillance department would remove staff involved in bilateral surveillance from area departments in which loan programs are designed and conditionality prescribed (Mussa 2002, 69–70).

Many analysts have devoted particular focus to reinvigorating the Fund's surveillance of exchange rates. Goldstein (2006) argues that the IMF needs to return to its traditional role of monitoring exchange rates, and that it has simply not been successful in pressuring countries—particularly, in recent years, China—to change their policies. He recommends the Fund issue reports on exchange-rate policies and that it shame countries using manipulative practices. Chinese officials, however, have understandably challenged the idea of pressing the Fund to focus on monitoring exchange rates, maintaining that their country needs to retain sovereignty in determining its exchange-rate policies (Zhou 2006, 4).

Others point out that, apart from macro-level surveillance of world economic trends, such as those found in its publication, *World Economic Outlook*, Fund staff concentrate their surveillance on a country-by-country basis. This practice has prevented staff from appreciating countries' policy linkages and their spillover effects; it might also explain why the staff's toolkit for warning of financial contagion remains weak.

In response to this criticism, Managing Director de Rato has announced the IMF would expand surveillance to include "multilateral consultations" —essentially a forum in which systematically important countries would discuss and debate specific issues of global economic significance in an effort to thwart the unraveling of the world economy, with the first multilateral consultation involving China, the euro area, Japan, Saudi Arabia, and the United States.[9] Some see this as a way of appeasing the United

---

9. "First Multilateral Consultation," *IMF Survey*, June 26, 2006, p. 179.

States by raising the issue of the overvalued Chinese currency, but de Rato has stated that the forum would also be used to tackle many global issues, including the effect of US current account deficits on external indebtedness (de Rato 2006a). More ambitiously, Camdessus argues that the IMF should take an active role in reinvigorating efforts to create a new Plaza or Louvre Accord. The IMF, he argues, is best suited to do this "because there is no other ... legitimate, global forum to tackle such a systemic problem" (Camdessus 2005, 4).

Devoting more attention to this kind of multilateral surveillance activity would be a shift in focus for the IMF; Lombardi and Woods (2006a) note that only 10 percent of the Executive Board's time is currently devoted to multilateral surveillance. Such a shift should, however, serve the IMF well. Since the IMF's birth, many other organizations have been created that engage in surveillance activities—including the Organisation for Economic Co-operation, the Bank for International Settlements, and the various G-groupings. But the Fund is uniquely well positioned to assume a lead role in this area at the multilateral level because of its more universal membership.

It is important, however, not to overstate the influence of the IMF's surveillance activities. Even in the bilateral context, the Fund's advice has generally had a significant impact only when backed up by the promise of loans. Without the financial carrot, and in an era when the quality of its advice is being questioned, an IMF focused more on surveillance activities might be an IMF with an increasingly marginal position in the world economy. To avoid this fate, the IMF should ensure that its advice is credible and useful to policymakers. This, in turn, might depend heavily on a successful implementation of some of the kinds of governance reforms outlined above.

The IMF's Lending and Crisis Management Role

What of the IMF's lending role? Many analysts have suggested that crisis lending is unlikely to be the main focus of the IMF's activities in the coming years because countries are finding alternative ways to insulate themselves from crises (see, for example, Dodge 2006; King 2006). It is worth remembering, however, that declining demand for IMF crisis lending is linked to the broader question of the IMF's legitimacy. Once again, if the kinds of governance reforms outlined above succeeded in restoring confidence in the institution, this trend could be reversed.

Even if there was new demand for IMF financing, other analysts question whether IMF support could have much of an impact in stemming crises because of the size of international capital flows today. To be effective in this task, IMF loans would need either to be very large or to act in a catalytic role vis-à-vis enormous private capital flows. Larger loans have become increasingly unlikely, however, in the wake of the political backlash in creditor countries against the large-scale bailouts of the 1990s. Moreover, evidence suggests that IMF lending does not generally play a positive catalytic role in generating private capital inflows (Bird and Rowlands 1997; Edwards 2006).

This need not imply, however, that IMF lending has no role to play in future financial crises. Willett (2006) argues that an international lender of last resort is needed because financial markets can be inefficient, although such a lender should not be used to protect pegged currencies under intense speculative attack. To make this work, Willett suggests the Fund add facilities that offer front-loaded financing on a short-term basis while demanding that members meet loan preconditions. De Rato (2006b) has also endorsed the IMF's role of providing crisis lending, and has called for a new type of arrangement to be developed to provide contingent financing for crisis prevention.

Many analysts note that IMF loans can still play an important role in facilitating debt restructuring, among them many who fiercely opposed the IMF's SDRM proposal—such as the Washington-based Institute of International Finance (IIF), a lobby group representing private international financial institutions. Since 2002, the IIF has been promoting the development of a voluntary code of conduct for debt restructuring that could be endorsed by both investors and developing country governments. The code—formally titled "Principles for Stable Capital Flows and Fair Debt Restructuring in Emerging Markets"—was initially designed as an alternative to the SDRM and to discourage future debtor governments from pursuing the kind of aggressive negotiating strategy with investors that Argentina engaged in after its default. The initiative has been quite successful. It was welcomed formally by the Group of Twenty major industrialized countries in November 2004, and is now supported by investor groups as well as more than 30 countries, including Mexico, Brazil, Turkey, and South Korea. Most of the provisions in the code concern the behavior of debtors and private creditors, but the principles also prescribe a role for the IMF in resolving future crises. The code notes that the IMF should not give "any appearance of encouraging a debtor to default," and strongly encourages the Fund to "lend in arrears"—that is, to provide financial support to sovereign debtors when good-faith negotiations with private creditors are under way and are backed by IMF economic programs (IIF 2005). De Rato (2006b, 7–8) has also suggested that the IMF devote more attention to clarifying its policy on lending into arrears.

In addition, de Rato has made the important suggestion that the IMF should be more open to supporting member governments' reserve pooling arrangements at the regional level, while singling out the need for the Fund to support existing arrangements such as the Chiang Mai Initiative. This support for pooling arrangements, he suggests, could come primarily through the Fund's surveillance role (as it already does in the case of the Chiang Mai Initiative):

> While it would be up to these groups to determine terms for access, the scope for expanding such [regional] safety nets would rise with a group's confidence in the economic policies of its members. The Fund can play a role, focusing on regular and intensive surveillance. It should explore modalities for further engagement in this area. (de Rato 2006b, 7)

De Rato's suggestion for pooling arrangements marks an important openness on the part of the Fund to working with, rather than resisting, recent calls for a more decentralized international monetary and financial system—a system where regional monetary funds would be first invoked and used in times of crisis. Regional organizations, some argue, are better able to represent their clients than institutions such as the IMF, which tend to reflect the interests of their key shareholders. Regional institutions could provide needed funds with less conditionality and more peer pressure while fostering greater policy ownership, which could be further used to achieve long-term development goals (Culpeper 2006). Proponents of the idea argue that regional funds would produce a competitive environment for both economic policy ideas and funds that could benefit emerging market economies. Others caution, however, that regional funds would be more susceptible to political considerations and, therefore, to moral hazards (De Gregorio et al. 1999, 103–04).

More generally, Porter (2006) also points out that the decentralization of global monetary and financial institutions would be in keeping with the similar devolution of global governance, and would offer advantages that the centralized, bureaucratic IMF should reflect on and assess in determining its own comparative advantage. There has been a proliferation of public and private institutions that overlap with the IMF's functions and scope, not just with respect to its lending role but also its surveillance and other activities. Many of these institutions are less prone than the IMF to legitimacy and accountability problems, and the Fund's capacity to develop formal and informal creative collaborative relationships with them— in effect, becoming more of a "node in a network" than a top-down bureaucracy—is crucial to its future.

Developing a more active relationship with regional initiatives thus represents an important step; however, some also question the effect of regional agreements on the IMF. Pauly (forthcoming), for example, cautions about the "erosion of normative solidarity" resulting from emerging regional competitor organizations. In a similar vein, Henning (2006) argues that the IMF needs to recognize regional initiatives while also assessing them on a set of agreed criteria. Such an approach, of course, is unlikely to evoke much sympathy from those who see regional arrangements as a way to insulate their countries from IMF dictates and advice.

What about the IMF's existing lending to low-income countries? Many critics have suggested that the IMF get out of the business of development lending altogether, arguing that the Fund lacks the expertise to advise low-income countries on development and trade policy—as evidenced by the failed conditionality and financial crises that have occurred under its watch (Akuyz 2005, 3). Debtor countries have long complained that the number and scope of conditions the IMF imposes on its loans are excessive and intrusive. Referring to "mission creep," critics of such conditions charge that the IMF has moved beyond its historical role of exchange-rate monitoring to prescribing policies that mirror those of other development agencies. In particular, the Fund's Poverty Reduction and Growth Facility has been highlighted for its intrusive and extensive conditionality, which has involved IMF staff in development issues beyond their expertise.

Horst Köhler, IMF managing director from 2000 to 2004, called during his tenure for a "more focused IMF," one that would "streamline conditionality"—especially the structural conditionality that developing countries found particularly intrusive (Köhler 2000). Fund staff were told that, in designing loan conditionality, they were to return to their core areas of expertise: exchange-rate policies, macroeconomic stabilization, and financial sector policies (IMF 2001, 34). Moreover, in response to criticism that IMF programs, especially those under the PRGF, tended to fail because member states lacked commitment to reforms, the IMF introduced the concept of "country ownership," whereby member states would "own" their programs by making greater commitments to their implementation. In 2002, the Fund created a new set of Guidelines on Conditionality, committing to increase member states' "ownership" of loan conditionality and implicitly reduce its intrusive structural conditionality.

Critics argue that PRGF programs continue to be poorly conceived and implemented. Kumar (2006) notes that the size of these programs is marginal relative to that of developing countries' budgets, which explains why many eligible countries, particularly the poorest, do not use them. Moreover, as Kumar suggests, the IMF itself has continuing difficulty actually internalizing the idea of conditionality ownership. Momani (2005a) attributes the organizational culture within the IMF for its staff's failure to adopt the political economy tools needed to evaluate and measure member countries' ownership of loan conditionality, and argues (2007) that the Fund's organizational culture needs to promote debate and foster diverse internal thinking.

Others point out that development lending is taking the IMF away from providing countries with its comparative advantage over other organizations: exchange-rate advice. Truman (2005) suggests that the role of development lending properly belongs to the World Bank, and that the IMF should focus on its bilateral and multilateral surveillance of low-income countries. In the Fund's defense, however, Boughton argues that the IMF still has a comparative advantage in being able to offer policy advice to low-income countries on how to improve governance, enhance revenue, and control spending. Indeed, in his view, the IMF is the only universal institution with the expertise to provide such advice (2005, 40).

The US government has generally endorsed the idea of reducing the Fund's role in development lending (Adams 2006). De Rato has also stressed that the IMF's role in low-income countries "needs to be better defined and less thinly spread." In his view, IMF support and advice for these countries should focus only on issues relating to its core mandate of macroeconomic policies. In so doing, he notes, the Fund would have to develop "clear understandings" with other development agencies because its narrow macroeconomic focus would "not necessarily translate into growth and poverty reduction unless a more multi-disciplinary view of development is taken" (2006, 9).

Conclusion

In our view, the current debate on reforming the IMF has been provoked mainly by two developments that have undermined the Fund's central position in global financial governance: the drift away from the institution by medium-income borrowers and the emergence of a more critical US view toward it. In this new political context, Fund management, key share-holders, and the concerned policy community have put forward a range of reform proposals primarily to restore and preserve the IMF's significance. Advocates of change focus particular attention on the need for process-oriented reforms that would change the nature of IMF governance as a means of restoring its legitimacy among many member governments. Also prominent are more outcome-oriented reforms that would make changes to the IMF's activities and performance.

It would be difficult to describe any of the prominent proposals in the current IMF reform debate as truly "transformative." Indeed, it is striking that none of the key participants in the current debate has proposed a dramatic expansion of the IMF's role and mandate in global financial governance. Instead, the focus has been a much less ambitious one of bolstering the IMF's legitimacy and encouraging it to fulfill its existing mandate more efficiently and effectively. Put a different way, the current reform debate has been driven primarily by the perceived failure of global governance, rather than by a demand for more global governance.

Whether these reform proposals are best seen as either "palliative" or "corrective" is a much more difficult question to answer. Often, the distinction is simply in the eye of the beholder. To their advocates, the proposals we have outlined in this paper correspond well with Stein's definition of "corrective" reforms: they are intended to the restore the IMF to its past healthy status. Most of the proposals, however, have been criticized as merely "palliative" and inadequate to address the institution's underlying problems. Our view of the content of the overall reform debate lies somewhere in the middle. A number of proposals, if implemented properly, could place the IMF once again in a more central role within global financial governance. Others, however, are much too limited to achieve this goal or are unlikely to be implemented.

One way to summarize our perspective on this issue is by addressing the following question: what kind of IMF is likely to emerge from this patchwork of reform proposals? Beyond the marginal changes to four countries' quotas implemented at the September 2006 Singapore meeting, it is difficult to predict which of these proposals, if any, the Fund is most likely to adopt. Still, some tentative lessons can be learned from Singapore and beyond. To begin, there is a remarkable degree of consensus that the IMF will become increasingly marginal unless it adopts serious governance reforms. Most attention has been given to the need to reallocate "chairs and shares," but this is also the area that will see the erection of many political roadblocks, even with the opportunity created by European integration. The potential significance of this reform—even given a major reallocation—for re-establishing the Fund's legitimacy is also easily overstated, and ignores problems with the quality of Fund advice. Of equal, if not greater, significance—and with fewer likely political roadblocks—could be other governance reforms, such as changing the selection process for the managing director, the constituency system, the mandate of the Executive Board, and the staffing of the institution.

If a significant package of governance reforms were implemented, the result would likely be a reinvigorated IMF. It would also likely be an IMF whose activities were somewhat different than those of a decade ago, when the Fund's reputation as a powerful international organization was based primarily on its lending capacity and associated (neoliberal) conditionality. If the IMF emerged from its current crisis reborn and strengthened, its surveillance functions would likely be more prominent, particularly in their multilateral dimensions, and the content of its advice would be less rigidly neoliberal. The Fund would still be involved in lending and crisis management, but its role in that respect would be both more collaborative with other private and public institutions and more focused on its core function of providing balance-of-payments support.

An alternative scenario, of course, would be no serious overhaul of the Fund's governance structure. In that event, the significance of reforms to the IMF's performance would diminish considerably. Without legitimacy, the Fund's ability to perform its surveillance role effectively—at both the bilateral and multilateral levels—would be severely constrained. Moreover, without trust in the institution, potential borrowers would only accelerate their drift away from it and increase their efforts to construct alternative crisis-management mechanisms (see Woods 2006, 188). In the words of Injoo Sohn (2005), potential borrowers would move from "rule takers" to "rule makers" in global financial governance, and the rules they make would assign only a small role to the IMF. Under that scenario, the IMF's influence would die, not with a bang, but with a whimper.

What are the broader lessons from this crisis moment for scholars of the IMF and of global governance more generally? First, the crisis has highlighted the vulnerability of the IMF's power. Historically, that power has stemmed from three sources: its material resources (that is, its lending), the authority derived from its technical expertise, and its delegated authority from member states.[10] In the current moment, all three sources of power are under serious challenge, generating a severe crisis for the institution.

Second, the crisis has highlighted some of the limitations of scholarly explanations of the IMF's changing global role that highlight the significance of bureaucratic culture. The most prominent explanation of this kind is offered by Barnett and Finnemore (2004), who attribute the expanding role of IMF conditionality into domestic affairs, particularly in the 1990s, partly to a bureaucratic logic—that is, in the face of persistent failure to

---

10. See Barnett and Finnemore (2004) for a discussion of these sources of power for international organizations.

stabilize balance-of-payments situations, IMF staff have pressed for an expansion of their mandate. Barnett and Finnemore add that Fund staff have had expertise authority, which states choose to listen to and learn from. As member states have become more open about criticizing the failures of Fund staff, they appear to have diminishing faith in the Fund's advice. Moreover, as states' preferences have changed, the Fund's ability to expand its mandate has also been constrained.

Also noteworthy is that the state preferences that now matter are not just those of the dominant countries. To be sure, to some extent the IMF's recent fate has been determined by the changing priorities of its dominant shareholder, the United States. But a number of lesser powers, particularly in East Asia and Latin America, have also had a decisive impact. Their new ability to influence the IMF's predicament is a product not just of a broader shift of power in the world economy toward "emerging markets" and the so-called BRICs (Brazil, Russia, India, and China)—a shift that is also influencing the governance of international trade in important ways. It is also a product of these lesser powers' new use of the political tool of "exit" through their boycotting of IMF borrowing, the creation of regional financial alternatives, and the unilateral accumulation of large foreign-exchange reserves.

Finally, even the role of the United States in this current crisis has been interesting. The shift in policy with respect to the IMF that has occurred during the Bush years has surprised many who assumed the United States would always have a positive view of the Fund as an institution that served its geopolitical and national economic interests. The shift reveals how the fate of international institutions can be strongly influenced by changing domestic US politics (see Broz and Hawes 2006). In addition, our reading of the period suggests that domestic political shifts reflect not just the material interests of various private actors, but also the important role of changing ideas.

References

Adams, Timothy. 2006. Statement by the Under Secretary for International Affairs in Advance of Meetings of the G7, IMF, and World Bank, April 19. Washington, DC: Department of the Treasury. Available at Web site: http://www.treasury.gov/press/releases/js4193.htm.

Akyuz, Yilmaz. 2005. "Reforming the IMF: Back to the Drawing Board." Research paper. Washington, DC: Intergovernmental Group of Twenty Four. Available at Web site: http://www.g24.org/Akyu0905.pdf.

Barnett, Michael, and Martha Finnemore. 2004. *Rules for the World: International Organizations in Global Politics*. Ithaca, NY: Cornell University Press.

Bird, Graham, and Dane Rowlands. 1997. "The Catalytic Effect of Lending by the International Financial Institutions." *World Economy* 20 (7): 967–91.

Bini Smaghi, Lorenzo. 2006. "IMF Governance and the Political Economy of a Consolidated EU Seat." In *Reforming the IMF for the 21st Century*, edited by Edwin Truman. Washington, DC: Institute for International Economics.

Birdsall, Nancy. 2003. "Why It Matters Who Runs the IMF and the World Bank." Working Paper 22. Washington, DC: Center for Global Development.

Blustein, Paul. 2001. *The Chastening: Inside the Crisis that Rocked the Global Financial System and Humbled the IMF*. New York: PublicAffairs.

Boughton, James. 2005. "Does the World Need a Universal Financial Institution?" *World Economics* 6 (2): 27–46.

Bradlow, Daniel D. 2006. "The Changing Role of the IMF in the Governance of the Global Economy and Its Consequences." Paper prepared for the Annual Banking Law Update, University of Johannesburg. Mimeographed.

Broz, J. Lawrence, and Michael Brewster Hawes. 2006. "Congressional Politics of Financing the International Monetary Fund." *International Organization* 60 (1): 367–99.

Buira, Ariel. 2002. "A New Voting Structure for the IMF." Washington, DC: Intergovernmental Group of Twenty Four. Available at Web site: http://www.g24.org/newvotig.pdf.

———. 2003. "The Governance of the International Monetary Fund." Washington, DC: Group of Twenty Four. Available at Web site: http://www.g24.org/imfgover.pdf.

Camdessus, Michel. 2005. "International Financial Institutions: Dealing with New Global Challenges." Washington, DC: Per Jacobsson Foundation. September 25. Available at Web site: http://www.perjacobsson.org/lectures/ 092505.pdf.

Cooper, Andrew F., and Bessma Momani. 2005. "Negotiating Out of Argentina's Financial Crisis: Segmenting the International Creditors." *New Political Economy* 10 (3): 305–20.

Culpeper, Roy. 2006. "Reforming the Global Financial Architecture: The Potential of Regional Institutions." Paper presented at the Centre for International Governance and Innovation workshop on "The Reform of Global Financial Governance: Whither the IMF?" Waterloo, ON, June 10. Available at Web site: http://igloo.org/imfreform.

Dabrowski, Marek. 2006. "Consolidating EU Votes Would Be More Symbolic than Real." *Europe's World*, Spring: 43–47.

De Gregorio, José, Barry Eichengreen, Takatoshi Ito, and Charles Wyplosz. 1999. *An Independent and Accountable IMF*. Geneva: Centre for Economic Policy Research.

de Rato, Rodrigo. 2006a. "How the IMF Can Help Promote a Collaborative Solution to Global Imbalances." Washington, DC: International Monetary Fund. April 14. Available at Web site: http://www.imf.org/external/np/speeches/ 2006/040406.htm.

———. 2006b. "The Managing Director's Report on Implementing the Fund's Medium-Term Strategy." Washington: International Monetary Fund. April 5.

Dodge, David. 2006. "The Evolving International Monetary Order and the Need for an Evolving IMF." Lecture to the Woodrow Wilson School of Public and International Affairs, Princeton University, Princeton, NJ, March 30.

Edwards, Martin. 2006. "Signaling Credibility? The IMF and Catalytic Finance." *Journal of International Relations and Development* 9 (1): 27–52.

European Parliament. 2006. *European Parliament Resolution on the Strategic Review of the International Monetary Fund*. Strasbourg. March 14. Available at Web site: http://www.globalpolicy.org/socecon/bwi-wto/imf/2006/ 0314euimfapproved.pdf.

Evans, Peter, and Martha Finnemore. 2001. "Organizational Reform and the Expansion of the South's Voice at the Fund." G24 Discussion Paper 15. Geneva: United Nations Conference on Trade and Development.

Fischer, Fritz. 2006. "Why Europe Should Spearhead IMF and World Bank Reform." *Europe's World*, Spring: 42–49.

Goldstein, Morris. 2006. "Currency Manipulation and Enforcing the Rules of the International Monetary System." In *Reforming the IMF for the 21st Century*, edited by Edwin Truman. Washington, DC: Institute for International Economics.

Helleiner, Eric. 2005. "The Strange Story of Bush and the Argentine Debt Crisis." *Third World Quarterly* 26 (6): 951–69.

———. 2006. "The Long and Winding Road to a Sovereign Debt Restructuring Regime." Paper presented to the Global Economic Governance Programme, Oxford University, May 12.

Helleiner, Eric, and Geoffrey Cameron. 2006. "Another World Order? The Bush Administration and HIPC Debt Cancellation." *New Political Economy* 11 (1): 125–40.

Henning, Randall. 2006. "Regional Arrangements and the International Monetary Fund." In *Reforming the IMF for the 21st Century*, edited by Edwin Truman. Washington, DC: Institute for International Economics.

IIF (Institute of International Finance). 2005. *Principles for Stable Capital Flows and Fair Debt Restructuring in Emerging Markets*. Washington, DC. Available at website: http://www.iif.com/data/public/principles-final_0305.pdf.

International Monetary Fund. 2001. Policy Development and Review Department. *Conditionality in Fund-Supported Programs: Policy Issues*. Washington, DC.

Kahler, Miles. 2002. *Leadership Selection in the Major Multilaterals*. Washington, DC: Institute for International Economics.

———. 2006. "Internal Governance and IMF Performance." In *Reforming the IMF for the 21st Century*, edited by Edwin Truman. Washington, DC: Institute for International Economics.

Kelkar, Vijay, Praveen Chaudhry, and Marta Vanduzer-Snow. 2005. "Time for a Change at the IMF." *Finance and Development* 41 (3): 21–23.

Kelkar, Vijay, Yikash Yadav, and Praveen Chaudhry. 2004. "Reforming the Governance of the International Monetary Fund." *World Economy* 27 (5): 727–43.

Kenen, Peter. 2006. "Comments on the Address of the Managing Director of the IMF." Remarks made at the book release of *Reforming the IMF for the 21st Century*, Institute for International Economics, Washington, DC, April 20.

King, Mervyn. 2006. "Reform of the International Monetary Fund." Speech at the Indian Council for Research on International Economic Relations, New Delhi, February 20. Available at Web site: http://www.bankofengland.co.uk/publications/speeches/2006/speech267.pdf.

Köhler, Horst. 2000. "Toward a More Focussed IMF." Luncheon Address at the International Monetary Conference, Paris, May 30. Available at Web site: http://www.imf.org/external/np/speeches/2000/053000.htm.

Krueger, Anne. 2001. *International Financial Architecture for 2002: A New Approach to Sovereign Debt Restructuring*. Washington, DC : International Monetary Fund.

Kumar, Ramesh. 2006. "Poverty Reduction and the Poverty Reduction Facility at the IMF: Carving a New Path or Losing Way." Paper presented at the Centre for International Governance and Innovation workshop on "The Reform of Global Financial Governance: Whither the IMF?" Waterloo, ON, June 10. Available at Web site: http://igloo.org/imfreform.

Lee, Yong Wook. 2006. "Japan and the Asian Monetary Fund." *International Studies Quarterly* 50 (2): 339–66.

Lombardi, Domenico and Ngaire Woods. 2006a. "Rethinking IMF Surveillance: A Political Economy Approach." Paper presented at the Centre for International Governance and Innovation workshop on "The Reform of Global Financial Governance: Whither the IMF?" Waterloo, ON, June 10. Available at Web site: http://igloo.org/imfreform.

———. 2006b. "Uneven Patterns of Governance: How Developing Countries Are Represented in the IMF." *Review of International Political Economy* 13 (3): 480–515.

Meltzer, Allan. 1995. "Why it is time to close down the IMF." *Financial Times*, June 16.

Momani, Bessma. 2004. "American Politicization of the International Monetary Fund." *Review of International Political Economy* 11 (5): 880–904.

———. 2005a. "Limits of Streamlining Fund Conditionality: The IMF's Organizational Culture." *Journal of International Relations and Development* 8 (2): 142–63.

———. 2005b. "Recruiting and Diversifying IMF Technocrats." *Global Society* 19 (2): 167–87.

————. 2007. "IMF Staff: Missing Link in IMF Reform Debates." *Review of International Organizations* 2 (1): 39–57.

————. Forthcoming. "Another Seat at the IMF Table: Russia's IMF Executive Director." *International Journal.*

Mussa, Michael. 2002. *Argentina and the Fund: From Triumph to Tragedy.* Washington, DC: Institute for International Economics.

Ostry, Jonathan, and Jeromin Zettelmeyer. 2005, "Strengthening IMF Crisis Prevention." IMF Working Paper WP/05/206. Washington, DC: International Monetary Fund.

Pauly, Louis. 1997. *Who Elected the Bankers?* Ithaca, NY: Cornell University Press.

————. Forthcoming. "IMF Surveillance and the Legacy of Bretton Woods." In *Bretton Woods Revisited*, edited by David Andrews. Ithaca, NY: Cornell University Press.

Porter, Tony. 2006. "Beyond the IMF: The Broader Institutional Arrangements in Global Financial Governance." Paper presented at the Centre for International Governance and Innovation workshop on "Reform of Global Financial Governance: Whither the IMF?" Waterloo, ON, June 10. Available at Web site: http://igloo.org/imfreform.

Ragan, Raghuram. 2006. "The Role of the International Monetary Fund in a Changing World." Speech to the Kiel Institute, Kiel, Germany, April 10. Available at Web site: http://www.imf.org/external/np/speeches/2006/041006.htm.

Rapkin, David, and Jonathan Strand. 2003. "Is East Asia Under-Represented in the International Monetary Fund?" *International Relations of the Asia-Pacific* 3 (1): 1–28.

Rustomjee, Cyrus. 2004. "Why Developing Countries Need a Stronger Voice." *Finance and Development* 41 (3): 21–23.

Saxton, James. 2002. Joint Economic Committee, US Congress. "IMF Sovereign Bankruptcy Supervision Is Unnecessary: New Analysis Rejects More IMF Mission Creep." Press release. United States Congress, Joint Economic Committee, Washington, DC. April 19.

Scholte, Jan Arte. 2002. *Civil Society Voices and the International Monetary Fund.* Ottawa: North-South Institute.

Snow, John W. 2006. "Testimony before the House Financial Services Committee on the International Financial System and the Global Economy." Press Release JS-4267. Washington, DC: Department of the Treasury. May 17.

Sohn, Injoo. 2005. "Asian Financial Cooperation: The Problem of Legitimacy in Global Financial Governance." *Global Governance* 11 (4): 487–504.

Suskind, Ron. 2004. *The Price of Loyalty: George W. Bush, the White House, and the Education of Paul O'Neill.* New York: Simon and Schuster.

Thirkell-White, Ben. 2004. "The International Monetary Fund and Civil Society." *New Political Economy* 9 (2): 251–70.

Truman, Edwin. 2006. *A Strategy for IMF Reform.* Washington, DC: Institute for International Economics.

United States. 2000. International Financial Institutions Advisory Committee. *Report.* Submitted to the US Congress and US Department of Treasury, March 8. Washington, DC.

Van Houtven, Leo. 2004. "Rethinking IMF Governance." *Finance and Development* 41 (3): 18–20.

Willett, Thomas. 2006. "A Likely Political Unrealistic Proposal to Make the IMF an Effective ILOLR and Increase the Effectiveness of Conditionality." Presentation at the Centre for International Governance and Innovation workshop on "Reform of Global Financial Governance: Whither the IMF?" Waterloo, ON, June 10. Available at Web site: http://igloo.org/imfreform.

Woods, Ngaire. 2006. *The Globalizers.* Ithaca, NY: Cornell University Press.

World Bank. 2006. *Global Development Finance.* Washington, DC: World Bank.

Zhou Xiaochuan. "IMFC Statement by the Governor, People's Bank of China." Washington, DC: International Monetary Fund. April 22. Available at Web site: http://www.imf.org/External/spring/2006/imfc/statement/eng/chn.pdf.

A Comment on the Effective Possibilities of Multilateralism

Patricia Goff

*   *   *

Reform has become something of a buzzword in debates about international organization and global governance. The United Nations needs reform, the International Monetary Fund (IMF), the World Trade Organization (WTO), and so on. But what does reform mean to the various parties involved? What does it entail or require? How might we bring it about? What specific outcomes are associated with reform? Daniel Drezner, John Ikenberry, Richard Rosecrance, James Fearon, and Arthur Stein cut into these questions from different angles, offering important insights in the process, but many questions remain. I outline some of them below.

The Role of the United States

Drezner, Ikenberry, Rosecrance, and Stein all put great emphasis on the role of the United States in reviving ailing institutions or creating new ones. The implication is that, if the United States wants to bring about reform, it will do so. If it does not perceive it to be in its national interest, then reform might be difficult. Certainly, this makes sense given both the role US officials played in creating the UN and the Bretton Woods institutions and the influence a hegemon wields. Nonetheless, it is worth pointing out that some changes have taken place that did not spring from US interests or actions.

The most obvious example concerns the rise of the BRICs (Brazil, Russia, India, and China). As several authors in this volume point out, inasmuch as we acknowledge a new distribution of power, it is not characterized solely by the singular prominence of the United States, but also by the emergence of India, Brazil, China, and others as strong economic players. This is important for at least two reasons. First, this shift has already had some very real consequences. In the context of the WTO, for example, the key deal makers have changed. In the past, we looked to the Quad (the European Union, the United States, Canada, and Japan) for cues on negotiating directions. More recently, it was the Five Interested Parties (the US, the EU, Brazil, India, and Australia), and now it is the G4 (the US, the EU, Brazil, and India) whose input is decisive. This development is particularly consequential for Canada and Japan, which have lost (or relinquished) a degree of influence in the trading regime as a result. The rise of the BRICs has arguably also had an effect on the IMF. As Eric Helleiner and Bessma Momani argue (in this volume), waning US support is only one reason the IMF is losing influence and legitimacy. An equally significant explanation lies in the fact that rising powers such as Argentina, Brazil, Indonesia, and various East Asian nations have found alternatives to Fund borrowing. A similar shift in power, however, has not manifested itself in other key international institutions—for example, at the United Nations, the BRICs have yet to be rewarded for their newfound status with Security Council seats. Nonetheless, in the case of both the WTO and IMF, significant change has already taken place as a result of a natural evolution in the dynamic relations among states.

The rise of the BRICs is also important because it is not yet clear what kind of *political* actors they will be (individually or collectively). Much ink has been spilled over their capacity in terms of economic growth and exports. In the case of China, its foreign reserves and its ability to finance US debt have been analyzed in depth. Less attention has been given to the foreign policy intentions and abilities of the BRICs, which makes it challenging to predict what may or may not be possible. Much has been assumed: it is not unusual to see articles in the popular press that discuss China in terms of a Cold War scenario. Meanwhile, the foreign ministers of India, Brazil, and South Africa have begun their own dialogue on issues of multilateralism and reform of the UN, among other international peace and development issues. (In shifting our attention to the *political*, might our attention more properly alight on Russia, a country that is rarely central to BRICs-oriented conversations that spring from perceptions of economic power?) What role might they play in global institutional reform? What is their vision? What is the nature and extent of their respective commitments to multilateralism generally or to a liberal multilateral order of the kind the United States is likely to support more specifically? As Drezner points out, in sponsoring the Shanghai Cooperation Organisation, China has already created new institutional structures outside of the US ambit. Stein notes that working around existing rules and institutions is not a luxury reserved to the hegemon or to powerful states. Therefore, too much emphasis on the United States or on BRICs as primarily economic actors might obscure key factors that can be mobilized for change or that must be acknowledged for a full understanding of change.

It is worth pointing out, too, that a focus on the United States can minimize the role of Europe. As Robert Wolfe notes (in this volume), "it is easy enough to see the General Agreement on Tariffs and Trade (GATT) of 1948 as a public good supplied by the United States alone, but by the 1960s the GATT could be seen as a bilateral agreement with Europe." Wolfe goes on to point out that any conclusion to the current round of trade talks would require the agreement of both (but not only) the United States and Europe. To be sure, the EU has not yet lived up to its potential as a foreign policy actor or as a counterweight to US power. Its influence is not equally significant across all international forums. It must, however, be factored into any serious discussion of global institutional reform.

A conversation about global institutional reform must also make room for nonstate actors. Traditional international relations theory argues that international rules and institutions spring from the interests of powerful states. Recent examples warn, however, against discounting smaller states and civil society actors. The obvious example is the Landmines Treaty, which emerged from concerted action by the Canadian government and nongovernmental organizations. Despite US unwillingness to ratify the Ottawa Convention, the treaty specifically and the movement to ban anti-personnel landmines more generally can boast many successes. Drezner adds a degree of subtlety in arguing that "[p]owerful international institutions are the creation of powerful governments." It may be true that the Ottawa Convention does not rank as a powerful instrument when we compare it to the WTO, for example. There is, nonetheless, a danger in overstating the degree to which US involvement determines the success of international efforts. Indeed, the appearance of a nascent framework of private authority adds another dimension to the conversation about non-state actors and their contribution to global institutional reform.

Of course, it would be naive to ignore the United States or to presume that its role is not important. Yet even here, the ways in which it is important deserve fuller attention. US choices are not dichotomous, but rather range along a continuum. In other words, even if one accepts the argument that US involvement in global governance structures is a function of national interest, the two choices are not US involvement in international institutions or US rejection of international institutions, based on its assessment of the tradeoff of institutional constraints versus gains from participation. Ikenberry captures an element of this when he shows that not only is the United States central to the multilateral system, but a robust multilateral system is key to restoring US legitimacy and credibility. In other words, opting out of the multilateral system is not nearly as straightforward as some might imply.

Equally interesting for the purposes of assessing the nature of and prospects for US involvement in global institutional reform is the work of Linda Weiss (2005). Whereas Ikenberry suggests that a changing international environment (and its concomitant change in incentive structure vis-à-vis international institutions) might disincline the United States from multilateral activity, Weiss suggests that domestic and international political and economic change lead states not to abandon international institutions, but to (re)shape them to their current needs. As she puts it,

> the rich nations as a group ... have carved out a multilateral order which best suits their current developmental trajectory, one that, on one hand, diminishes space for promoting more labour- and capital-intensive industries critical to their climb up the developmental ladder and, on the other hand, increases space for sponsoring the technology—or knowledge-intensive industries that are now deemed critical to securing national prosperity. (2005, 724)

Weiss concentrates on the WTO, and it is safe to say that her argument does not travel easily to other international institutions. Nonetheless, her observation of "heightened (more strategically focused) activism in the context of tighter multilateral discipline" (739) is instructive, dovetailing in some ways with Stein's claim (in this volume) that multilateralism is an existential reality.

Even if we are persuaded that US involvement is absolutely crucial to global institutional reform and that the United States appears reticent at the moment, all is not lost. Constructivist theorizing in international relations has shown us that interests evolve (Klotz 1995). Helleiner and Momani (in this volume) provide an illustration of this, showing that a shift in US domestic politics has led to a rethinking of whether support for the IMF continues to be in the US national interest. Sometimes interests evolve as a result of an explicit, hard-headed assessment of a prevailing situation; at other times, it might be harder to identify an overt process as states make adjustments on the fly as a result of interaction with others—which might include states and institutions. States evaluate on an ongoing basis what they are relative to other states, and that evaluation informs perceptions of interests and, by extension, state policies and practices. The point is that US interests likely cannot remain fixed even if US officials want them to. The fluidity of global politics almost guarantees it.

Whither Multilateralism?

In recent years, there appears to have been a renewed interest in multilateralism. Nearly 15 years ago, John Ruggie wrote that "curiously, little explicit and detailed analytical attention has been paid in this literature to a core feature of current international institutional arrangements: their multilateral form" (1993, 5). Ruggie noted that there seemed to be a preference among international relations scholars for terms such as "cooperation" and "institution." Why, then, are we giving new consideration to multilateralism? Partly this has to do with the difficulties that key multilateral institutions (the IMF, WTO, UN) face. Partly it has to do with a proliferation of regional and bilateral efforts, which are perceived as opposing multilateralism. But perhaps mostly it has to do with the actions of the George W. Bush administration in Iraq, which have led many to question whether the United States remains committed to multilateralism. The most common answer to this question seems to be "most of the time." Paul Heinbecker (and Richard Haass before him) calls the Bush administration's approach "multilateralism à la carte": "a selective instrument for validating US action when Washington so wanted and to be ignored when it proved uncooperative" (2004, 12). (Interestingly, Ferry de Kerckhove in this volume uses the same term to capture UN involvement in Iraq.) Quoting Francis Fukuyama, Drezner (in this volume) refers to US "multi-multilateralism," which roughly corresponds to forum shopping.

Questioning whether the United States is still committed to multilateral action is not unimportant, but preoccupation with this question can divert attention away from important issues about multilateralism writ large— issues that might get us closer to understanding what a truly transformative change to the global institutional order might look like. Before we broach these larger issues, let us explore the various ways in which the term "multilateralism" is typically used. Recognizing the various uses or definitions of the concept is important because, among other things, it helps us identify what is in opposition to multilateralism or what constitutes a deviation from it.

Indeed, not everyone uses the term in the same way: it means different things in different national contexts. In the United States, multilateralism tends to refer to a conception of "the overall relations among states" (Ruggie 1993, 12) that might or might not implicate institutions; here, multilateralism is opposed to "going it alone." In Canada, on the other hand, multilateralism is at least partly equated with institutions or international organizations. When certain actors sidestep institutions, Canadians assume they have rejected multilateralism, which might be only partly true (or might not necessarily be true). In recognition of this logic, Stein (in this volume) cautions against "those who want international cooperation and mistake international institutions as international cooperation." In the Canadian context, it is actually support for rules-based international structures that multilateralism is likely meant to capture, but the slippage is not uncommon: as de Kerckhove argues (in this volume), the failure to date of UN reform has led to a questioning of multilateral action more generally.

Notions of multilateralism that circulate in various national contexts also differ from the one that many political scientists accept. The definition of multilateralism that Ruggie (1993) offered when he sought to correct the lack of attention given to the concept by the field of international relations has two components. The first pertains to relations among three or more parties. But more than just coordinating the actions of multiple states, the term also embodies *principles and rules of conduct that are applicable to all countries*. Theoretically, these rules and principles transcend the particular interests of individual participants in the multilateral system (1993, 11). As Finnemore puts it, "multilateralism involves acting according to a mutually agreed-upon set of principles and rules. It has never meant that all decisions get made by committee nor has it demanded that states abandon all independent action" (2005, 16).

So, when we look at the multilateral system that was put in place following World War II, we see coordination of state action via several robust international institutions and we see that the nature of that coordination was specific and specified. By way of illustration, Ruggie lists among the generalized principles of conduct that operate in the multilateral trade regime, "the norm of [most-favored-nation] treatment, corresponding rules about reciprocal tariff reductions and the application of safeguards, and collectively sanctioned procedures for implementing the rules" (1993, 13). These organizing principles, intended to operate regardless of the power capabilities of individual participants, represent an aspect of multilateralism that is often lost in contemporary debates.

A focus on Ruggie's definition of the concept of multilateralism gets us to the ideas underpinning the system. Contemporary debates about the United States' commitment to multilateralism often focus on the size and composition of the coalition the Bush administration assembled in support of the Iraq invasion. They rarely examine inadvertent or intentional efforts by the administration to change the principles and goals of the multilateral system, yet a transformative change to the multilateral system lies here, not in whether the United States allied with two or ten states. Ikenberry, Rosecrance, and Stein each in their way argue that multilateralism is desirable, necessary, or even inevitable. But to what end? Here may be where some of the most significant changes have occurred, for good and bad.

The United States did not have the support of many of its traditional allies in going into Iraq. In part, this support was withheld because the Bush administration pursued what many perceived to be a *preventive* war, which the UN Charter does not sanction. An argument can be made that the Canadians, Europeans, and others withheld their support, not because US action was not in their respective interests, but because US action represented a departure from accepted international practice, from the recognized rules, organizing principles, and goals of the multilateral order. If the United States can be said to have moved away from multilateralism in this instance, it did not do so because it acted unilaterally or with only a small coalition but because it deviated from the generally recognized purpose of multilateral action. Indeed, even if the United States had boasted 100 percent adhesion by its allies, *the shift in its intent* toward preventive war could signal a change in the rules of conduct or the aspirations underpinning the multilateral order.

I am not suggesting that a single instance of preventive war necessarily constitutes a durable change to the system. I am, however, pointing out that a fulsome discussion of multilateralism should reference the evolving and possibly contested purposes to which that order is perceived to be put. The criteria by which we judge the robustness of the multilateral system must move beyond counting coalition members. Multilateralism is not dead because US officials refer to the United Nations as a "talk shop." The multilateral order that was instituted after World War II, however, might be dead if agreement over the goals or policy ends toward which multilateral action (via institutions or not) is working breaks down or becomes reconfigured. The corollary to this is that, even in a unipolar configuration, a continuing commitment to the ideas underpinning the multilateral order would keep a particular multilateral order alive.

Interestingly, when the G20 countries walked out of the Cancún WTO ministerial, analysts did not immediately question the robustness of multilateralism. I would argue that this was because the G20 representatives were demanding that their negotiating partners adhere to the rules of the WTO and live up to the commitments, goals, and aspirations associated with participation in the trading regime. They were not questioning the very ideas underpinning the multilateral order; rather, they sought to uphold them.

That the Bush administration is prosecuting a preventive war is not the only evidence that the ideas underpinning the multilateral order are shifting. The prominence of human rights discourse and the burgeoning effort to institutionalize a commitment to protect populations whose governments are unwilling or unable to do so also suggest an evolution in our understanding of the justification for the use of force. What is new about multilateralism is not strictly the fact that it will operate in the foreseeable future against the backdrop of a unipolar distribution of power, but also that the principles and goals that have underpinned the multilateral order in the security realm are now in dispute. Ikenberry comes to the conclusion that if the United States were once again to act as a rule maker, allies who have defected would return. However, a fuller definition of multilateralism, such as Ruggie offers, cautions that this would depend on the rules being made. We can infer from the Ikenberry piece that he favors something like what animated post–World War II US policy, in which case he might be correct. Multilateralism might be an existential reality, but which version of multilateralism? How will the principles underpinning the multilateral order ultimately be redefined, and by whom?

It is revealing to note that suggesting that the United States has turned its back on multilateralism has become an indictment in itself. Of course, there are those who object to the substance of US action (just as there are those who support it). But there are others for whom the term "unilateral" is pejorative. This is perhaps because multilateralism has come to be equated with principled action—with action that is not *solely* in the national interest. As Drezner points out (in this volume), international institutions (as one component of multilateralism) have come to be associated with rules-based outcomes (good) as opposed to power-based outcomes (bad). The former serves the collective interest as opposed to narrower national interests, often pursued at the expense of others. As Stein puts it (in this volume), "[w]hen people talk about multilateralism, then, they mean more than a set of states that combine their capabilities to achieve some objective. They also have in mind the legitimacy that comes from states acting in concert because their objectives are not particularistic national interests but common interests." Heinbecker (2004) and Ikenberry (in this volume) argue that multilateral action has greater legitimacy. In his analysis of the Iraq War, Heinbecker suggests that "legitimacy is a prerequisite to broad-based, effective cooperation in the management of the war's aftermath" (2004, 4). Of course, the connotation we attach to the term "multilateralism" can cut both ways—those who are multilateralist can be accused of being too idealistic and perhaps naive. What is interesting from my perspective is that there is a connotation attached at all.

There are many ways to achieve desired ends in the international arena. As Barnett and Finnemore (1999) point out, international institutions exhibit "pathologies." Drezner (in this volume) argues from a different angle that institutionalization can have negative consequences—or, at least, might not always have positive consequences. In his analysis, a proliferation of instruments can look a lot like the state of anarchy—the lack of an overarching authority or, in Weber's (2001) formulation, the lack of an "orderer"—in the international arena that realists believe preceded institutionalization and multilateralism. Drezner is not alone in raising the possibility that cooperative action, institutions, and/or multilateralism might lead to negative outcomes—Stein (in this volume) also gestures at this. Given this possibility and the many other examples of where cooperative action and/or institutions have produced less than optimal outcomes, it is curious that multilateralism is perceived in such a positive light. Indeed, in some quarters, it seems multilateral action is legitimate precisely because it is multilateral.

This is likely the legacy of the post–World War II period. Multilateral activity was so successful in that instance that multilateral activity generally has come to be perceived as good. In the same way that the concept of protectionism has been unable to shake the negative legacy of Smoot-Hawley, so multilateralism continues to be equated with the economic and security successes of the post–World War II period. This is understandable, but valuing multilateralism intrinsically, as if it were an end in itself, might not advance a discussion of global institutional reform. Admitting multilateralism to the pantheon of hallowed concepts is risky because it can foreclose or devalue options that are not multilateral in nature without ensuring that multilateralism will always produce the most desirable outcomes.

The alternative is to shift our focus to outcomes and to the ideas, goals, and aspirations underpinning multilateral action. What do we want to achieve? What are the principles and goals that we would like to see underpinning the multilateral order and what are we going to do to bring them about? We have some idea of the principles and goals that the United States favors as the multilateral system evolves. Given this evolving configuration, where can we be effective? Which channels are open to us and which are not?

Apples and Oranges

What does it mean to say that an institution is in crisis? What counts as reform? Drezner points to a "sclerosis" in global institutions. Rosecrance talks about "democratizing" institutions so that the leadership of international organizations is more reflective of shifts in the distribution of power. The debate about global institutional reform has proceeded along several tracks. Included in these are a general discussion about multilateralism and participation in the global governance architecture. Alongside this important discussion is a series of institution-specific debates that might lead some to question whether a holistic approach to global institutional reform will get us where we need to go. Some key questions are present in both conversations: what is not working? why is reform required? what form should reform take? what is the goal of reform? Interestingly, the answers to these questions are quite different if we apply them to the United Nations, for example, versus if we apply them to the IMF or the WTO.

The example of the WTO is instructive. Weiss (2005, 725) argues that "the new trade regime represents a quantum leap in global regulation," suggesting that states have agreed to an extensive set of rules that can be quite constraining. The same cannot be said for the United Nations, which lacks enforcement mechanisms and whose General Assembly resolutions rely on moral suasion. Ikenberry (in this volume) suggests that the WTO "might be used to address wider global challenges," challenges typically associated with the UN—such as arms control and nonproliferation—suggesting a different level of confidence in the WTO than in the UN. Rosecrance (in this volume) advocates a new Concert of Great Powers, although he admits this is not necessary for the smooth functioning of the WTO; it is, however, more important for Security Council decisions at the UN. At a minimum, then, inasmuch as international institutions encumber states, they do so differently, and states respond to that constraint differently. (Of course, institutions can also enable state activity.) In part, this view relies on the age-old distinction between the high politics realm of security and the "less high politics" realm of political economy. But even this formulation gets us only so far.

Just as different institutions restrict states differently, so the challenges that bedevil these institutions are qualitatively different. The WTO has reached an impasse in the current round of negotiations, as the interests of developing and developed countries have diverged. As Wolfe (in this volume) puts it,

> [m]embers are at vastly different levels of development, their political and legal systems are based on divergent premises, and while they are unequally penetrated by the social and economic forces of globalization, they must cope with overlapping regulatory domains. The WTO universe is certainly plural if not medieval.

The organization, however, in no way risks becoming obsolete. It continues to be the centerpiece of the trade regime, despite a proliferation of regional agreements. Its dispute settlement mechanism continues to provide a useful and legitimate forum for resolving differences. It "does indeed work rather well on a day-to-day basis" (Wolfe, in this volume). The same cannot be said for the IMF, which has suffered considerably in terms of credibility. Countries that have reached a higher stage of development no longer require the Fund's services. More worrisome, however, are those countries that must borrow but that have found alternatives to the IMF, thus threatening to make it obsolete as its resources are largely given over to servicing a single key borrower, Turkey. A comparison between the WTO and the IMF evokes Stein's claim (in this volume) that "dissatisfaction does not necessarily equal failure that requires reform." Dissatisfaction seems closer to failure for the IMF than for the WTO.

The case of the United Nations might be even more complicated. Not only does it lend itself to an analysis that differs from that of the Bretton Woods institutions, but also there is not necessarily consensus on its central "problems." For example, many commentators have suggested that US skepticism about the UN threatens its ability to be a real contributor to international security and development issues. While this argument is not unpersuasive, it risks missing other challenges that, in the long run, might be more problematic for the UN than ambivalent US support. For example, James Fearon (in this volume) points to the fact that not only has the UN's membership grown considerably since its inception, but the body also could be hampered in reaching key goals by the fact that not all members share a commitment to democracy. From another perspective, Paul Heinbecker, Canada's former ambassador to the UN, argues that "the fundamental political and legal challenge facing the UN is to determine when and under what conditions the international community is justified in intervening in the internal affairs of member states" (2004, 19). Heinbecker's comments spring from the failure of the UN to prevent genocide in Rwanda and Darfur. Yet this conversation implicates much more than the UN. These failures have as much to do with our ongoing commitment to the notion of sovereignty as they do with the UN's lack of capacity. Understanding the failures in Rwanda and Darfur also requires recognition that we have entered an era characterized by challenges for which the UN was not designed or equipped—civil wars and failed states among them. The reform focus in these instances shifts away from whether the UN can rely on hegemonic leadership to how we can empower the UN to act in combat or post-conflict reconstruction situations or to how we can translate into practice the now-codified concept of the Responsibility to Protect. In other words, how we define the "problem" determines the range of reform solutions we entertain.

That the challenges facing key global institutions are not identical makes it tempting to look at reform on an ad hoc basis, and on some level this is wise. Such an ad hoc approach, however, must also acknowledge the increasingly important conversation about the need for coherence across the system. An effective IMF is appealing so long as it does not work at cross purposes to the UN or the WTO. A WTO that effectively promotes trade liberalization is appealing if it does not do so at the expense of development as promoted by the UN or the World Bank. Our conversation about global institutional reform, then, must occur on two levels. The first must capture the nuance and uniqueness of the challenges facing specific institutions designed to perform particular tasks. The second must take a more holistic view of the global governance architecture and our overall efforts to achieve dearly held goals. Identifying these goals might not be difficult—any list would include security, development, and justice, among others. Agreeing on their definition, rank order, and the best path to their attainment, however, might be more challenging and might be where the real work of reform resides.

References

Barnett, Michael, and Martha Finnemore. 1999. "The Politics, Power, and Pathologies of International Organizations." *International Organization* 53 (4): 699–732.

Finnemore, Martha. 2005. "Fights about Rules: The Role of Efficacy and Power in Changing Multilateralism." *Review of International Studies* 31 (December): 187–206.

Heinbecker, Paul. 2004. "The UN in the Twenty-First Century: Canada Needs This Old Dog to Learn New Tricks." In *Canada among Nations, 2004*, edited by David Carment, Fen Osler Hampson, and Norman Hillmer (Montreal; Kingston, ON: McGill-Queen's University Press.

Klotz, Audie. 1995. *Norms in International Relations: The Struggle against Apartheid*. Ithaca, NY: Cornell University Press.

Ruggie, John Gerard. 1993. "Multilateralism: The Anatomy of an Institution." In *Multilateralism Matters: The Theory and Praxis of an Institutional Forum*, edited by John Gerard Ruggie. New York: Columbia University Press.

Weber, Cynthia. 2001. *International Relations Theory: A Critical Introduction*. London: Routledge.

Weiss, Linda. 2005. "Global Governance, National Strategies: How Industrialized States Make Room to Move under the WTO." *Review of International Political Economy* 12 (5): 723–49.

Conclusion

Alan S. Alexandroff

*   *   *

Can the world be governed? After all the chapters in this volume, one might think that the answer was obvious. Yet, even with the views of the international relations experts expressed in these pages and the recommendations of the extensive literature on global governance reform to which they refer, uncertainty remains.

In part, the difficulty is definitional. As I suggested in the Introduction, in looking at the global governance issue, one's focus is blurred by the wide diversity of international organizations and institutions—a diversity that is mirrored in this volume. And even as most of the authors consciously focus on multilateralism—on international organizations and institutions, both formal and informal, and on the rules, principles, and norms that constitute global governance—our colleague from the Canadian government, Ferry de Kerckhove, raises a much broader concept: "a move from a multilateral system at the service of national interests to a true system of world governance."

In this volume, most of the analyses focus on the variety of international organizations, both formal and informal, and institutions, rules, principles, and norms that constitute global governance. Notwithstanding the plethora of definitions and the emergence of new, nonstate actors, especially in the global economy, that appear to have had an effect on global governance,[1] international organizations and institutions remain tethered to state behavior and to the national interest of states. So, while unilateral action is possible, it is equally likely that states will choose a multilateral approach.

Now, it might be a simple matter of self-selection, but the view that arises from the chapters in this volume is that multilateral organizations can and do overcome the problem of collective action—not all the time, nor in all fields, nor necessarily effectively, but international organizations and institutions provide the setting and the incentive for states to cooperate, even where power is evidently unequally spread among states. States employ multilateralism across the international system: they act collectively to promote stability and curtail conflict. They also focus on global prosperity issues or, as Paul Collier notes, they collectively attack the development problem of divergence between rich and poor states. All these and other state actions are taken on a largely collaborative and multilateral basis.

The question, then, comes down to this: can the international system generate "effective multilateralism." as several of our authors and the volume's subtitle suggest? If so, how? Daniel Drezner offers a slightly more poetic goal: "to build a better mousetrap on the global stage." But is "effective multilateralism" that mousetrap? A better mousetrap would be one built on the capacity for collective action—that is, on a willingness to exercise collective action. Effective multilateralism would then be far less likely to be measured on the congruence between leadership and the distribution of power than on the construction of a grouping of states that expressed a collective determination of leadership legitimacy. Such multilateral action, moreover, would have to be in furtherance of the expressed goals or mandate of the organization or institution. These criteria would again be used in determining global governance reform.

But in proposing this perspective on effective multilateralism and global governance reform, one recognizes that there is no unanimity of approach—indeed, in this volume and elsewhere, many different analytic perspectives are advanced. For some analysts, the structure of multilateralism is built principally on the distribution of power. And with the redistribution of power that is occurring in the contemporary international system, the

---

1. See, particularly, the writings of John Ruggie (2003, 93); see also Slaughter (2004).

analysis of global governance effectiveness and reform grows ever more complicated and uncertain. Drezner points to a contemporary structural reality in which there is too often a mismatch between governance structures and the distribution of power in international relations. Many organizations and institutions that were created after World War II still reflect the distribution of leadership power that existed more than 50 years ago. The task of identifying effective multilateralism is made no easier when analysts or decision makers address legitimacy in the construction of international organizations. Restructuring governance, or insisting on reform, is both thankless and frequently unachievable—at least it would seem so. The classic case for this, in some ways, is the reform of the UN Security Council and the inability to revise its leadership significantly. The repeated failure to secure changes to the ranks of the Permanent Five is a continuing warning to those who demand reform. Even where membership is constructed around effectiveness, reform—or, possibly more precisely, commitment—is not easily achieved in international relations. Arthur Stein (p. 30 in this volume) suggests that the contemporary task of effective, or what he calls "new," multilateralism is the following:

> historical organizations are dealing with a quite different distribution of power, and any new institutional arrangement will be constructed in the shadow of hegemony. The challenge of today is how to adapt existing organizations so that they remain compatible with the incentives of the United States, and how to fashion new multilateral arrangements in a unipolar age.

Now, it may be that we are looking at the wrong constellation of state actors. Perhaps the United States is yesterday's concern. Certainly, Patricia Goff points to the importance, for example, of Brazil, Russia, India, and China—the so-called BRICs.[2] Further she extends the influence of actors

---

2. Nomenclature is quite confusing here. Furthermore, these new collectives vary because of a shifting emphasis away from economics and diplomacy. Goldman Sachs, the US investment banking house, has produced a series of "terrain-altering" reports on the emergence and impact of the BRICs—see O'Neil (2001); Wilson and Purushothaman (2003); Goldman Sachs Global Economic Group (2006). Here at the Centre for International Governance Innovation (CIGI), we first identified "BRICSAM"—Brazil, Russia, India, China, South

on the contemporary global governance scene to nonstate actors, as well as to newly emerging state actors or not quite formed ones such as the European Union. As she declares, "[t]here is, nonetheless, a danger in overstating the degree to which the US involvement determines the success of international efforts" (p. 392 in this volume). While the constellation of great powers is more uncertain in contemporary international relations, in contrast to, say, the Cold War decades, it is unlikely that effective multilateralism could be achieved without attention to US interests and US incentive compatibility. That is certainly the way the analysis in this Conclusion proceeds.

Notwithstanding the challenges—changes in the distribution of power in the international system; concern for or, perhaps more accurately, the lack of concern for leadership and the legitimate coalition of states; the commitment to economic growth, development or security—the answer to "can the world be governed?" is, in my view, "yes, but …"

I can hear the muttering arising from such an equivocal answer. Yet, in the following analysis, I try to suggest the contingent factors that can debilitate, inhibit, or at least delay effective multilateralism. And it will be evident that there are significant hurdles to global governance reform and the creation of multilateral incentive compatibility. But in the face of these uncertainties with respect to approach, behavior, and outcomes, I believe that the answer, however equivocal, is an optimistic conclusion drawn on the best data we currently possess.

The Supply and Demand for Global Governance Reform

Today, we hear the hue and cry: "reform is critical to global governance, and it is required now!" A recent example, just one among many, is that

---

Africa, the ASEAN countries, and Mexico; later, Andrew Cooper, a CIGI Distinguished Fellow, identified "B(R)ICSAM," separating out Russia due to its almost-established role in the G7/8—see Antkiewicz and Whalley (2005); Cooper, Antkiewicz, and Shaw (2006); Cooper (2007). Still others suggest that the collective identity of newly emerging large economies should be restricted to just India and China, or "Chindia," in recognition of the focus on these two large transitional economies, which far outdistance the others in the group in size.

of Anne-Marie Slaughter and John Ikenberry, both of the Woodrow Wilson School and co-directors of the Princeton Project on National Security, who wrote early in their recent Final Report (2006, 7):

> The system of international institutions that the United States and its allies built after World War II and steadily expanded over the course of the Cold War is broken. Every major institution—the United Nations, the International Monetary Fund, the World Bank, the World Trade Organization, the North Atlantic Treaty Organization—and countless smaller ones face calls for major reform.

Indeed, calls are in the air for reform not just in the realm of security but across the global governance spectrum, from trade to the environment, from humanitarian intervention to international financial institutions. As Stein notes (p. 19 in this volume), "[a] great deal of dissatisfaction with global governance exists today, and many proposals for reform of international organizations continue to be proffered." Moreover, and as Stein highlights, it is not exactly clear why all this clamor is occurring now. Are the numerous calls for reform and the many reform proposals "bubbling up" because institutions are perceived to be failing to achieve their objectives? Or could it be that "success" has given rise to calls for more international institutions? And then we should probably separate out legitimate calls for significant reform from what Stein identifies as "feigned dissatisfaction" on the part of politicians who, needing scapegoats, loudly decry the effectiveness of various international organizations and institutions and demand their reform.

One reason for such demands has already been noted: we are increasingly uncertain of the sustainability of US hegemony. Particularly in the light of the emergence of large new economies—those of China and India, in particular—it is not surprising that leadership in various international organizations created decades earlier would be questioned.

In addition, and again as Stein notes, the motivations that drive national reform proposals can be quite varied and can include a desire to promote, at least to a national audience, those that are not likely to succeed or that have little or no chance of being implemented. Indeed, a cursory, "back of the envelope" assessment of the flood of reform proposals likely would reveal that the number that would be either corrective or transformative would be less than overwhelming. Further, as Drezner and others point out, proposals that call for more "legitimate" leadership—the UN Security Council-type reforms—frequently lead to failure or stalemate. In the light of the failure of the Leaders' Summit of 2005, it is more than slightly sobering to reflect on a previous volume by Heinbecker and Goff (2005) and statements by officials, both national and international, urging the need to reform, among other things, the makeup of the Security Council. This failure serves to underline Stein's recognition of an apparent reversal of roles in the examination of global governance reform: today, it is international officials and national politicians who call for dramatic reform, while academics, perhaps acknowledging that large-scale reform is unlikely, prefer to offer up more limited proposals.

Notwithstanding the difficulties and, indeed, failures to date in changing leadership at the United Nations, for example, there are those who still argue for leadership change and significant reform of that body. In this volume (p. 130), John Ikenberry suggests the need to "build agreements and commitments within the 'community of democracies'." He suggests that such a commitment would make the United States more likely to support institutional commitments to states that are democracies and to strengthen an organization that is committed to the community of democracies. James Fearon, in his an analytic effort to construct a new UN-like body, raises the possibility that membership in a new Security Council-like body, not to mention a wider General Assembly-like institution, arguably could be limited to certified democracies. Fearon is alert to the reality that such an enterprise would exclude China and, increasingly likely, Russia. Nevertheless, such an organization, or even the threat of one, might well encourage leadership change, notwithstanding the difficulties of forum shopping that its creation could engender. Such a body, according to Fearon, presumably could better promote peace and security in the long run and potentially be based on the legitimacy of people rather than on states. Moreover, in the face of a growing focus on an international human rights agenda, there might be no alternative to such an evolving global governance organization.

Evolving Organizations and Institutions?

The structure of global governance plays a significant role in the analysis of global governance outcomes (see Table 1 in the Introduction). Analysts generally begin their study by examining the distribution of power in the international system. Often, they see and describe a "balance of power" that imparts a dynamic quality to both state power and international configurations that make up leadership in multilateral organizations and institutions. Recently, international relations experts have paid close attention to unipolarity and the effect of US hegemony. In this volume, for example, Ikenberry argues that the growing US ambivalence toward multilateralism arises in part from US hegemony—the current unipolarity. The structure of global governance appears to shift along a continuum from multipolarity through bipolarity to unipolarity built on the strength US hegemony.

Although there is much comment on unilateralism in this volume and more generally in the current examination of global governance—in part, engendered by the current US administration's behavior and rhetoric with respect to unilateral action—there is an equally strong theme, which Stein raises, that multilateralism is an "existential reality" in international relations. It is not that states are unwilling to take unilateral action—for they are, and not only the United States—but that they are equally willing to exercise collaborative and collective behavior in international relations, subject to incentive compatibility.

Global governance in the international system, however, can be described from a slightly different structural perspective and continuum as well. Stein sees multilateralism as reflecting a weak confederal system. A number of international relations experts have looked at various structural configurations in the international system. For example, Deudney (1995) looks at the early United States as an international subsystem and chronicles its transformation from a weak confederal structure of states, under its first constitution, the Articles of Confederation, to a far more tightly knit and rather strong federal structure—a structure that no multilateral organization or institution even faintly looks like. Then there is the European Union. Seen through the eyes of international relations experts, the EU is a "strong" confederal system, with the participating states limiting national sovereignty and constructing collective interests that they exercise through various EU organs (see Kagan 2002, 2003). Further along this structural continuum are the majority of multilateral organizations and institutions, displaying what Stein calls "weak" confederal structures. Some are formal—among them the UN Security Council, the World Trade Organization (WTO), and the International Monetary Fund (IMF)—while others are largely informal, such as Great Power coalitions, "coalitions of the willing," and alliances of every kind.

Richard Rosecrance, in this volume, divides global governance structures less along formal versus informal lines and more along a universal-effectiveness continuum, with a focus on governance procedures and approaches and a differentiation of the constraints on the behavior of individual states. Thus, his soft institutional procedures are universal, though weak. An instance of this "soft" structure is reflected in the UN or in international law. Medium approaches, according to Rosecrance, are the WTO or the IMF, where the scope of the organization is not truly universal, if only because of limitations on the scope of their governance, although the ties might be effective within the organization's jurisdiction. Thus, for example, the WTO is restricted to trade and a number of trade-plus issues, while the IMF is restricted to debt and financial issues. And then there are "hard" institutional approaches: UN Security Council decisions, for example—especially binding Chapter VII-type decisions.

Although there is no analytic agreement yet on how to characterize and differentiate global governance organizations, it appears that the current forms of global governance are situated somewhere along the weak confederal end of the spectrum. This raises the question of whether shifting global governance structures along this continuum would enhance effective multilateralism. If so, how could such shift be engineered?

In the contemporary setting, a reasonable construction of multilateralism, as Stein suggests, is built on at least two principles: an existential reality, and incentive compatibility. At the heart of this multilateral motivation, then, is the need to construct global governance such that states prefer to achieve national outcomes in international relations in the context of collaboration and multilateral organizations. But constructing incentive compatibility is at the heart of my "yes, but…" contingent conclusion.

My focus on the United States is not principally concerned with whether that country is the hegemon of the system. The United States is, and for the foreseeable future will remain, at least a key actor and influence in global governance, and one can imagine few instances of effective multilateralism that would exclude US participation—one need only look at the Kyoto Accord or the International Criminal Court. US participation is not a sufficient condition for effective multilateralism but US participation creates close to a necessary one. As a number of the contributors to this volume—Ikenberry, in particular—suggest, it is evident that the United States is ambivalent about multilateralism. Yet this ambivalence and the United States' adoption of unilateral action, as Ikenberry points out, comes at a cost, including a closer scrutiny by other states of US behavior, reduced cooperation, and a loss of legitimacy. Incentives to spur greater US multilateralism might arise from exactly these efforts to restore US legitimacy, create efficiencies, and reduce enforcement costs. Indeed, as Ikenberry also notes, the higher the perceived cost of acting unilaterally, the more US leadership might be encouraged to initiate and promote multilateral approaches.

Thus, global governance is, in part, dependent on the perceived cost to US leadership of unilateral action. The current burden of largely unilateral action in Iraq, for instance, might well encourage some reassessment of the cost of such action. And, of course, the effectiveness calculation could be recalibrated with new US leadership. But the calculation of the cost of unilateral action extends beyond the life of any particular administration. As Stein points out, it is evident that a number of US multilateral initiatives have been stymied as much by the lack of congressional support as by hesitance on the part of the executive branch. The strong current of national sovereignty in the legislative branch and in the two major political parties is a continuing check on US multilateral participation. So, it would be incautious to believe that US global governance participation is simply a function of a change in administration. The strong national sovereignty current in US politics thus emphasizes the basis for my contingent answer to the global governance question.[3]

3. The decline in bipartisan support for what is described as liberal institutionalism has led Charles Kupchan and Peter Trubowitz (2007) to argue that liberal internationalism—the US use of power and international cooperation—has died in US foreign policy.

In cautioning us not to overemphasize the US role in global governance analysis, Goff raises the importance of Europe and the possible influence of Europe—principally the EU—on global governance. The EU, as has been pointed out, is characterized as a strong confederal subsystem in the global context, yet recent EU behavior suggests one should adopt a degree of skepticism about its collective global role. On key global issues, especially international security, the EU's collective leadership seems blunted, and doubts abound about the European security commitment, whether in NATO or in some stand-alone European defense force. It may become necessary—in the context of the potential acquisition of nuclear weapons by Iran, for example—to look at the influence of individual member countries such as France, Germany, and the United Kingdom rather than the EU itself.

Then there are the BRICs, whose larger players, India and China, have an evident presence when one considers effective multilateralism. Indeed, as Robert Wolfe points out, major emerging economies such as India, China, and Brazil are playing a significant role in the Doha Round of multilateral trade negotiations. At the same time, however, the Doha Round underlines the limits on the influence of these and possibly other emerging economies: they might be able to block progress on a particular outcome but they appear unwilling to become rule makers. Former US deputy secretary of state Robert Zoellick urged China to become a "responsible stakeholder," but the comment is applicable to all the BRICs, which seem unwilling to "step up to the plate" on questions of global governance. Indeed, they appear to regard multilateral initiatives with great suspicion, as designed to benefit the developed or even colonial or imperialist powers; instead, they express highly traditional national sovereignty positions. Thus, on Burma and Darfur, for example, China has expressed concerns about intervention and an unwillingness to become involved in what it regards as the internal matters of sovereign states.

Thus, while there is doubt about the commitment of the BRICs to effective multilateralism, what about the likelihood of their acting in a more collective manner with a collective view? Do they see themselves as reflecting a group perspective on global governance issues and initiatives? These new Great Powers, acting individually or as group, are likely to have a significant impact on global governance, as we hope to show in future studies. Their stepping up to the plate and developing a sense of ownership of issues will be critical to our understanding of how to achieve successful global governance in the near term. It may be that, as Rosecrance suggests, the war against terrorism, the effort to avoid further nuclear proliferation, and rules and actions to promote economic prosperity will provide the basis for collective action on the part of the BRICs. Yet, human rights, humanitarian intervention, the reduction of economic protectionism, and the curbing of carbon-producing energy sources are but a few of the issues that pose incentive compatibility questions for the BRICs and challenge their participation in global governance. Paul Collier makes clear the enormity and complexity of successful development action. Yet it is unclear that current governance organizations or institutions—whether the G8, P5, or some expanded version of either, if such a creation were even possible—can successfully provide the collective action required.

A final point warrants mention. Several of our contributors note that the future might not look like the present with respect to global governance. Ikenberry suggests that we are likely to see more informal, bilateral, and domestic organizations and institutions—it may well be that the various exercises in leadership and legitimacy redistribution will enervate future efforts to reform international organizations and institutions. Fearon raises the prospect that the G8 or some extended G-something organization could move us to a more democratic leadership forum. Rosecrance suggests that Great Power leadership might provide the necessary global governance means. Thus, informal, more narrowly purposed instruments might well become the means to tackle global governance issues, notwithstanding the prospect of increased forum shopping. Some time ago, political scientist Charles Lipson examined the concept and the ubiquity of informal agreements in international relations. As he pointed out,

[i]nformal accords among states and transnational actors are not exceptional. The scale and the diversity of such accords indicate that they are an important feature of world politics, not rare and peripheral. The very informality of so many agreements illuminates basic features of international politics. It highlights the continuing search for international cooperation, the profusion of forms it takes, and the serious obstacles to more durable commitments. (1991, 498)

Lipson confined himself to agreements, but agreements are tied in many instances to less formal organizations and institutions. Indeed, institutions consisting of rules, principles, and norms frequently are built on informal agreements. Here again, as with the examination of the BRICs, we hope in a follow-up exercise to examine just how these new global governance structures are being created and where they might be gaining effectiveness, and to determine the influence they could have on future global governance.

In summary, in the near future, global governance and global governance reform are likely to be influenced by:

- acknowledging that the sources of reform are varied and include motivations other than achieving effective global governance reform;
- growing support in the United States for reducing the cost of unilateral action, leading, if only grudgingly, to a greater emphasis on collective action;
- accepting, particularly in the United States, that the increasing engagement of the BRICs in international organizations and institutions is not just a zero-sum exercise and will not come merely at the cost of the diminution of US influence; and
- the growing recognition in the BRICs, particularly China and India, that organizations and rules that govern the actions of nation-states are compatible with their own national interests—such a shift would entail a growing sense of ownership of global governance on the part of the BRICs, as well as, perhaps, some reconfiguration of the rules, principles, and norms of global governance organizations.

The prospect of global governance remains; the hows and whys have yet to be explored. In the end, however, we return to the contingent expression of optimism about whether the world can be governed: "yes, but …"

References

Antkiewicz, Agata, and John Whalley. 2005. "BRICSAM and the Non-WTO." CIGI Working Paper 3. Waterloo, ON: Centre for International Governance Innovation. October.

Cooper, Andrew. 2007. "The Logic of the B(R)ICSAM Model for G8 Reform." Policy Brief in International Governance 1. Waterloo, ON: Centre for International Governance Innovation. May.

Cooper, Andrew, Agata Antkiewicz, and Timothy Shaw. 2006. "Economic Size Trumps All Else? Lessons from BRICSAM." CIGI Working Paper 12. Waterloo, ON: Centre for International Governance Innovation. December.

Deudney, David. 1995. "The Philadelphia System: Sovereignty, Arms Control and Balance of Power in the American States-Union Circa 1787-1861." *International Organization* 49 (2): 191–225.

Goldman Sachs Global Economic Group. 2006. *The World and the BRICs Dream*. New York: Goldman Sachs.

Heinbecker, Paul, and Patricia Goff, eds. 2005. *Irrelevant or Indispensable? The United Nations in the 21st Century*. Waterloo, ON: Wilfrid Laurier University Press.

Ikenberry, G. John, and Anne-Marie Slaughter. 2006. *Forging a World of Liberty under Law: U.S. National Security in the 21st Century*. Final Report of the Princeton Project on National Security. Princeton, NJ: Princeton University, Woodrow Wilson School of Public and International Affairs.

Kagan, Robert. 2002. "Power and Weakness." *Policy Review* 113 (June/July): 3–28.

———. 2003. *Of Paradise and Power: America and Europe in the New World Order*. New York: Alfred A. Knopf.

Kupchan, Charles, and Peter Trubowitz. 2007. "Dead Center: The Demise of Liberal Institutionalism." *International Security* 32 (2): 7–44.

Lipson, Charles. 1991. "Why Are Some International Agreements Informal?" *International Organization* 45 (4): 495–538.

O'Neill, Jim. 2001. "Building Better Global Economic BRICs." Global Economics Paper 66. New York: Goldman Sach. November.

Ruggie, John. 2003. "Taking Embedded Liberalism Global: The Corporate Connection." In *Taming Globalization: Frontiers of Governance*, edited by David Held and Mathias Koenig-Archibugi. Cambridge, UK: Polity Press.

Slaughter, Anne-Marie. 2004. *A New World Order*. Princeton, NJ: Princeton University Press.

Wilson, Dominic, and Roopa Purushothaman. 2003. "Dreaming with BRICs: The Path to 2050." Global Economics Paper 99. New York: Goldman Sachs. October.

Contributors

*   *   *

Alan S. Alexandroff is research director for the Program on Conflict Management and Negotiation at the Munk Centre for International Studies, University of Toronto. He has taught international trade and politics, conflict management, and dispute resolution at a number of North American institutions, including Queen's University (Kingston, Ontario), McGill University, and the University of California at Los Angeles, as well as at the University of Toronto. His research and writing interests include trade, investment, and trade policy in North America; the multilateral trading system; China's accession to the World Trade Organization and its integration into the global economy; and conflict management in the international system, including the reform of global governance. Dr. Alexandroff is a senior fellow at the Centre for International Governance Innovation. His most recent publication is *Trends in World Trade: Essays in Honor of Sylvia Ostry* (2007), for which he served as editor and contributor.

Paul Collier is professor of economics and director of the Centre for the Study of African Economies at Oxford University. From 1998 to 2003 he was director of the Development Research Group of the World Bank. Professor Collier is a specialist in the political, economic, and developmental predicaments of poor countries. He holds a Distinction Award from Oxford

University, and in 1988 he was awarded the Edgar Graham Book Prize for the co-written *Labour and Poverty in Rural Tanzania*. He is also the author of *The Bottom Billion: Why the Poorest Countries Are Failing and What Can Be Done about It* (2007), in which he discusses the pros and cons of developmental aid to developing countries.

Ferry de Kerckhove is director general of the International Organizations Bureau, part of the Canadian Department of Foreign Affairs and International Trade, and the personal representative of the prime minister of Canada for *la Francophonie*, the international organization of French-speaking countries. He is responsible for the programs and specialized agencies of the UN covered by Canada's missions in New York, Geneva, Paris, and Rome, and for relations between Canada, the Commonwealth, and *la Francophonie*. Born in Belgium, Mr. de Kerckhove has a B.Soc. Sc. (Honours) in economics and an M.A. in political science from the University of Ottawa and pursued Ph.D. studies at Université Laval in Quebec City. In 1973 he entered the Canadian foreign service, where he has had a distinguished career, having held posts as minister and deputy head of mission in Moscow, high commissioner to Pakistan, and ambassador to both Indonesia and East Timor. In September 2003, he joined the School of Political Studies at the University of Ottawa as diplomat in residence. He has published several papers on international relations and Islamic fundamentalism in specialized journals.

Daniel W. Drezner is associate professor of international politics at the Fletcher School, Tufts University. He received his B.A. from Williams College and his Ph.D. in political science from Stanford University. He previously taught at the University of Chicago and the University of Colorado at Boulder. He is the author of *All Politics Is Global* (2007), *U.S. Trade Policy* (2006), and *The Sanctions Paradox* (1999). Professor Drezner has published articles in numerous scholarly journals as well as in the *New York Times,* the *Washington Post,* and *Foreign Affairs*. He has received fellowships from the German Marshall Fund of the United States, the Council on Foreign Relations, and Harvard University, and has held positions with the Civic Education Project, the RAND Corporation, and the US Treasury Department. He keeps a daily weblog at www.danieldrezner.com.

James D. Fearon is Theodore and Frances Geballe Professor in the School of Humanities and Sciences and professor of political science at Stanford

University. His research has focused on democracy and international disputes, explanations for interstate wars, and the causes of civil and especially ethnic violence. Representative publications include "Neotrusteeship and the Problem of Weak States" (*International Security*, Spring 2004), "Ethnicity, Insurgency, and Civil War" (*American Political Science Review*, February 2003), and "Iraq's Civil War" (*Foreign Affairs*, March/April 2007). He was elected a fellow of the American Academy of the Arts and Sciences in 2002.

Patricia M. Goff is associate professor of political science at Wilfrid Laurier University and a senior fellow at the Centre for International Governance Innovation. Her fields of expertise include international relations and international political economy. She is co-editor (with Kevin Dunn) of *Identity and Global Politics: Empirical and Theoretical Elaborations* (2004) and (with Paul Heinbecker) *Irrelevant or Indispensable? The United Nations in the 21st Century* (2005), and the author of *Limits to Liberalization: Local Culture in a Global Marketplace* (2007). Dr. Goff holds a Ph.D. in political science from Northwestern University, a Diplôme études approfondies in comparative politics from the University of Paris, an M.A. in French literature from McMaster University, and a B.A. (Honours) from the University of Western Ontario. She is associate editor of *Behind the Headlines*, a publication of the Canadian Institute of International Affairs, and executive director of the Academic Council on the United Nations System.

Eric Helleiner is CIGI (Centre for International Governance Innovation) Chair in International Governance and professor in the Department of Political Science, University of Waterloo. He is also director of the M.A. program at Waterloo and of the Ph.D. program in global governance at both Waterloo and Wilfrid Laurier University. His research focuses on North–South international financial relations. He is currently a Trudeau Foundation fellow and co-editor of the book series Cornell Studies in Money. He is the author of *States and the Reemergence of Global Finance* (1994), *The Making of National Money* (2003), and *Towards North American Monetary Union?* (2006), for which he received the Donner Prize for the best book on Canadian public policy. He is also co-editor of *Nation-States and Money* (1999) and *Economic Nationalism in a Globalizing World* (2005), and has received the Marvin Gelber Essay Prize in International Relations from the Canadian Institute for International Affairs.

G. John Ikenberry is Albert G. Milbank Professor of Politics and International Affairs at Princeton University. He is author of *After Victory: Institutions, Strategic Restraint, and the Rebuilding of Order after Major War* (2001), which won the 2002 Schroeder-Jervis Award presented by the American Political Science Association for the best book in international history and politics. He is currently writing a sequel to this book, *Liberal Leviathan: The Origins, Crisis, and Transformation of the American System*. A collection of his essays, *Liberal Order and Imperial Ambition: American Power and International Order*, was published in 2006 by Polity Press. Among his many activities, Professor Ikenberry served as a member of an advisory group at the US State Department in 2003–04. He has lectured throughout the United States, Europe, and Asia. He is also the reviewer of books on political and legal affairs for *Foreign Affairs*.

Bessma Momani is an assistant professor in the Departments of Political Science and History at the University of Waterloo and a senior fellow at the Centre for International Governance and Innovation. She specializes in the International Monetary Fund (IMF) and Middle East economic liberalization. Co-author of the textbook *Twentieth-Century World History*, she has published a monograph entitled *IMF–Egyptian Debt Negotiations*. Dr. Momani has also published articles about the IMF in *Review of International Political Economy, Asian Affairs, Global Society, Journal of International Relations and Development, New Political Economy, Canadian Journal of Political Science,* and *Review of International Organizations*. On economic liberalization in the Middle East, she has published in *Middle East Review of International Affairs, World Economy,* and *World Economics*.

Richard Rosecrance is adjunct professor in public policy at Harvard University, research professor of political science at the University of California, and senior fellow in the Belfer Center for Science and International Affairs. He was formerly director of the Burkle Center for International Relations at UCLA. He has written widely on international topics. Among his publications are *The Rise of the Trading State* (1986), *America's Economic Resurgence* (1990), *The Domestic Bases of Grand Strategy* (co-editor, 1993), *The Rise of the Virtual State* (1999), *The Costs of Conflict* (co-editor, 1999), *The New Great Power Coalition* (editor, 2001), and *No More States? Globalization, Self-Determination, and Terrorism* (co-editor, 2006). His next book is entitled *Mergers among Nations*. Professor Rosecrance served on the Policy Planning Council of the US State Department and has received Guggenheim, Rockefeller, Ford, Carnegie, and many other fellowships. He has held regular university posts at Cornell University and the University of California at Berkeley and visiting positions at the International Institute for Strategic Studies, Kings College (London), London School of Economics, European University Institute (Florence), and Australian National University.

Arthur A. Stein is professor of political science, University of California at Los Angeles. He has an A.B. from Cornell University, and a Ph.D. from Yale University. He has written widely on international economic and strategic affairs and is the author of *The Nation at War* (1980) and *Why Nations Cooperate* (1991), and co-editor of *The Domestic Bases of Grand Strategy* (1993) and *No More States? Globalization, National Self-Determination, and Terrorism* (2006). He has served on the Policy Planning Staff of the US State Department and consulted for US defense and intelligence agencies. Professor Stein has also been a guest scholar at the Brookings Institution and an international affairs fellow of the Council on Foreign Relations. He is currently a co-editor of the *American Political Science Review.*

Robert Wolfe is professor in the School of Policy Studies, Queen's University (Kingston, Ontario), where he is director of the Master of Public Administration teaching program. He was a foreign service officer for many years, serving abroad in Bangladesh and in the Canadian delegation to the Organisation for Economic Co-operation and Development in Paris. Since joining Queen's in 1995, he has published widely on Canadian trade policy and on the World Trade Organization. His most recent publications are "Decision-Making and Transparency in the 'Medieval' WTO" (*Journal of International Economic Law*), "See You in Geneva? Legal (Mis)Representations of the Trading System" (*European Journal of International Relations*), and a book entitled *Process Matters: Sustainable Development and Domestic Trade Transparency* (co-edited with Mark Halle, 2007).

Index

*   *   *

A
Afghanistan, 65, 95, 164, 167, 190, 204–206, 233, 254, 290

Africa: agriculture in, 253, 265; autocracies in, 254, 269–70, 276–77; civil war in, 255, 258–59, 268–69; decolonization in, 163; democracies in, 251, 253–54, 269–71; development of, 9–10, 241–85; and environmental issues, 214–15, 220; former French colonies of, 25n9, 255, 268–69; G8 activities in, 173; genocide in, and multilateralism, 44, 203–204, 268–69, 271, 400–401; governance in, 251, 253–54, 261, 275–79; natural resources in, 253–54, 257, 260, 264, 273–74, 275, 277, 280; NGOs in, 271, 280; peacekeeping/peace building in, 173, 190, 269–70; sub-Saharan, and IMF, 357–58, 364–65; and UN representation, 174. *See also entries immediately below*

Africa, security issues in: and aid, 262–63; and arms trade, 274–75, 280; budgeting for, 281; and civil war, 255, 258–59, 268–69, 401; and coups, 268, 270–71; in failing states, 279–80, 282–83, 401; and genocide, 44, 203–204, 268–69, 271, 400–401; and military intervention, 268–72, 400–401; and peacekeeping/peace building, 173, 190, 269–70

Africa, standards for companies in, 272–75, 280; and arms trade, 274–75, 280; and foreign banks, 272–73, 280; and resource extraction companies, 273–74, 280

Africa, standards for governments in, 275–79; and budget transparency, 275–76; and free/fair elections, 276–77; and post-conflict situations, 278–79; and rights of foreign investors, 277–78

Africa Growth and Opportunity Act (U.S. statute), 266–68

African aid, 261–65, 280–82, 284–85; as counterproductive, 261–62; and failing states, 263–64; as percentage of GDP, 247–48, 250–51; security implications of, 262–63

African development, 9–10, 241–85; and issue of divergence, 9, 241, 242–51, 283–85; OECD instruments for, 9–10, 241, 260–83, 284–85; and problems for autonomous handling of, 251–59, 260

Books in the Studies in International Governance Series

Alan S. Alexandroff, editor
Can the World Be Governed? Possibilities for Effective Multilateralism / 2008 / vi + 438 pp. / ISBN 978-1-55458-041-5

Paul Heinbecker and Patricia Goff, editors
Irrelevant or Indispensable? The United Nations in the 21st Century / 2005 / xii + 196 pp. / ISBN 0-88920-493-4

Paul Heinbecker and Bessma Momani, editors
Canada and the Middle East: In Theory and Practice / 2007 / ix + 232 pp. / ISBN-13: 978-1-55458-024-8 / ISBN-10: 1-55458-024-2

Yasmine Shamsie and Andrew S. Thompson, editors
Haiti: Hope for a Fragile State / 2006 / xvi + 131 pp. / ISBN-13: 978-0-88920-510-9 / ISBN-10: 0-88920-510-8

James W. St.G. Walker and Andrew S. Thompson, editors
Critical Mass: The Emergence of Global Civil Society / 2008 / xxvii + 302 pp. / ISBN-13: 978-1-55458-022-4 / ISBN-10: 1-55458-022-6

Jennifer Welsh and Ngaire Woods, editors
Exporting Good Governance: Temptations and Challenges in Canada's Aid Program / 2007 / xx + 343 pp. / ISBN-13: 978-1-55458-029-3 / ISBN-10: 1-55458-029-3